TAILS DON'T LIE

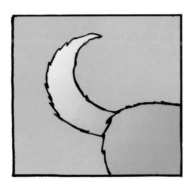

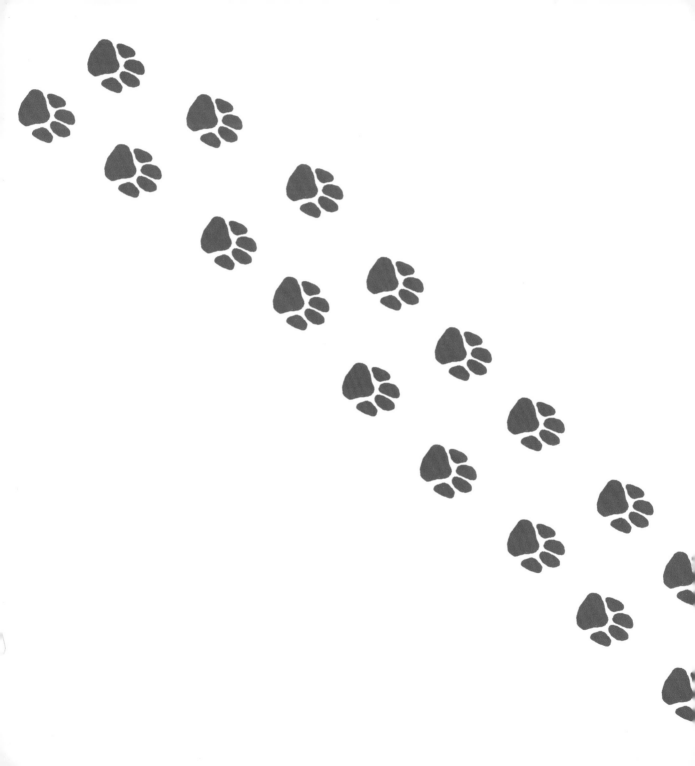

TAILS DON'T LIE

A Decade of Dog Cartoons

(70 in Dog Years)

ADRIAN RAESIDE

HARBOUR
PUBLISHING

To Koko and Sakura—
who have both since passed over to the Rainbow Bridge, where I'm sure Sakura is
chasing anyone bigger than herself and Koko has found a warm flowerbed to sleep on.

HARBOUR PUBLISHING CO. LTD.
P.O. Box 219, Madeira Park, BC,
V0N 2H0, Canada
www.harbourpublishing.com

Book cover and page layout
by Teresa Karbashewski

This book was printed
with soy-based inks on
chlorine-free paper made from
10% post-consumer waste

Printed and bound in Canada

Harbour Publishing acknowledges financial support from the Government of Canada through the Canada Book Fund and the Canada Council for the Arts, and from the Province of British Columbia through the BC Arts Council and the Book Publishing Tax Credit.

 Canada Council **Conseil des Arts** **for the Arts** **du Canada**    BRITISH COLUMBIA ARTS COUNCIL
An agency of the Province of British Columbia

Library and Archives Canada Cataloguing in Publication

Raeside, Adrian, 1957-
        Tails don't lie : a decade of dog cartoons (70 in dog years) / Adrian Raeside.
ISBN 978-1-55017-599-8

        1. Dogs–Caricatures and cartoons. 2. Canadian wit and humor, Pictorial. I. Title.
II. Title: Dog cartoons. III. Title: Adrian Raeside's dog cartoons.

NC1449.R34A4 2013   741.5'6971   C2012-908232-5

Introduction

Dogs.

Why do they look so pleased with themselves when they sit in the driver's seat?

Why is it that no matter how many times you tell them to get off the couch, they will eventually wear you down, and take over the couch?

Why is it that no matter how much mud they track in the house or food they sneak off the counter, they will always end up getting away with it?

Why are small dogs usually more assertive than big dogs? (One shudders to think of what would happen if a chihuahua got its paws on a thermonuclear device—and dinner was late by five minutes…) And how do they know the EXACT minute when it's their dinner time?

Compiled from ten years of *The Other Coast* comic strip, *Tails Don't Lie* is a collection of cartoons on all things doggy— a sideways look at the shedding, drooling, farting, bed-hogging, hairy contradictions we share our lives with.

And if you don't have a dog, get one. You don't know what you're missing.

—ADRIAN RAESIDE

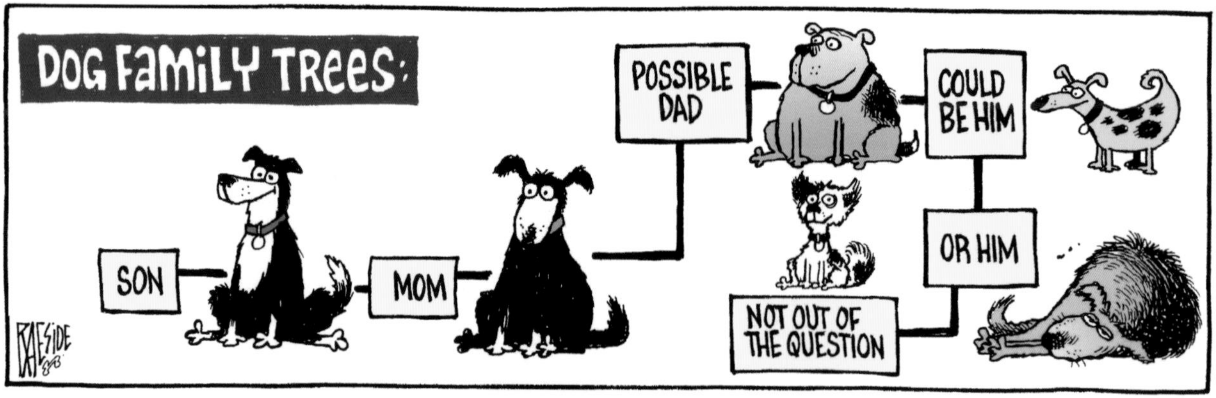
DOG FAMILY TREES:
SON
MOM
POSSIBLE DAD
COULD BE HIM
OR HIM
NOT OUT OF THE QUESTION

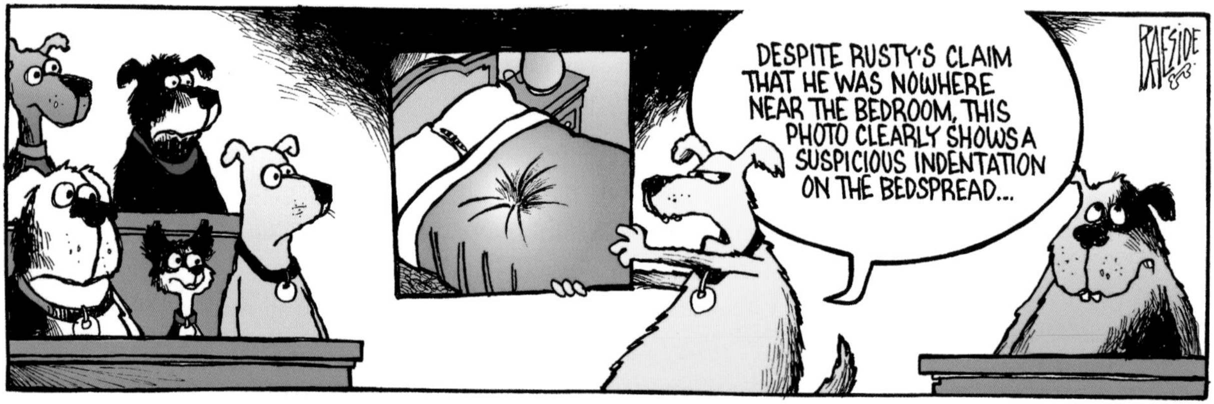
DESPITE RUSTY'S CLAIM THAT HE WAS NOWHERE NEAR THE BEDROOM, THIS PHOTO CLEARLY SHOWS A SUSPICIOUS INDENTATION ON THE BEDSPREAD...

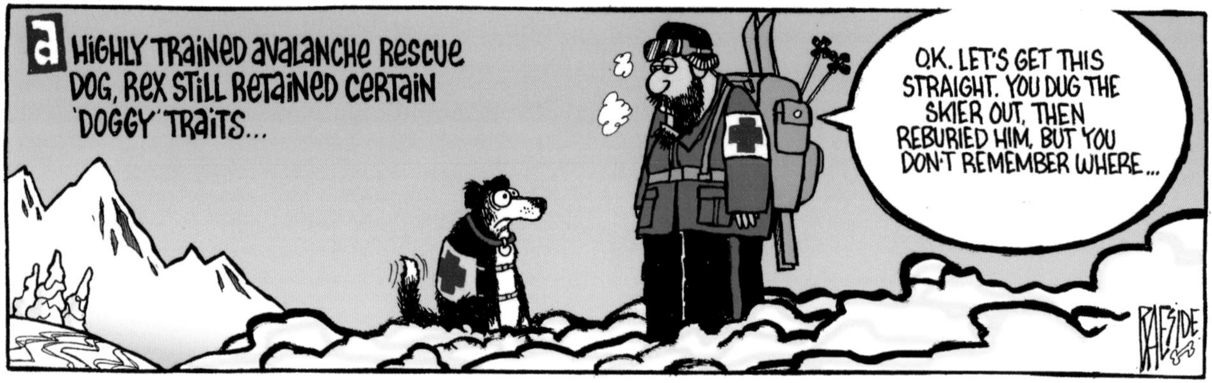
A HIGHLY TRAINED AVALANCHE RESCUE DOG, REX STILL RETAINED CERTAIN 'DOGGY' TRAITS...
O.K. LET'S GET THIS STRAIGHT. YOU DUG THE SKIER OUT, THEN REBURIED HIM, BUT YOU DON'T REMEMBER WHERE...

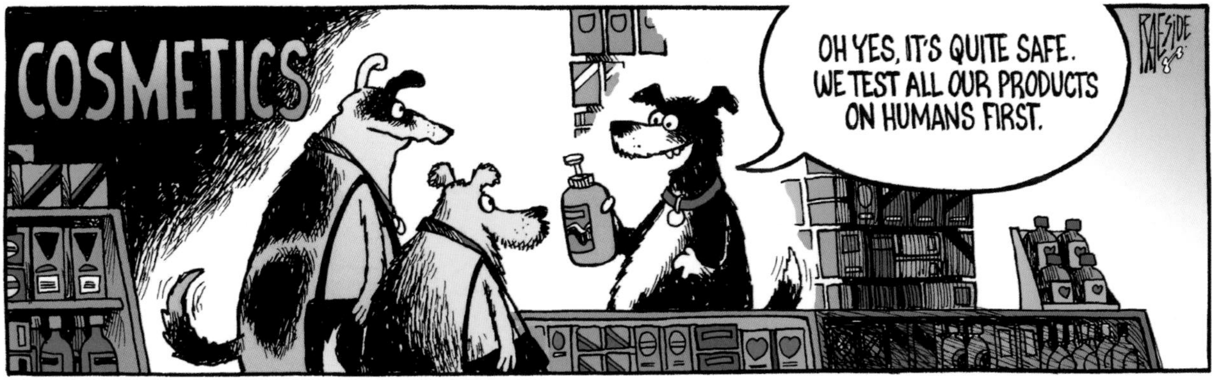
COSMETICS
RAESIDE
OH YES, IT'S QUITE SAFE. WE TEST ALL OUR PRODUCTS ON HUMANS FIRST.

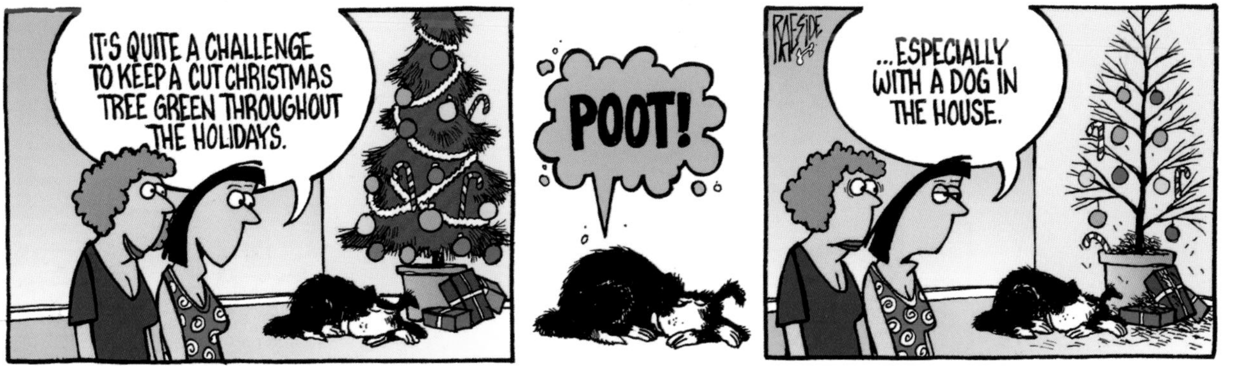
IT'S QUITE A CHALLENGE TO KEEP A CUT CHRISTMAS TREE GREEN THROUGHOUT THE HOLIDAYS.
POOT!
RAESIDE
...ESPECIALLY WITH A DOG IN THE HOUSE.

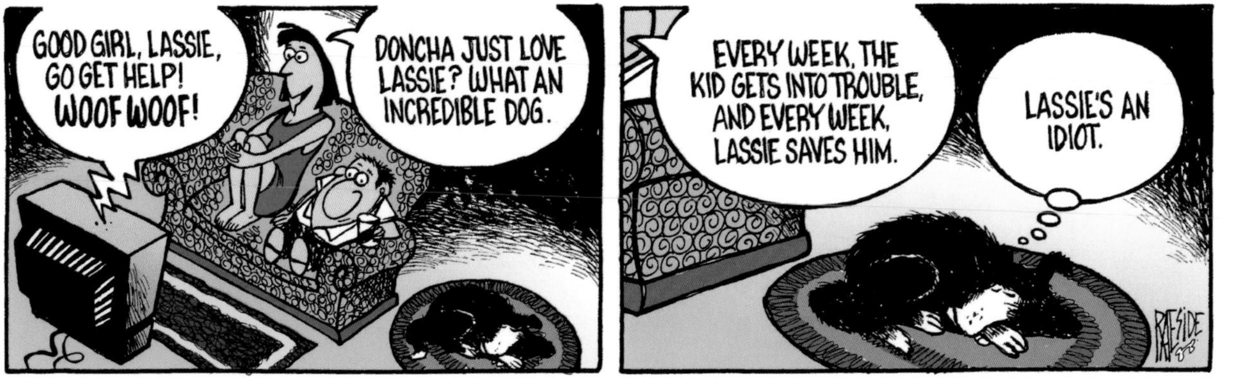
GOOD GIRL, LASSIE, GO GET HELP! WOOF WOOF!
DONCHA JUST LOVE LASSIE? WHAT AN INCREDIBLE DOG.
EVERY WEEK, THE KID GETS INTO TROUBLE, AND EVERY WEEK, LASSIE SAVES HIM.
LASSIE'S AN IDIOT.
RAESIDE

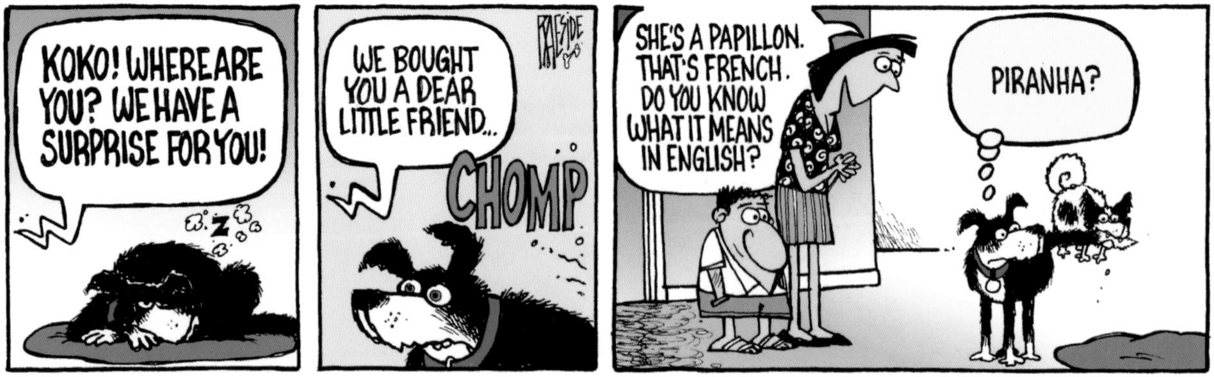
KOKO! WHERE ARE YOU? WE HAVE A SURPRISE FOR YOU!
Z
WE BOUGHT YOU A DEAR LITTLE FRIEND...
CHOMP
SHE'S A PAPILLON. THAT'S FRENCH. DO YOU KNOW WHAT IT MEANS IN ENGLISH?
PIRANHA?

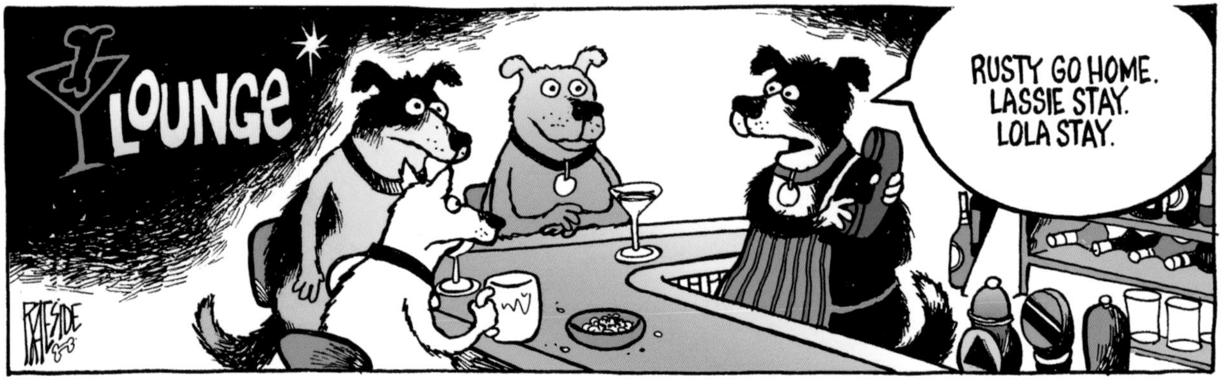
LOUNGE
RUSTY GO HOME. LASSIE STAY. LOLA STAY.

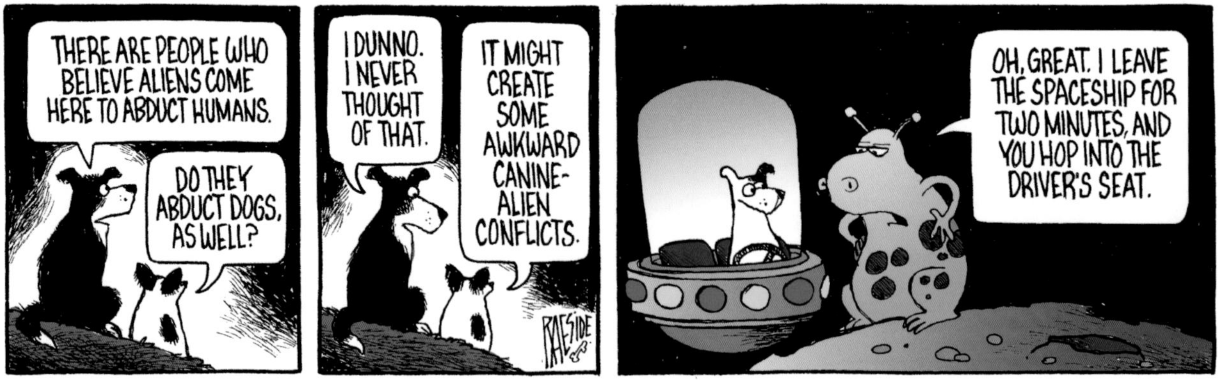
THERE ARE PEOPLE WHO BELIEVE ALIENS COME HERE TO ABDUCT HUMANS.
DO THEY ABDUCT DOGS, AS WELL?
I DUNNO. I NEVER THOUGHT OF THAT.
IT MIGHT CREATE SOME AWKWARD CANINE-ALIEN CONFLICTS.
OH, GREAT. I LEAVE THE SPACESHIP FOR TWO MINUTES, AND YOU HOP INTO THE DRIVER'S SEAT.

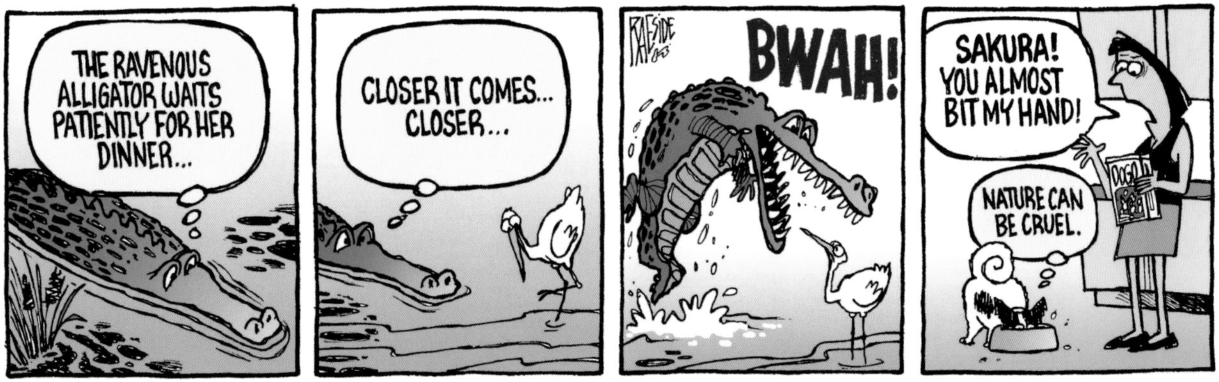
THE RAVENOUS ALLIGATOR WAITS PATIENTLY FOR HER DINNER...
CLOSER IT COMES... CLOSER...
BWAH!
SAKURA! YOU ALMOST BIT MY HAND!
NATURE CAN BE CRUEL.

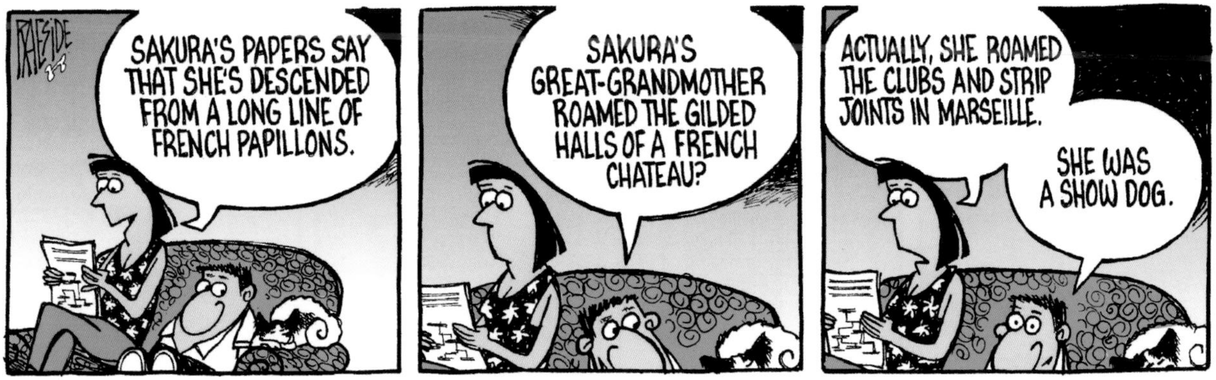
SAKURA'S PAPERS SAY THAT SHE'S DESCENDED FROM A LONG LINE OF FRENCH PAPILLONS.
SAKURA'S GREAT-GRANDMOTHER ROAMED THE GILDED HALLS OF A FRENCH CHATEAU?
ACTUALLY, SHE ROAMED THE CLUBS AND STRIP JOINTS IN MARSEILLE.
SHE WAS A SHOW DOG.

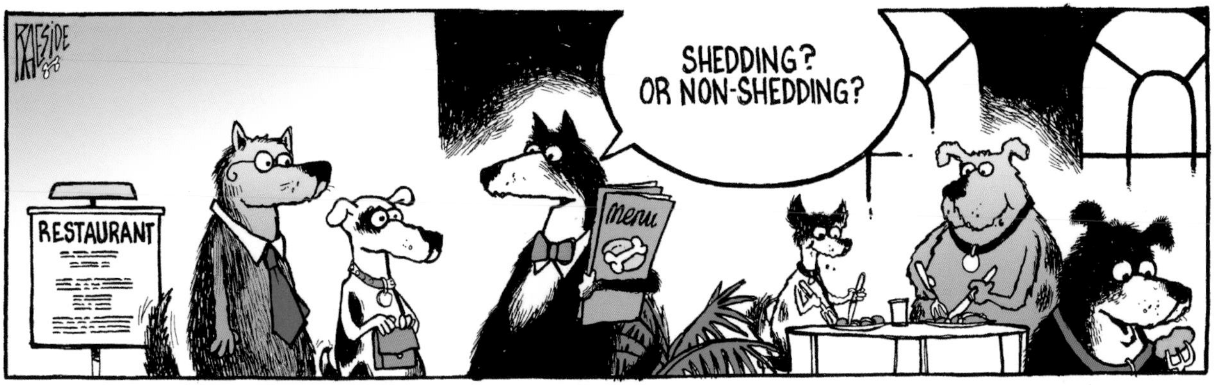
RESTAURANT
SHEDDING? OR NON-SHEDDING?
Menu

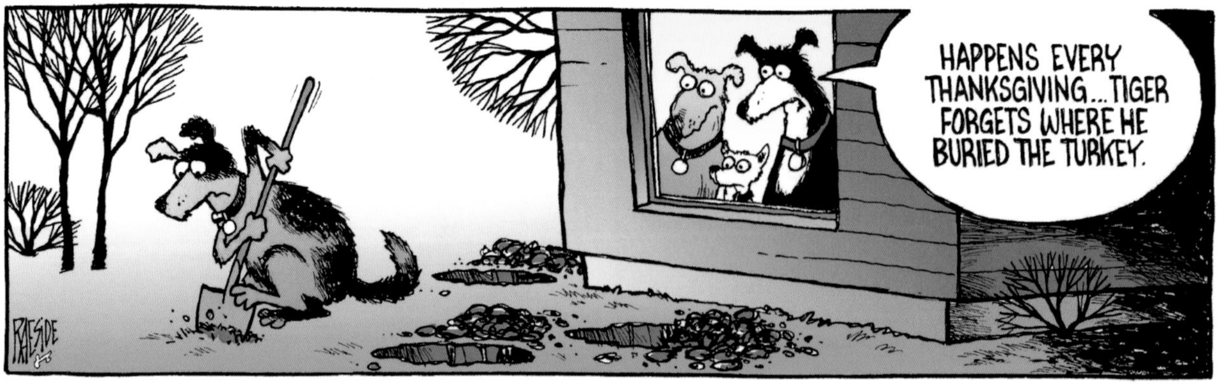
HAPPENS EVERY THANKSGIVING... TIGER FORGETS WHERE HE BURIED THE TURKEY.

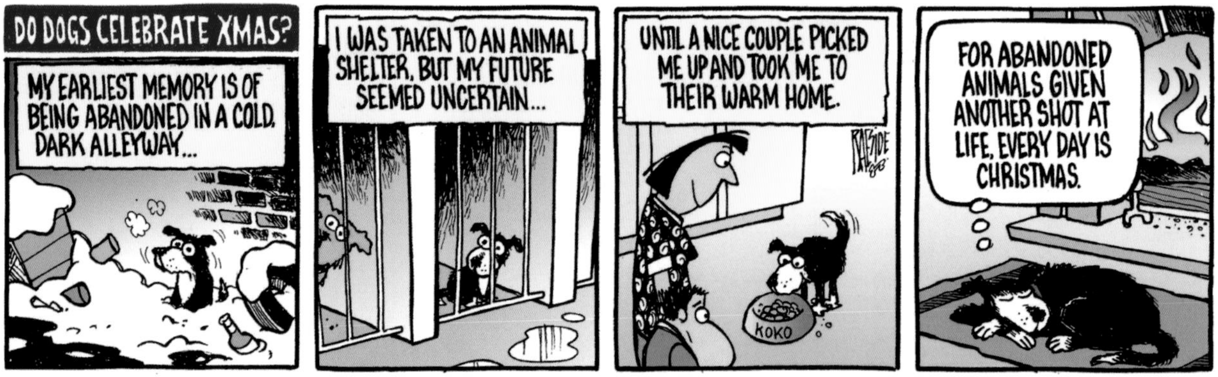
DO DOGS CELEBRATE XMAS?
MY EARLIEST MEMORY IS OF BEING ABANDONED IN A COLD, DARK ALLEYWAY...
I WAS TAKEN TO AN ANIMAL SHELTER, BUT MY FUTURE SEEMED UNCERTAIN...
UNTIL A NICE COUPLE PICKED ME UP AND TOOK ME TO THEIR WARM HOME.
KOKO
FOR ABANDONED ANIMALS GIVEN ANOTHER SHOT AT LIFE, EVERY DAY IS CHRISTMAS.

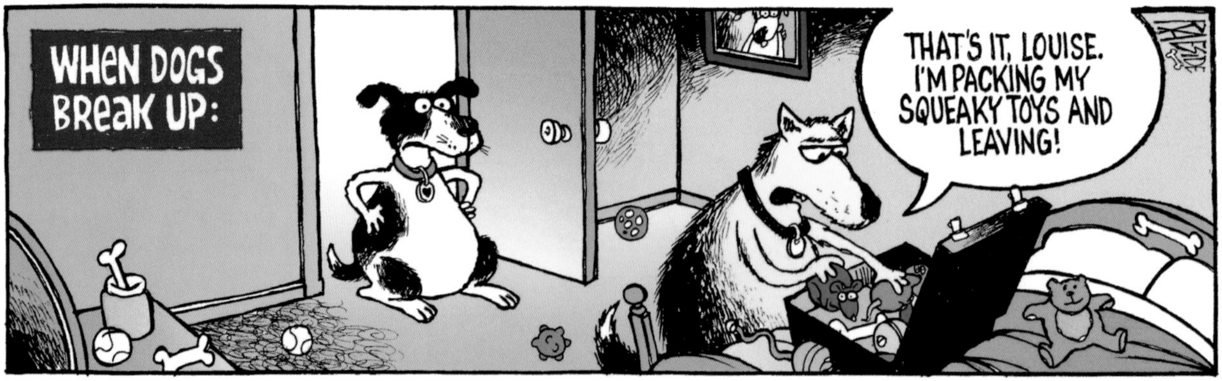
WHEN DOGS BREAK UP:
THAT'S IT, LOUISE. I'M PACKING MY SQUEAKY TOYS AND LEAVING!

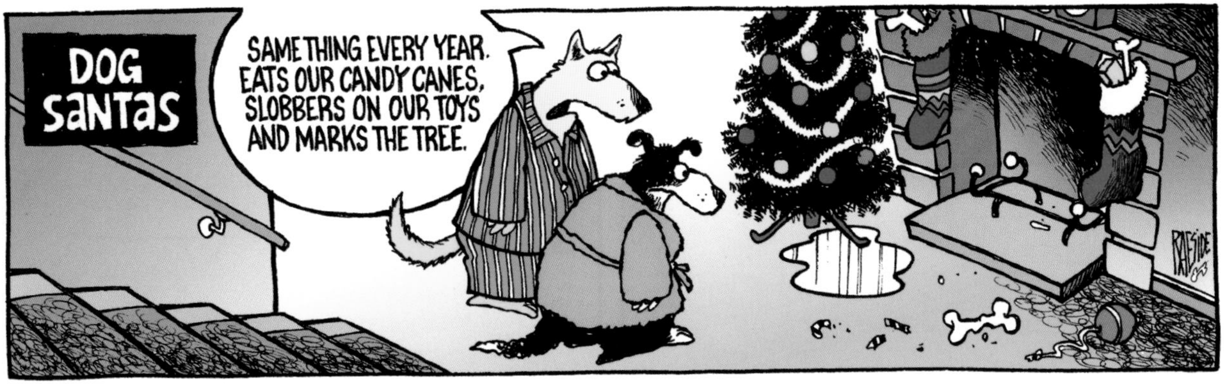
DOG SANTAS
SAME THING EVERY YEAR. EATS OUR CANDY CANES, SLOBBERS ON OUR TOYS AND MARKS THE TREE.
RAESIDE

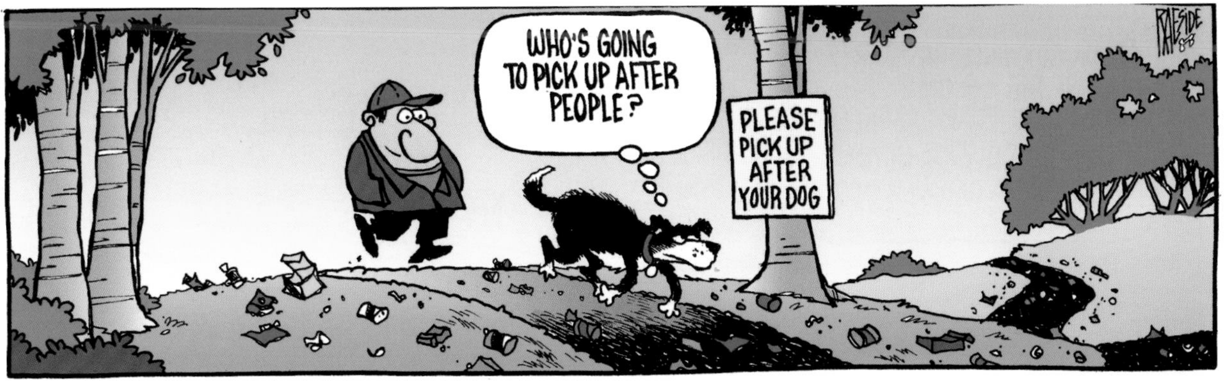
WHO'S GOING TO PICK UP AFTER PEOPLE?
PLEASE PICK UP AFTER YOUR DOG
RAESIDE

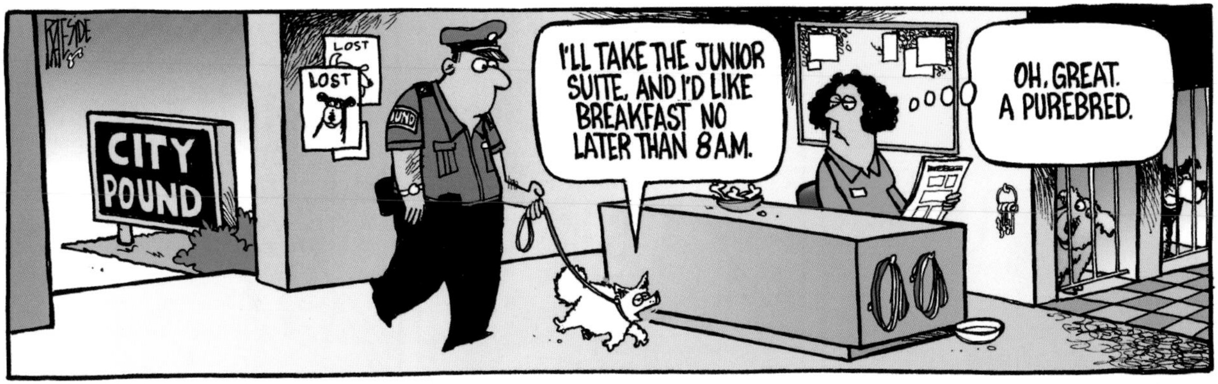
RAESIDE
CITY POUND
LOST
LOST
I'LL TAKE THE JUNIOR SUITE, AND I'D LIKE BREAKFAST NO LATER THAN 8 A.M.
OH, GREAT. A PUREBRED.

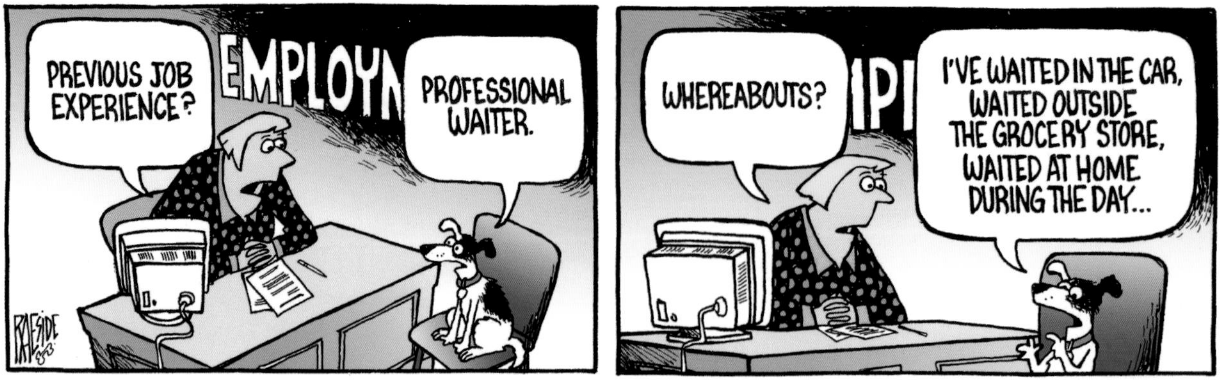
PREVIOUS JOB EXPERIENCE?
PROFESSIONAL WAITER.
WHEREABOUTS?
I'VE WAITED IN THE CAR, WAITED OUTSIDE THE GROCERY STORE, WAITED AT HOME DURING THE DAY...

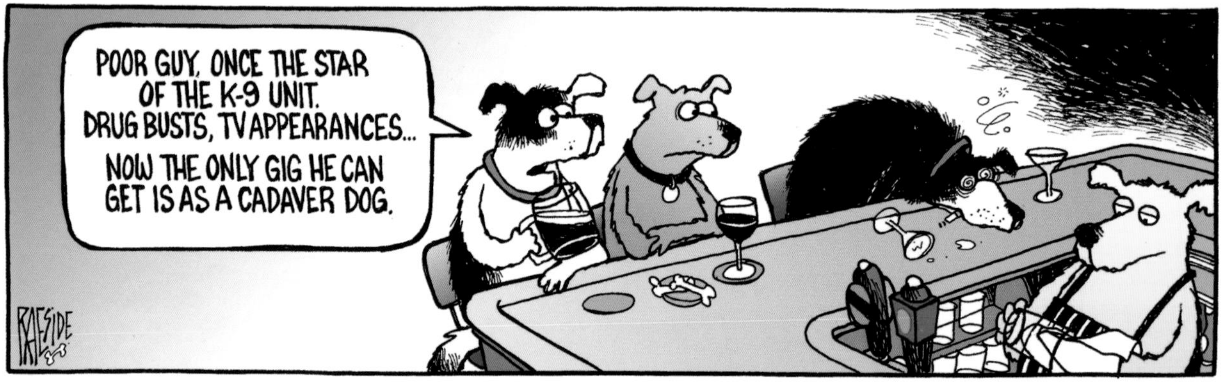
POOR GUY, ONCE THE STAR OF THE K-9 UNIT. DRUG BUSTS, TV APPEARANCES...
NOW THE ONLY GIG HE CAN GET IS AS A CADAVER DOG.

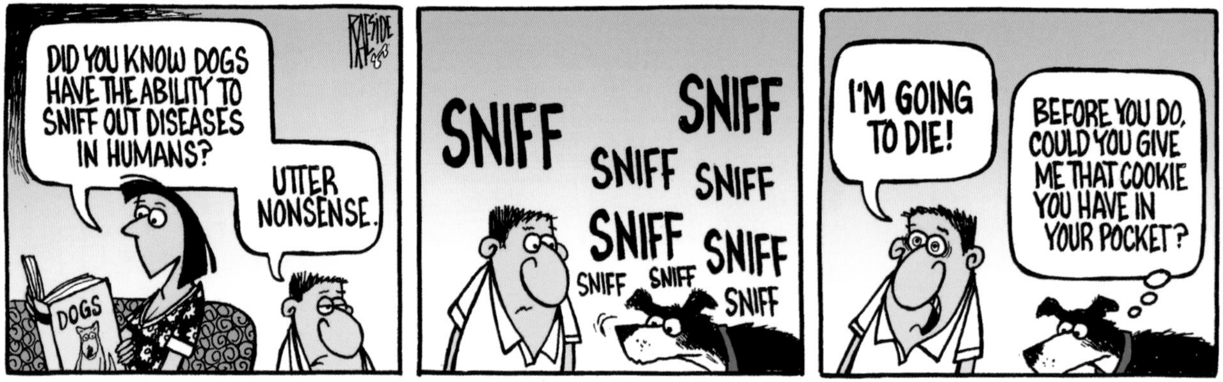
DID YOU KNOW DOGS HAVE THE ABILITY TO SNIFF OUT DISEASES IN HUMANS?
UTTER NONSENSE.
DOGS
SNIFF SNIFF SNIFF SNIFF SNIFF SNIFF SNIFF SNIFF SNIFF
I'M GOING TO DIE!
BEFORE YOU DO, COULD YOU GIVE ME THAT COOKIE YOU HAVE IN YOUR POCKET?

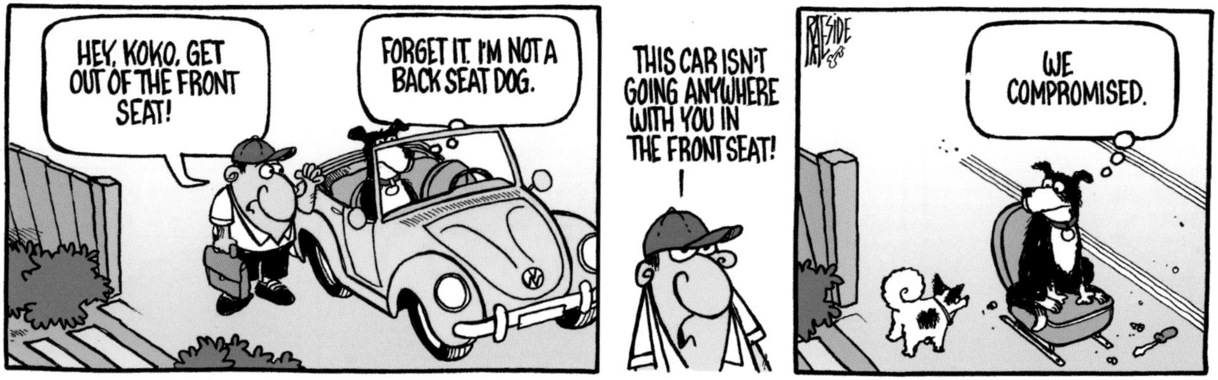
HEY, KOKO, GET OUT OF THE FRONT SEAT!
FORGET IT. I'M NOT A BACK SEAT DOG.
THIS CAR ISN'T GOING ANYWHERE WITH YOU IN THE FRONT SEAT!
WE COMPROMISED.

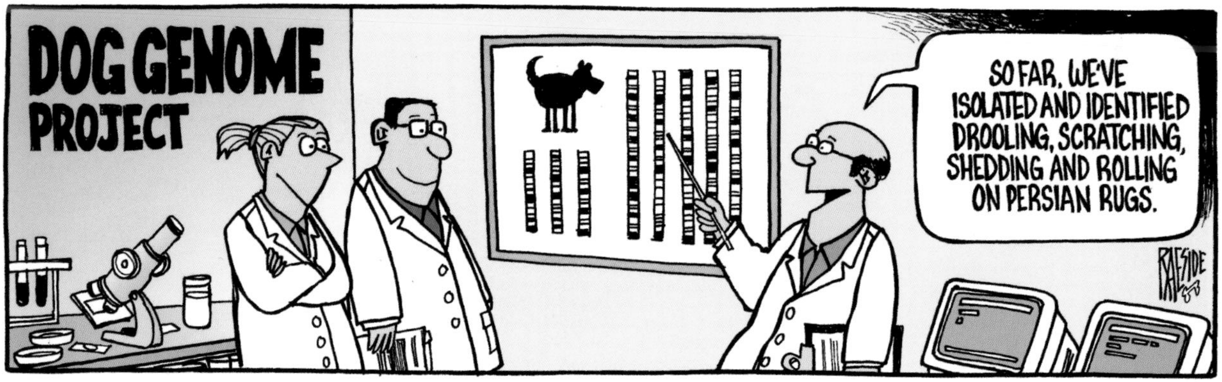
DOG GENOME PROJECT
SO FAR, WE'VE ISOLATED AND IDENTIFIED DROOLING, SCRATCHING, SHEDDING AND ROLLING ON PERSIAN RUGS.

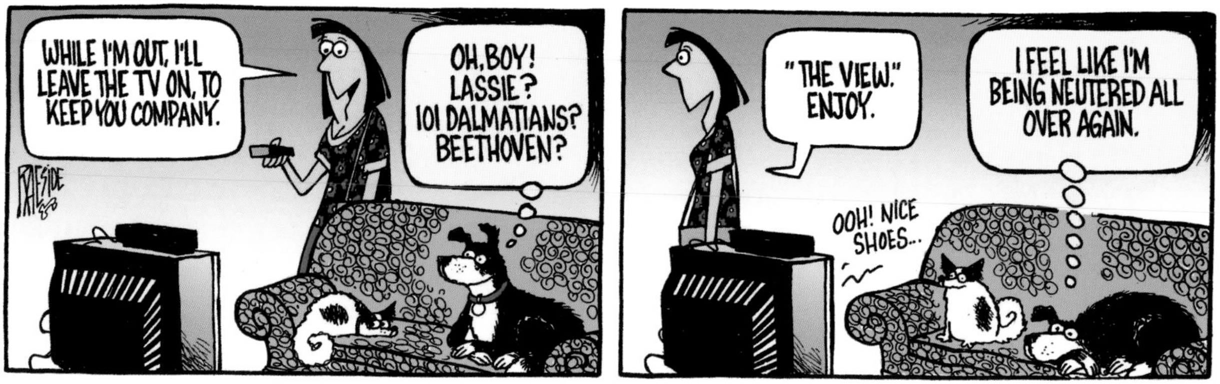
WHILE I'M OUT, I'LL LEAVE THE TV ON, TO KEEP YOU COMPANY.
OH, BOY! LASSIE? 101 DALMATIANS? BEETHOVEN?
"THE VIEW." ENJOY.
OOH! NICE SHOES...
I FEEL LIKE I'M BEING NEUTERED ALL OVER AGAIN.

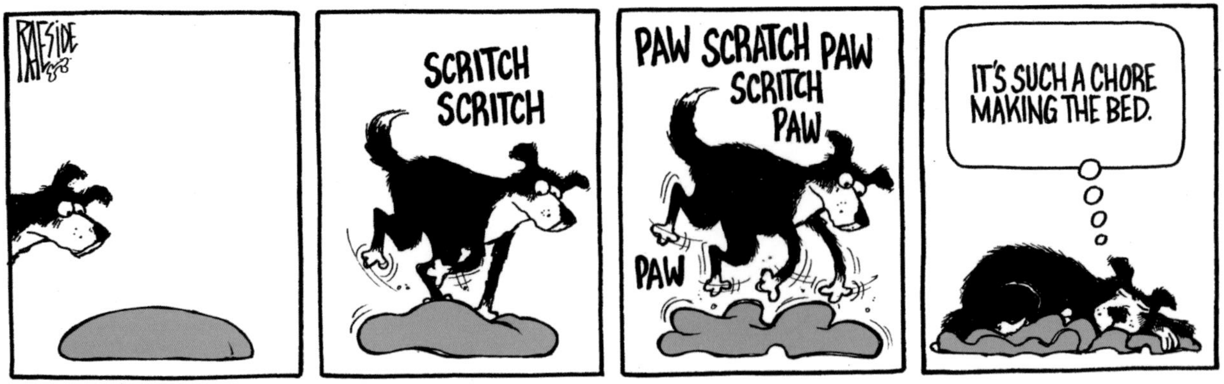
SCRITCH
SCRITCH
PAW SCRATCH PAW
SCRITCH
PAW
PAW
IT'S SUCH A CHORE MAKING THE BED.

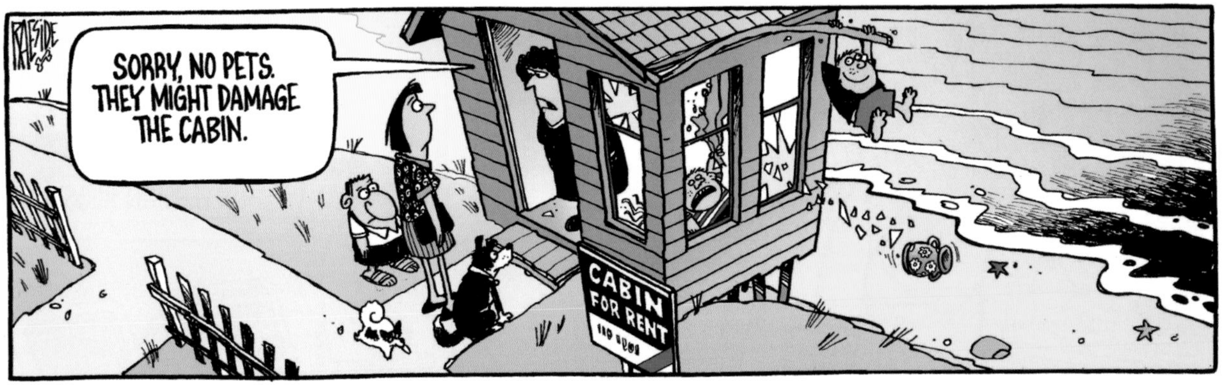
SORRY, NO PETS. THEY MIGHT DAMAGE THE CABIN.
CABIN FOR RENT

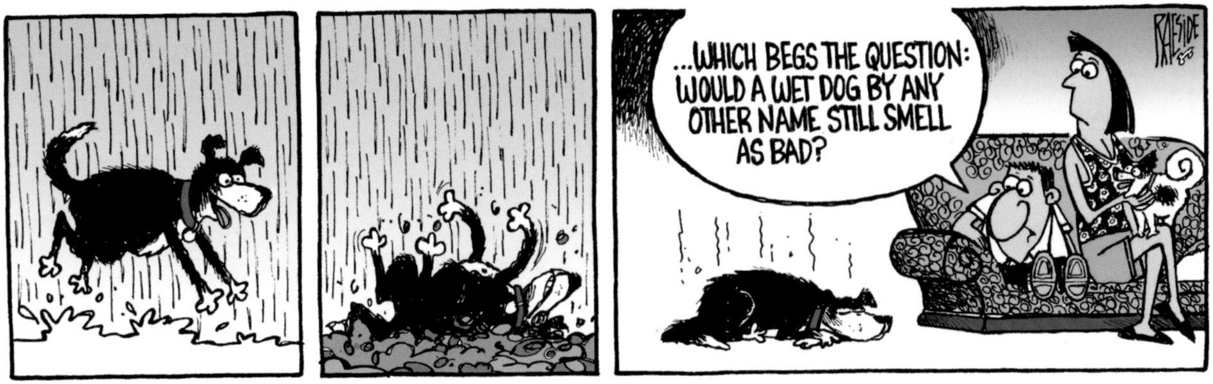
...WHICH BEGS THE QUESTION: WOULD A WET DOG BY ANY OTHER NAME STILL SMELL AS BAD?

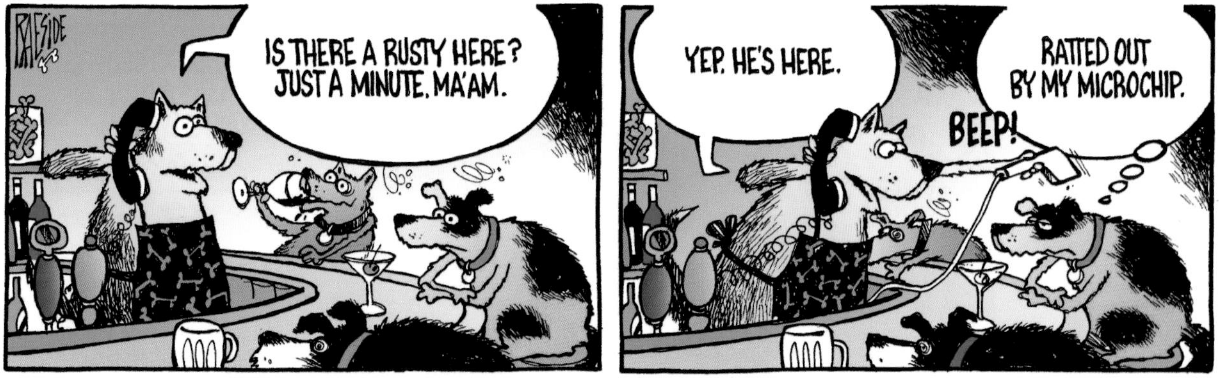
IS THERE A RUSTY HERE? JUST A MINUTE, MA'AM.
YEP. HE'S HERE.
BEEP!
RATTED OUT BY MY MICROCHIP.

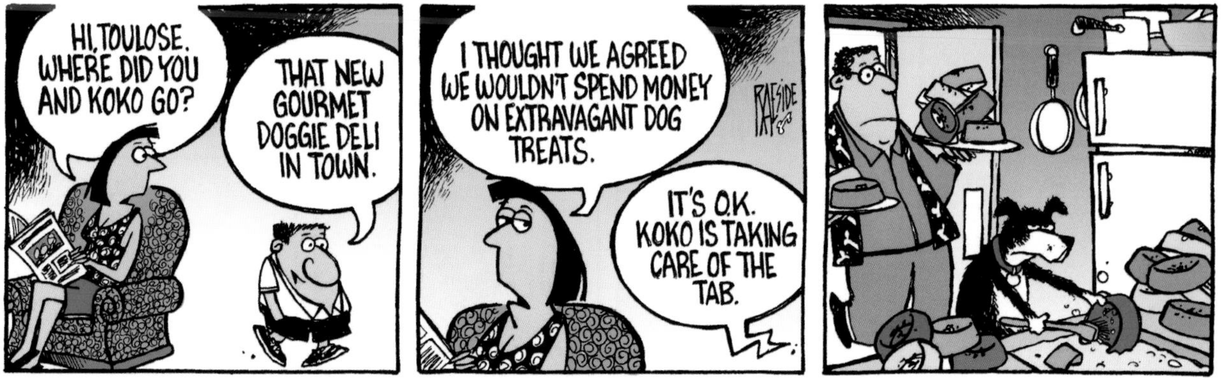
HI, TOULOSE. WHERE DID YOU AND KOKO GO?
THAT NEW GOURMET DOGGIE DELI IN TOWN.
I THOUGHT WE AGREED WE WOULDN'T SPEND MONEY ON EXTRAVAGANT DOG TREATS.
IT'S O.K. KOKO IS TAKING CARE OF THE TAB.

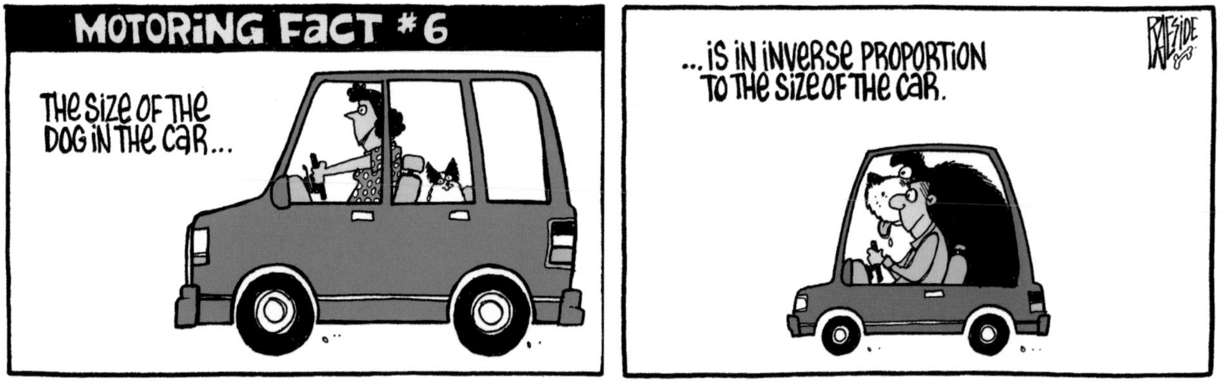
MOTORING FACT #6
The size of the dog in the car...
...is in inverse proportion to the size of the car.

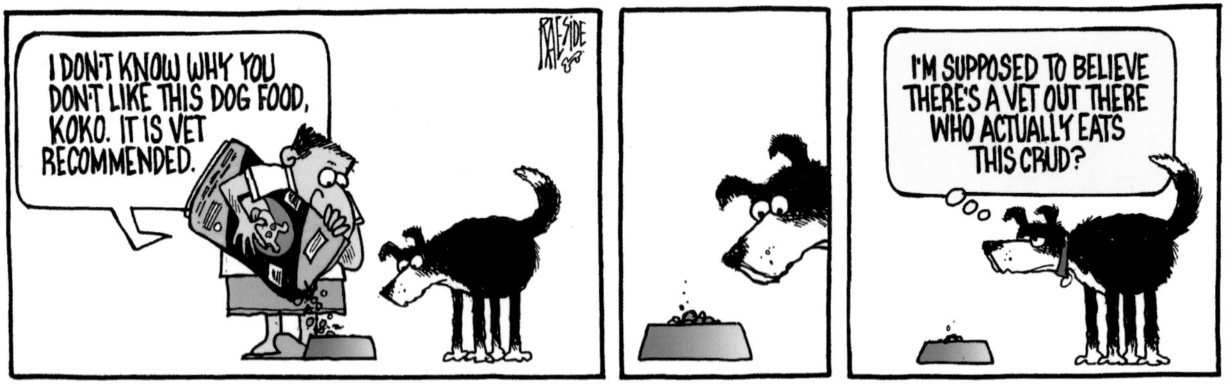
I DON'T KNOW WHY YOU DON'T LIKE THIS DOG FOOD, KOKO. IT IS VET RECOMMENDED.
I'M SUPPOSED TO BELIEVE THERE'S A VET OUT THERE WHO ACTUALLY EATS THIS CRUD?

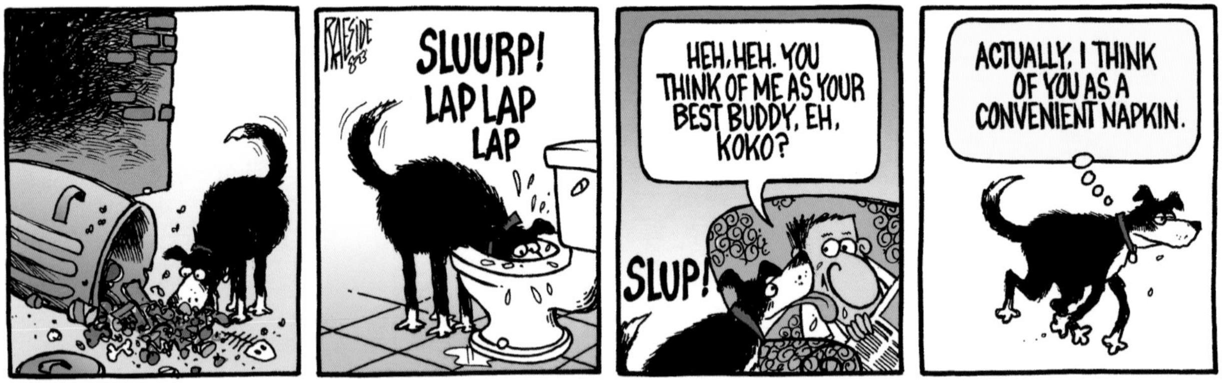
SLUURP!
LAP LAP LAP
HEH, HEH. YOU THINK OF ME AS YOUR BEST BUDDY, EH, KOKO?
SLUP!
ACTUALLY, I THINK OF YOU AS A CONVENIENT NAPKIN.

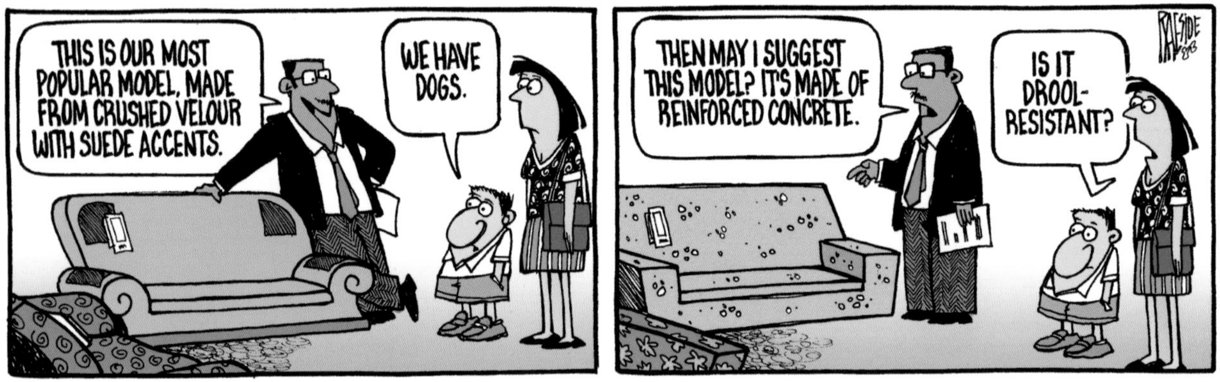
THIS IS OUR MOST POPULAR MODEL, MADE FROM CRUSHED VELOUR WITH SUEDE ACCENTS.
WE HAVE DOGS.
THEN MAY I SUGGEST THIS MODEL? IT'S MADE OF REINFORCED CONCRETE.
IS IT DROOL-RESISTANT?

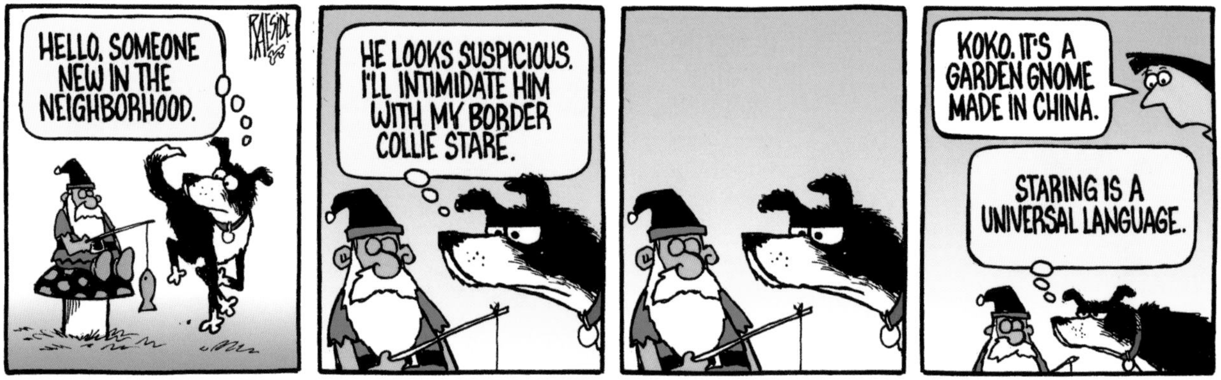
HELLO, SOMEONE NEW IN THE NEIGHBORHOOD.
HE LOOKS SUSPICIOUS. I'LL INTIMIDATE HIM WITH MY BORDER COLLIE STARE.
KOKO. IT'S A GARDEN GNOME MADE IN CHINA.
STARING IS A UNIVERSAL LANGUAGE.

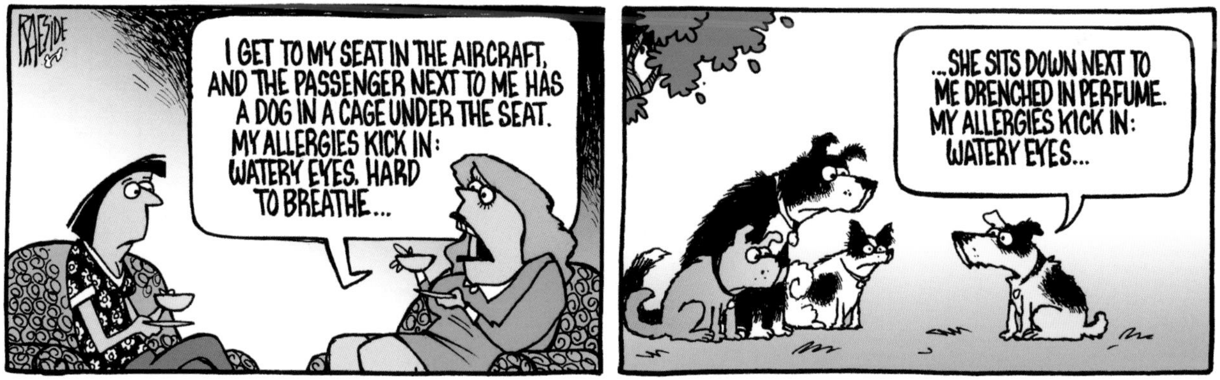
I GET TO MY SEAT IN THE AIRCRAFT, AND THE PASSENGER NEXT TO ME HAS A DOG IN A CAGE UNDER THE SEAT. MY ALLERGIES KICK IN: WATERY EYES. HARD TO BREATHE...
...SHE SITS DOWN NEXT TO ME DRENCHED IN PERFUME. MY ALLERGIES KICK IN: WATERY EYES...

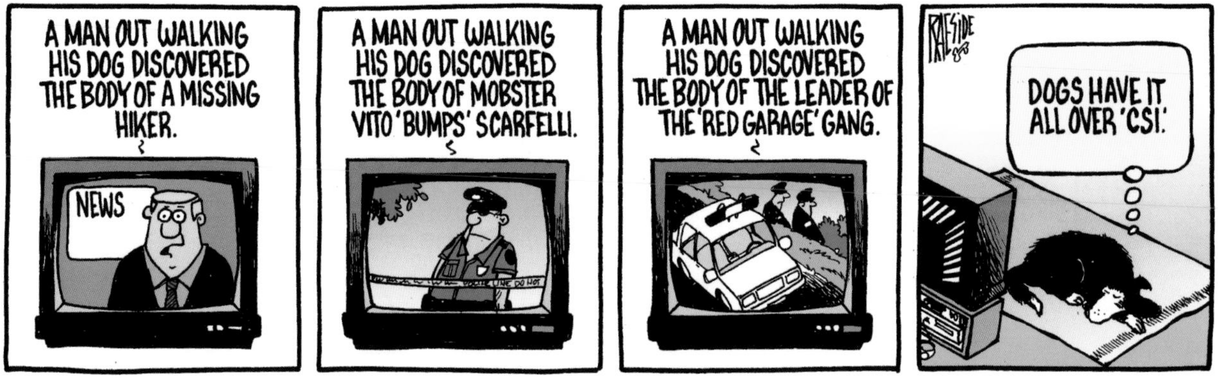
A MAN OUT WALKING HIS DOG DISCOVERED THE BODY OF A MISSING HIKER.
NEWS
A MAN OUT WALKING HIS DOG DISCOVERED THE BODY OF MOBSTER VITO 'BUMPS' SCARFELLI.
A MAN OUT WALKING HIS DOG DISCOVERED THE BODY OF THE LEADER OF THE 'RED GARAGE' GANG.
DOGS HAVE IT ALL OVER 'CSI.'

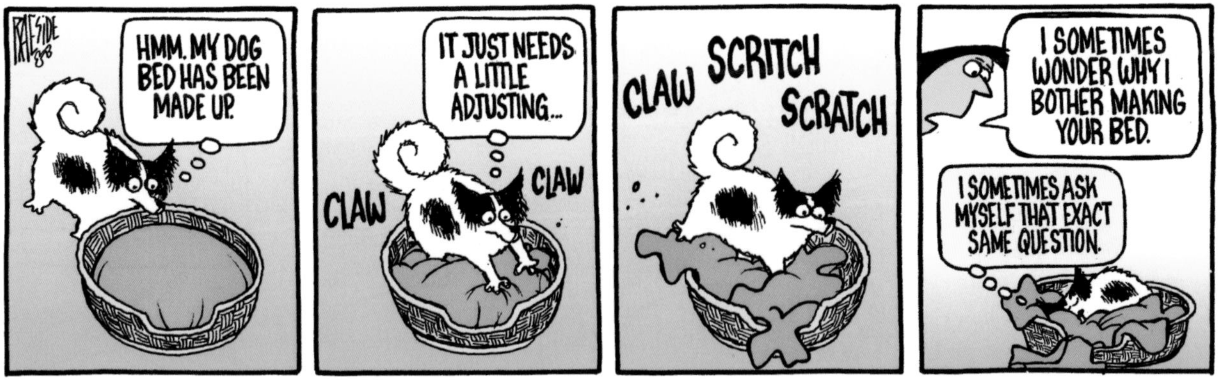
HMM. MY DOG BED HAS BEEN MADE UP.
IT JUST NEEDS A LITTLE ADJUSTING...
CLAW
CLAW
CLAW
SCRITCH
SCRATCH
I SOMETIMES WONDER WHY I BOTHER MAKING YOUR BED.
I SOMETIMES ASK MYSELF THAT EXACT SAME QUESTION.

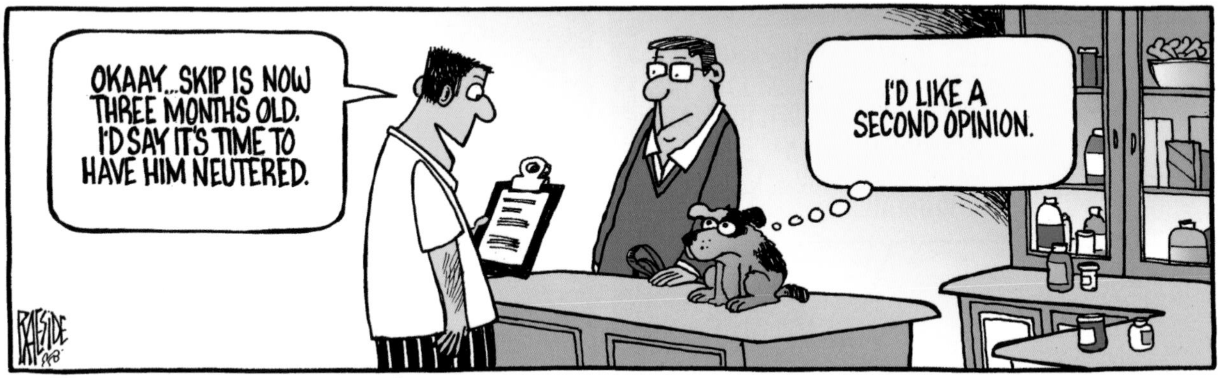
OKAAY...SKIP IS NOW THREE MONTHS OLD. I'D SAY IT'S TIME TO HAVE HIM NEUTERED.
I'D LIKE A SECOND OPINION.

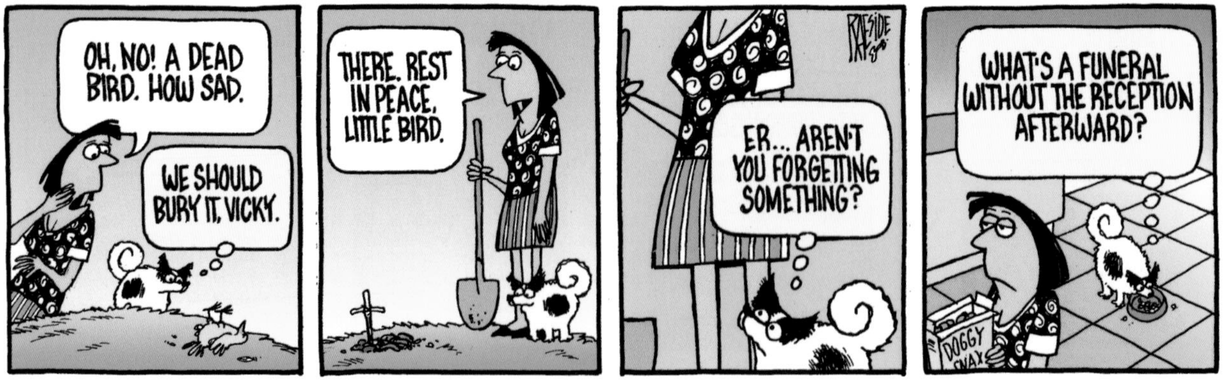
OH, NO! A DEAD BIRD. HOW SAD.
WE SHOULD BURY IT, VICKY.
THERE. REST IN PEACE, LITTLE BIRD.
ER... AREN'T YOU FORGETTING SOMETHING?
WHAT'S A FUNERAL WITHOUT THE RECEPTION AFTERWARD?
DOGGY SNAX

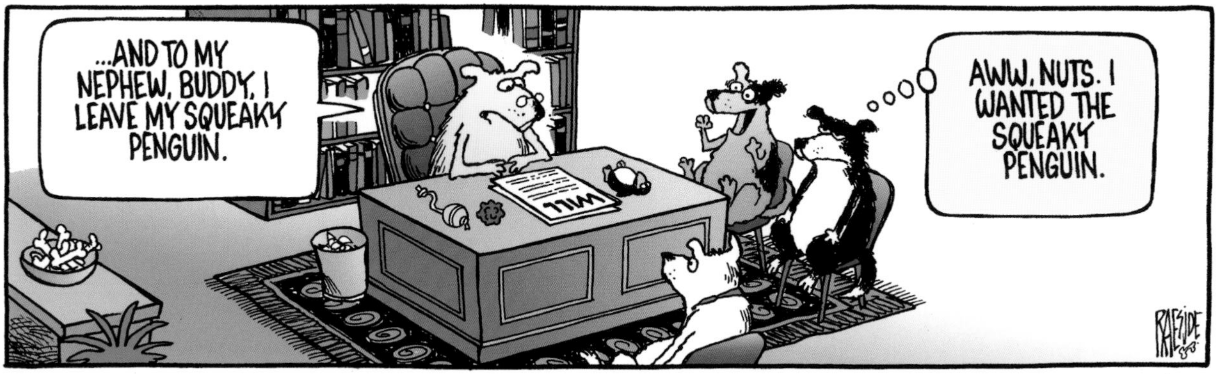
...AND TO MY NEPHEW, BUDDY, I LEAVE MY SQUEAKY PENGUIN.
WILL
AWW, NUTS. I WANTED THE SQUEAKY PENGUIN.

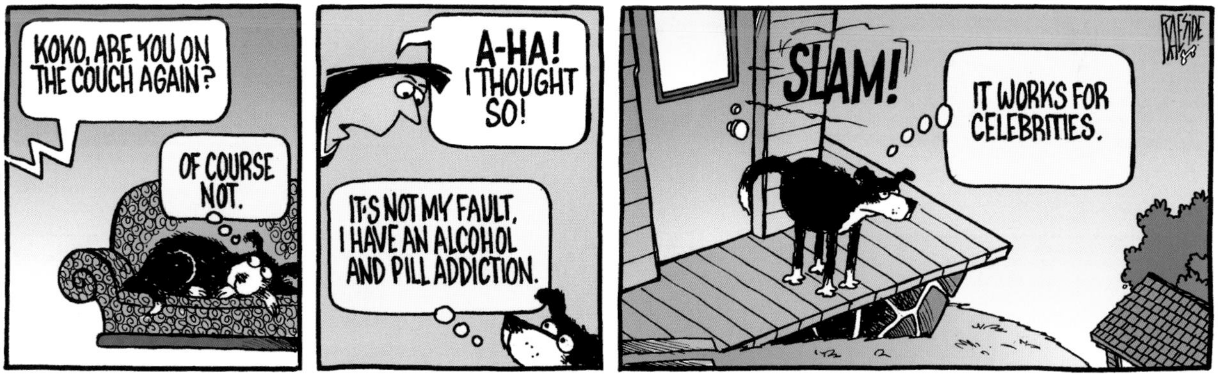
KOKO, ARE YOU ON THE COUCH AGAIN?
OF COURSE NOT.
A-HA! I THOUGHT SO!
IT'S NOT MY FAULT, I HAVE AN ALCOHOL AND PILL ADDICTION.
SLAM!
IT WORKS FOR CELEBRITIES.

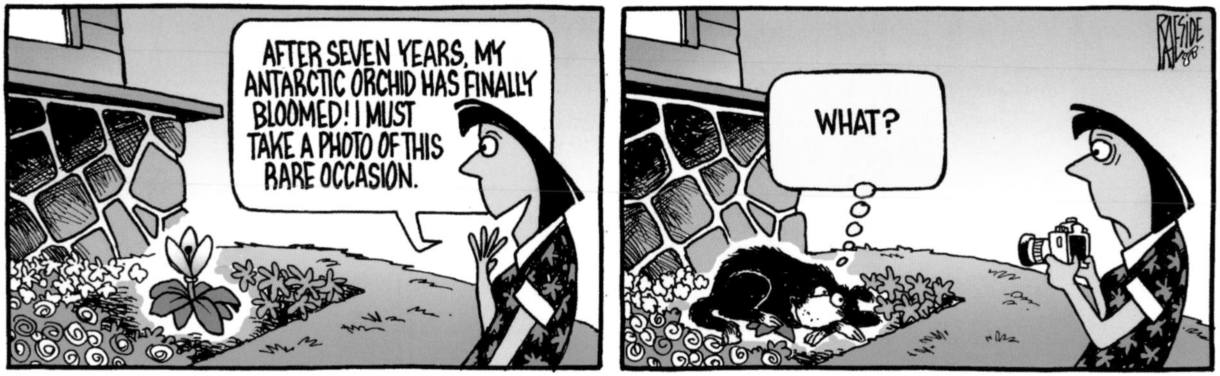
AFTER SEVEN YEARS, MY ANTARCTIC ORCHID HAS FINALLY BLOOMED! I MUST TAKE A PHOTO OF THIS RARE OCCASION.
WHAT?

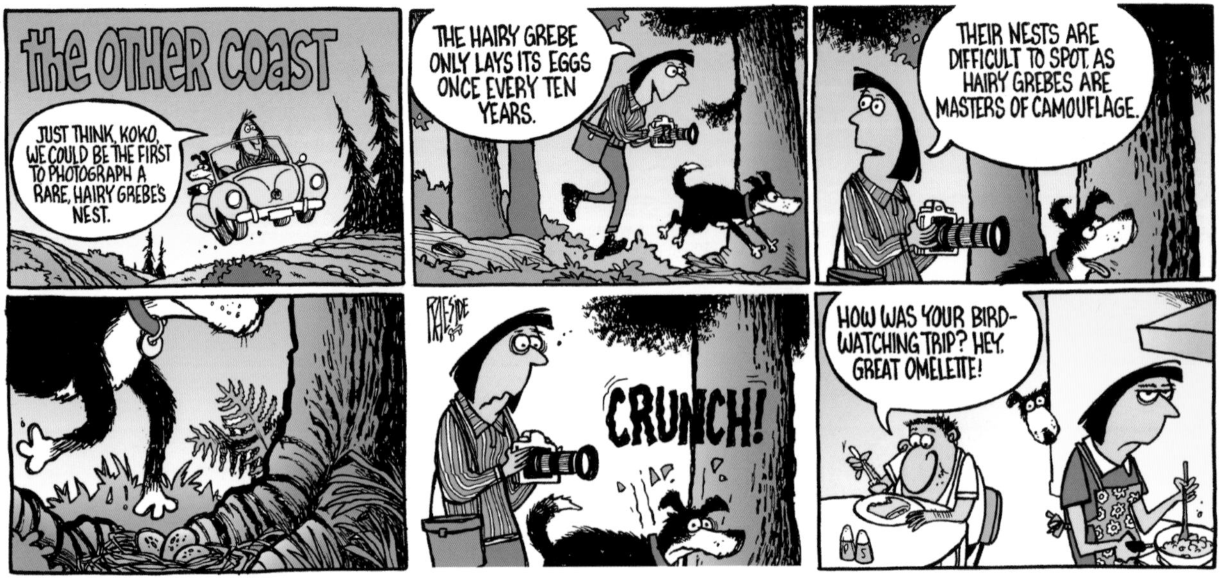
the OTHER COAST
JUST THINK, KOKO, WE COULD BE THE FIRST TO PHOTOGRAPH A RARE, HAIRY GREBE'S NEST.
THE HAIRY GREBE ONLY LAYS ITS EGGS ONCE EVERY TEN YEARS.
THEIR NESTS ARE DIFFICULT TO SPOT, AS HAIRY GREBES ARE MASTERS OF CAMOUFLAGE.
CRUNCH!
HOW WAS YOUR BIRD-WATCHING TRIP? HEY, GREAT OMELETTE!

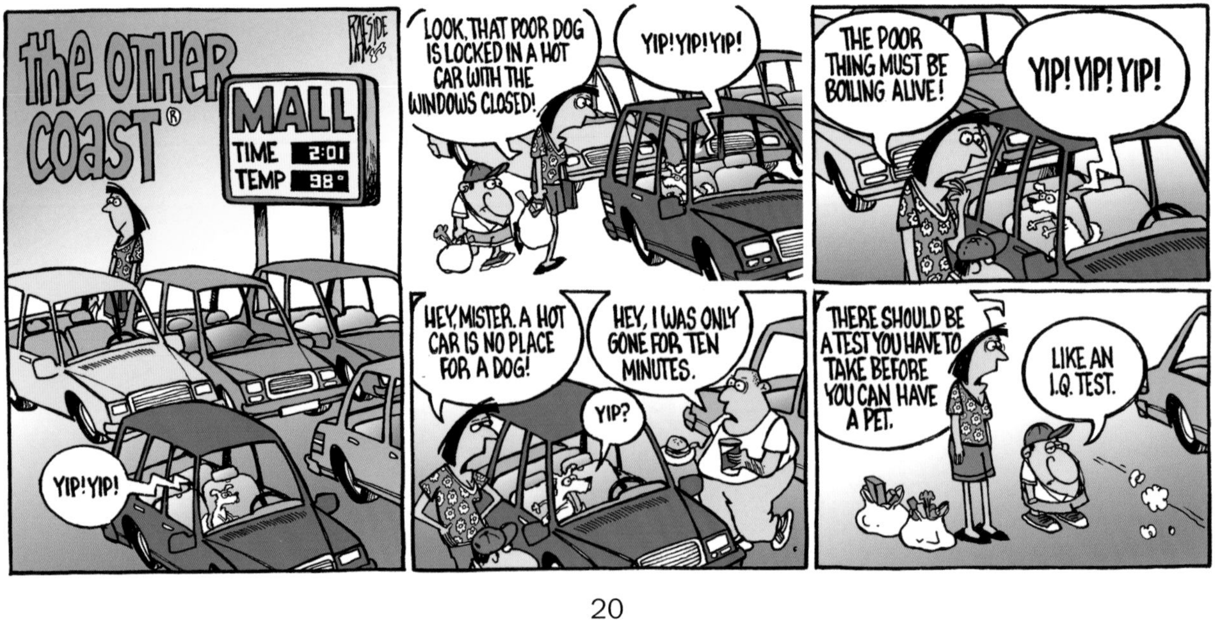
the OTHER COAST®
MALL
TIME 2:01
TEMP 98°
YIP! YIP!
LOOK, THAT POOR DOG IS LOCKED IN A HOT CAR WITH THE WINDOWS CLOSED!
YIP! YIP! YIP!
THE POOR THING MUST BE BOILING ALIVE!
YIP! YIP! YIP!
HEY, MISTER. A HOT CAR IS NO PLACE FOR A DOG!
HEY, I WAS ONLY GONE FOR TEN MINUTES.
YIP?
THERE SHOULD BE A TEST YOU HAVE TO TAKE BEFORE YOU CAN HAVE A PET.
LIKE AN I.Q. TEST.

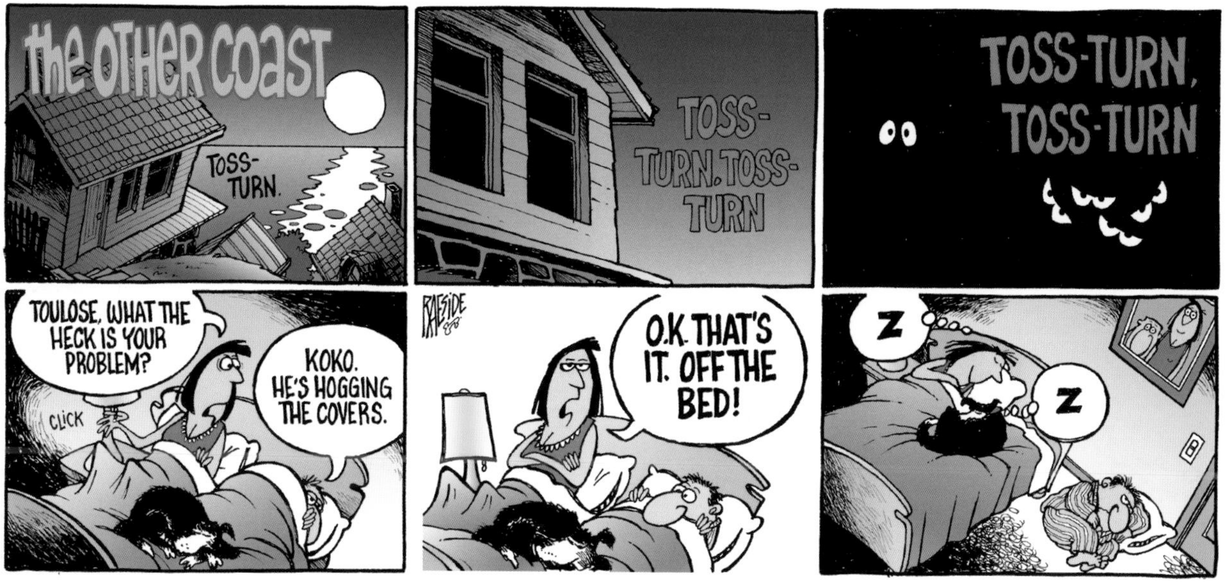

the OTHER COAST
TOSS-TURN.
TOSS-TURN, TOSS-TURN
TOSS-TURN, TOSS-TURN, TOSS-TURN
TOULOSE, WHAT THE HECK IS YOUR PROBLEM?
CLICK
KOKO. HE'S HOGGING THE COVERS.
O.K. THAT'S IT. OFF THE BED!
Z
Z

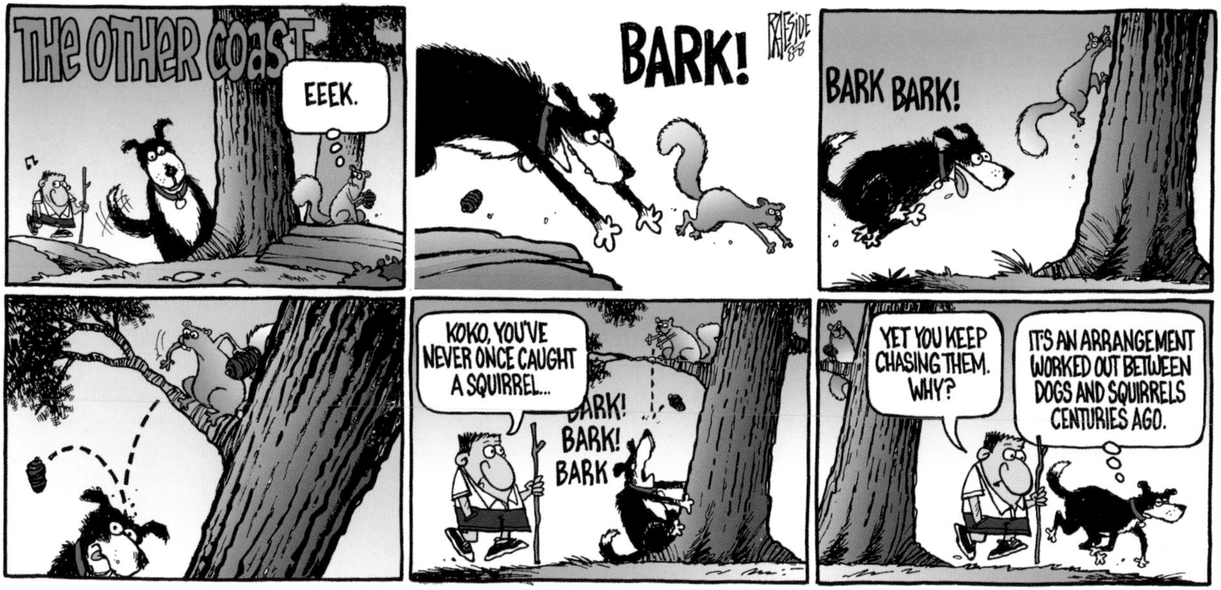

THE OTHER COAST
EEEK.
BARK!
BARK BARK!
KOKO, YOU'VE NEVER ONCE CAUGHT A SQUIRREL...
BARK! BARK! BARK
YET YOU KEEP CHASING THEM. WHY?
IT'S AN ARRANGEMENT WORKED OUT BETWEEN DOGS AND SQUIRRELS CENTURIES AGO.

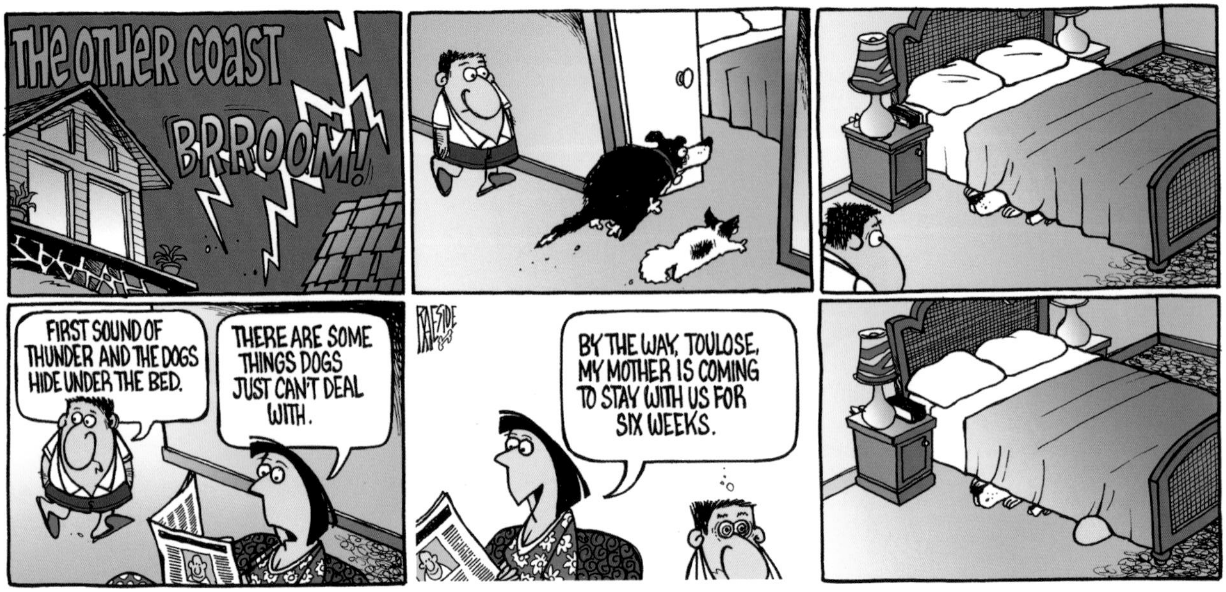
THE OTHER COAST
BRROOM!
FIRST SOUND OF THUNDER AND THE DOGS HIDE UNDER THE BED.
THERE ARE SOME THINGS DOGS JUST CAN'T DEAL WITH.
BY THE WAY, TOULOSE, MY MOTHER IS COMING TO STAY WITH US FOR SIX WEEKS.

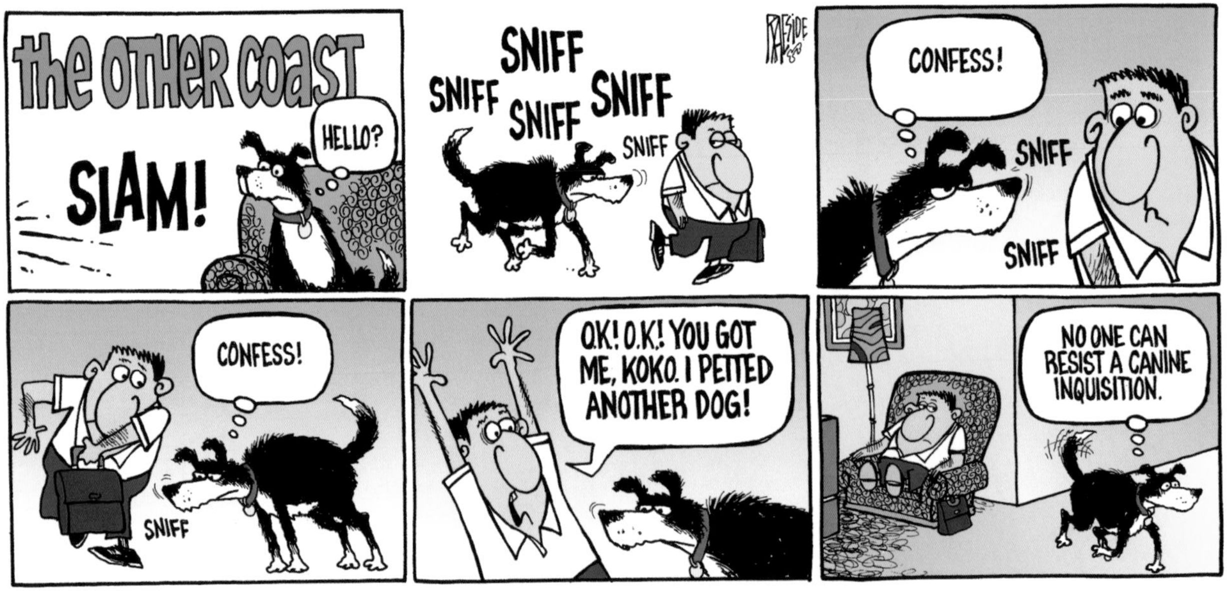
the OTHER COAST
SLAM!
HELLO?
SNIFF
SNIFF
SNIFF
SNIFF
SNIFF
CONFESS!
SNIFF
SNIFF
CONFESS!
SNIFF
O.K! O.K! YOU GOT ME, KOKO. I PETTED ANOTHER DOG!
NO ONE CAN RESIST A CANINE INQUISITION.

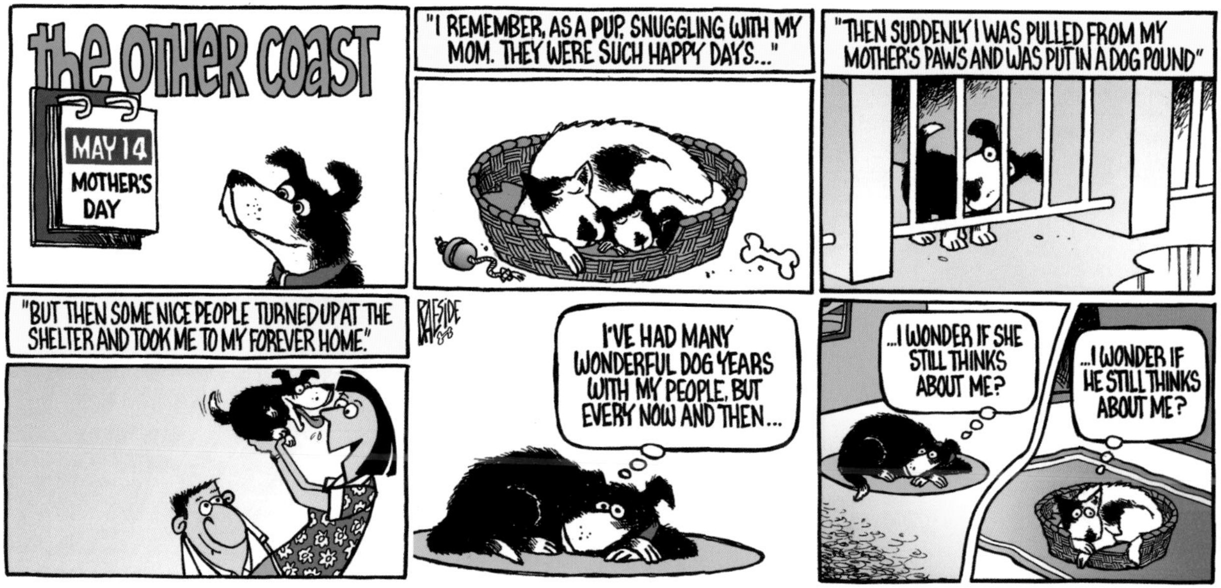
THE OTHER COAST
MAY 14
MOTHER'S DAY
"I REMEMBER, AS A PUP, SNUGGLING WITH MY MOM. THEY WERE SUCH HAPPY DAYS..."
"THEN SUDDENLY I WAS PULLED FROM MY MOTHER'S PAWS AND WAS PUT IN A DOG POUND"
"BUT THEN SOME NICE PEOPLE TURNED UP AT THE SHELTER AND TOOK ME TO MY FOREVER HOME."
I'VE HAD MANY WONDERFUL DOG YEARS WITH MY PEOPLE, BUT EVERY NOW AND THEN...
...I WONDER IF SHE STILL THINKS ABOUT ME?
...I WONDER IF HE STILL THINKS ABOUT ME?

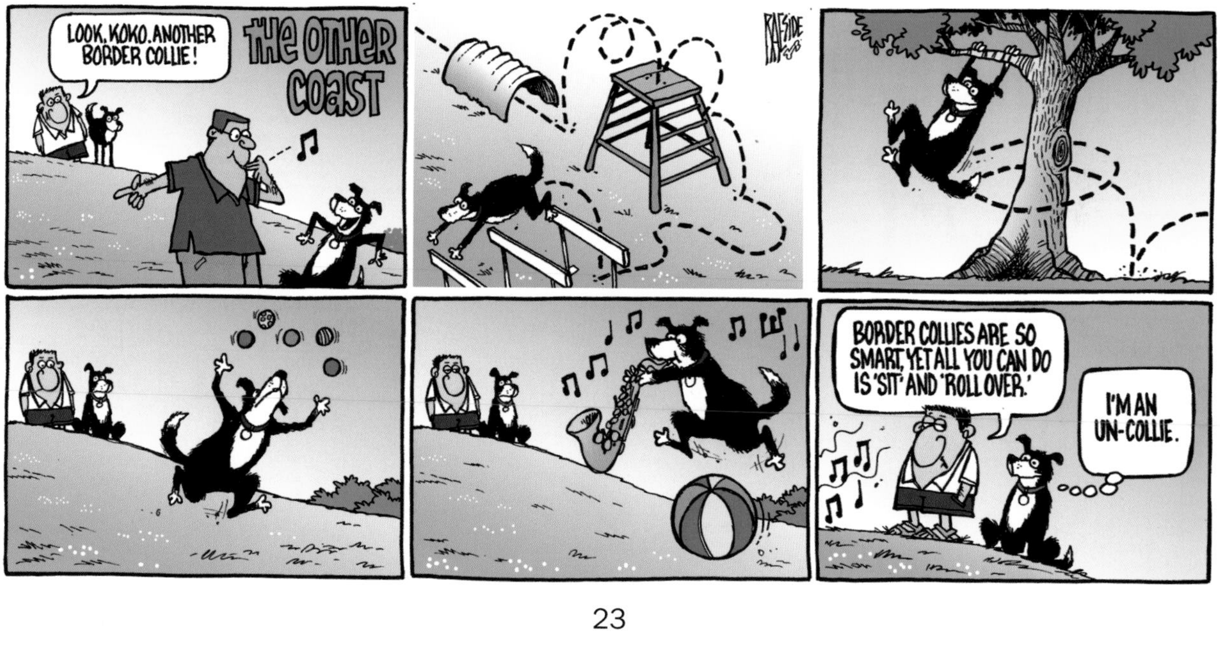
LOOK, KOKO. ANOTHER BORDER COLLIE!
THE OTHER COAST
BORDER COLLIES ARE SO SMART, YET ALL YOU CAN DO IS 'SIT' AND 'ROLL OVER.'
I'M AN UN-COLLIE.

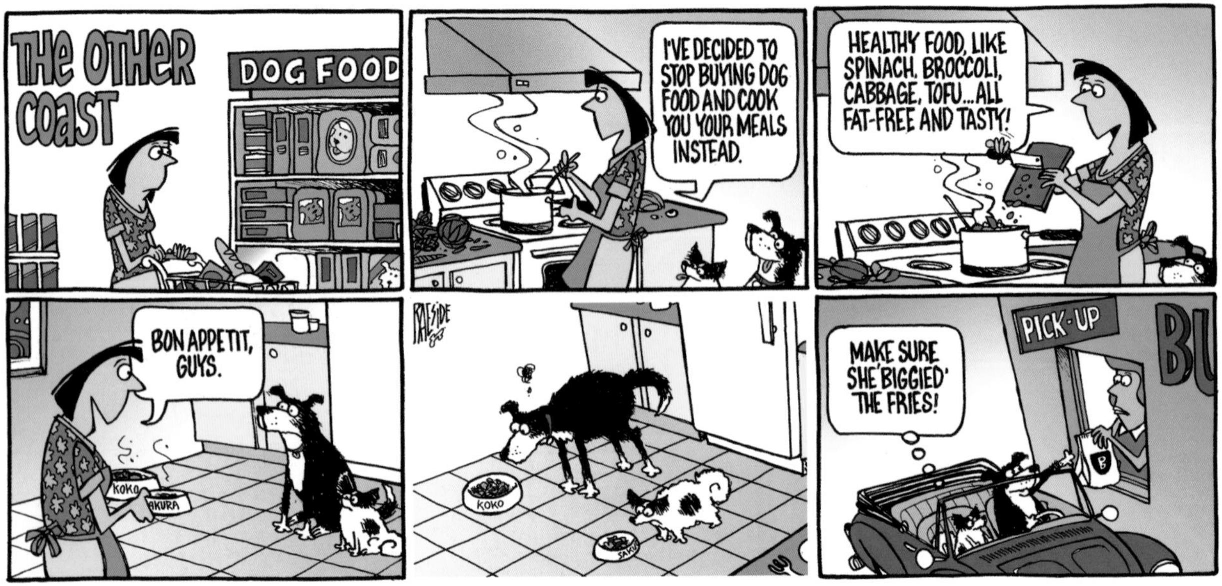
THE OTHER COAST
DOG FOOD
I'VE DECIDED TO STOP BUYING DOG FOOD AND COOK YOU YOUR MEALS INSTEAD.
HEALTHY FOOD, LIKE SPINACH, BROCCOLI, CABBAGE, TOFU...ALL FAT-FREE AND TASTY!
BON APPETIT, GUYS.
KOKO
KOKO
PICK-UP
MAKE SURE SHE 'BIGGIED' THE FRIES!
B

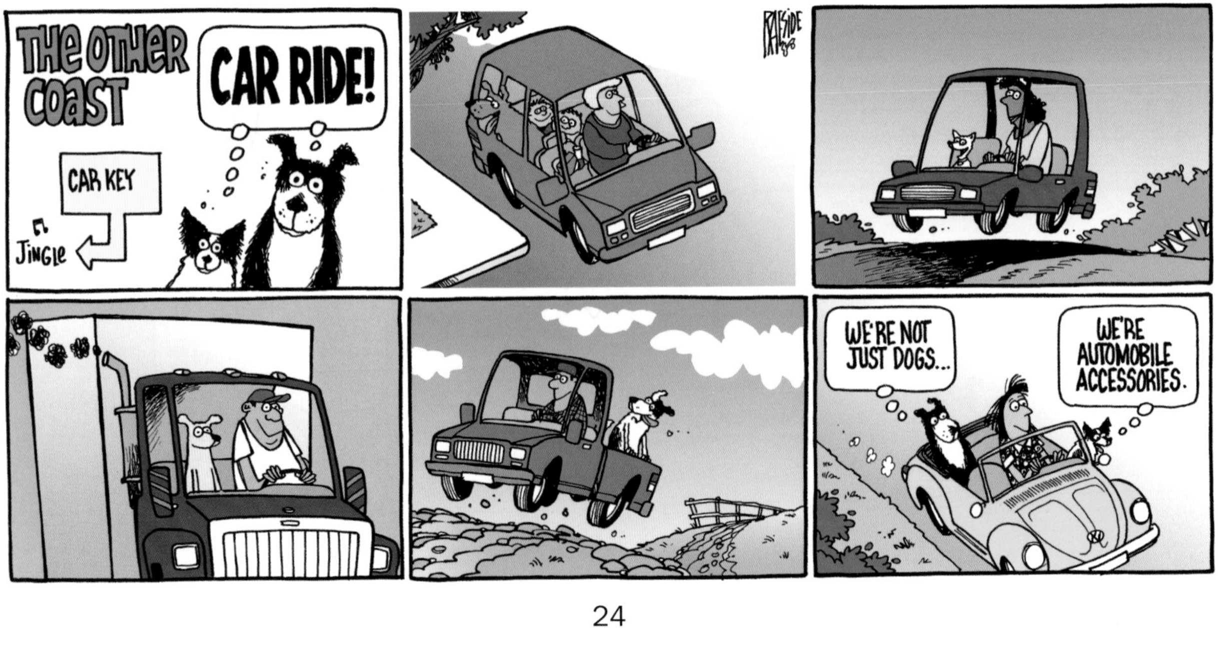
THE OTHER COAST
CAR RIDE!
CAR KEY
JINGLE
WE'RE NOT JUST DOGS...
WE'RE AUTOMOBILE ACCESSORIES.

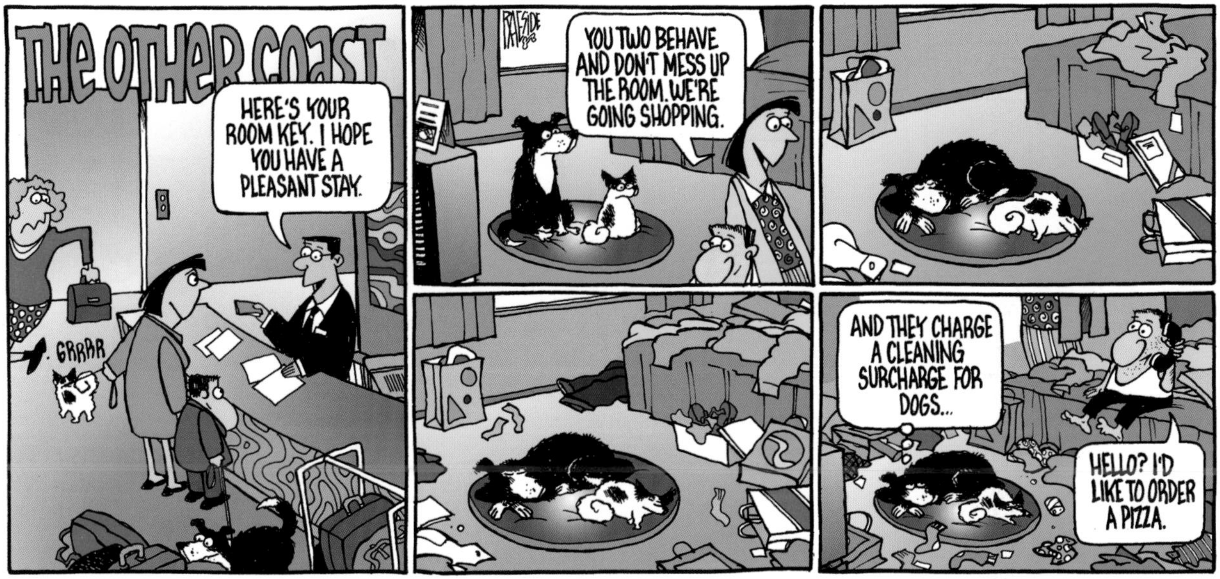
THE OTHER COAST
HERE'S YOUR ROOM KEY. I HOPE YOU HAVE A PLEASANT STAY.
GRRRR
YOU TWO BEHAVE AND DON'T MESS UP THE ROOM. WE'RE GOING SHOPPING.
AND THEY CHARGE A CLEANING SURCHARGE FOR DOGS...
HELLO? I'D LIKE TO ORDER A PIZZA.

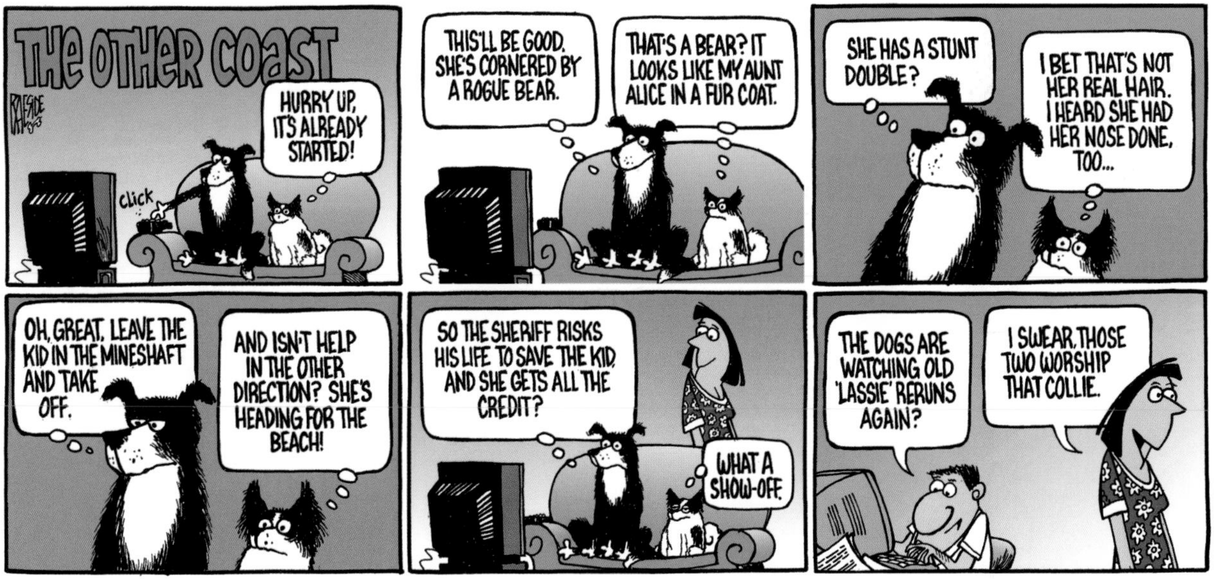
THE OTHER COAST
HURRY UP, IT'S ALREADY STARTED!
CLICK
THIS'LL BE GOOD. SHE'S CORNERED BY A ROGUE BEAR.
THAT'S A BEAR? IT LOOKS LIKE MY AUNT ALICE IN A FUR COAT.
SHE HAS A STUNT DOUBLE?
I BET THAT'S NOT HER REAL HAIR. I HEARD SHE HAD HER NOSE DONE, TOO...
OH, GREAT, LEAVE THE KID IN THE MINESHAFT AND TAKE OFF.
AND ISN'T HELP IN THE OTHER DIRECTION? SHE'S HEADING FOR THE BEACH!
SO THE SHERIFF RISKS HIS LIFE TO SAVE THE KID, AND SHE GETS ALL THE CREDIT?
WHAT A SHOW-OFF.
THE DOGS ARE WATCHING OLD 'LASSIE' RERUNS AGAIN?
I SWEAR, THOSE TWO WORSHIP THAT COLLIE.

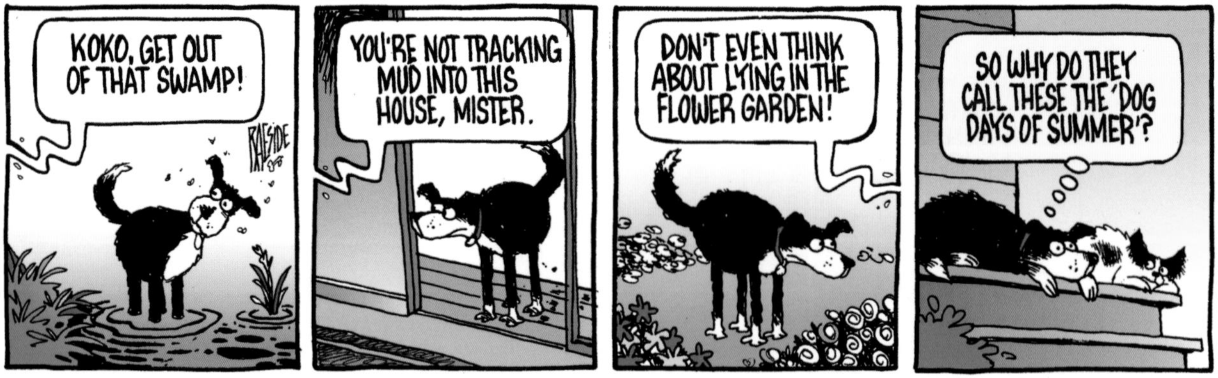
KOKO, GET OUT OF THAT SWAMP!
YOU'RE NOT TRACKING MUD INTO THIS HOUSE, MISTER.
DON'T EVEN THINK ABOUT LYING IN THE FLOWER GARDEN!
SO WHY DO THEY CALL THESE THE 'DOG DAYS OF SUMMER'?

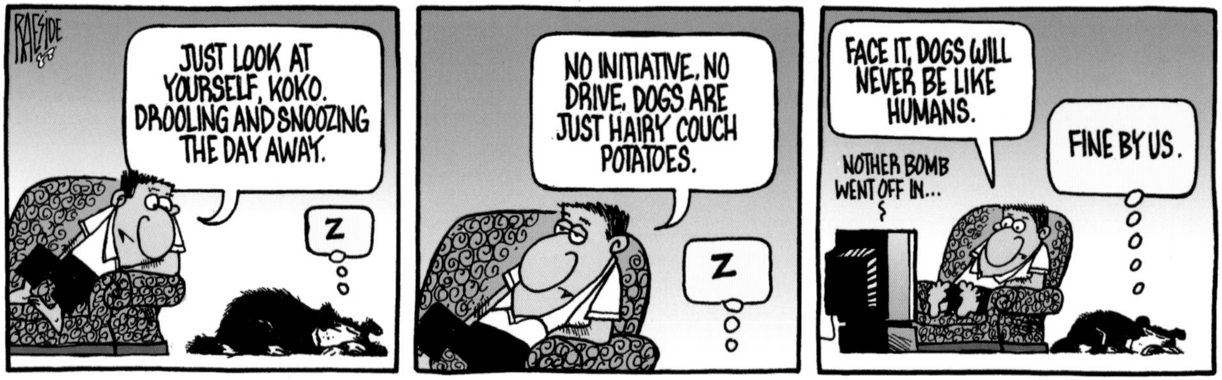
JUST LOOK AT YOURSELF, KOKO. DROOLING AND SNOOZING THE DAY AWAY.
Z
NO INITIATIVE, NO DRIVE, DOGS ARE JUST HAIRY COUCH POTATOES.
Z
FACE IT, DOGS WILL NEVER BE LIKE HUMANS.
NOTHER BOMB WENT OFF IN...
FINE BY US.

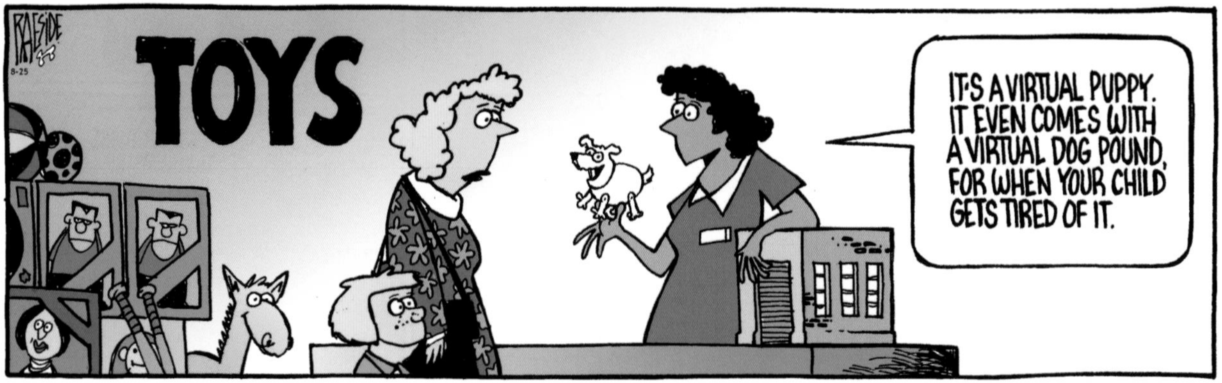
TOYS
IT'S A VIRTUAL PUPPY. IT EVEN COMES WITH A VIRTUAL DOG POUND, FOR WHEN YOUR CHILD GETS TIRED OF IT.

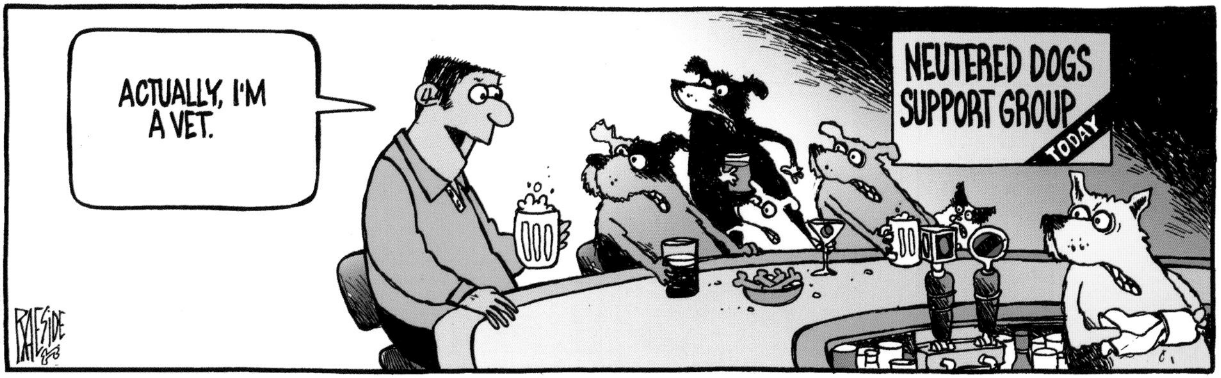
ACTUALLY, I'M A VET.
NEUTERED DOGS SUPPORT GROUP
TODAY

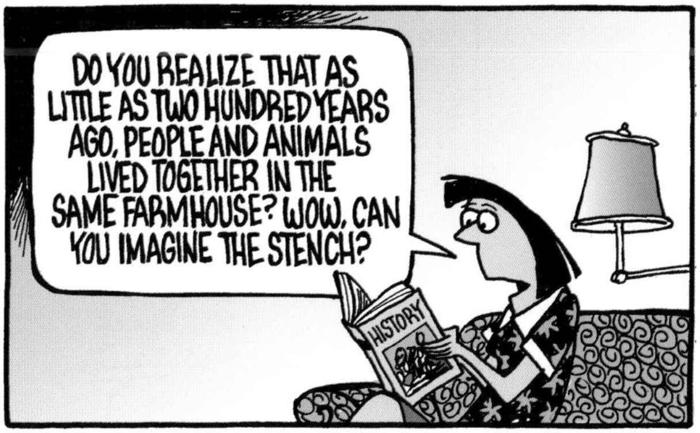
DO YOU REALIZE THAT AS LITTLE AS TWO HUNDRED YEARS AGO, PEOPLE AND ANIMALS LIVED TOGETHER IN THE SAME FARMHOUSE? WOW, CAN YOU IMAGINE THE STENCH?
HISTORY

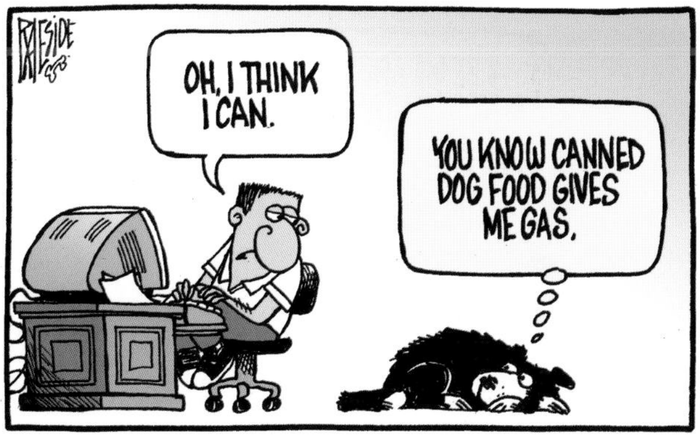
OH, I THINK I CAN.
YOU KNOW CANNED DOG FOOD GIVES ME GAS.

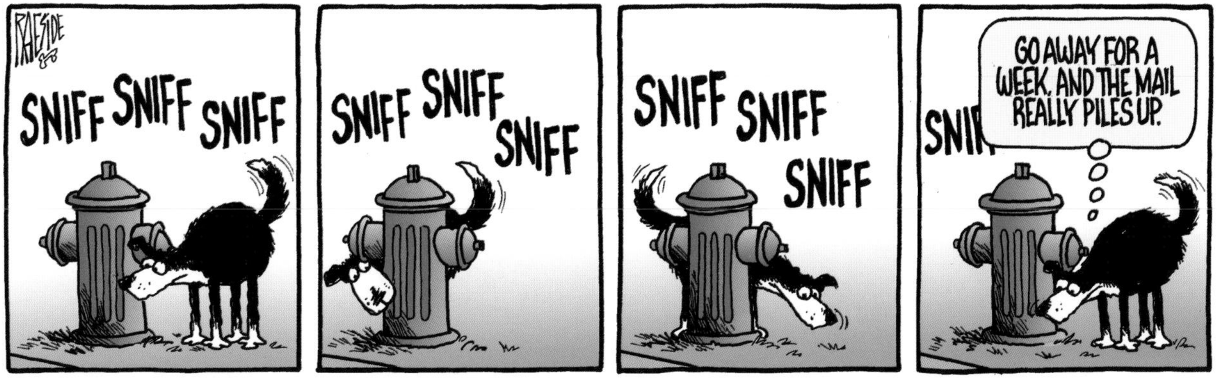
SNIFF SNIFF SNIFF
SNIFF SNIFF SNIFF
SNIFF SNIFF SNIFF
GO AWAY FOR A WEEK, AND THE MAIL REALLY PILES UP.

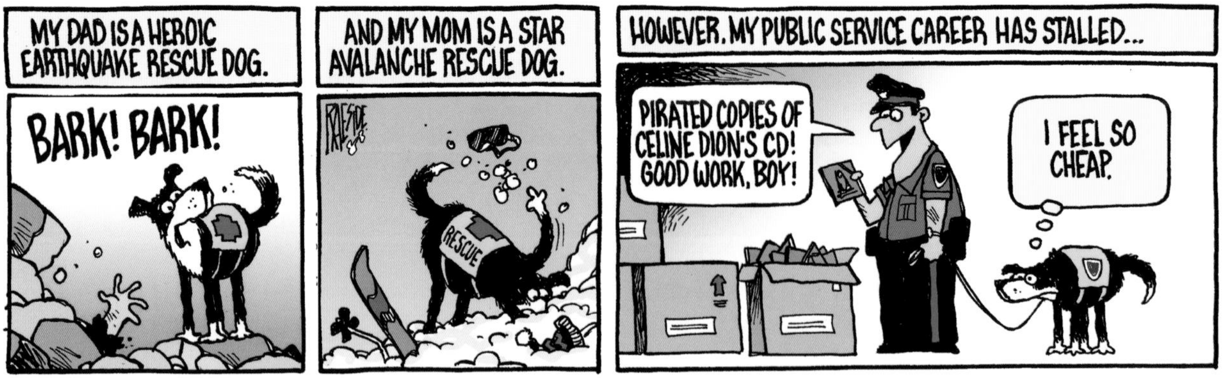
MY DAD IS A HEROIC EARTHQUAKE RESCUE DOG.
BARK! BARK!
AND MY MOM IS A STAR AVALANCHE RESCUE DOG.
RESCUE
HOWEVER, MY PUBLIC SERVICE CAREER HAS STALLED...
PIRATED COPIES OF CELINE DION'S CD! GOOD WORK, BOY!
I FEEL SO CHEAP.

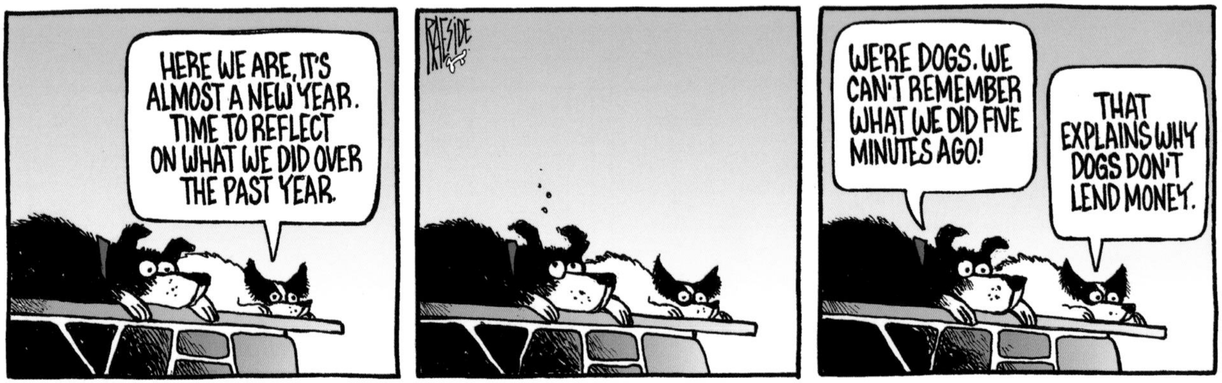
HERE WE ARE, IT'S ALMOST A NEW YEAR. TIME TO REFLECT ON WHAT WE DID OVER THE PAST YEAR.
WE'RE DOGS. WE CAN'T REMEMBER WHAT WE DID FIVE MINUTES AGO!
THAT EXPLAINS WHY DOGS DON'T LEND MONEY.

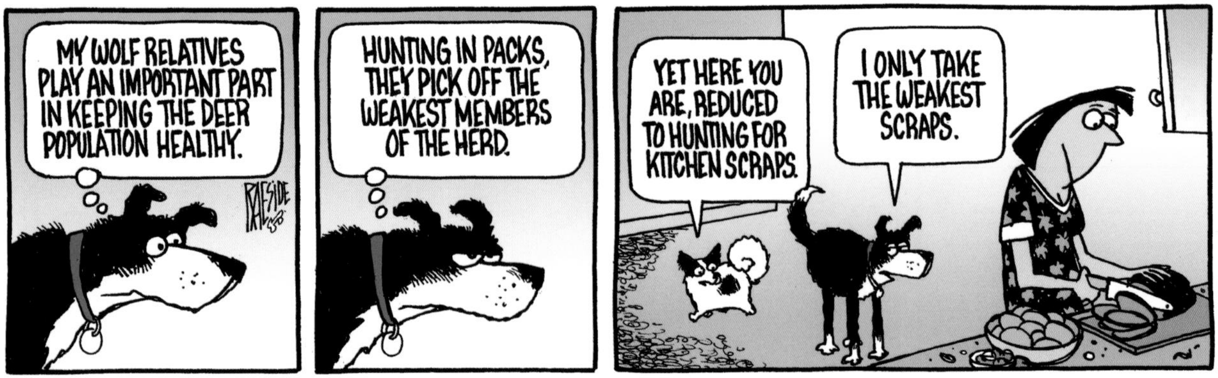
MY WOLF RELATIVES PLAY AN IMPORTANT PART IN KEEPING THE DEER POPULATION HEALTHY.
HUNTING IN PACKS, THEY PICK OFF THE WEAKEST MEMBERS OF THE HERD.
YET HERE YOU ARE, REDUCED TO HUNTING FOR KITCHEN SCRAPS.
I ONLY TAKE THE WEAKEST SCRAPS.

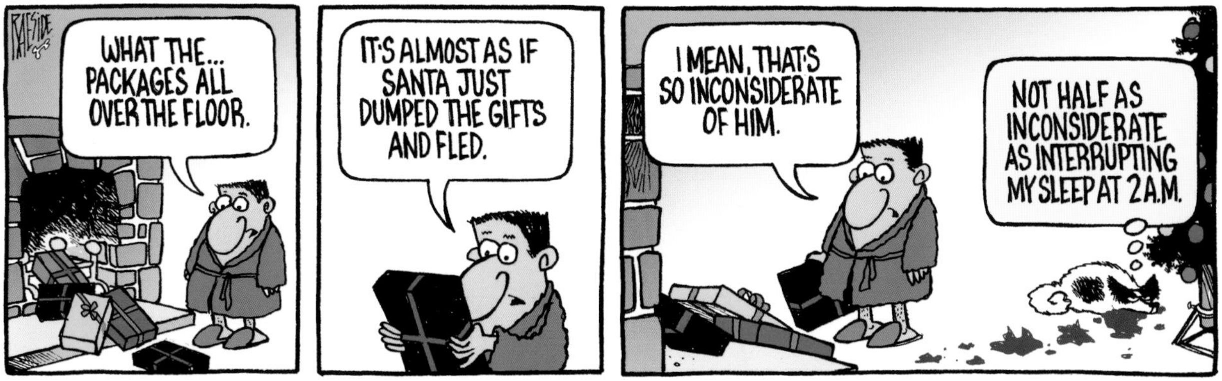
WHAT THE... PACKAGES ALL OVER THE FLOOR.
IT'S ALMOST AS IF SANTA JUST DUMPED THE GIFTS AND FLED.
I MEAN, THAT'S SO INCONSIDERATE OF HIM.
NOT HALF AS INCONSIDERATE AS INTERRUPTING MY SLEEP AT 2 A.M.

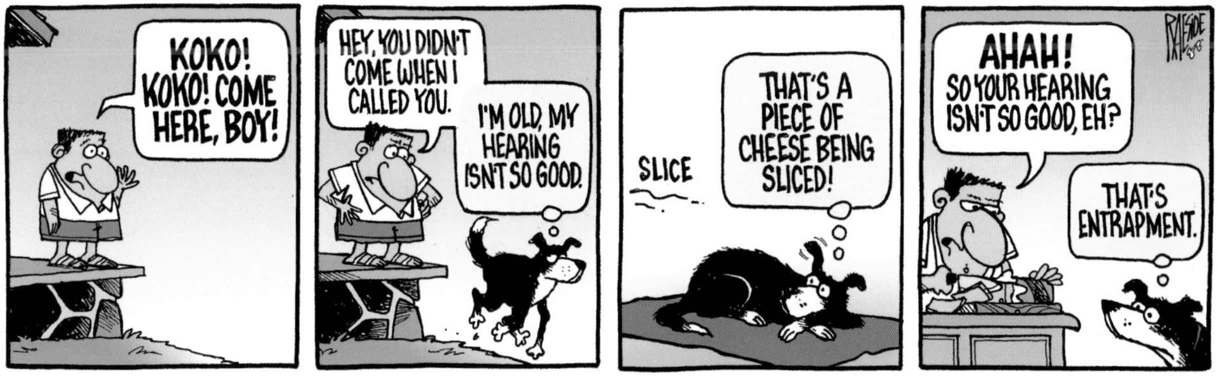
KOKO! KOKO! COME HERE, BOY!
HEY, YOU DIDN'T COME WHEN I CALLED YOU.
I'M OLD, MY HEARING ISN'T SO GOOD.
SLICE
THAT'S A PIECE OF CHEESE BEING SLICED!
AHAH! SO YOUR HEARING ISN'T SO GOOD, EH?
THAT'S ENTRAPMENT.

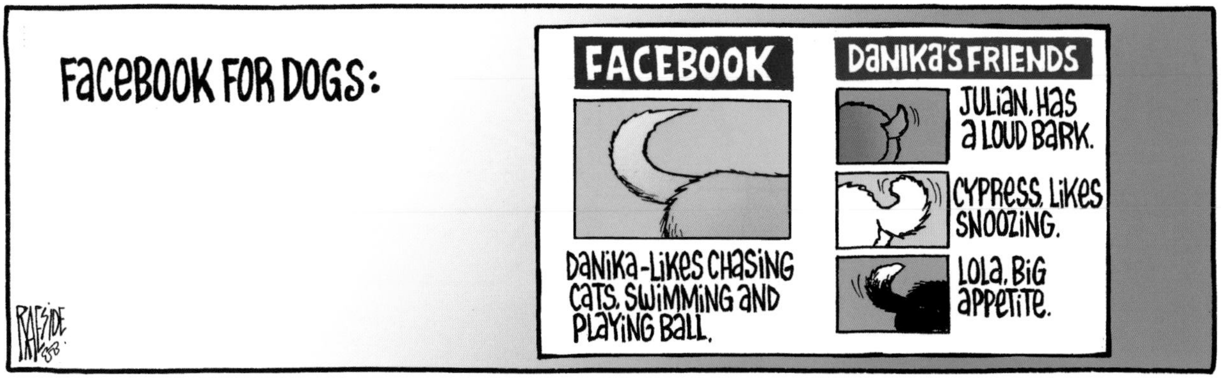
FACEBOOK FOR DOGS:
FACEBOOK
DANIKA-LIKES CHASING CATS, SWIMMING AND PLAYING BALL.
DANIKA'S FRIENDS
JULIAN, HAS A LOUD BARK.
CYPRESS, LIKES SNOOZING.
LOLA, BIG APPETITE.

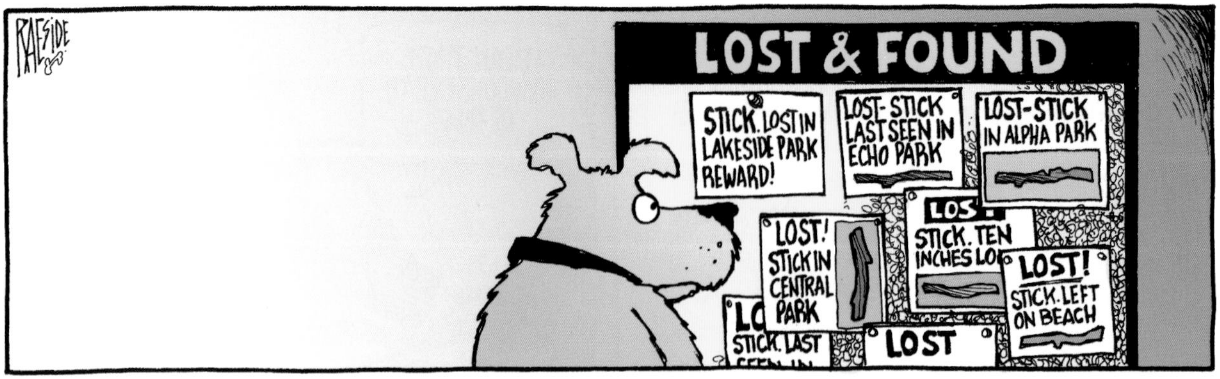
RAESIDE
LOST & FOUND
STICK. LOST IN LAKESIDE PARK REWARD!
LOST- STICK LAST SEEN IN ECHO PARK
LOST-STICK IN ALPHA PARK
LOST! STICK IN CENTRAL PARK
STICK. TEN INCHES LO
LOST! STICK. LEFT ON BEACH
STICK. LAST
LOST

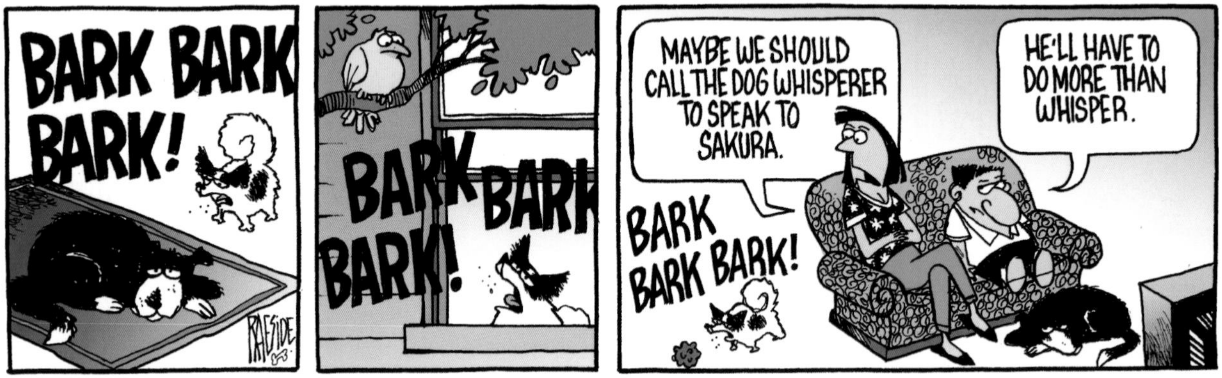
BARK BARK BARK!
RAESIDE
BARK BARK BARK!
MAYBE WE SHOULD CALL THE DOG WHISPERER TO SPEAK TO SAKURA.
HE'LL HAVE TO DO MORE THAN WHISPER.
BARK BARK BARK!

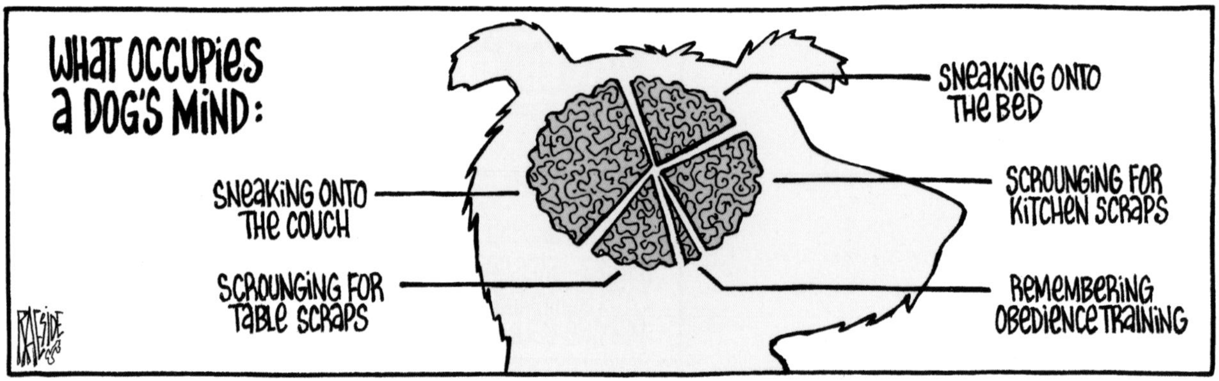
WHAT OCCUPIES A DOG'S MIND:
SNEAKING ONTO THE BED
SNEAKING ONTO THE COUCH
SCROUNGING FOR KITCHEN SCRAPS
SCROUNGING FOR TABLE SCRAPS
REMEMBERING OBEDIENCE TRAINING
RAESIDE

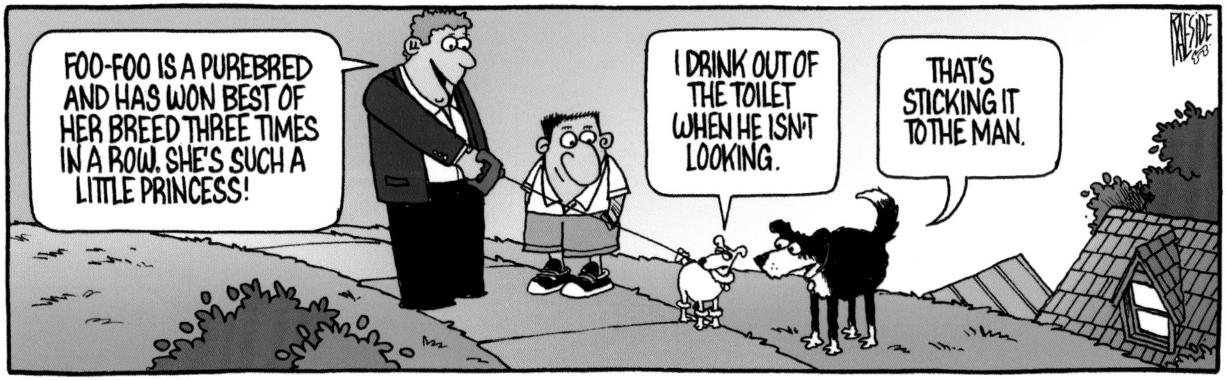
FOO-FOO IS A PUREBRED AND HAS WON BEST OF HER BREED THREE TIMES IN A ROW. SHE'S SUCH A LITTLE PRINCESS!
I DRINK OUT OF THE TOILET WHEN HE ISN'T LOOKING.
THAT'S STICKING IT TO THE MAN.

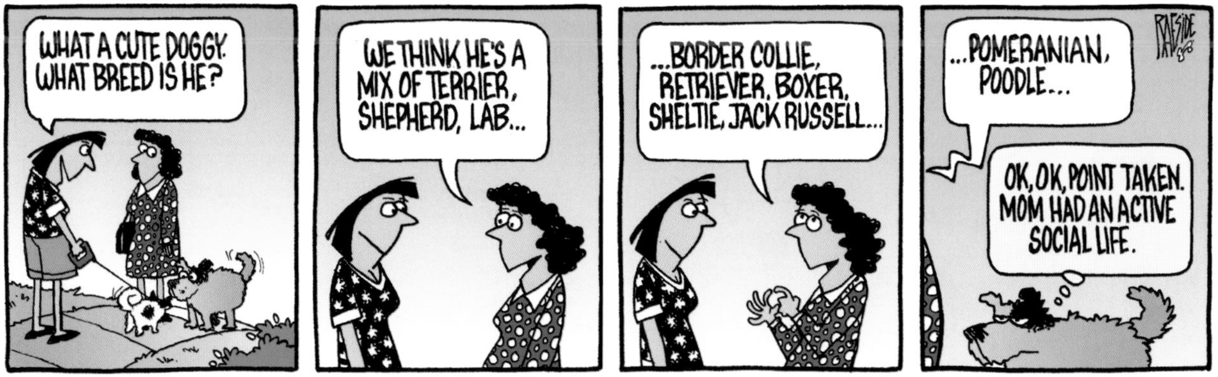
WHAT A CUTE DOGGY. WHAT BREED IS HE?
WE THINK HE'S A MIX OF TERRIER, SHEPHERD, LAB...
...BORDER COLLIE, RETRIEVER, BOXER, SHELTIE, JACK RUSSELL...
...POMERANIAN, POODLE...
OK, OK, POINT TAKEN. MOM HAD AN ACTIVE SOCIAL LIFE.

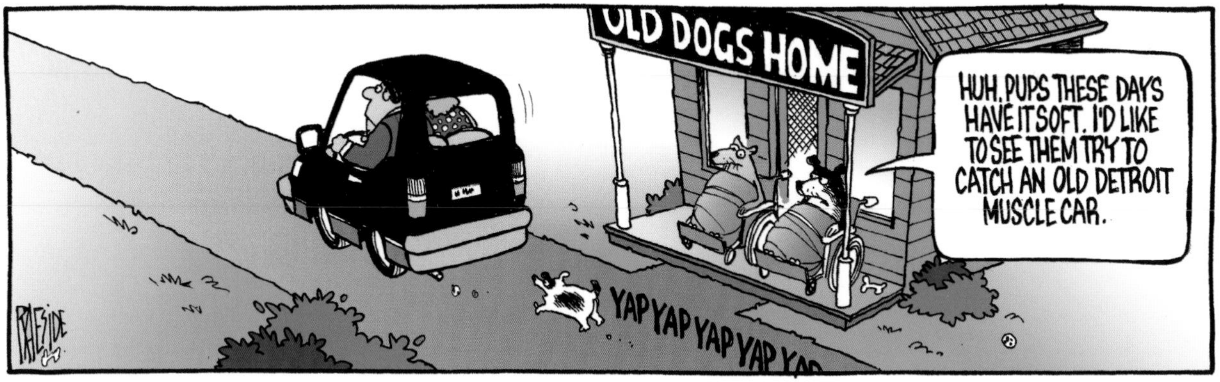
OLD DOGS HOME
HUH. PUPS THESE DAYS HAVE IT SOFT. I'D LIKE TO SEE THEM TRY TO CATCH AN OLD DETROIT MUSCLE CAR.
YAP YAP YAP YAP

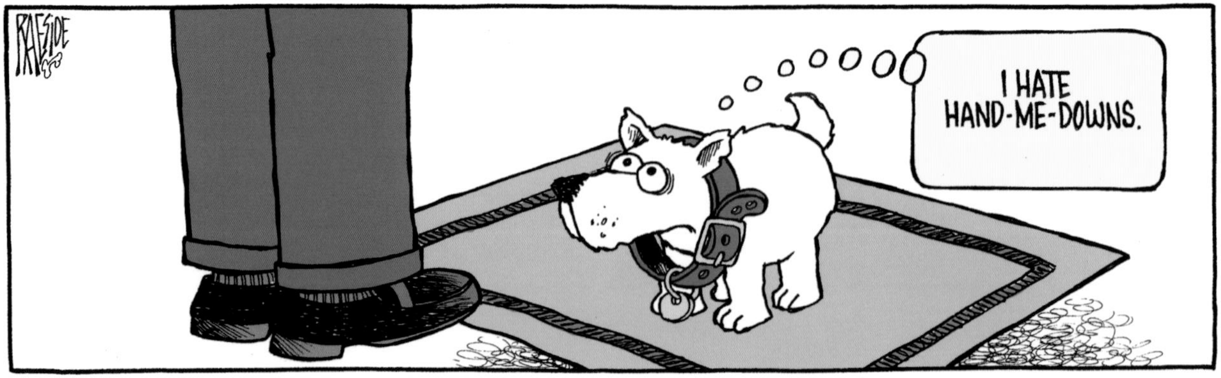
RAESIDE
I HATE HAND-ME-DOWNS.

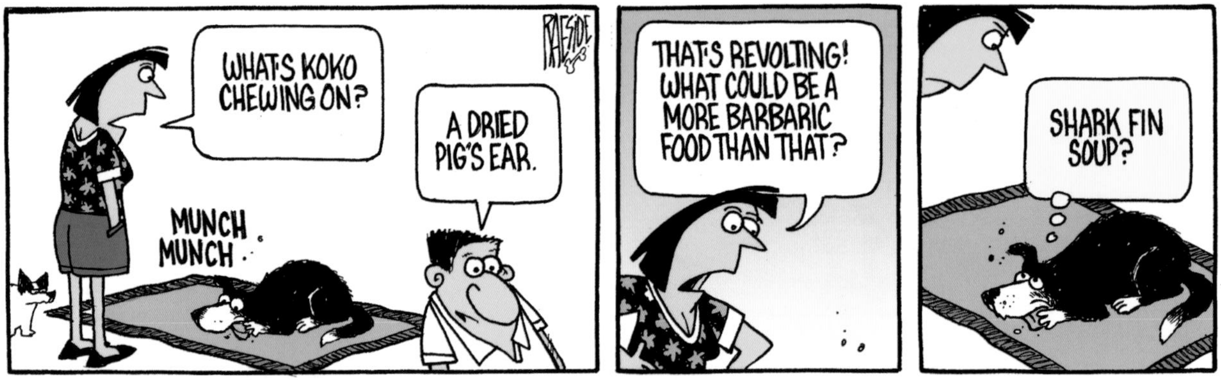
RAESIDE
WHAT'S KOKO CHEWING ON?
A DRIED PIG'S EAR.
MUNCH MUNCH
THAT'S REVOLTING! WHAT COULD BE A MORE BARBARIC FOOD THAN THAT?
SHARK FIN SOUP?

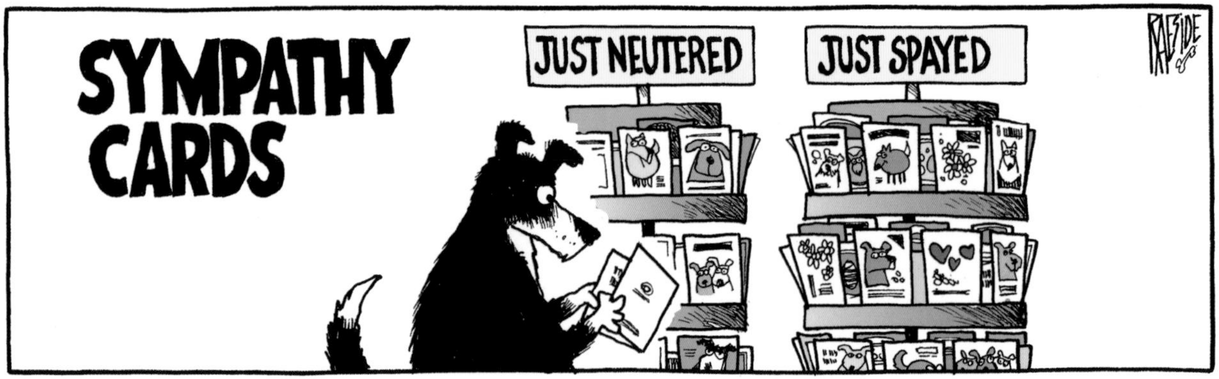
SYMPATHY CARDS
JUST NEUTERED
JUST SPAYED
RAESIDE

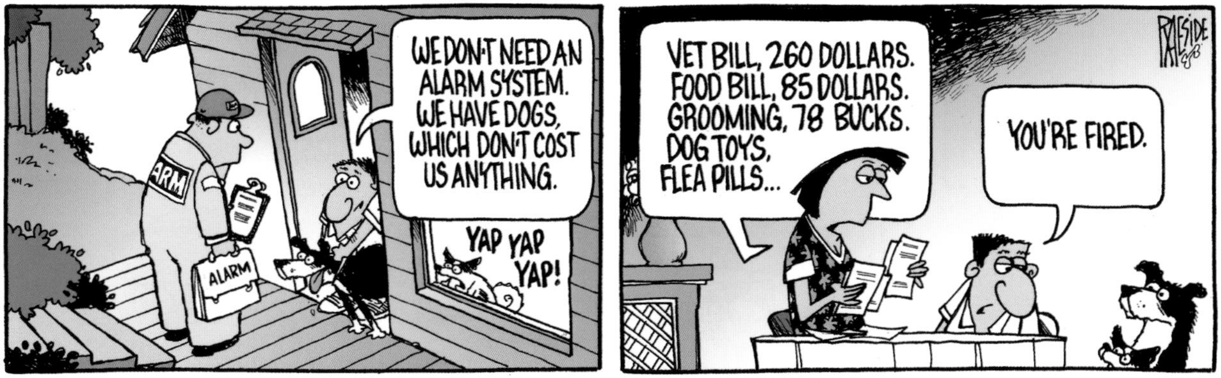
WE DON'T NEED AN ALARM SYSTEM. WE HAVE DOGS, WHICH DON'T COST US ANYTHING.
YAP YAP YAP!
VET BILL, 260 DOLLARS. FOOD BILL, 85 DOLLARS. GROOMING, 78 BUCKS. DOG TOYS, FLEA PILLS...
YOU'RE FIRED.

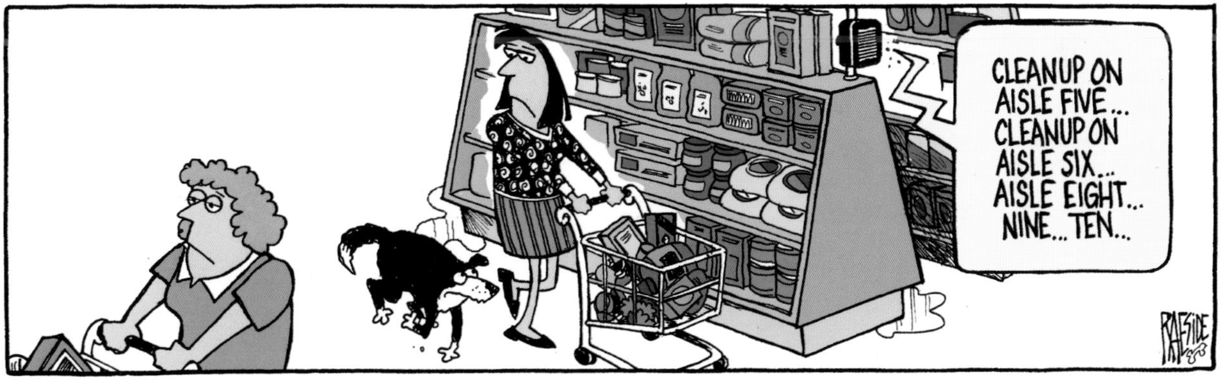
CLEANUP ON AISLE FIVE... CLEANUP ON AISLE SIX... AISLE EIGHT... NINE... TEN...

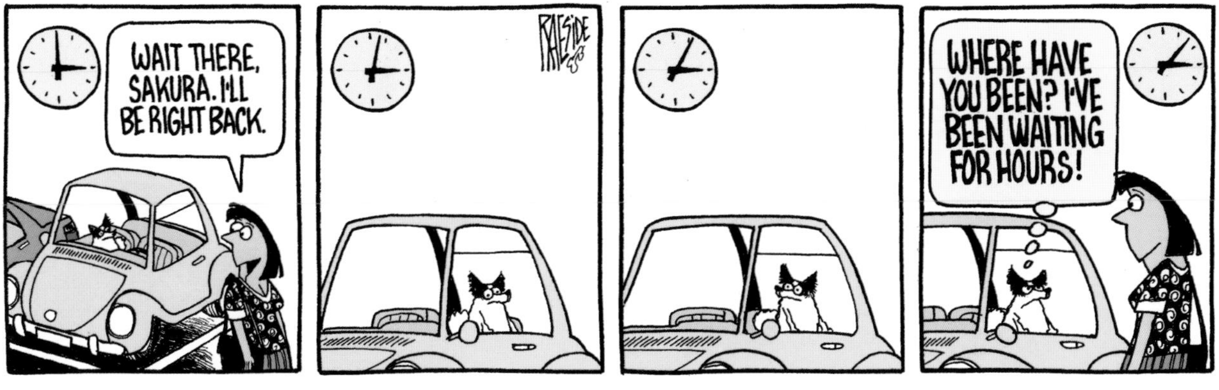
WAIT THERE, SAKURA. I'LL BE RIGHT BACK.
WHERE HAVE YOU BEEN? I'VE BEEN WAITING FOR HOURS!

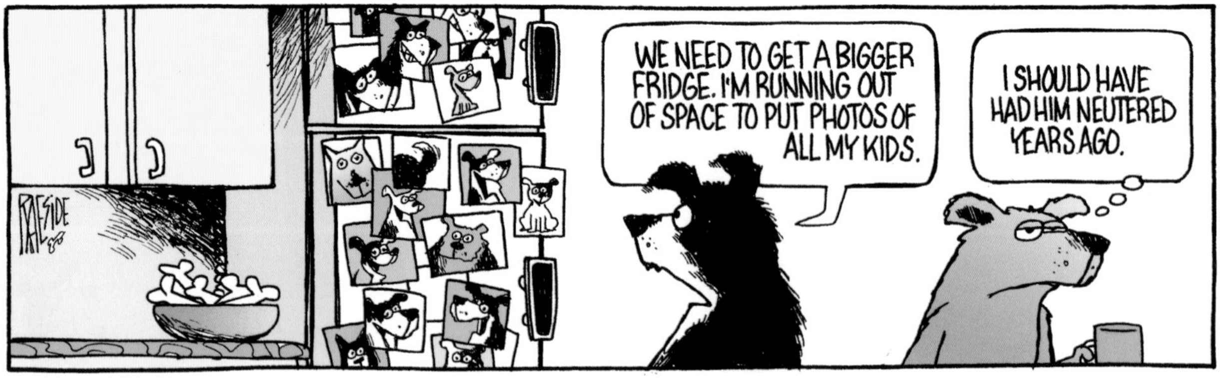
WE NEED TO GET A BIGGER FRIDGE. I'M RUNNING OUT OF SPACE TO PUT PHOTOS OF ALL MY KIDS.
I SHOULD HAVE HAD HIM NEUTERED YEARS AGO.

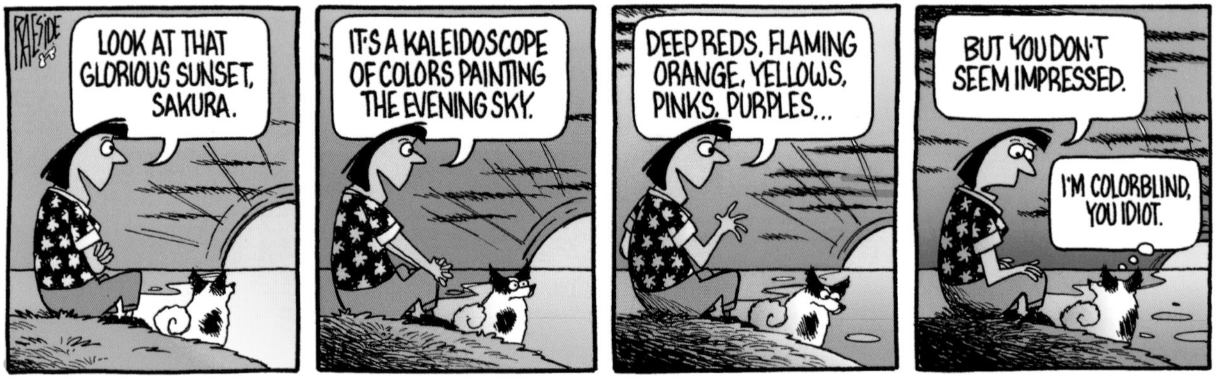
LOOK AT THAT GLORIOUS SUNSET, SAKURA.
IT'S A KALEIDOSCOPE OF COLORS PAINTING THE EVENING SKY.
DEEP REDS, FLAMING ORANGE, YELLOWS, PINKS, PURPLES...
BUT YOU DON'T SEEM IMPRESSED.
I'M COLORBLIND, YOU IDIOT.

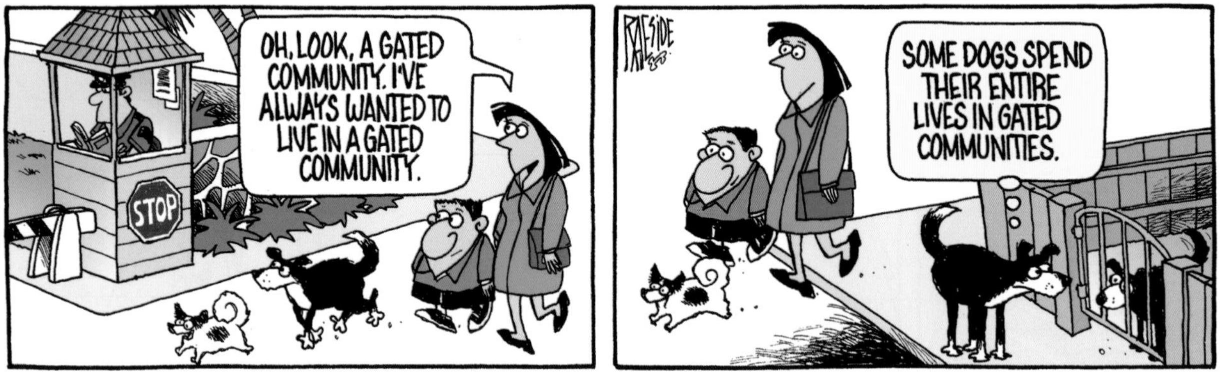
STOP
OH, LOOK, A GATED COMMUNITY. I'VE ALWAYS WANTED TO LIVE IN A GATED COMMUNITY.
SOME DOGS SPEND THEIR ENTIRE LIVES IN GATED COMMUNITIES.

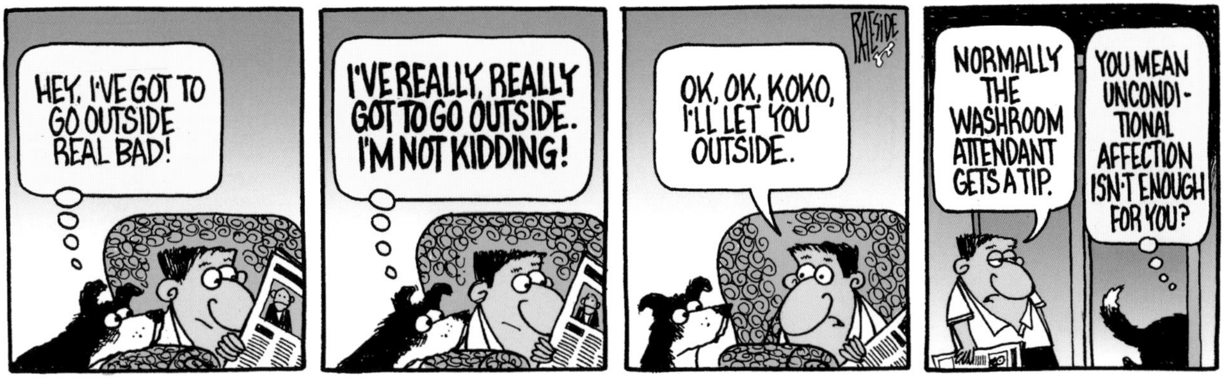
HEY, I'VE GOT TO GO OUTSIDE REAL BAD!
I'VE REALLY, REALLY GOT TO GO OUTSIDE. I'M NOT KIDDING!
RAESIDE
OK, OK, KOKO, I'LL LET YOU OUTSIDE.
NORMALLY THE WASHROOM ATTENDANT GETS A TIP.
YOU MEAN UNCONDI-TIONAL AFFECTION ISN'T ENOUGH FOR YOU?

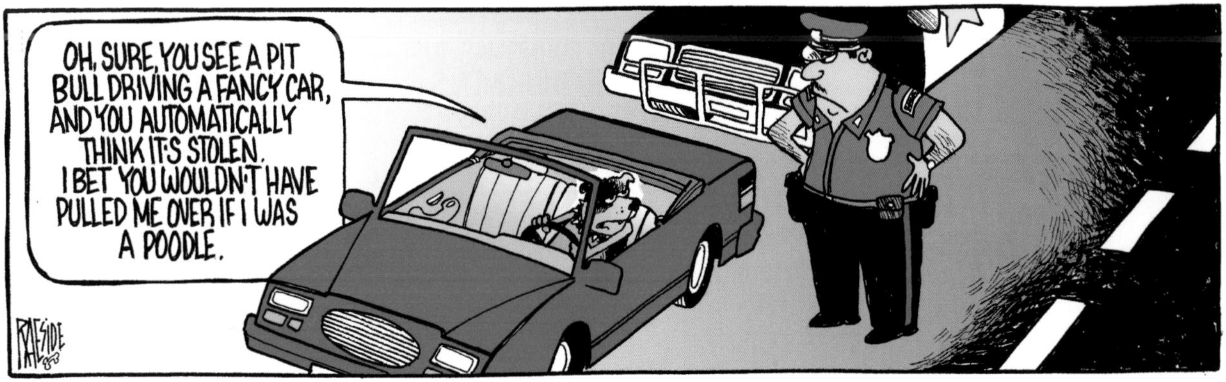
OH, SURE, YOU SEE A PIT BULL DRIVING A FANCY CAR, AND YOU AUTOMATICALLY THINK IT'S STOLEN. I BET YOU WOULDN'T HAVE PULLED ME OVER IF I WAS A POODLE.
RAESIDE

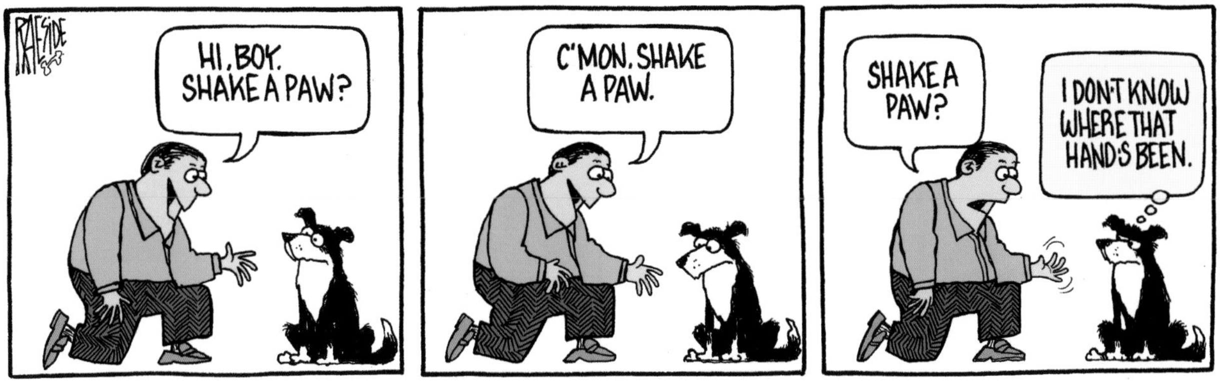
RAESIDE
HI, BOY. SHAKE A PAW?
C'MON. SHAKE A PAW.
SHAKE A PAW?
I DON'T KNOW WHERE THAT HAND'S BEEN.

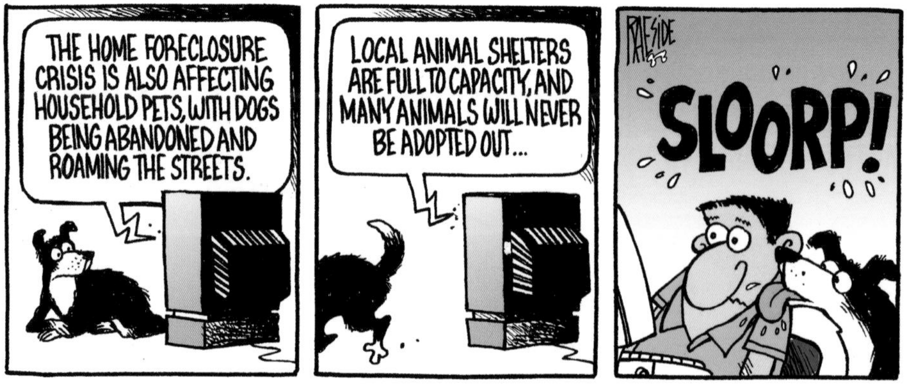
THE HOME FORECLOSURE CRISIS IS ALSO AFFECTING HOUSEHOLD PETS, WITH DOGS BEING ABANDONED AND ROAMING THE STREETS.
LOCAL ANIMAL SHELTERS ARE FULL TO CAPACITY, AND MANY ANIMALS WILL NEVER BE ADOPTED OUT...
SLOORP!
WHAT WAS THAT FOR?
TAKING A CHANCE ON ME THAT DAY YOU SAW ME IN THE CITY POUND.

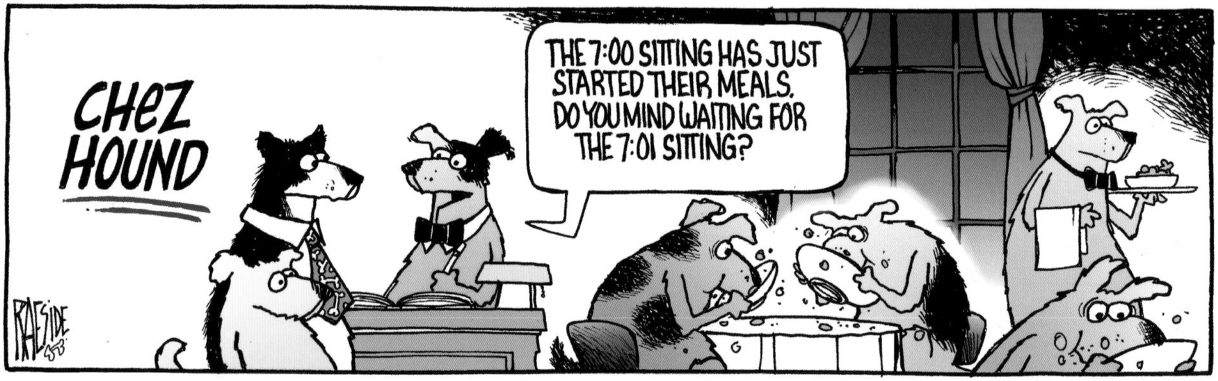
CHEZ HOUND
THE 7:00 SITTING HAS JUST STARTED THEIR MEALS. DO YOU MIND WAITING FOR THE 7:01 SITTING?

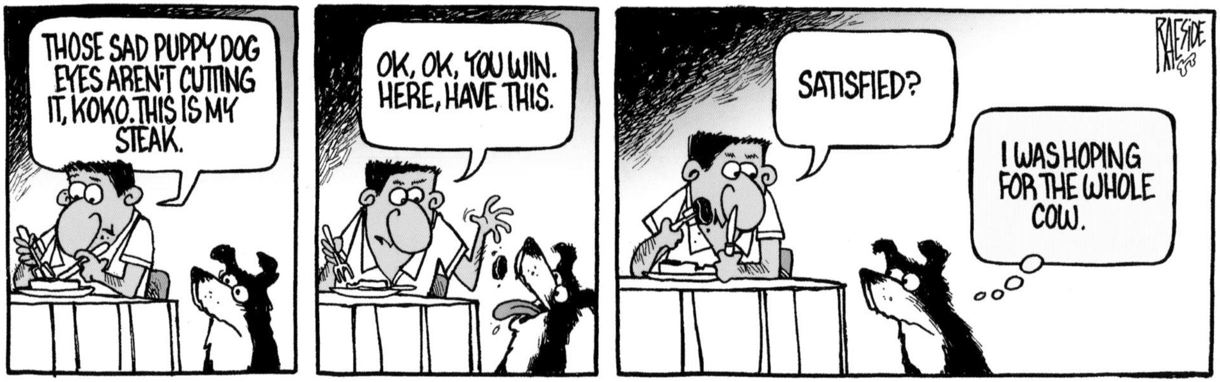
THOSE SAD PUPPY DOG EYES AREN'T CUTTING IT, KOKO. THIS IS MY STEAK.
OK, OK, YOU WIN. HERE, HAVE THIS.
SATISFIED?
I WAS HOPING FOR THE WHOLE COW.

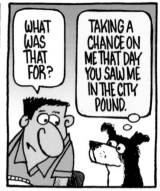

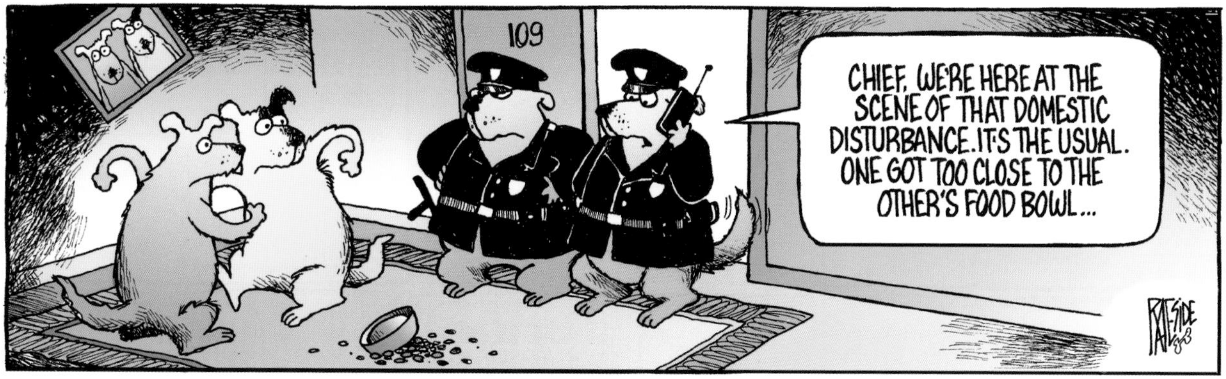
109
CHIEF, WE'RE HERE AT THE SCENE OF THAT DOMESTIC DISTURBANCE. IT'S THE USUAL. ONE GOT TOO CLOSE TO THE OTHER'S FOOD BOWL...

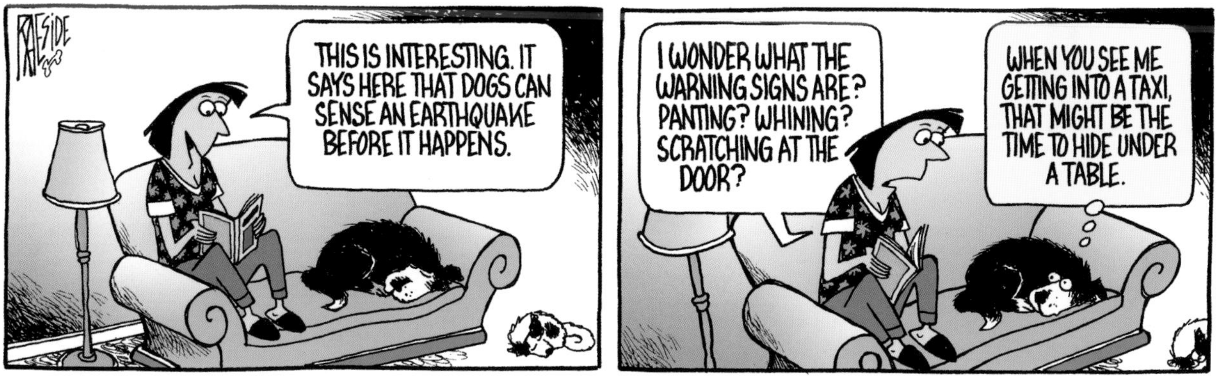
THIS IS INTERESTING. IT SAYS HERE THAT DOGS CAN SENSE AN EARTHQUAKE BEFORE IT HAPPENS.
I WONDER WHAT THE WARNING SIGNS ARE? PANTING? WHINING? SCRATCHING AT THE DOOR?
WHEN YOU SEE ME GETTING INTO A TAXI, THAT MIGHT BE THE TIME TO HIDE UNDER A TABLE.

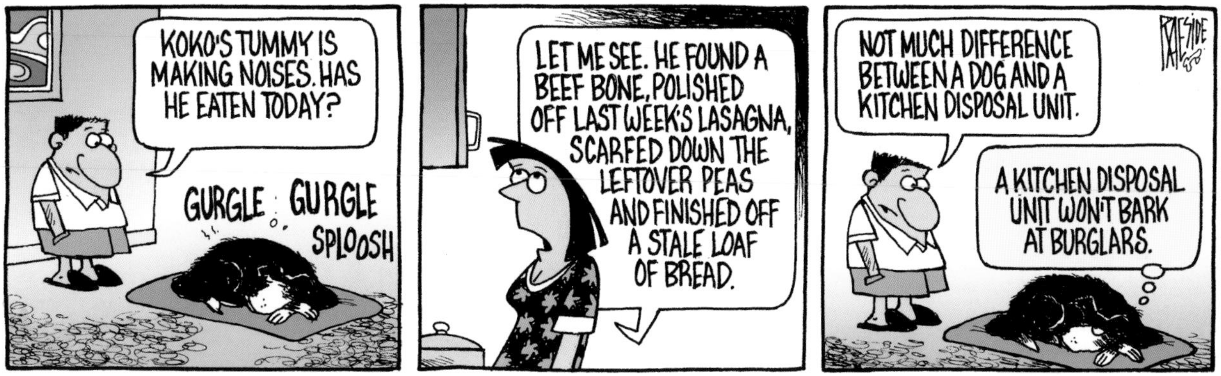
KOKO'S TUMMY IS MAKING NOISES. HAS HE EATEN TODAY?
GURGLE GURGLE
SPLOOSH
LET ME SEE. HE FOUND A BEEF BONE, POLISHED OFF LAST WEEK'S LASAGNA, SCARFED DOWN THE LEFTOVER PEAS AND FINISHED OFF A STALE LOAF OF BREAD.
NOT MUCH DIFFERENCE BETWEEN A DOG AND A KITCHEN DISPOSAL UNIT.
A KITCHEN DISPOSAL UNIT WON'T BARK AT BURGLARS.

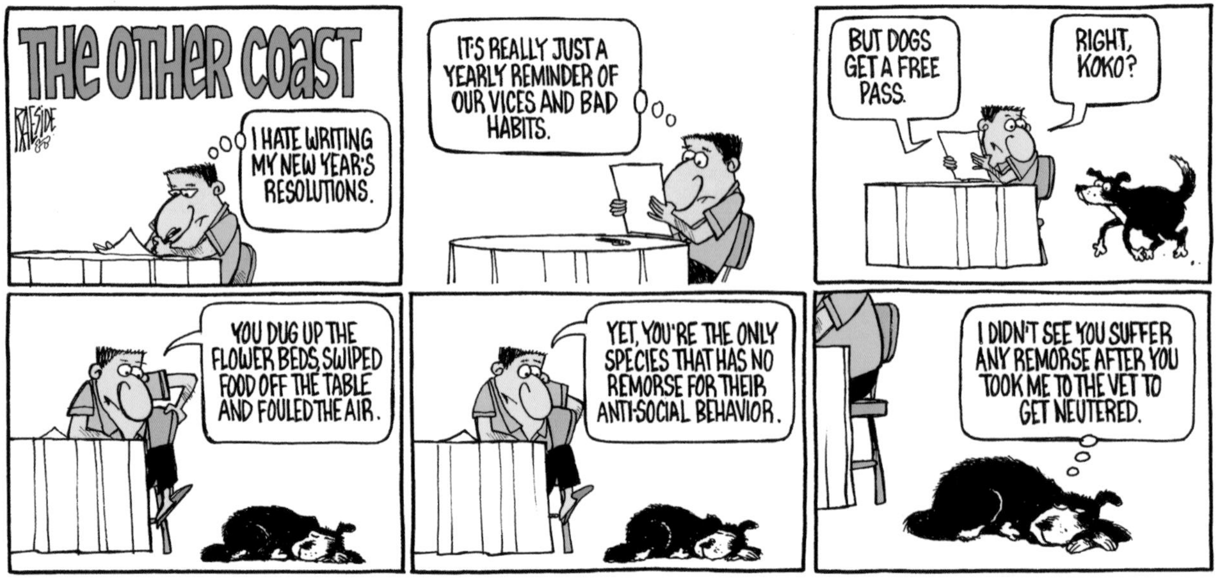
THE OTHER COAST
RAESIDE
I HATE WRITING MY NEW YEAR'S RESOLUTIONS.
IT'S REALLY JUST A YEARLY REMINDER OF OUR VICES AND BAD HABITS.
BUT DOGS GET A FREE PASS.
RIGHT, KOKO?
YOU DUG UP THE FLOWER BEDS, SWIPED FOOD OFF THE TABLE AND FOULED THE AIR.
YET, YOU'RE THE ONLY SPECIES THAT HAS NO REMORSE FOR THEIR ANTI-SOCIAL BEHAVIOR.
I DIDN'T SEE YOU SUFFER ANY REMORSE AFTER YOU TOOK ME TO THE VET TO GET NEUTERED.

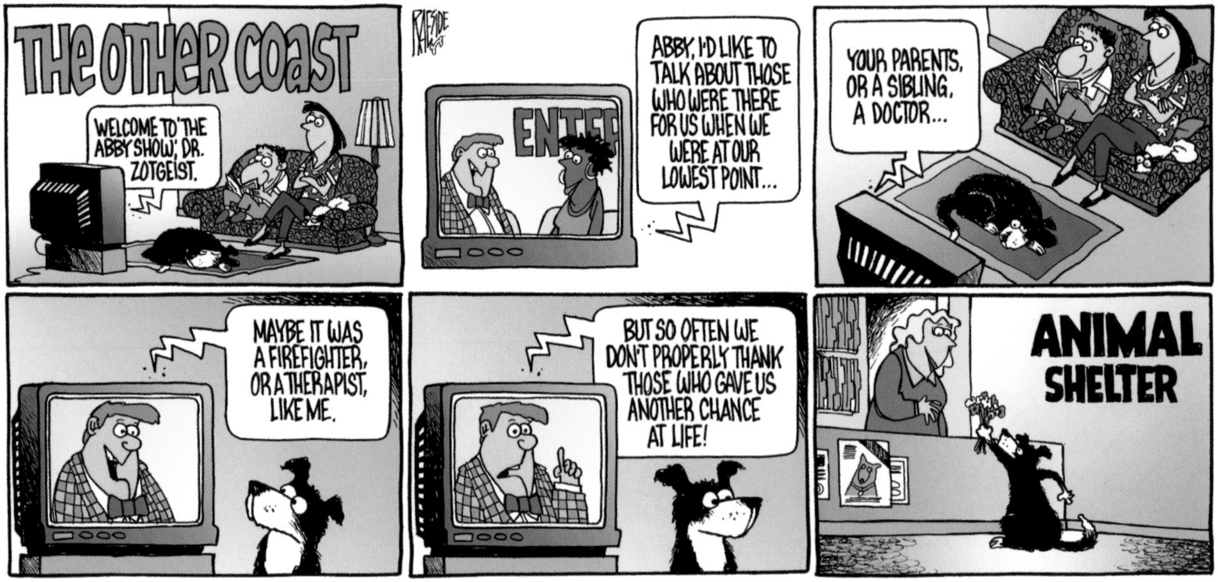
THE OTHER COAST
WELCOME TO 'THE ABBY SHOW,' DR. ZOTGEIST.
RAESIDE
ABBY, I'D LIKE TO TALK ABOUT THOSE WHO WERE THERE FOR US WHEN WE WERE AT OUR LOWEST POINT...
YOUR PARENTS, OR A SIBLING, A DOCTOR...
MAYBE IT WAS A FIREFIGHTER, OR A THERAPIST, LIKE ME.
BUT SO OFTEN WE DON'T PROPERLY THANK THOSE WHO GAVE US ANOTHER CHANCE AT LIFE!
ANIMAL SHELTER

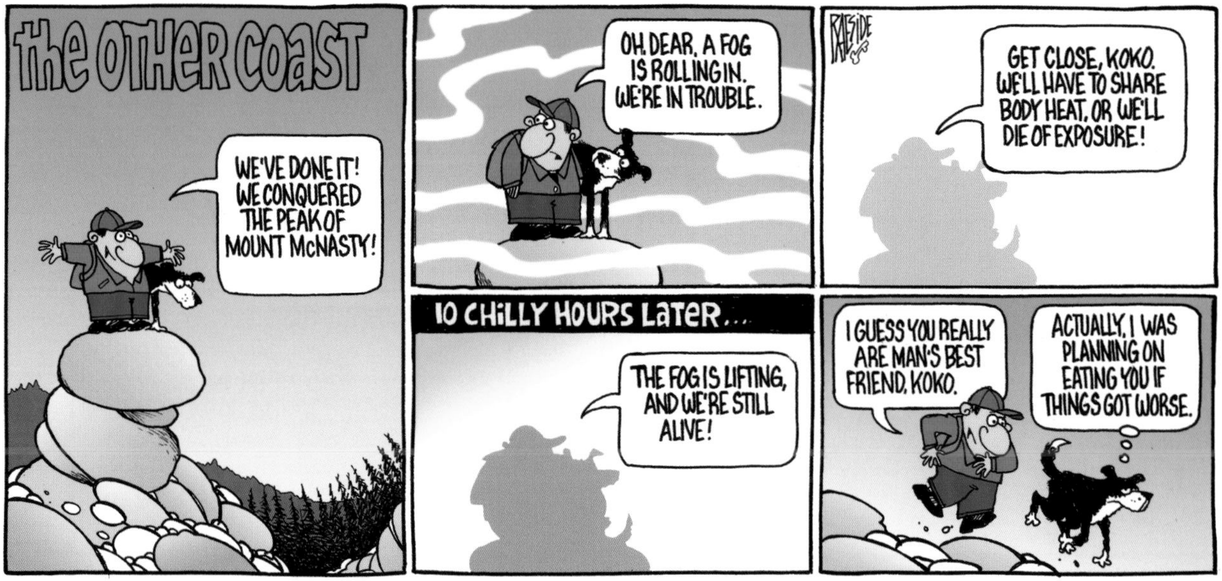
the OTHER COAST
WE'VE DONE IT! WE CONQUERED THE PEAK OF MOUNT McNASTY!
OH, DEAR, A FOG IS ROLLING IN. WE'RE IN TROUBLE.
RAESIDE
GET CLOSE, KOKO. WE'LL HAVE TO SHARE BODY HEAT, OR WE'LL DIE OF EXPOSURE!
10 CHILLY HOURS LATER...
THE FOG IS LIFTING, AND WE'RE STILL ALIVE!
I GUESS YOU REALLY ARE MAN'S BEST FRIEND, KOKO.
ACTUALLY, I WAS PLANNING ON EATING YOU IF THINGS GOT WORSE.

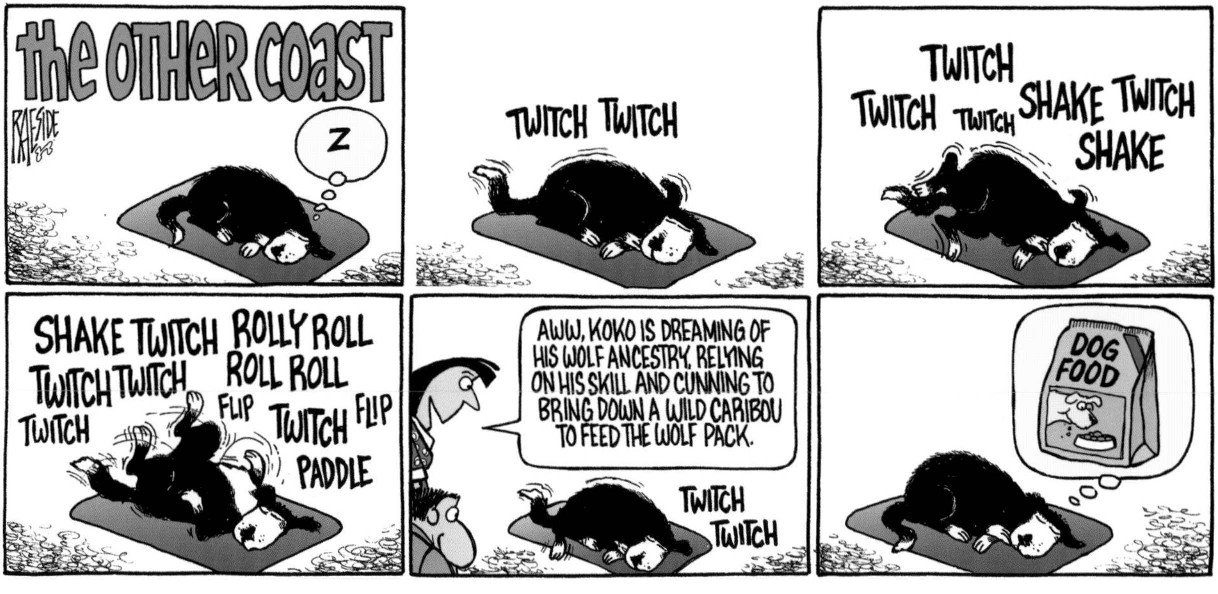
the OTHER COAST
RAESIDE
Z
TWITCH TWITCH
TWITCH
TWITCH TWITCH SHAKE TWITCH
SHAKE
SHAKE TWITCH ROLLY ROLL
TWITCH TWITCH ROLL ROLL
TWITCH FLIP TWITCH FLIP
PADDLE
AWW, KOKO IS DREAMING OF HIS WOLF ANCESTRY, RELYING ON HIS SKILL AND CUNNING TO BRING DOWN A WILD CARIBOU TO FEED THE WOLF PACK.
TWITCH TWITCH
DOG FOOD

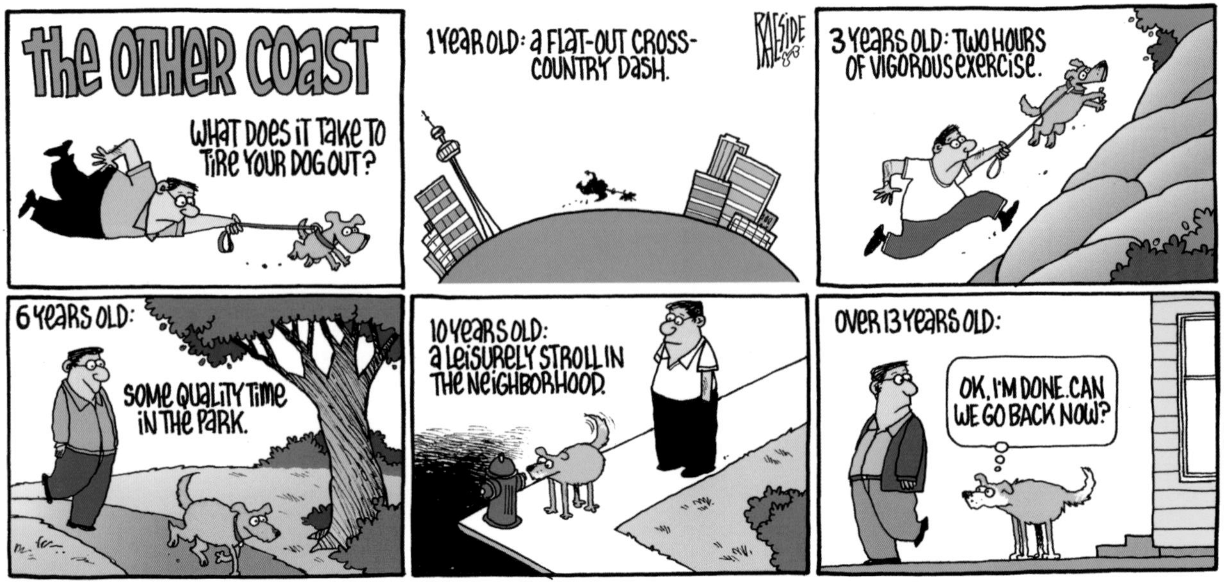
the OTHER COAST
WHAT DOES IT TAKE TO TIRE YOUR DOG OUT?
1 YEAR OLD: A FLAT-OUT CROSS-COUNTRY DASH.
RAESIDE
3 YEARS OLD: TWO HOURS OF VIGOROUS EXERCISE.
6 YEARS OLD:
SOME QUALITY TIME IN THE PARK.
10 YEARS OLD: A LEISURELY STROLL IN THE NEIGHBORHOOD.
OVER 13 YEARS OLD:
OK, I'M DONE. CAN WE GO BACK NOW?

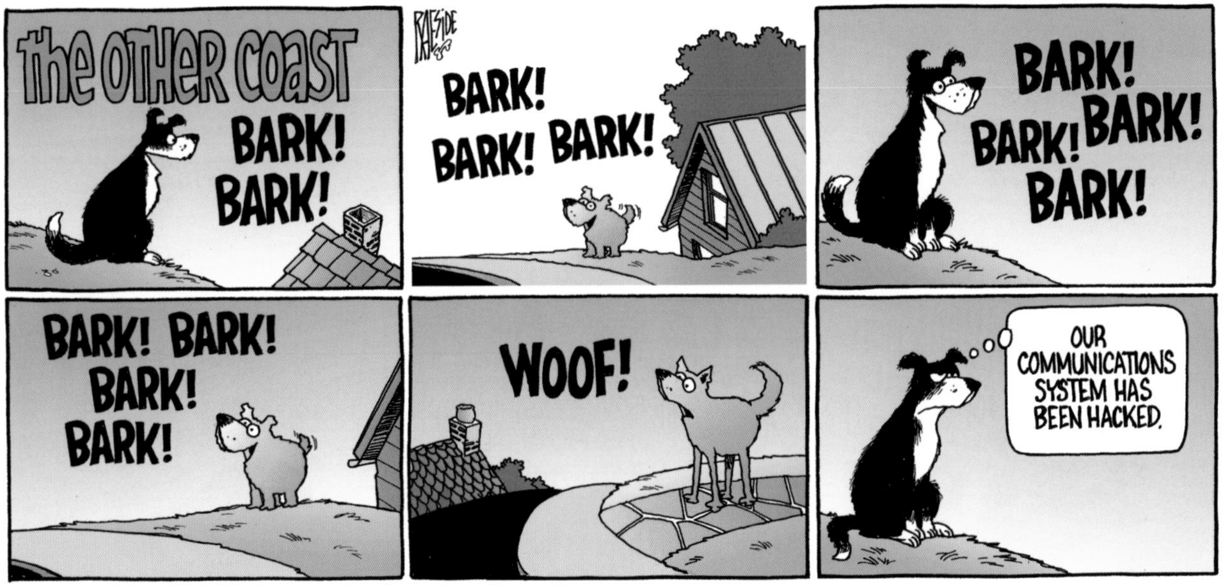
the OTHER COAST
BARK! BARK!
RAESIDE
BARK! BARK! BARK!
BARK! BARK! BARK! BARK!
BARK! BARK! BARK! BARK!
WOOF!
OUR COMMUNICATIONS SYSTEM HAS BEEN HACKED.

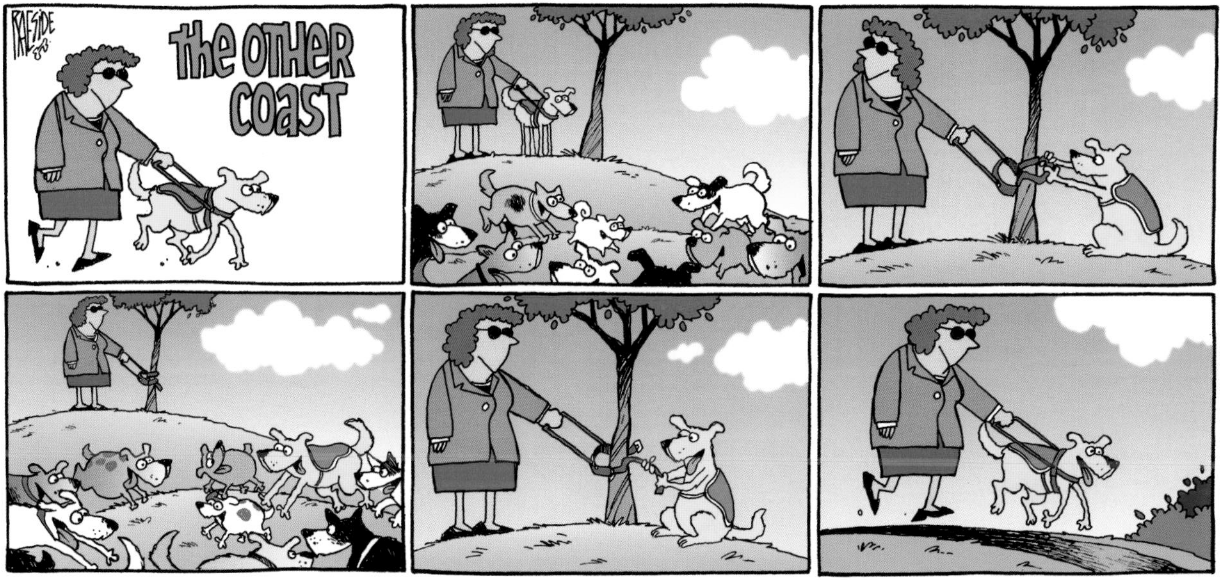
RAESIDE '88
the OTHER COAST

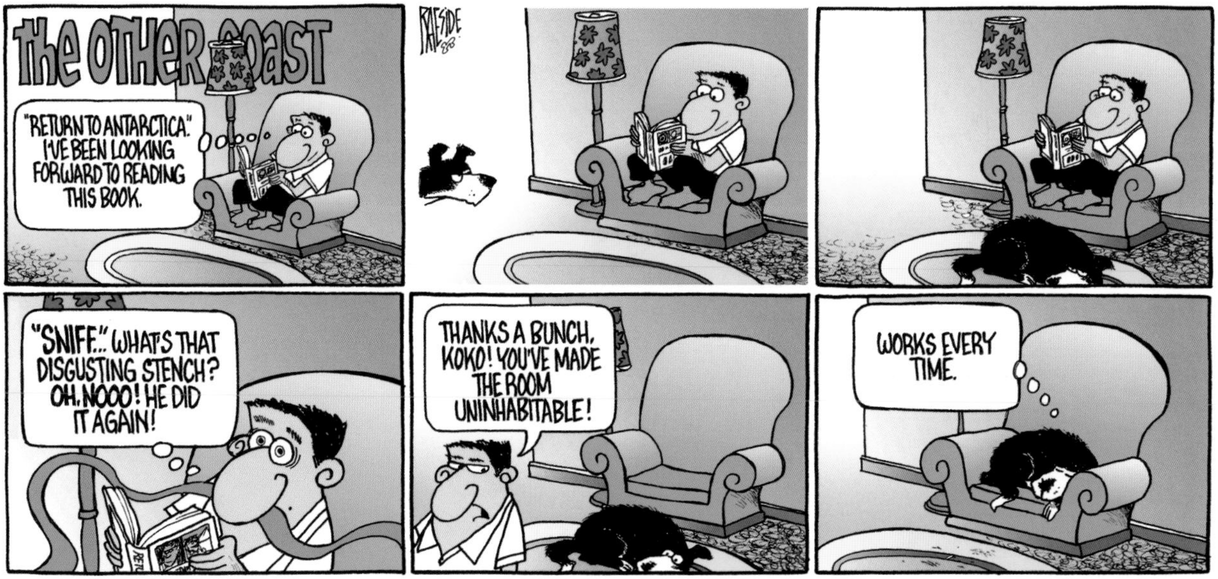
the OTHER COAST
"RETURN TO ANTARCTICA." I'VE BEEN LOOKING FORWARD TO READING THIS BOOK.
RAESIDE '88
"SNIFF..." WHAT'S THAT DISGUSTING STENCH? OH, NOOO! HE DID IT AGAIN!
THANKS A BUNCH, KOKO! YOU'VE MADE THE ROOM UNINHABITABLE!
WORKS EVERY TIME.

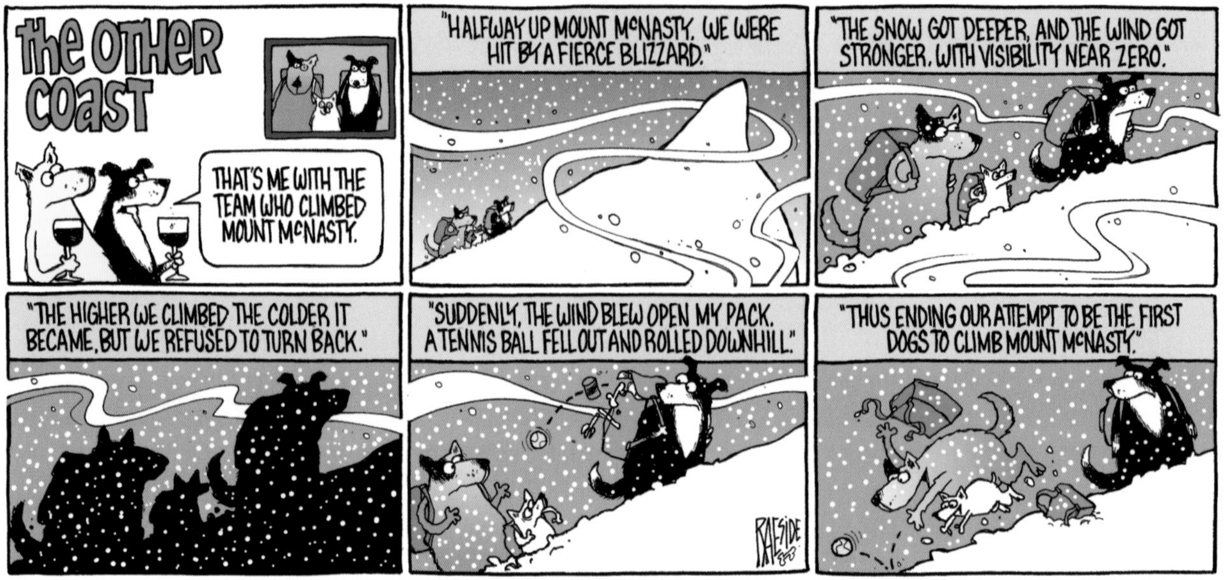
the OTHER COAST
THAT'S ME WITH THE TEAM WHO CLIMBED MOUNT McNASTY.
"HALFWAY UP MOUNT McNASTY, WE WERE HIT BY A FIERCE BLIZZARD."
"THE SNOW GOT DEEPER, AND THE WIND GOT STRONGER, WITH VISIBILITY NEAR ZERO."
"THE HIGHER WE CLIMBED THE COLDER IT BECAME, BUT WE REFUSED TO TURN BACK."
"SUDDENLY, THE WIND BLEW OPEN MY PACK. A TENNIS BALL FELL OUT AND ROLLED DOWNHILL."
"THUS ENDING OUR ATTEMPT TO BE THE FIRST DOGS TO CLIMB MOUNT McNASTY."
RAESIDE

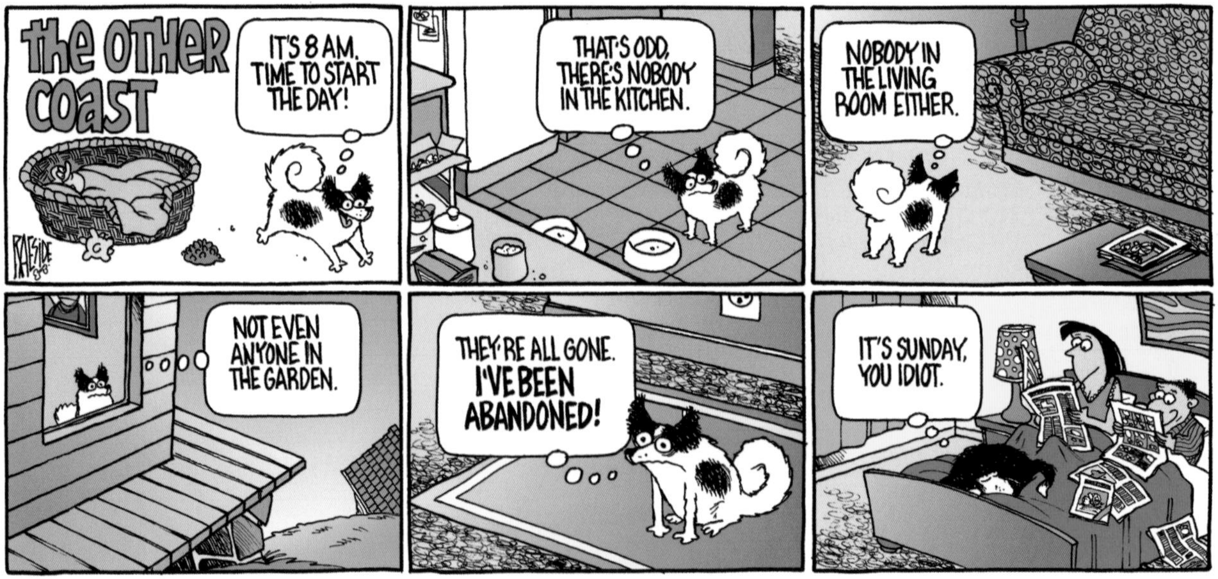
the OTHER COAST
IT'S 8 AM, TIME TO START THE DAY!
RAESIDE
THAT'S ODD, THERE'S NOBODY IN THE KITCHEN.
NOBODY IN THE LIVING ROOM EITHER.
NOT EVEN ANYONE IN THE GARDEN.
THEY'RE ALL GONE. I'VE BEEN ABANDONED!
IT'S SUNDAY, YOU IDIOT.

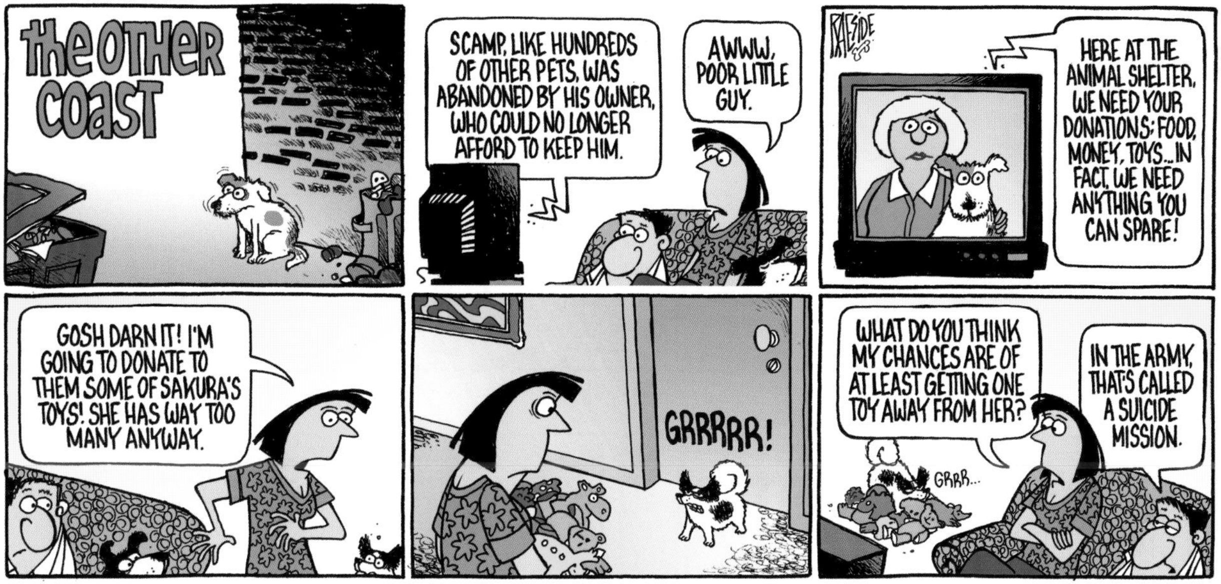
the OTHER COAST
SCAMP, LIKE HUNDREDS OF OTHER PETS, WAS ABANDONED BY HIS OWNER, WHO COULD NO LONGER AFFORD TO KEEP HIM.
AWWW, POOR LITTLE GUY.
HERE AT THE ANIMAL SHELTER, WE NEED YOUR DONATIONS; FOOD, MONEY, TOYS... IN FACT, WE NEED ANYTHING YOU CAN SPARE!
GOSH DARN IT! I'M GOING TO DONATE TO THEM SOME OF SAKURA'S TOYS! SHE HAS WAY TOO MANY ANYWAY.
GRRRRR!
WHAT DO YOU THINK MY CHANCES ARE OF AT LEAST GETTING ONE TOY AWAY FROM HER?
GRRR...
IN THE ARMY, THAT'S CALLED A SUICIDE MISSION.

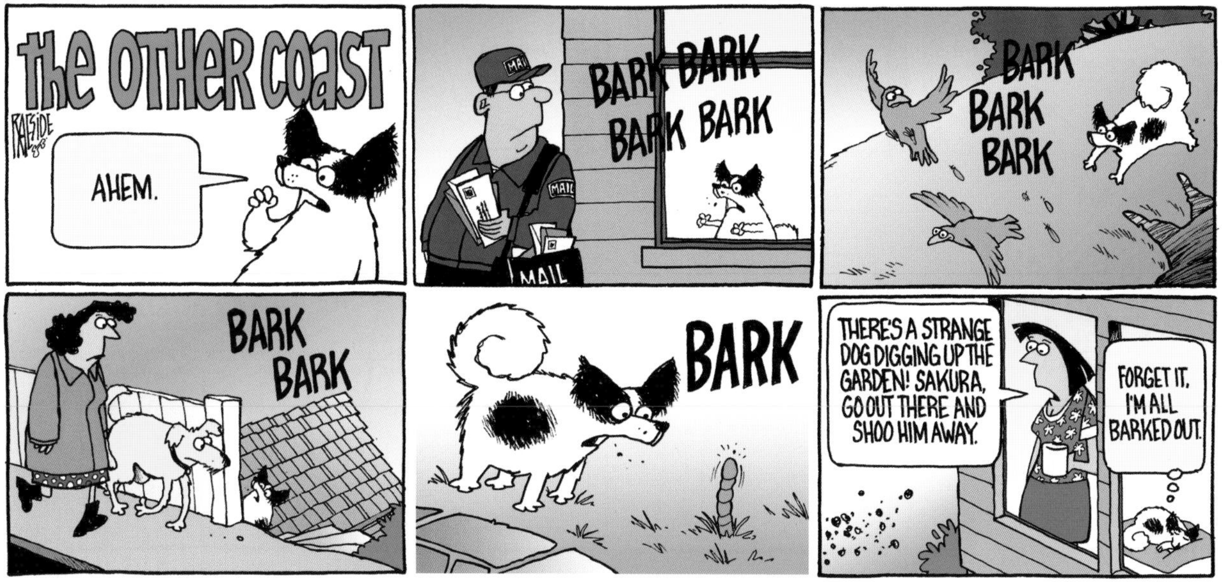
the OTHER COAST
AHEM.
MAIL
BARK BARK
BARK BARK
MAIL
MAIL
BARK
BARK
BARK
BARK
BARK
BARK
THERE'S A STRANGE DOG DIGGING UP THE GARDEN! SAKURA, GO OUT THERE AND SHOO HIM AWAY.
FORGET IT. I'M ALL BARKED OUT.

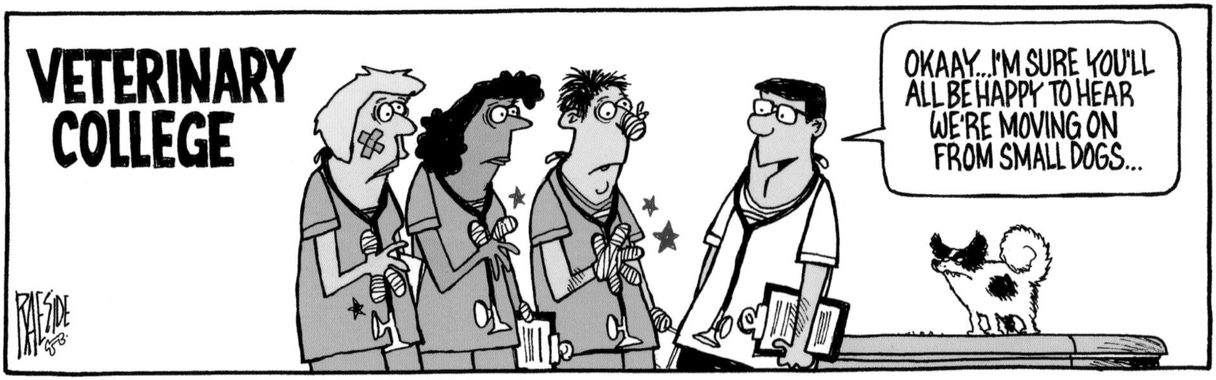
VETERINARY COLLEGE
OKAAY...I'M SURE YOU'LL ALL BE HAPPY TO HEAR WE'RE MOVING ON FROM SMALL DOGS...
RAESIDE

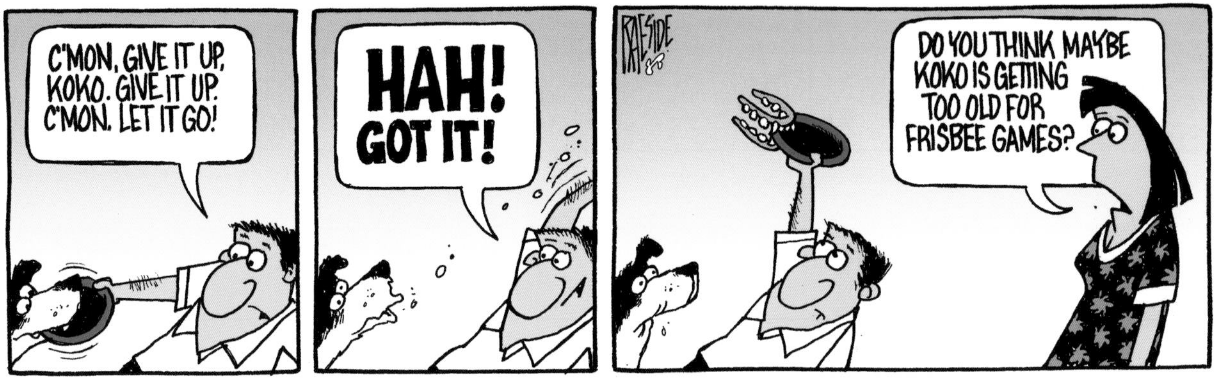
C'MON, GIVE IT UP, KOKO. GIVE IT UP. C'MON. LET IT GO!
HAH! GOT IT!
RAESIDE
DO YOU THINK MAYBE KOKO IS GETTING TOO OLD FOR FRISBEE GAMES?

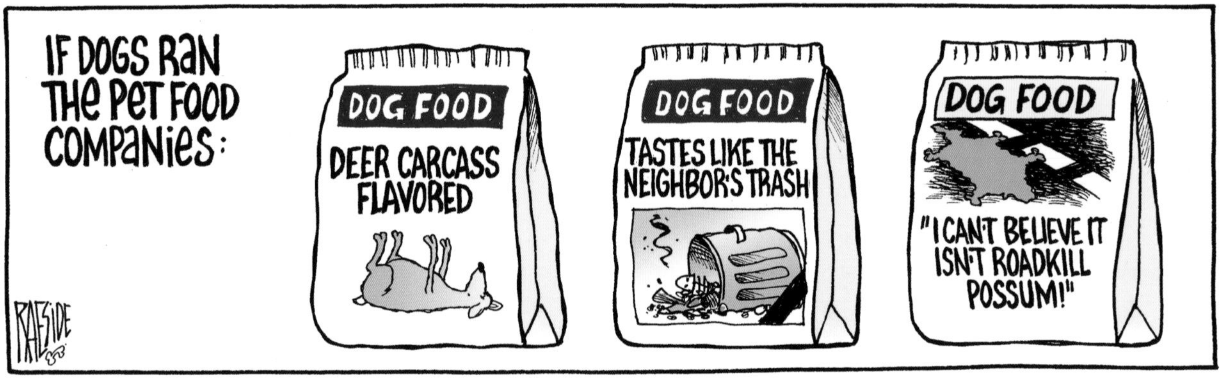
IF DOGS RAN THE PET FOOD COMPANIES:
DOG FOOD
DEER CARCASS FLAVORED
DOG FOOD
TASTES LIKE THE NEIGHBOR'S TRASH
DOG FOOD
"I CAN'T BELIEVE IT ISN'T ROADKILL POSSUM!"
RAESIDE

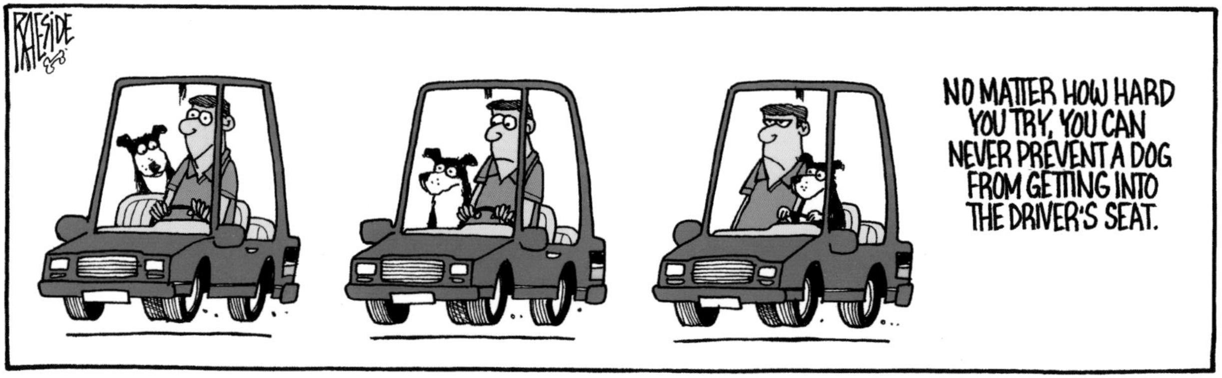
RAESIDE
NO MATTER HOW HARD YOU TRY, YOU CAN NEVER PREVENT A DOG FROM GETTING INTO THE DRIVER'S SEAT.

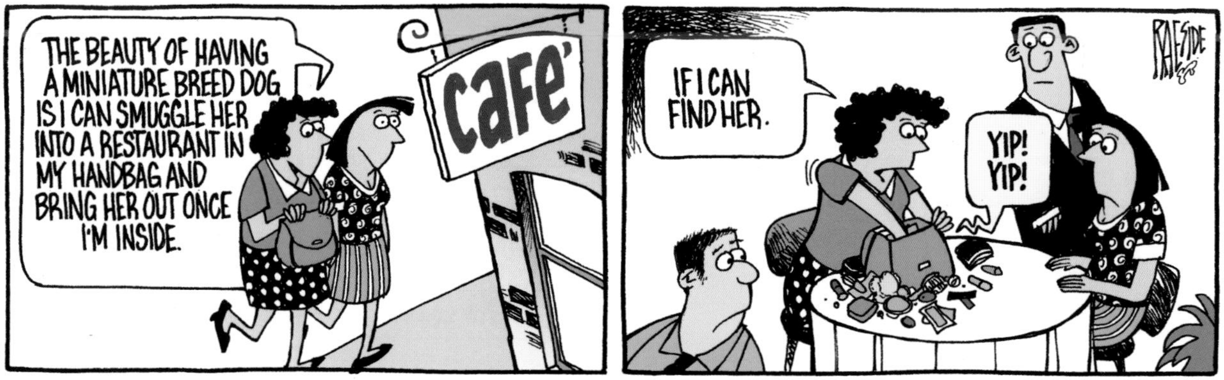
THE BEAUTY OF HAVING A MINIATURE BREED DOG IS I CAN SMUGGLE HER INTO A RESTAURANT IN MY HANDBAG AND BRING HER OUT ONCE I'M INSIDE.
CAFE'
IF I CAN FIND HER.
YIP! YIP!
RAESIDE

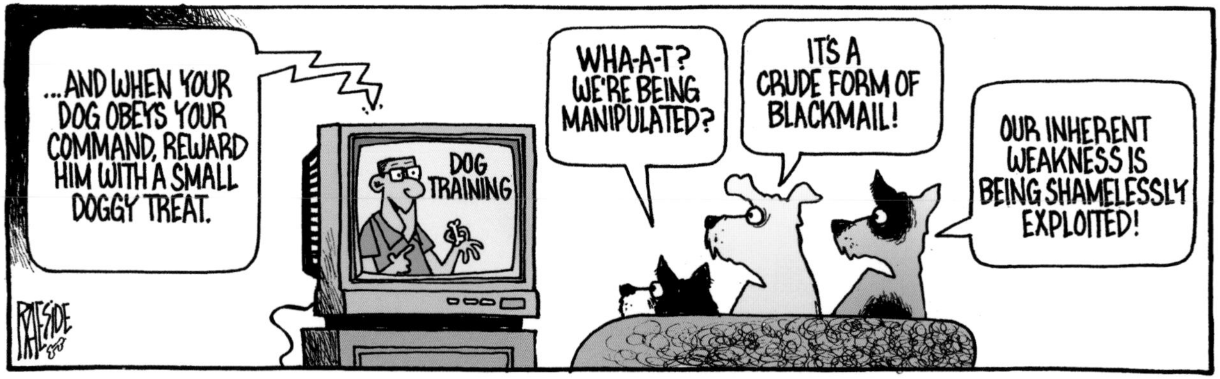
...AND WHEN YOUR DOG OBEYS YOUR COMMAND, REWARD HIM WITH A SMALL DOGGY TREAT.
DOG TRAINING
WHA-A-T? WE'RE BEING MANIPULATED?
IT'S A CRUDE FORM OF BLACKMAIL!
OUR INHERENT WEAKNESS IS BEING SHAMELESSLY EXPLOITED!
RAESIDE

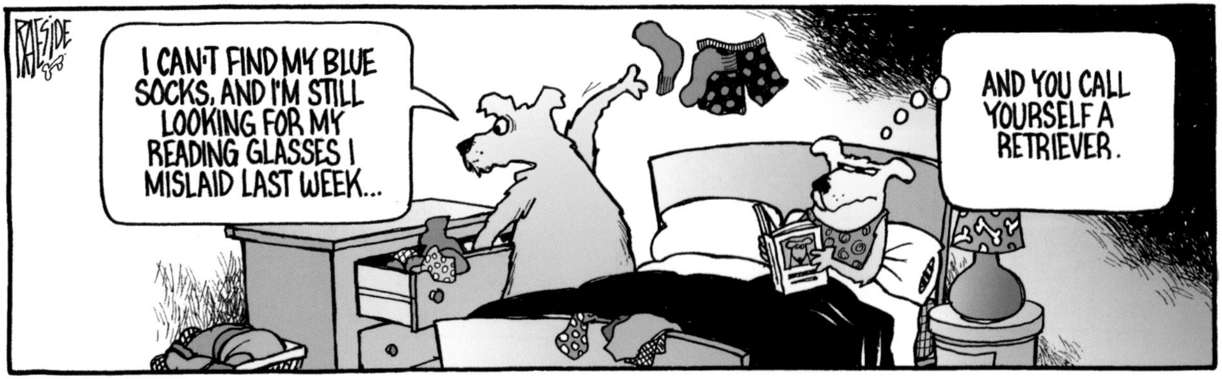
I CAN'T FIND MY BLUE SOCKS, AND I'M STILL LOOKING FOR MY READING GLASSES I MISLAID LAST WEEK...
AND YOU CALL YOURSELF A RETRIEVER.

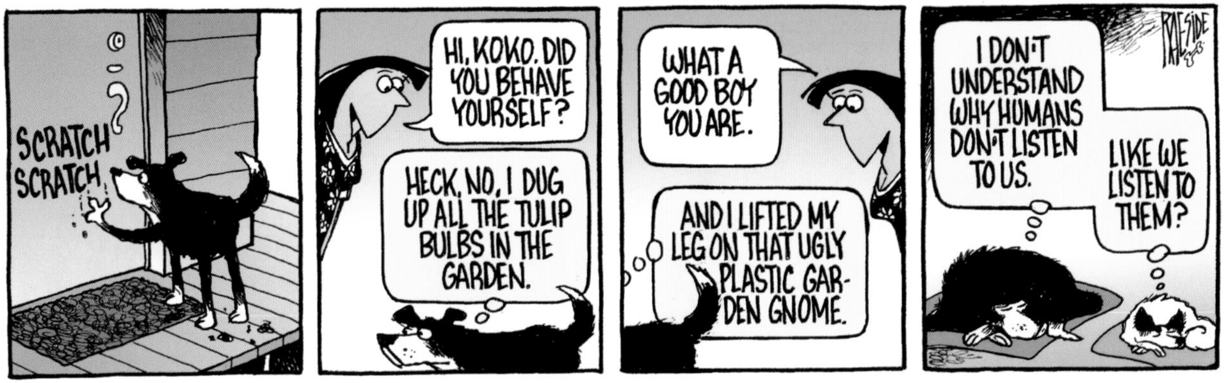
SCRATCH SCRATCH
HI, KOKO. DID YOU BEHAVE YOURSELF?
HECK, NO, I DUG UP ALL THE TULIP BULBS IN THE GARDEN.
WHAT A GOOD BOY YOU ARE.
AND I LIFTED MY LEG ON THAT UGLY PLASTIC GARDEN GNOME.
I DON'T UNDERSTAND WHY HUMANS DON'T LISTEN TO US.
LIKE WE LISTEN TO THEM?

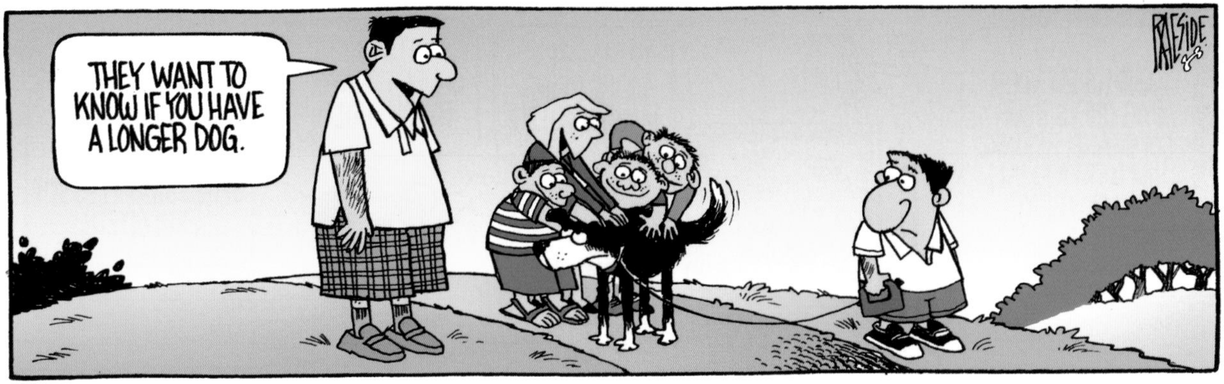
THEY WANT TO KNOW IF YOU HAVE A LONGER DOG.

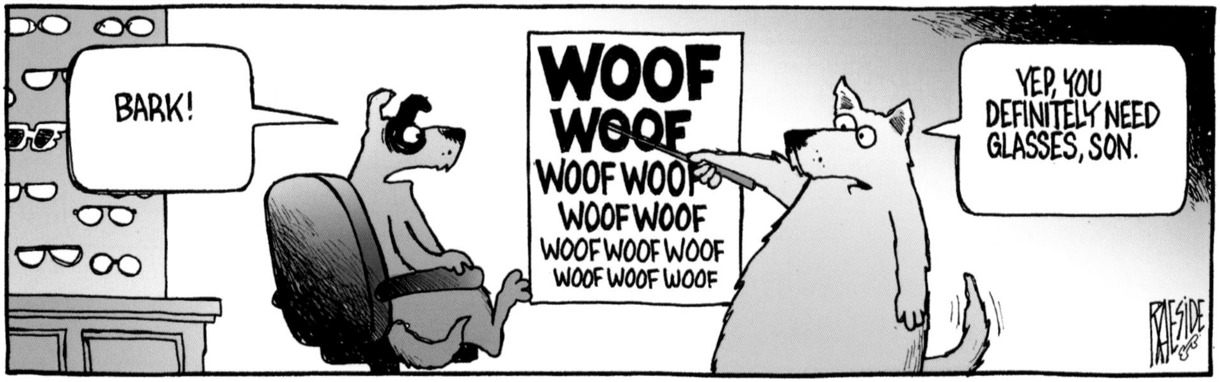
BARK!
WOOF
WOOF
WOOF WOOF
WOOF WOOF
WOOF WOOF WOOF
WOOF WOOF WOOF
YEP, YOU DEFINITELY NEED GLASSES, SON.
RAESIDE

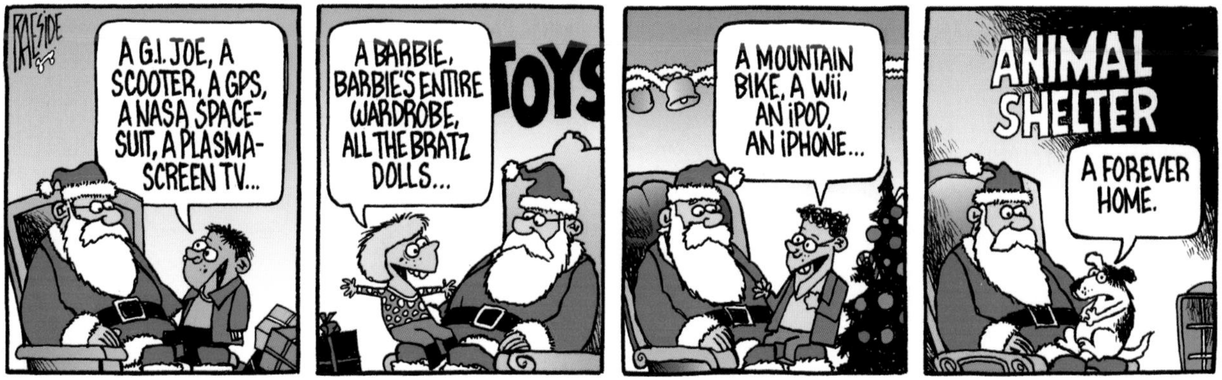
RAESIDE
A G.I. JOE, A SCOOTER, A GPS, A NASA SPACE-SUIT, A PLASMA-SCREEN TV...
TOYS
A BARBIE, BARBIE'S ENTIRE WARDROBE, ALL THE BRATZ DOLLS...
A MOUNTAIN BIKE, A Wii, AN iPOD, AN iPHONE...
ANIMAL SHELTER
A FOREVER HOME.

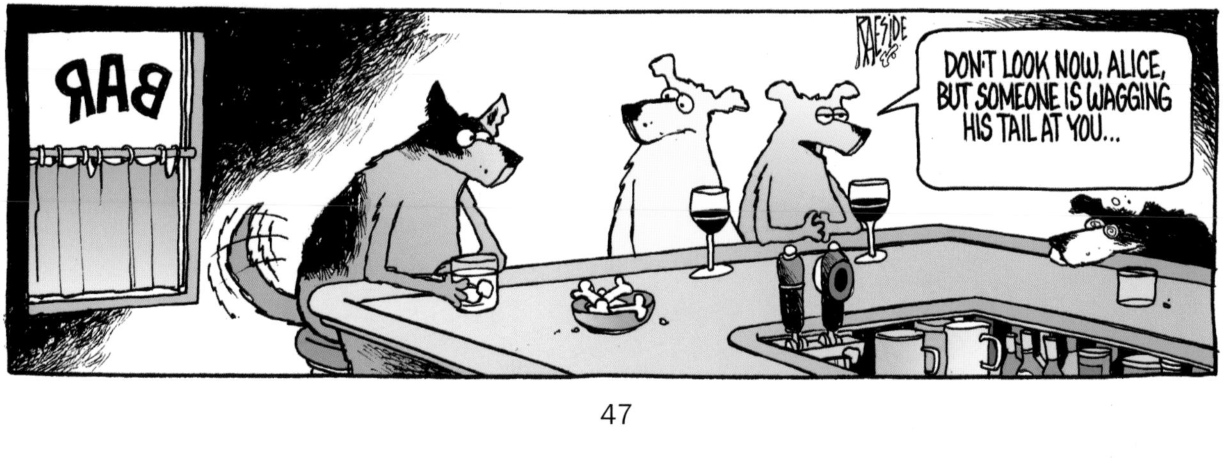
BAR
RAESIDE
DON'T LOOK NOW, ALICE, BUT SOMEONE IS WAGGING HIS TAIL AT YOU...

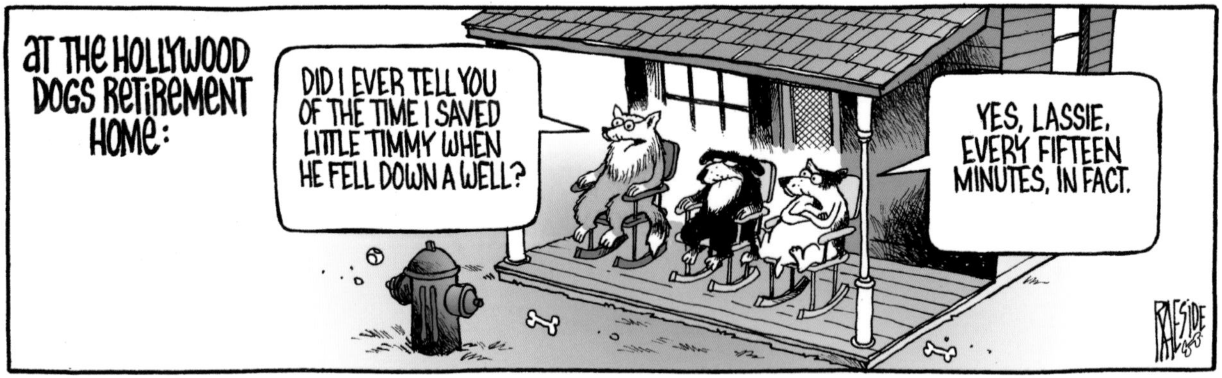
AT THE HOLLYWOOD DOGS RETIREMENT HOME:
DID I EVER TELL YOU OF THE TIME I SAVED LITTLE TIMMY WHEN HE FELL DOWN A WELL?
YES, LASSIE, EVERY FIFTEEN MINUTES, IN FACT.

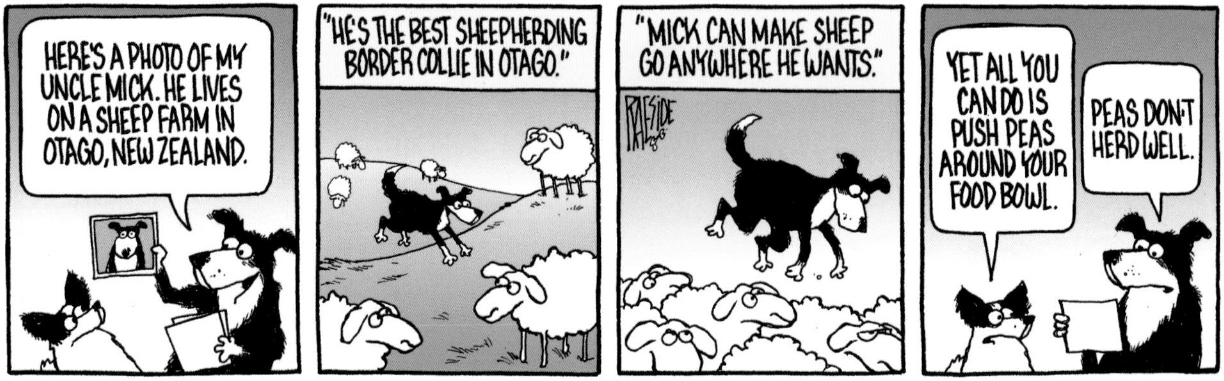
HERE'S A PHOTO OF MY UNCLE MICK. HE LIVES ON A SHEEP FARM IN OTAGO, NEW ZEALAND.
"HE'S THE BEST SHEEPHERDING BORDER COLLIE IN OTAGO."
"MICK CAN MAKE SHEEP GO ANYWHERE HE WANTS."
YET ALL YOU CAN DO IS PUSH PEAS AROUND YOUR FOOD BOWL.
PEAS DON'T HERD WELL.

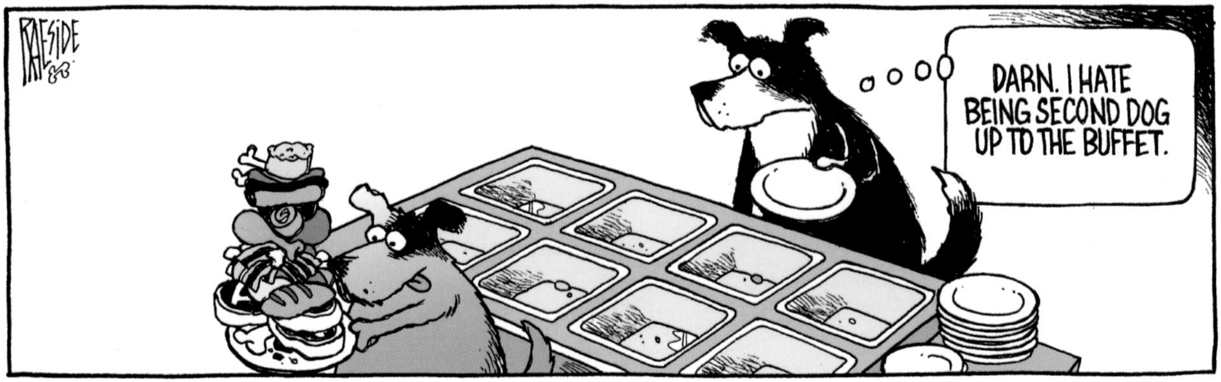
DARN. I HATE BEING SECOND DOG UP TO THE BUFFET.

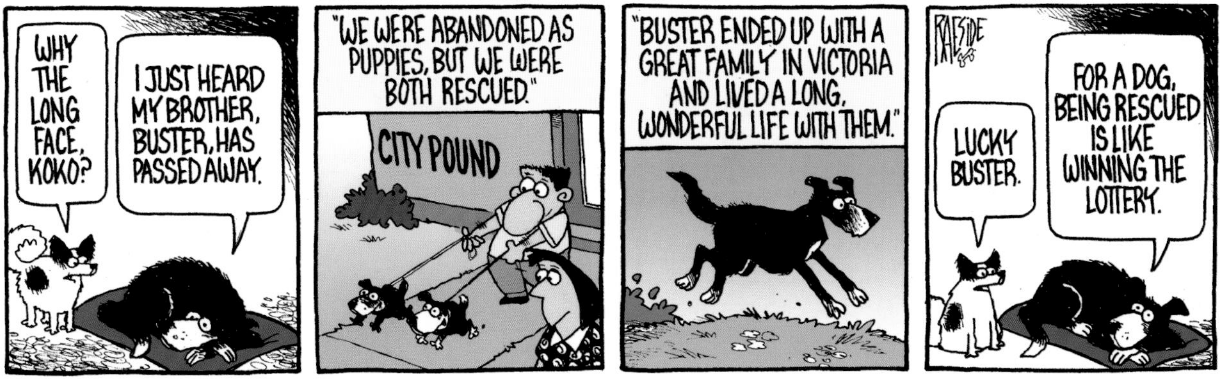
WHY THE LONG FACE, KOKO?
I JUST HEARD MY BROTHER, BUSTER, HAS PASSED AWAY.
"WE WERE ABANDONED AS PUPPIES, BUT WE WERE BOTH RESCUED."
CITY POUND
"BUSTER ENDED UP WITH A GREAT FAMILY IN VICTORIA AND LIVED A LONG, WONDERFUL LIFE WITH THEM."
LUCKY BUSTER.
FOR A DOG, BEING RESCUED IS LIKE WINNING THE LOTTERY.

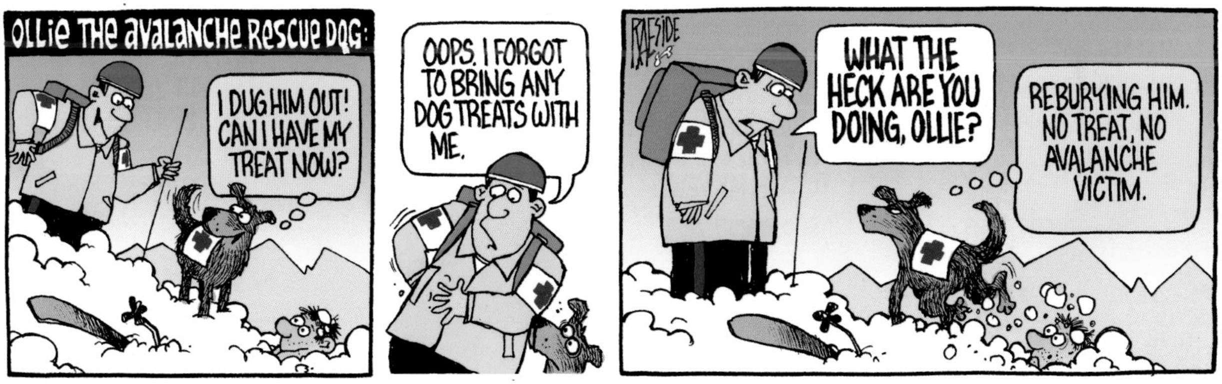
OLLIE THE AVALANCHE RESCUE DOG:
I DUG HIM OUT! CAN I HAVE MY TREAT NOW?
OOPS. I FORGOT TO BRING ANY DOG TREATS WITH ME.
WHAT THE HECK ARE YOU DOING, OLLIE?
REBURYING HIM. NO TREAT, NO AVALANCHE VICTIM.

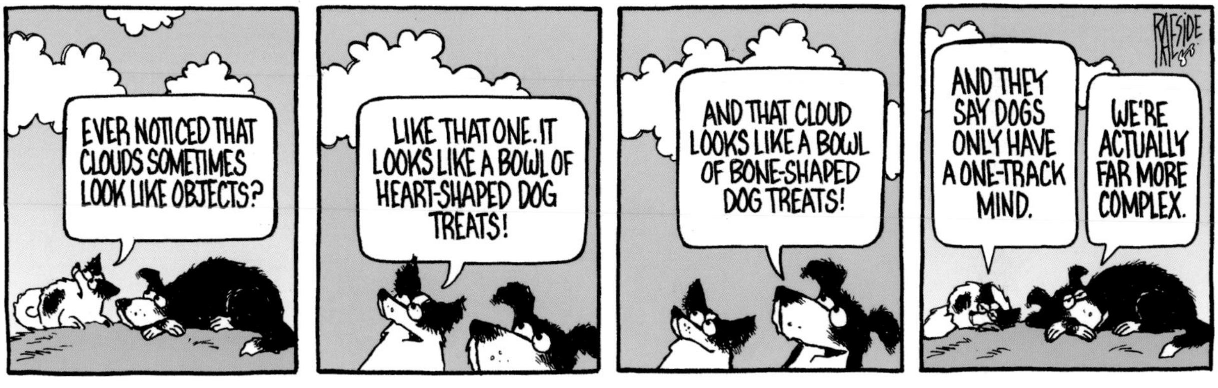
EVER NOTICED THAT CLOUDS SOMETIMES LOOK LIKE OBJECTS?
LIKE THAT ONE. IT LOOKS LIKE A BOWL OF HEART-SHAPED DOG TREATS!
AND THAT CLOUD LOOKS LIKE A BOWL OF BONE-SHAPED DOG TREATS!
AND THEY SAY DOGS ONLY HAVE A ONE-TRACK MIND.
WE'RE ACTUALLY FAR MORE COMPLEX.

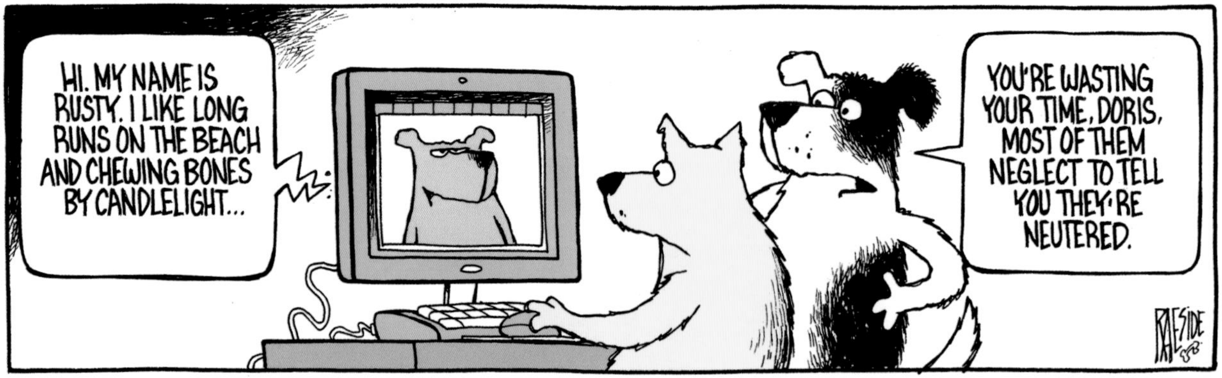
HI. MY NAME IS RUSTY. I LIKE LONG RUNS ON THE BEACH AND CHEWING BONES BY CANDLELIGHT...
YOU'RE WASTING YOUR TIME, DORIS. MOST OF THEM NEGLECT TO TELL YOU THEY'RE NEUTERED.

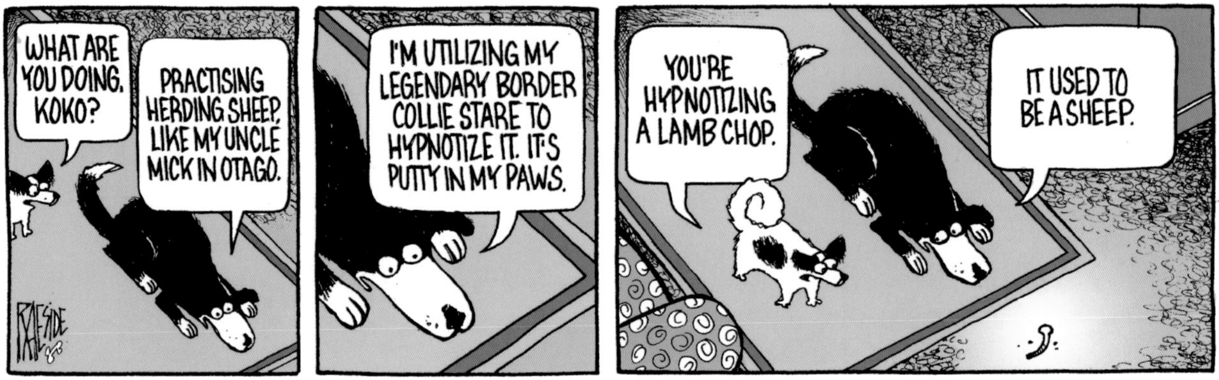
WHAT ARE YOU DOING, KOKO?
PRACTISING HERDING SHEEP, LIKE MY UNCLE MICK IN OTAGO.
I'M UTILIZING MY LEGENDARY BORDER COLLIE STARE TO HYPNOTIZE IT. IT'S PUTTY IN MY PAWS.
YOU'RE HYPNOTIZING A LAMB CHOP.
IT USED TO BE A SHEEP.

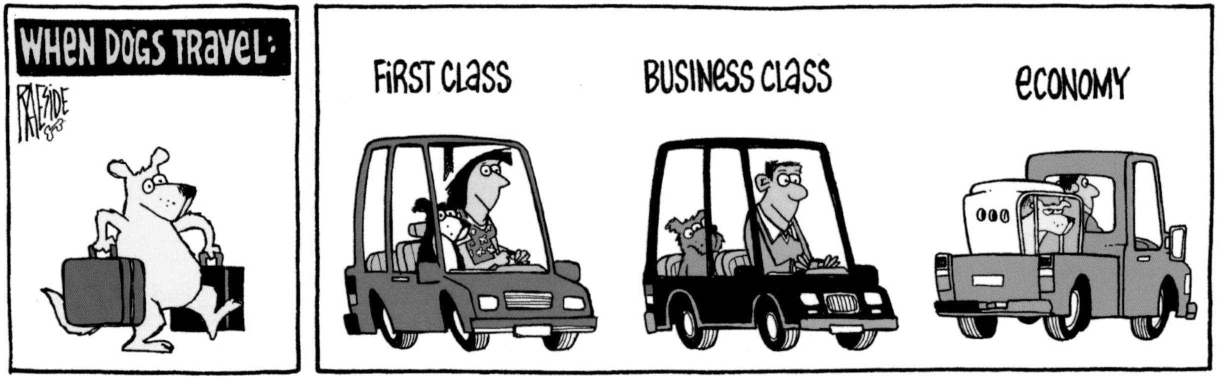
WHEN DOGS TRAVEL:
FIRST CLASS
BUSINESS CLASS
ECONOMY

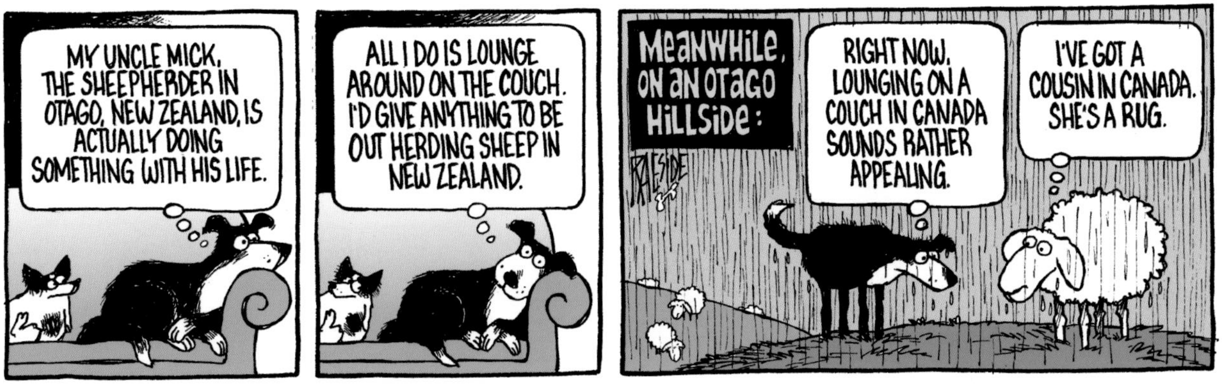
MY UNCLE MICK, THE SHEEPHERDER IN OTAGO, NEW ZEALAND, IS ACTUALLY DOING SOMETHING WITH HIS LIFE.
ALL I DO IS LOUNGE AROUND ON THE COUCH. I'D GIVE ANYTHING TO BE OUT HERDING SHEEP IN NEW ZEALAND.
MEANWHILE, ON AN OTAGO HILLSIDE:
RIGHT NOW, LOUNGING ON A COUCH IN CANADA SOUNDS RATHER APPEALING.
I'VE GOT A COUSIN IN CANADA. SHE'S A RUG.

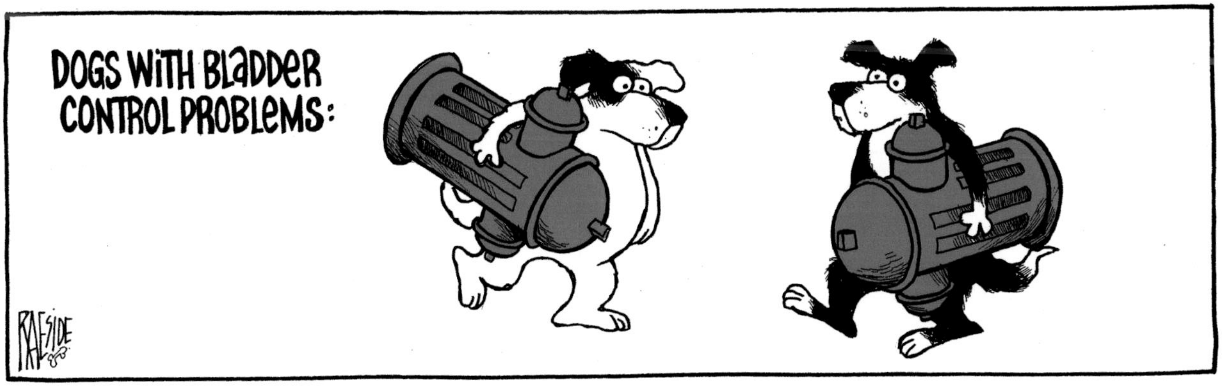
DOGS WITH BLADDER CONTROL PROBLEMS:

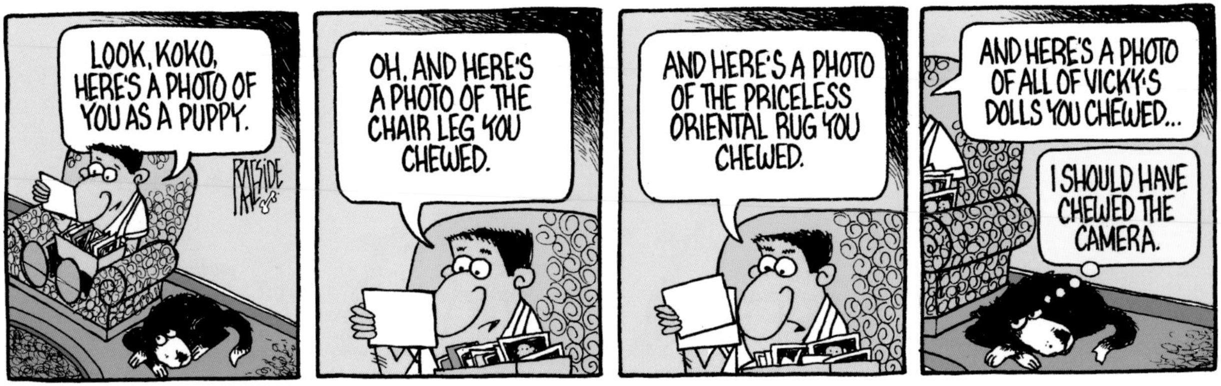
LOOK, KOKO, HERE'S A PHOTO OF YOU AS A PUPPY.
OH, AND HERE'S A PHOTO OF THE CHAIR LEG YOU CHEWED.
AND HERE'S A PHOTO OF THE PRICELESS ORIENTAL RUG YOU CHEWED.
AND HERE'S A PHOTO OF ALL OF VICKY'S DOLLS YOU CHEWED...
I SHOULD HAVE CHEWED THE CAMERA.

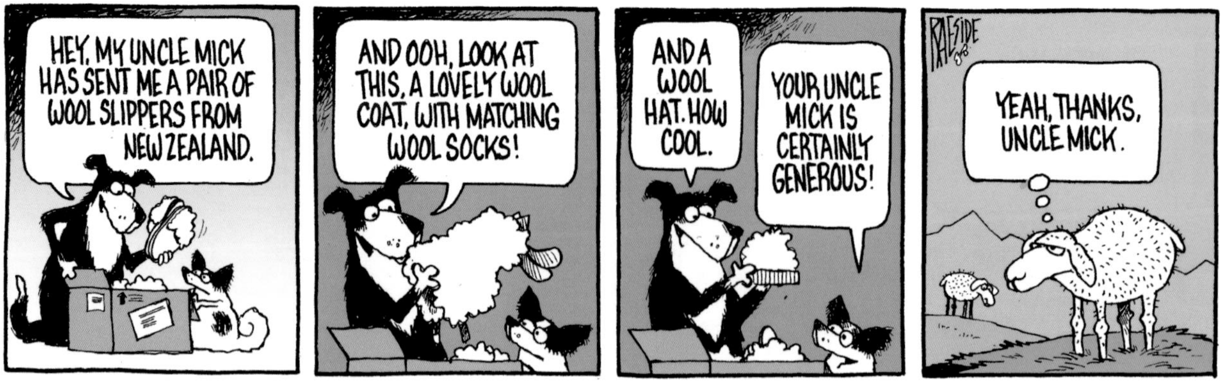
HEY, MY UNCLE MICK HAS SENT ME A PAIR OF WOOL SLIPPERS FROM NEW ZEALAND.
AND OOH, LOOK AT THIS, A LOVELY WOOL COAT, WITH MATCHING WOOL SOCKS!
AND A WOOL HAT. HOW COOL.
YOUR UNCLE MICK IS CERTAINLY GENEROUS!
YEAH, THANKS, UNCLE MICK.

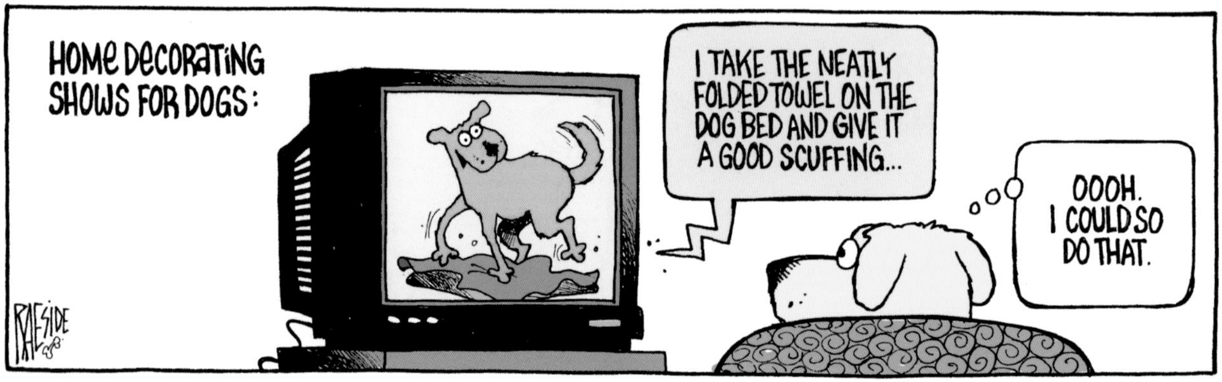
HOME DECORATING SHOWS FOR DOGS:
I TAKE THE NEATLY FOLDED TOWEL ON THE DOG BED AND GIVE IT A GOOD SCUFFING...
OOOH. I COULD SO DO THAT.

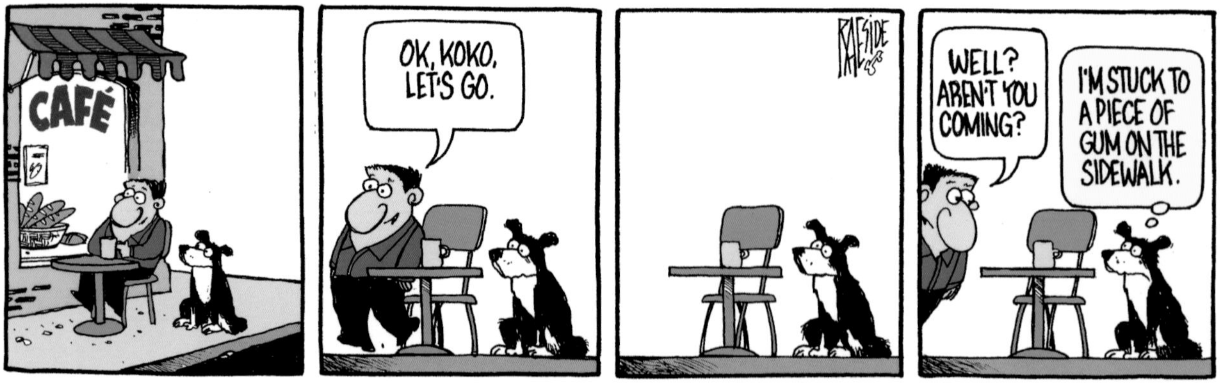
CAFÉ
OK, KOKO, LET'S GO.
WELL? AREN'T YOU COMING?
I'M STUCK TO A PIECE OF GUM ON THE SIDEWALK.

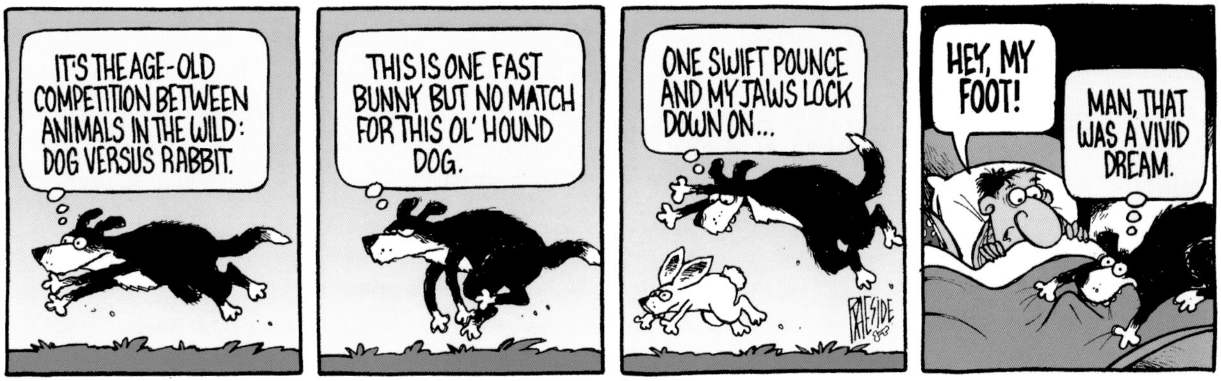
IT'S THE AGE-OLD COMPETITION BETWEEN ANIMALS IN THE WILD: DOG VERSUS RABBIT.
THIS IS ONE FAST BUNNY BUT NO MATCH FOR THIS OL' HOUND DOG.
ONE SWIFT POUNCE AND MY JAWS LOCK DOWN ON...
HEY, MY FOOT!
MAN, THAT WAS A VIVID DREAM.

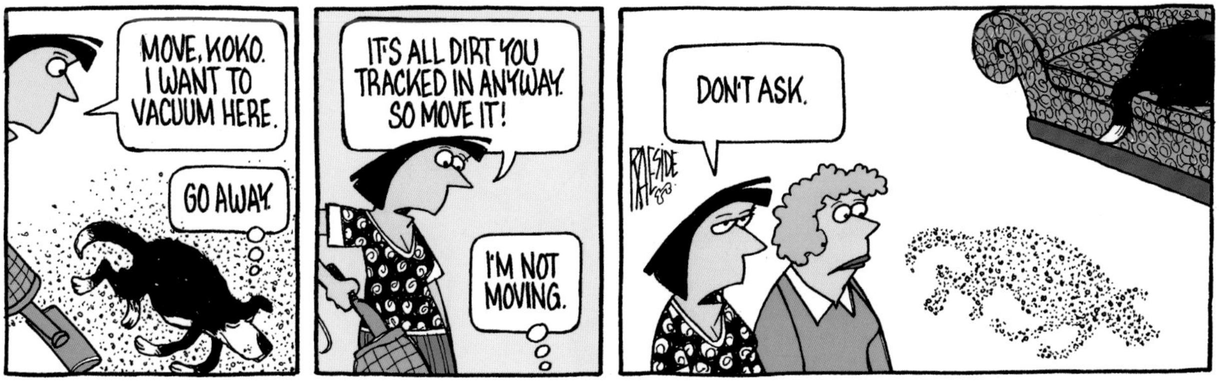
MOVE, KOKO. I WANT TO VACUUM HERE.
GO AWAY.
IT'S ALL DIRT YOU TRACKED IN ANYWAY. SO MOVE IT!
I'M NOT MOVING.
DON'T ASK.

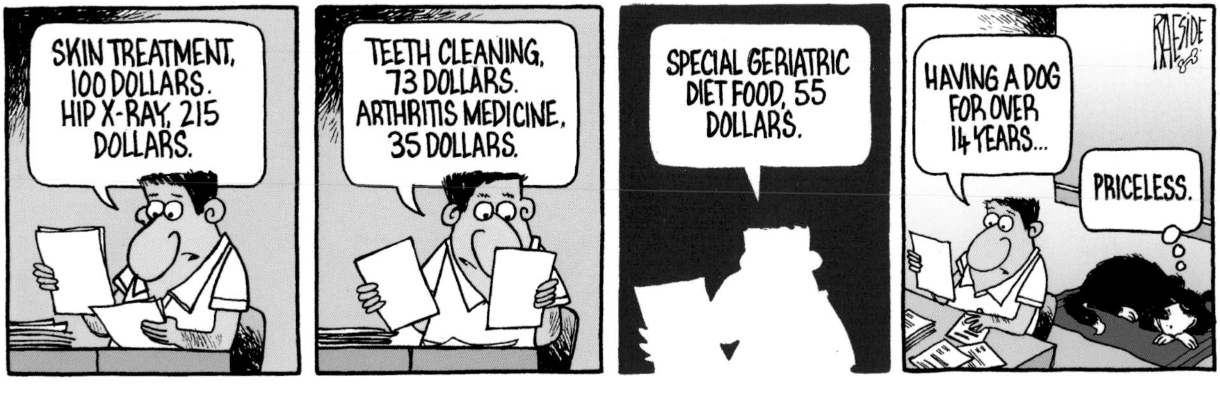
SKIN TREATMENT, 100 DOLLARS. HIP X-RAY, 215 DOLLARS.
TEETH CLEANING, 73 DOLLARS. ARTHRITIS MEDICINE, 35 DOLLARS.
SPECIAL GERIATRIC DIET FOOD, 55 DOLLARS.
HAVING A DOG FOR OVER 14 YEARS...
PRICELESS.

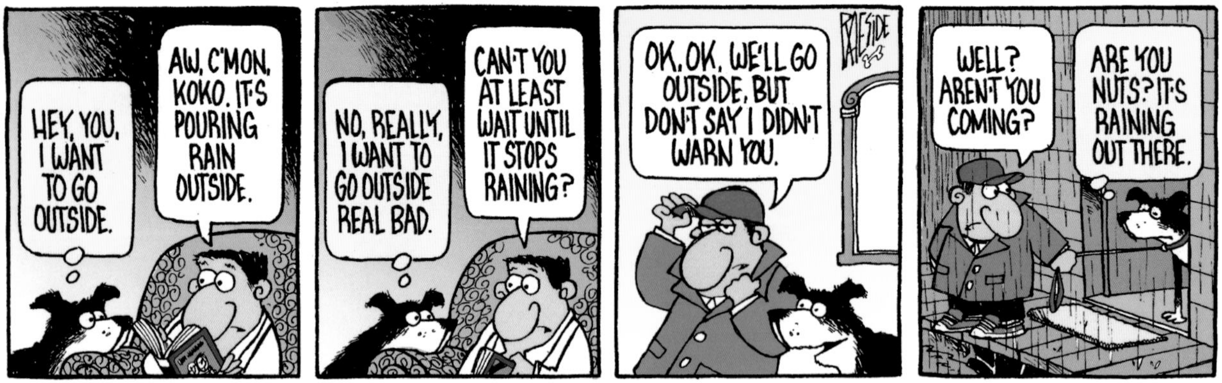
HEY, YOU, I WANT TO GO OUTSIDE.
AW, C'MON, KOKO. IT'S POURING RAIN OUTSIDE.
NO, REALLY, I WANT TO GO OUTSIDE REAL BAD.
CAN'T YOU AT LEAST WAIT UNTIL IT STOPS RAINING?
OK, OK, WE'LL GO OUTSIDE, BUT DON'T SAY I DIDN'T WARN YOU.
WELL? AREN'T YOU COMING?
ARE YOU NUTS? IT'S RAINING OUT THERE.

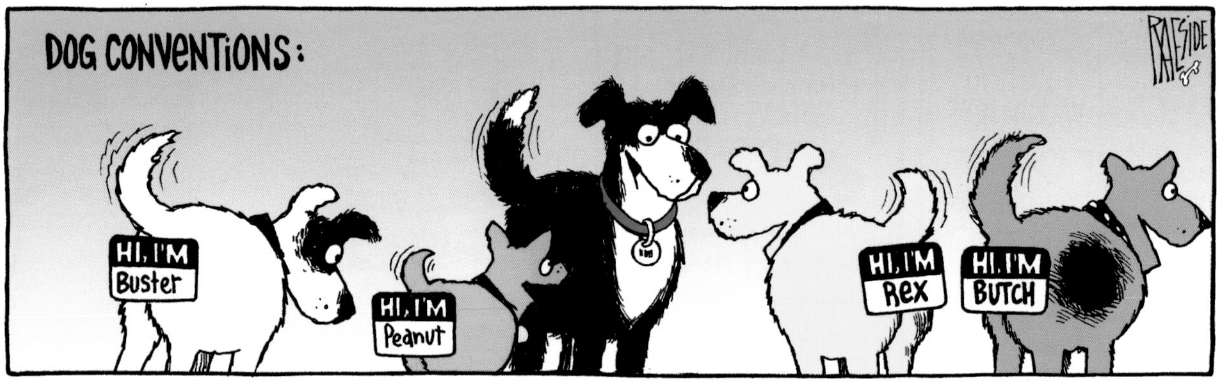
DOG CONVENTIONS:
HI, I'M Buster
HI, I'M Peanut
HI, I'M Rex
HI, I'M BUTCH

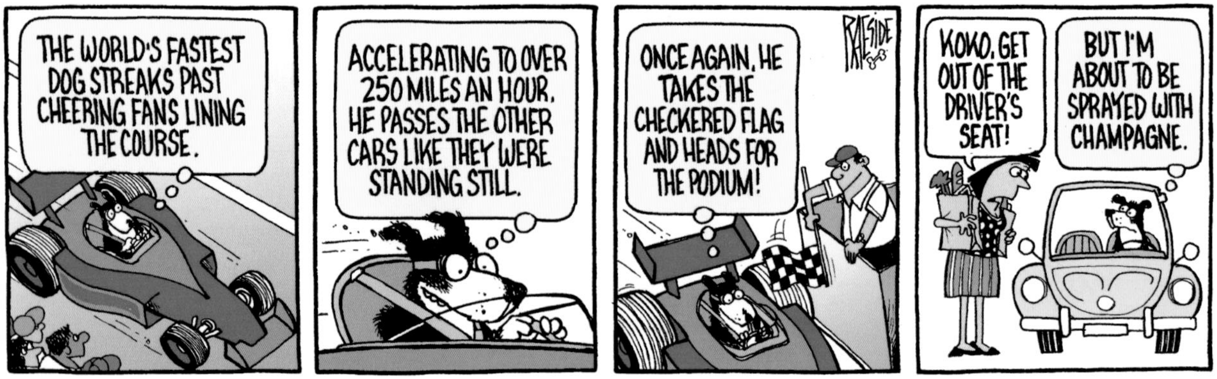
THE WORLD'S FASTEST DOG STREAKS PAST CHEERING FANS LINING THE COURSE.
ACCELERATING TO OVER 250 MILES AN HOUR, HE PASSES THE OTHER CARS LIKE THEY WERE STANDING STILL.
ONCE AGAIN, HE TAKES THE CHECKERED FLAG AND HEADS FOR THE PODIUM!
KOKO, GET OUT OF THE DRIVER'S SEAT!
BUT I'M ABOUT TO BE SPRAYED WITH CHAMPAGNE.

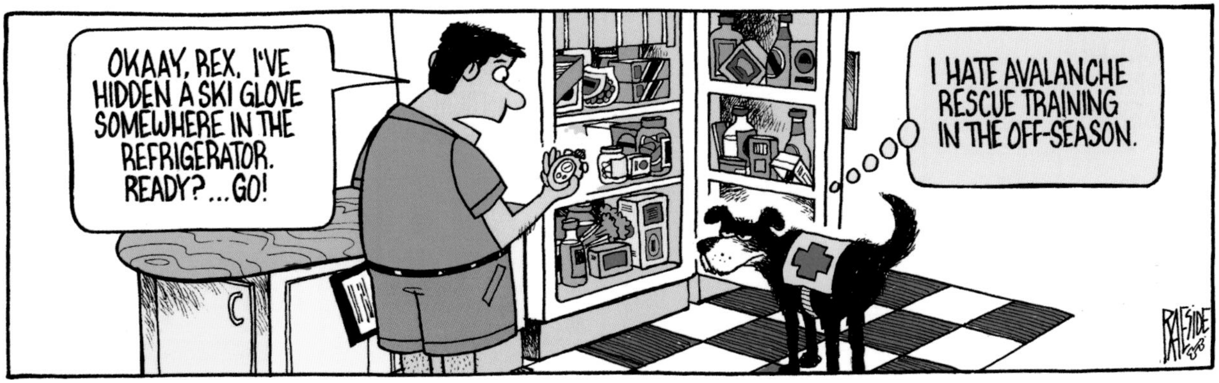
OKAAY, REX, I'VE HIDDEN A SKI GLOVE SOMEWHERE IN THE REFRIGERATOR. READY?...GO!
I HATE AVALANCHE RESCUE TRAINING IN THE OFF-SEASON.

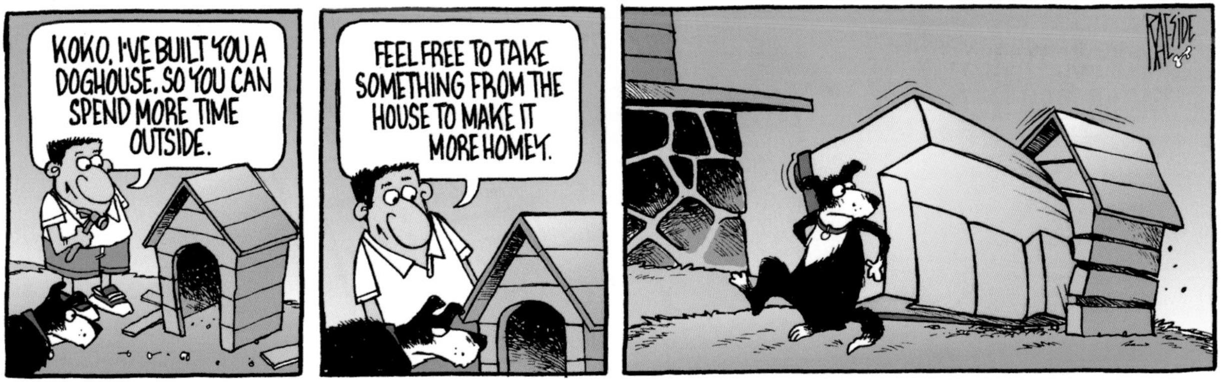
KOKO, I'VE BUILT YOU A DOGHOUSE, SO YOU CAN SPEND MORE TIME OUTSIDE.
FEEL FREE TO TAKE SOMETHING FROM THE HOUSE TO MAKE IT MORE HOMEY.

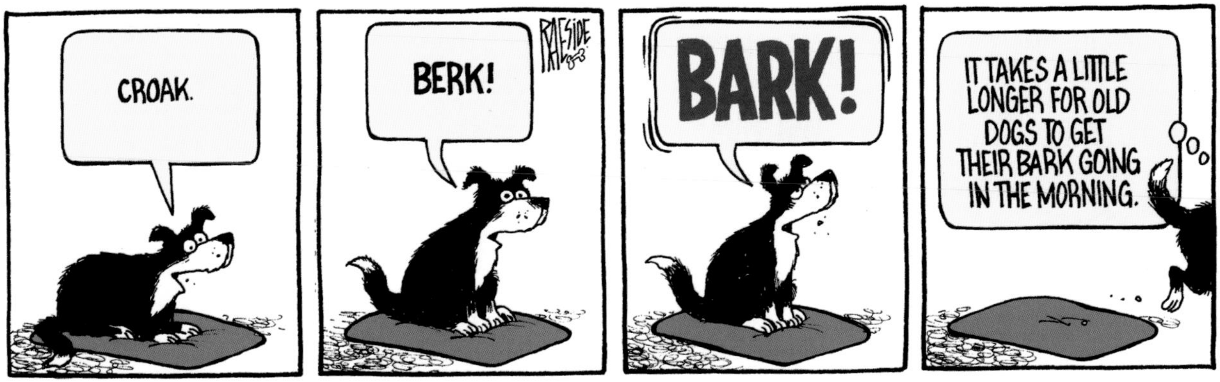
CROAK.
BERK!
BARK!
IT TAKES A LITTLE LONGER FOR OLD DOGS TO GET THEIR BARK GOING IN THE MORNING.

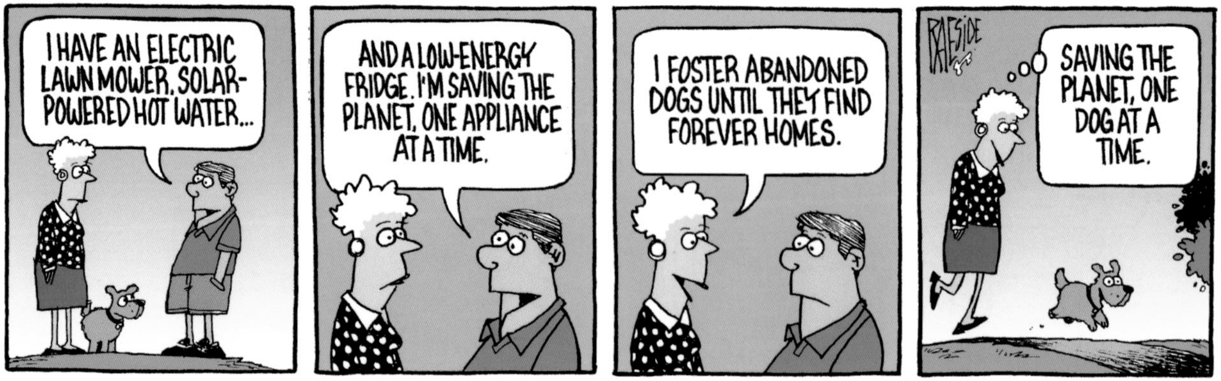
I HAVE AN ELECTRIC LAWN MOWER, SOLAR-POWERED HOT WATER...
AND A LOW-ENERGY FRIDGE. I'M SAVING THE PLANET, ONE APPLIANCE AT A TIME.
I FOSTER ABANDONED DOGS UNTIL THEY FIND FOREVER HOMES.
RAESIDE
SAVING THE PLANET, ONE DOG AT A TIME.

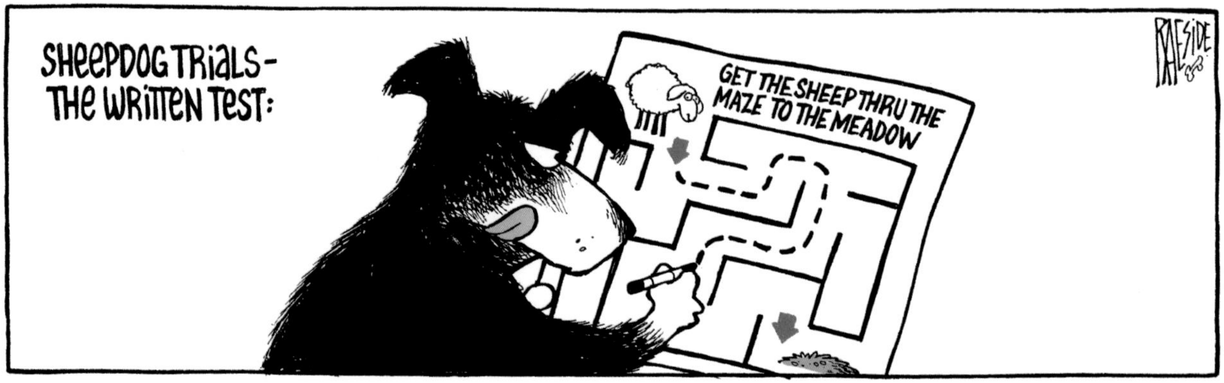
SHEEPDOG TRIALS - THE WRITTEN TEST:
GET THE SHEEP THRU THE MAZE TO THE MEADOW
RAESIDE

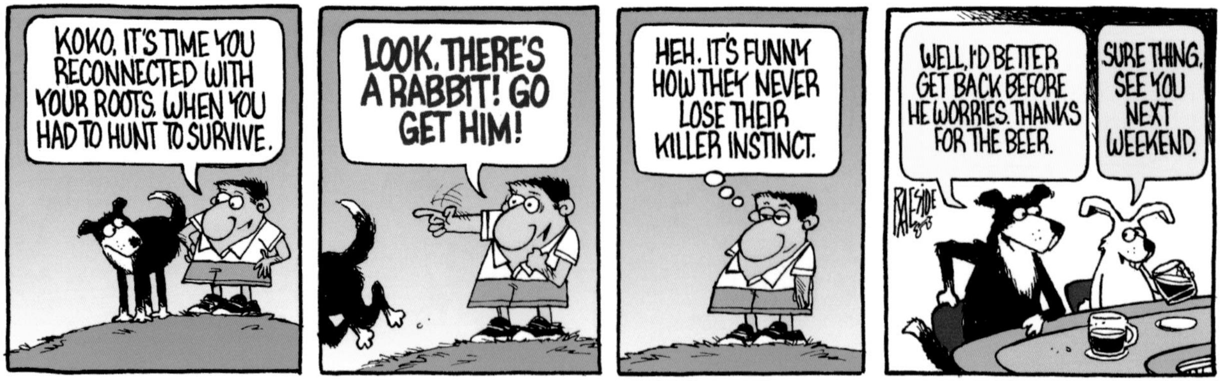
KOKO, IT'S TIME YOU RECONNECTED WITH YOUR ROOTS. WHEN YOU HAD TO HUNT TO SURVIVE.
LOOK, THERE'S A RABBIT! GO GET HIM!
HEH. IT'S FUNNY HOW THEY NEVER LOSE THEIR KILLER INSTINCT.
WELL, I'D BETTER GET BACK BEFORE HE WORRIES. THANKS FOR THE BEER.
SURE THING. SEE YOU NEXT WEEKEND.
RAESIDE

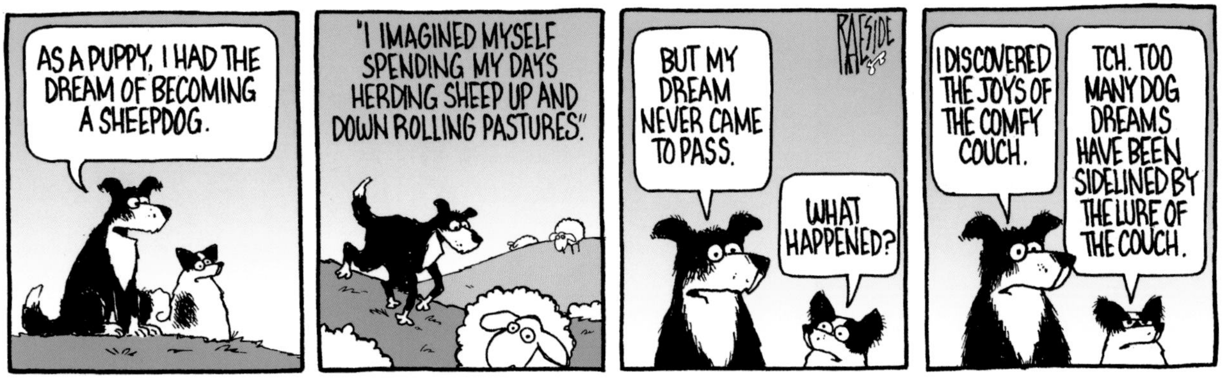
AS A PUPPY, I HAD THE DREAM OF BECOMING A SHEEPDOG.
"I IMAGINED MYSELF SPENDING MY DAYS HERDING SHEEP UP AND DOWN ROLLING PASTURES."
BUT MY DREAM NEVER CAME TO PASS.
WHAT HAPPENED?
I DISCOVERED THE JOYS OF THE COMFY COUCH.
TCH. TOO MANY DOG DREAMS HAVE BEEN SIDELINED BY THE LURE OF THE COUCH.

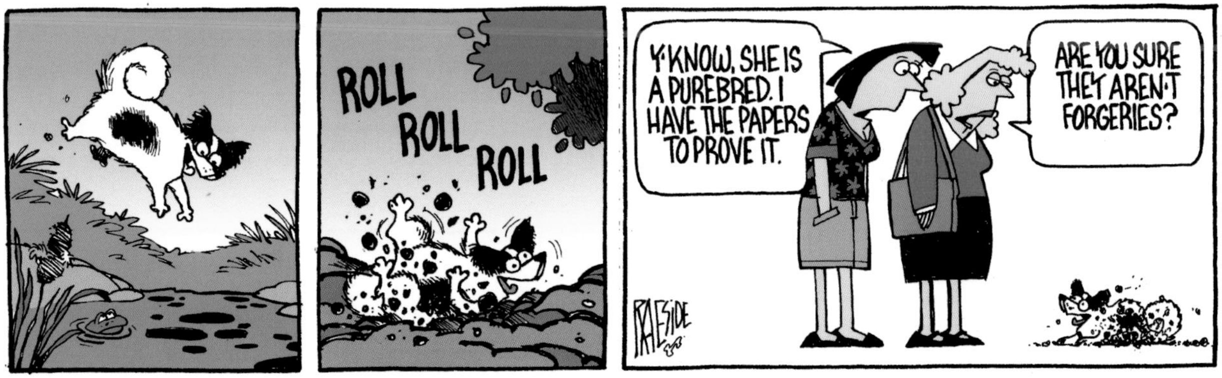
ROLL
ROLL
ROLL
Y'KNOW, SHE IS A PUREBRED. I HAVE THE PAPERS TO PROVE IT.
ARE YOU SURE THEY AREN'T FORGERIES?

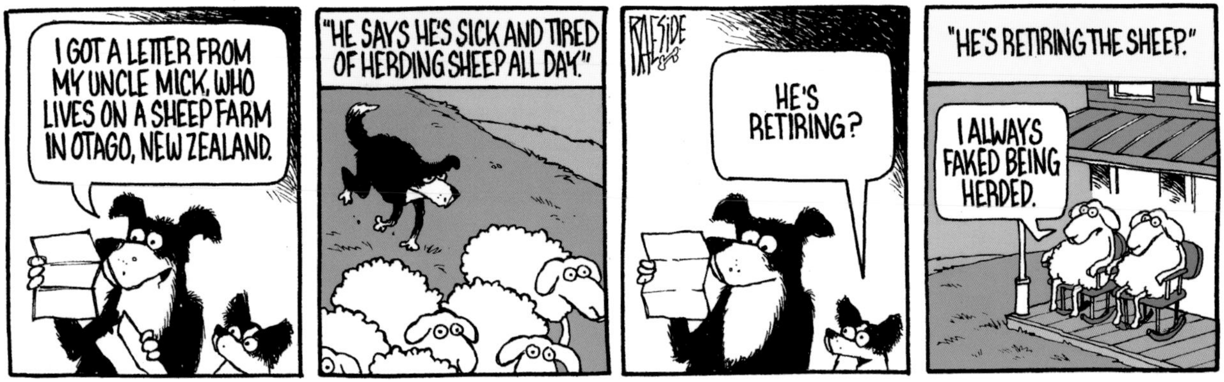
I GOT A LETTER FROM MY UNCLE MICK, WHO LIVES ON A SHEEP FARM IN OTAGO, NEW ZEALAND.
"HE SAYS HE'S SICK AND TIRED OF HERDING SHEEP ALL DAY."
HE'S RETIRING?
"HE'S RETIRING THE SHEEP."
I ALWAYS FAKED BEING HERDED.

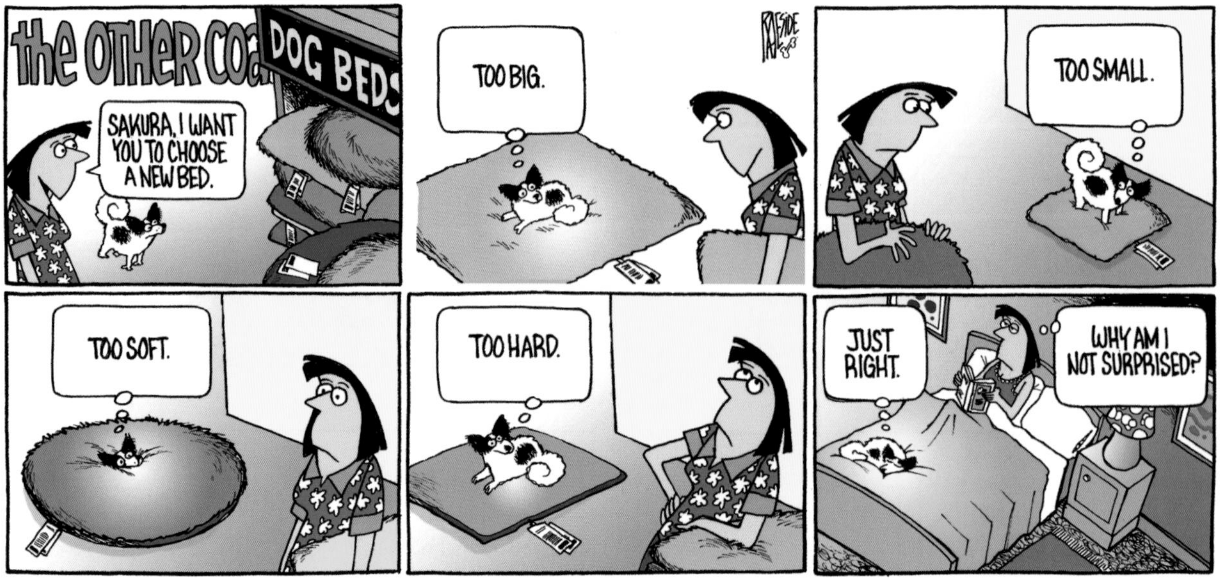
the OTHER COAST
DOG BEDS
SAKURA, I WANT YOU TO CHOOSE A NEW BED.
TOO BIG.
TOO SMALL.
TOO SOFT.
TOO HARD.
JUST RIGHT.
WHY AM I NOT SURPRISED?

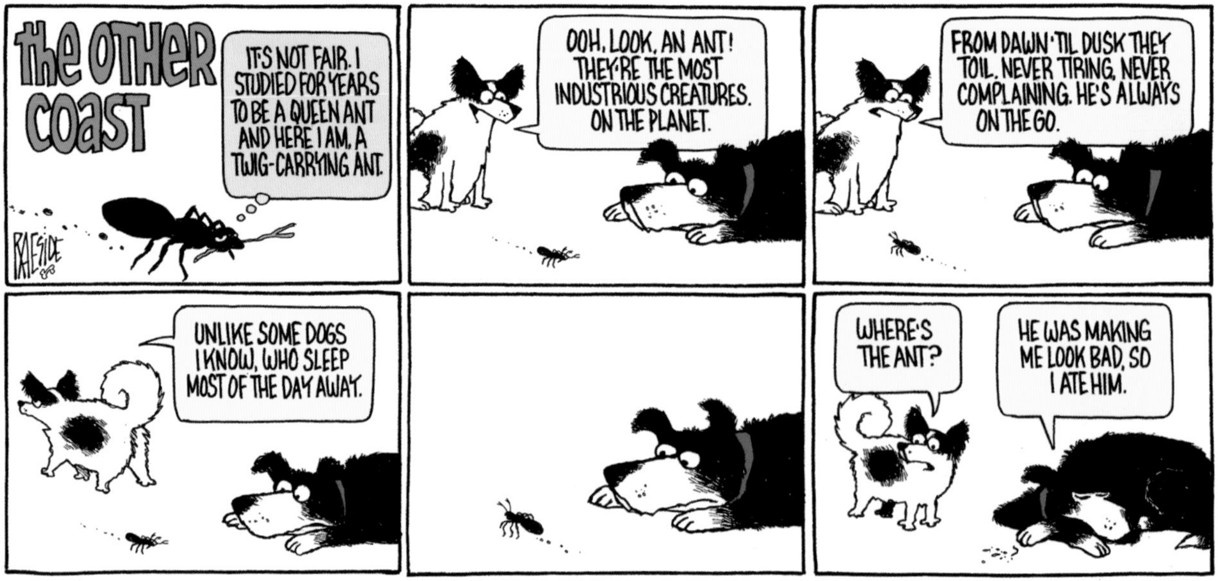
the OTHER COAST
IT'S NOT FAIR. I STUDIED FOR YEARS TO BE A QUEEN ANT AND HERE I AM, A TWIG-CARRYING ANT.
OOH, LOOK, AN ANT! THEY'RE THE MOST INDUSTRIOUS CREATURES. ON THE PLANET.
FROM DAWN 'TIL DUSK THEY TOIL. NEVER TIRING, NEVER COMPLAINING. HE'S ALWAYS ON THE GO.
UNLIKE SOME DOGS I KNOW, WHO SLEEP MOST OF THE DAY AWAY.
WHERE'S THE ANT?
HE WAS MAKING ME LOOK BAD, SO I ATE HIM.

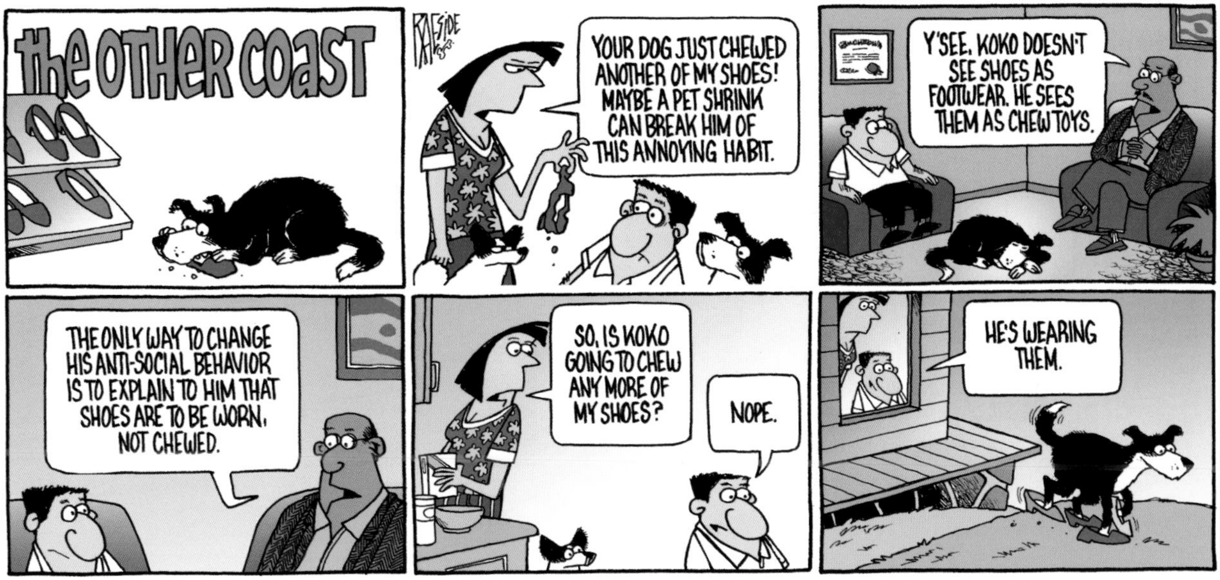
the OTHER COAST
RAESIDE
YOUR DOG JUST CHEWED ANOTHER OF MY SHOES! MAYBE A PET SHRINK CAN BREAK HIM OF THIS ANNOYING HABIT.
Y'SEE, KOKO DOESN'T SEE SHOES AS FOOTWEAR. HE SEES THEM AS CHEW TOYS.
THE ONLY WAY TO CHANGE HIS ANTI-SOCIAL BEHAVIOR IS TO EXPLAIN TO HIM THAT SHOES ARE TO BE WORN, NOT CHEWED.
SO, IS KOKO GOING TO CHEW ANY MORE OF MY SHOES?
NOPE.
HE'S WEARING THEM.

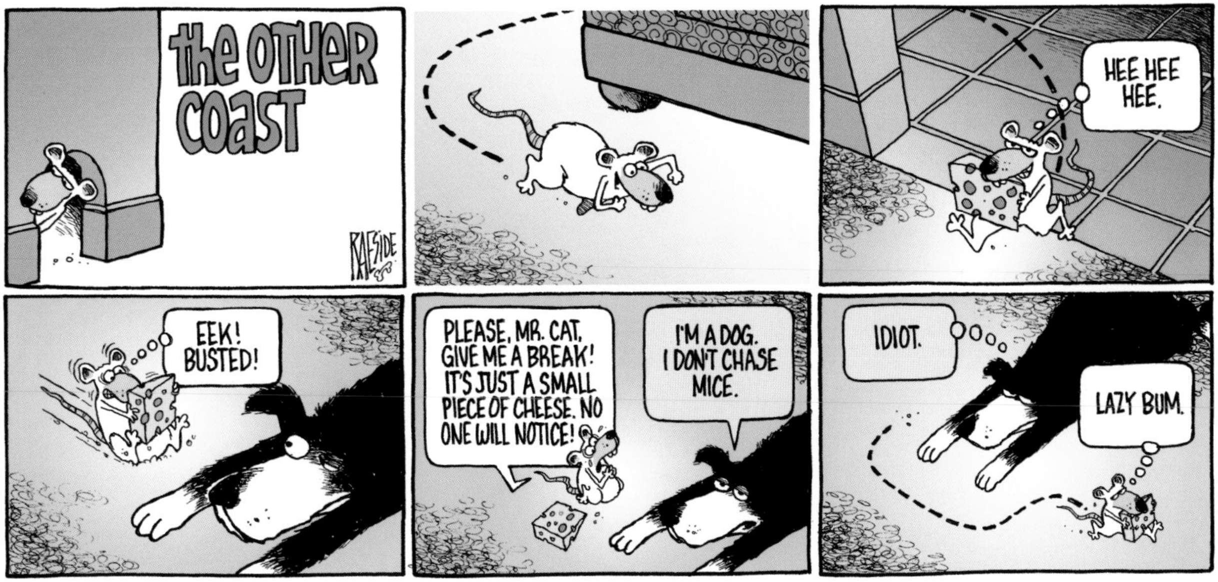
the OTHER COAST
RAESIDE
HEE HEE HEE.
EEK! BUSTED!
PLEASE, MR. CAT, GIVE ME A BREAK! IT'S JUST A SMALL PIECE OF CHEESE. NO ONE WILL NOTICE!
I'M A DOG. I DON'T CHASE MICE.
IDIOT.
LAZY BUM.

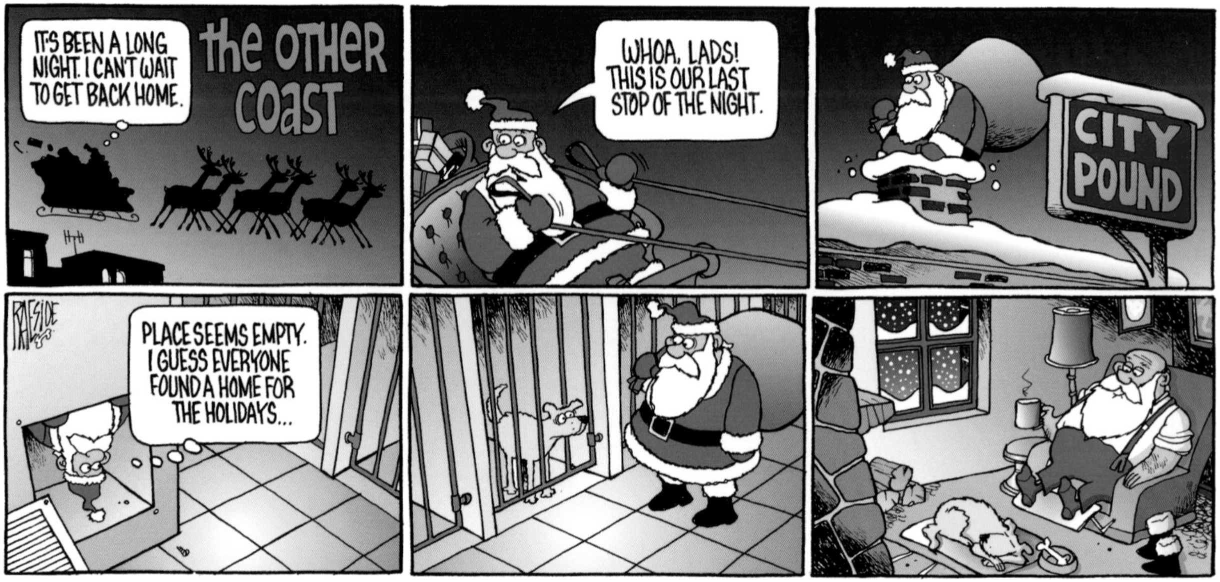
IT'S BEEN A LONG NIGHT. I CAN'T WAIT TO GET BACK HOME.
the OTHER COAST
WHOA, LADS! THIS IS OUR LAST STOP OF THE NIGHT.
CITY POUND
PLACE SEEMS EMPTY. I GUESS EVERYONE FOUND A HOME FOR THE HOLIDAYS...

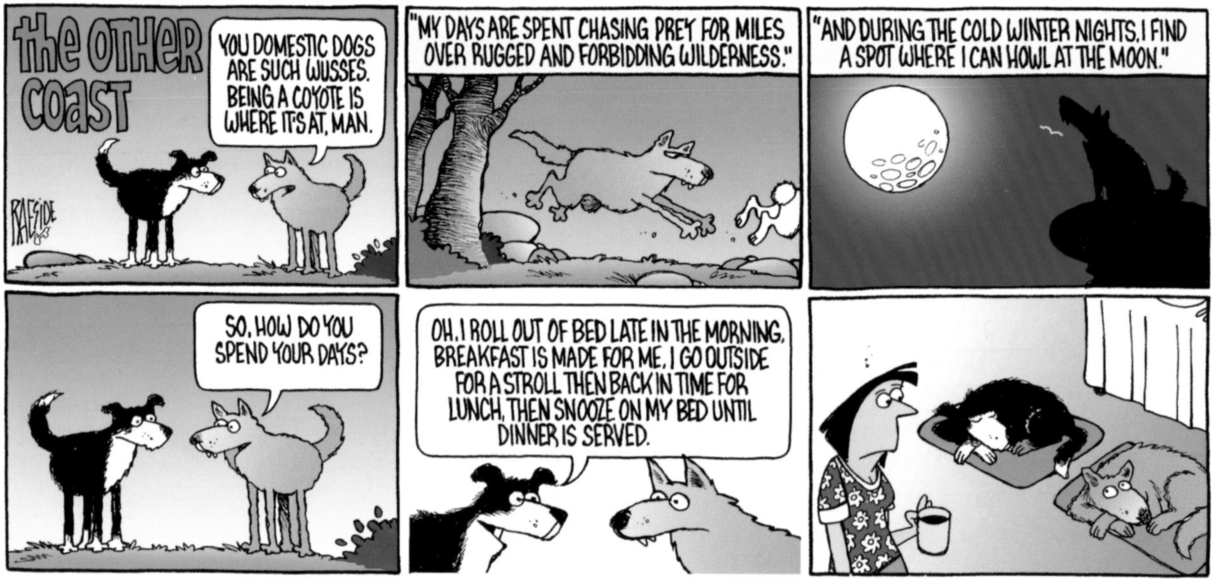
the OTHER COAST
YOU DOMESTIC DOGS ARE SUCH WUSSES. BEING A COYOTE IS WHERE IT'S AT, MAN.
"MY DAYS ARE SPENT CHASING PREY FOR MILES OVER RUGGED AND FORBIDDING WILDERNESS."
"AND DURING THE COLD WINTER NIGHTS, I FIND A SPOT WHERE I CAN HOWL AT THE MOON."
SO, HOW DO YOU SPEND YOUR DAYS?
OH, I ROLL OUT OF BED LATE IN THE MORNING, BREAKFAST IS MADE FOR ME, I GO OUTSIDE FOR A STROLL THEN BACK IN TIME FOR LUNCH, THEN SNOOZE ON MY BED UNTIL DINNER IS SERVED.

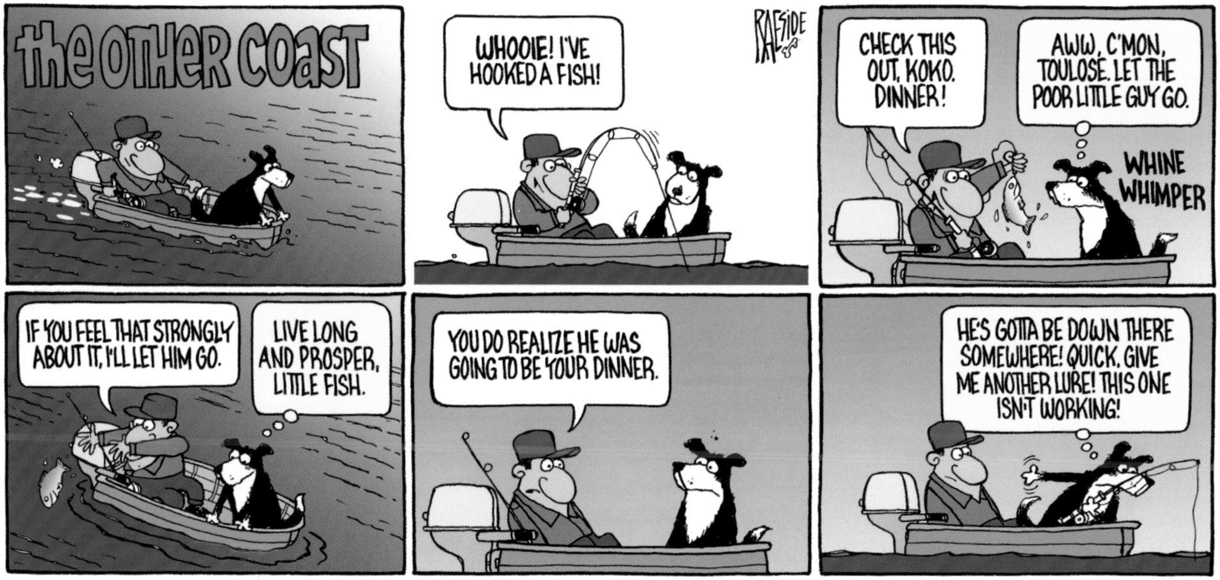
the OTHER COAST
RAESIDE
WHOOIE! I'VE HOOKED A FISH!
CHECK THIS OUT, KOKO. DINNER!
AWW, C'MON, TOULOSE. LET THE POOR LITTLE GUY GO.
WHINE
WHIMPER
IF YOU FEEL THAT STRONGLY ABOUT IT, I'LL LET HIM GO.
LIVE LONG AND PROSPER, LITTLE FISH.
YOU DO REALIZE HE WAS GOING TO BE YOUR DINNER.
HE'S GOTTA BE DOWN THERE SOMEWHERE! QUICK, GIVE ME ANOTHER LURE! THIS ONE ISN'T WORKING!

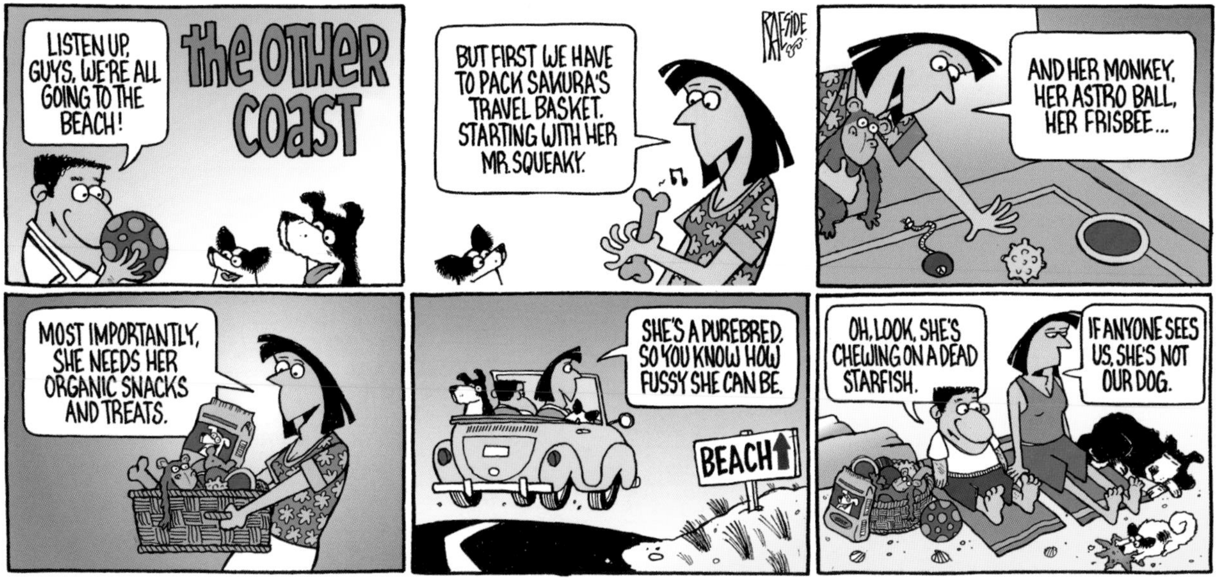
LISTEN UP, GUYS, WE'RE ALL GOING TO THE BEACH!
the OTHER COAST
RAESIDE
BUT FIRST WE HAVE TO PACK SAKURA'S TRAVEL BASKET. STARTING WITH HER MR. SQUEAKY.
AND HER MONKEY, HER ASTRO BALL, HER FRISBEE...
MOST IMPORTANTLY, SHE NEEDS HER ORGANIC SNACKS AND TREATS.
SHE'S A PUREBRED, SO YOU KNOW HOW FUSSY SHE CAN BE.
BEACH
OH, LOOK, SHE'S CHEWING ON A DEAD STARFISH.
IF ANYONE SEES US, SHE'S NOT OUR DOG.

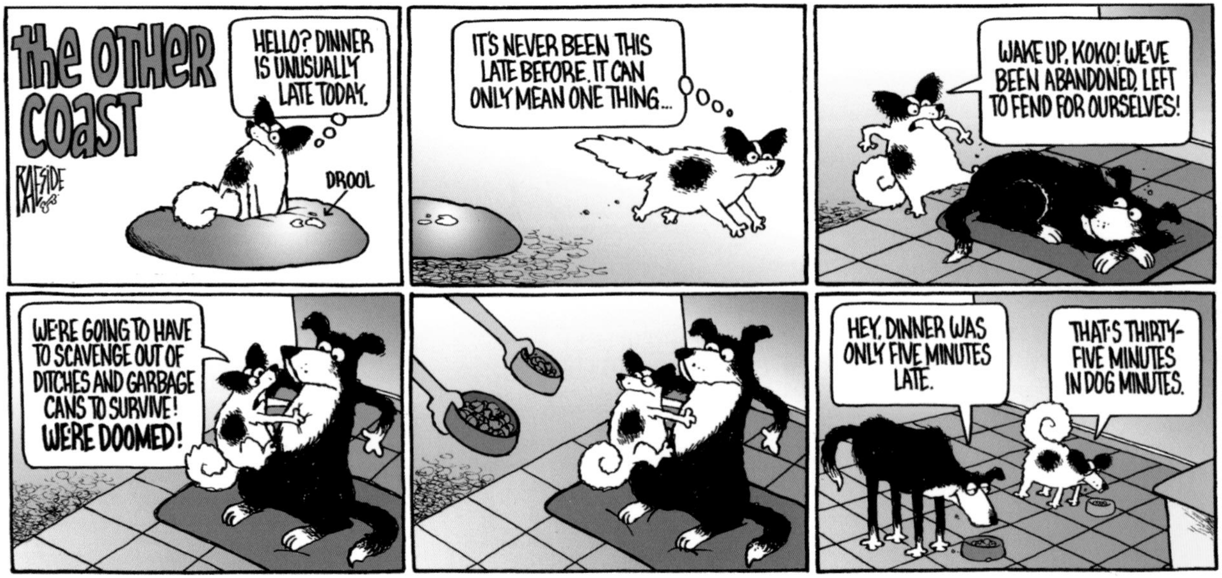
the OTHER COAST
RAESIDE
HELLO? DINNER IS UNUSUALLY LATE TODAY.
DROOL
IT'S NEVER BEEN THIS LATE BEFORE. IT CAN ONLY MEAN ONE THING...
WAKE UP, KOKO! WE'VE BEEN ABANDONED, LEFT TO FEND FOR OURSELVES!
WE'RE GOING TO HAVE TO SCAVENGE OUT OF DITCHES AND GARBAGE CANS TO SURVIVE! WE'RE DOOMED!
HEY, DINNER WAS ONLY FIVE MINUTES LATE.
THAT'S THIRTY-FIVE MINUTES IN DOG MINUTES.

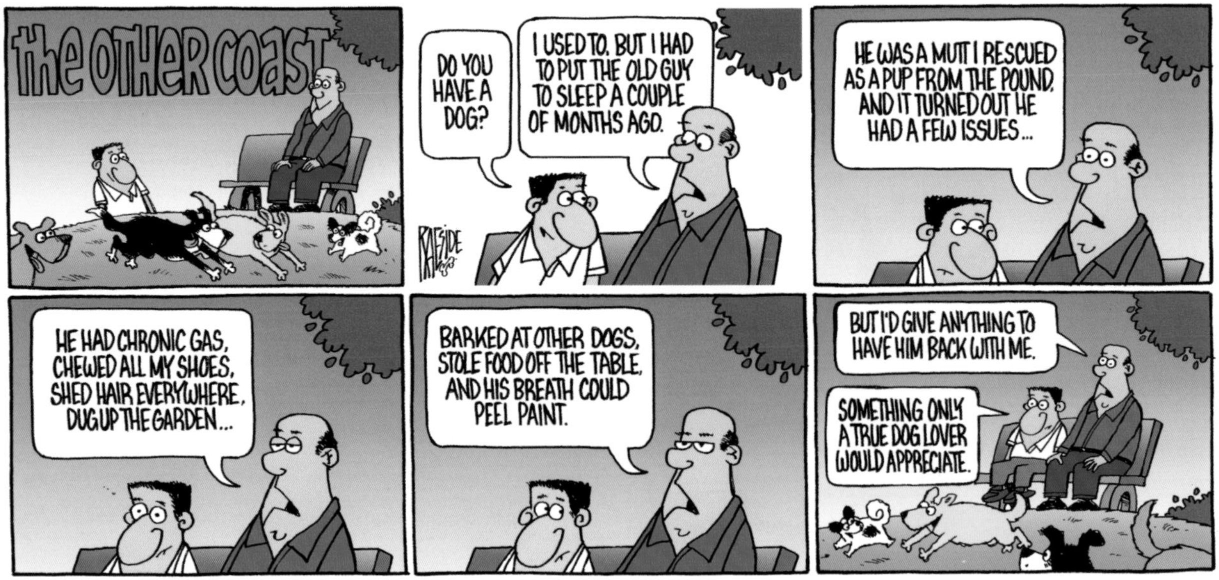
the OTHER COAST
DO YOU HAVE A DOG?
I USED TO, BUT I HAD TO PUT THE OLD GUY TO SLEEP A COUPLE OF MONTHS AGO.
RAESIDE
HE WAS A MUTT I RESCUED AS A PUP FROM THE POUND, AND IT TURNED OUT HE HAD A FEW ISSUES...
HE HAD CHRONIC GAS, CHEWED ALL MY SHOES, SHED HAIR EVERYWHERE, DUG UP THE GARDEN...
BARKED AT OTHER DOGS, STOLE FOOD OFF THE TABLE, AND HIS BREATH COULD PEEL PAINT.
BUT I'D GIVE ANYTHING TO HAVE HIM BACK WITH ME.
SOMETHING ONLY A TRUE DOG LOVER WOULD APPRECIATE.

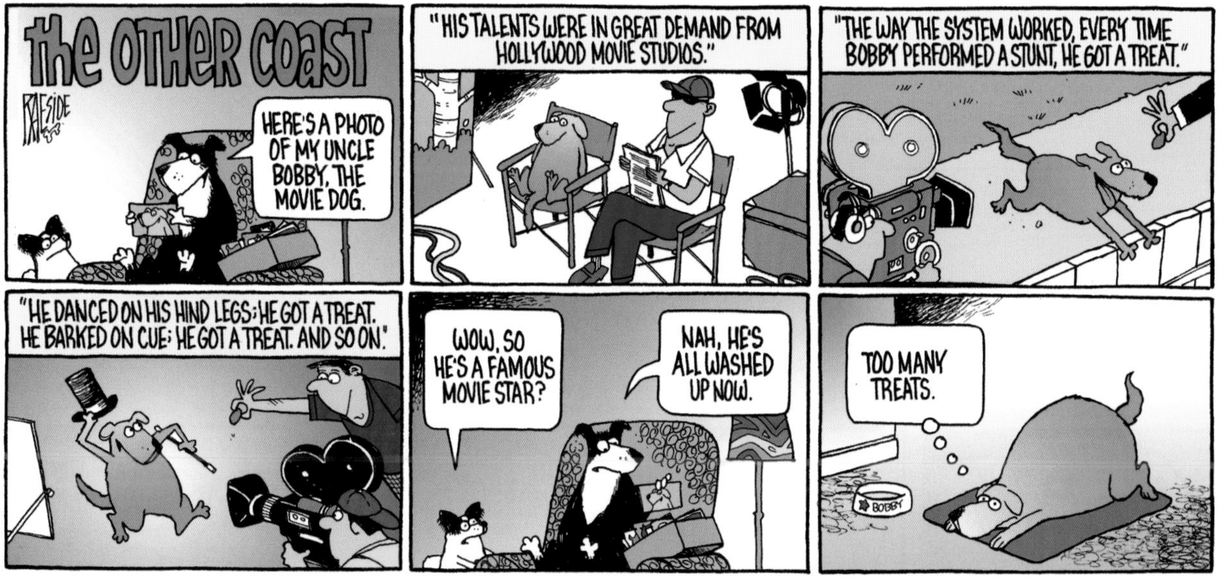
the OTHER COAST
RAESIDE
HERE'S A PHOTO OF MY UNCLE BOBBY, THE MOVIE DOG.
"HIS TALENTS WERE IN GREAT DEMAND FROM HOLLYWOOD MOVIE STUDIOS."
"THE WAY THE SYSTEM WORKED, EVERY TIME BOBBY PERFORMED A STUNT, HE GOT A TREAT."
"HE DANCED ON HIS HIND LEGS; HE GOT A TREAT. HE BARKED ON CUE; HE GOT A TREAT. AND SO ON."
WOW, SO HE'S A FAMOUS MOVIE STAR?
NAH, HE'S ALL WASHED UP NOW.
TOO MANY TREATS.
BOBBY

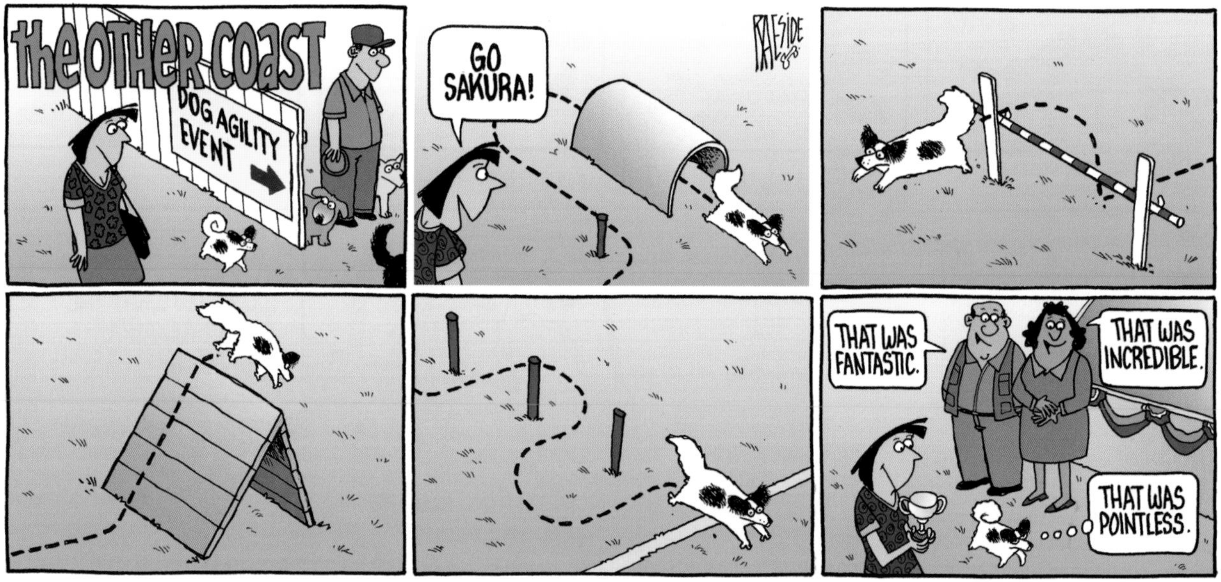
the OTHER COAST
DOG AGILITY EVENT
GO SAKURA!
RAESIDE
THAT WAS FANTASTIC.
THAT WAS INCREDIBLE.
THAT WAS POINTLESS.

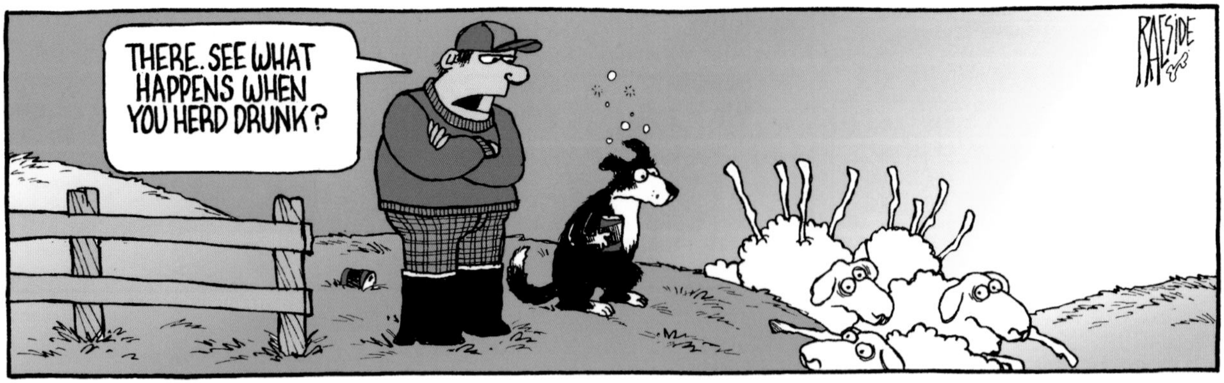
THERE. SEE WHAT HAPPENS WHEN YOU HERD DRUNK?
RAESIDE

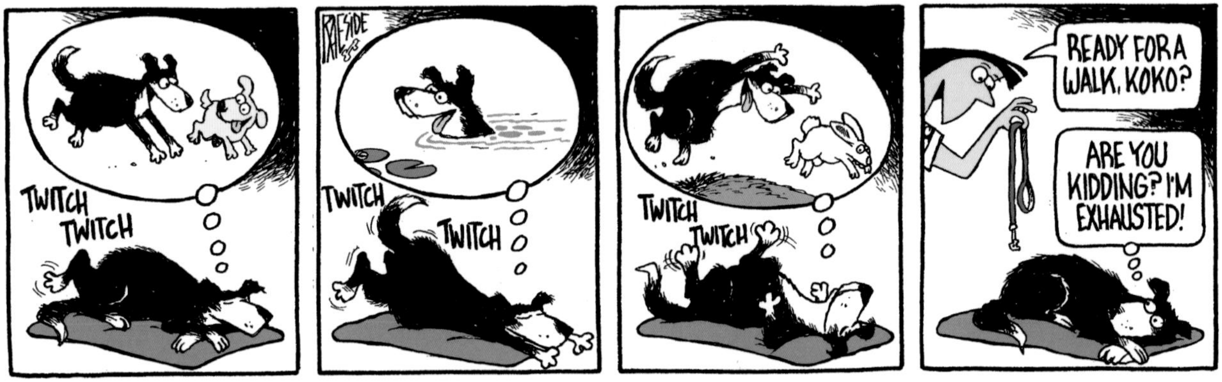
TWITCH
TWITCH
RAESIDE
TWITCH
TWITCH
TWITCH
TWITCH
READY FOR A WALK, KOKO?
ARE YOU KIDDING? I'M EXHAUSTED!

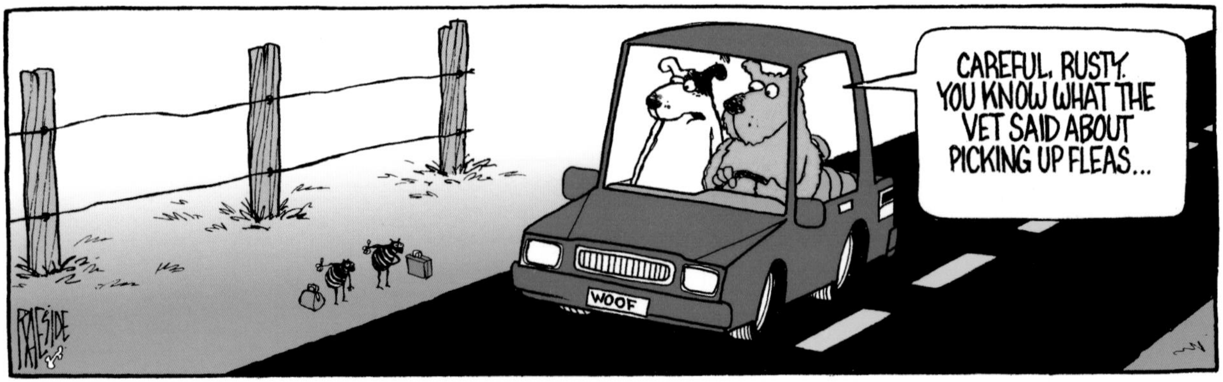
CAREFUL, RUSTY. YOU KNOW WHAT THE VET SAID ABOUT PICKING UP FLEAS...
WOOF
RAESIDE

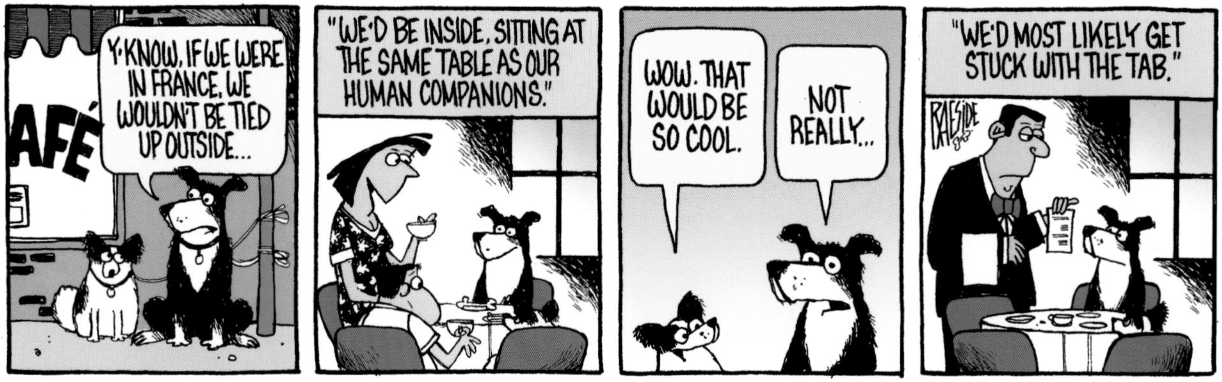
AFÉ
Y'KNOW, IF WE WERE IN FRANCE, WE WOULDN'T BE TIED UP OUTSIDE...
"WE'D BE INSIDE, SITTING AT THE SAME TABLE AS OUR HUMAN COMPANIONS."
WOW. THAT WOULD BE SO COOL.
NOT REALLY...
"WE'D MOST LIKELY GET STUCK WITH THE TAB."
RAESIDE

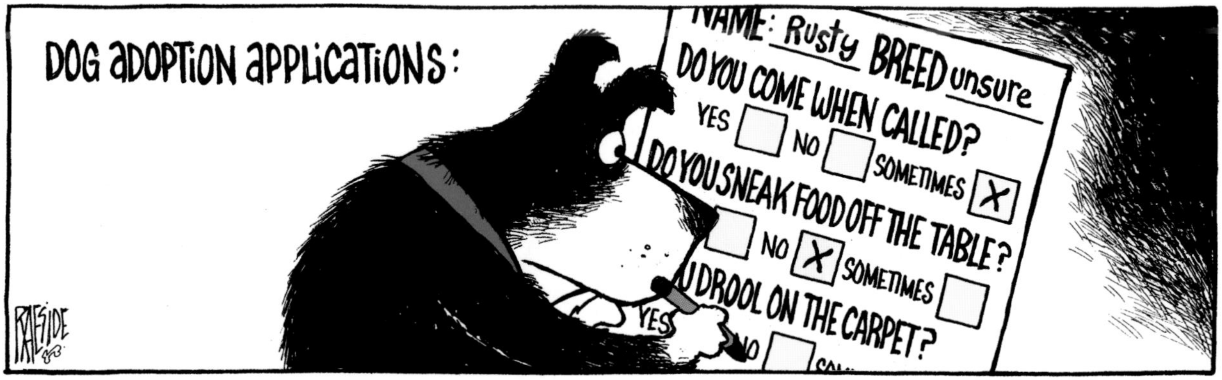
DOG adoption applications:
NAME: Rusty BREED unsure
DO YOU COME WHEN CALLED?
YES NO SOMETIMES X
DO YOU SNEAK FOOD OFF THE TABLE?
NO X SOMETIMES
U DROOL ON THE CARPET?
YES
RAESIDE

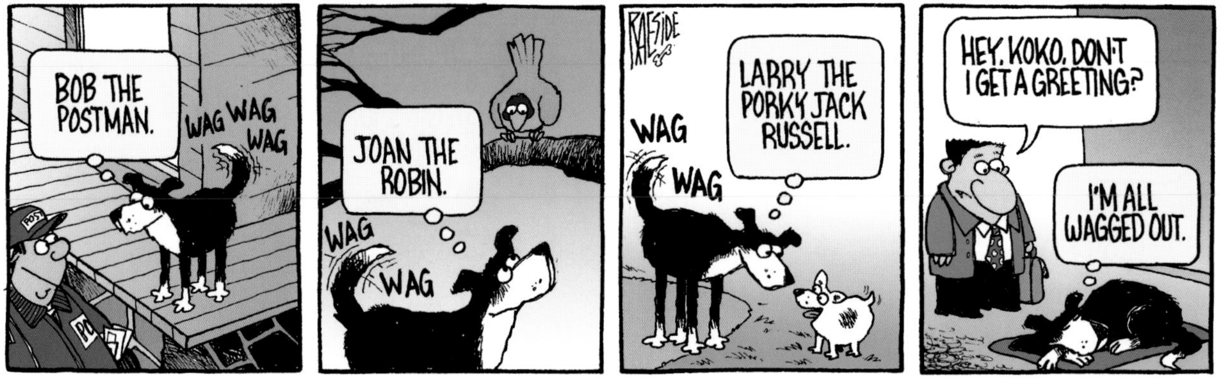
BOB THE POSTMAN.
WAG WAG WAG
JOAN THE ROBIN.
WAG
WAG
RAESIDE
WAG
LARRY THE PORKY JACK RUSSELL.
WAG
HEY, KOKO, DON'T I GET A GREETING?
I'M ALL WAGGED OUT.

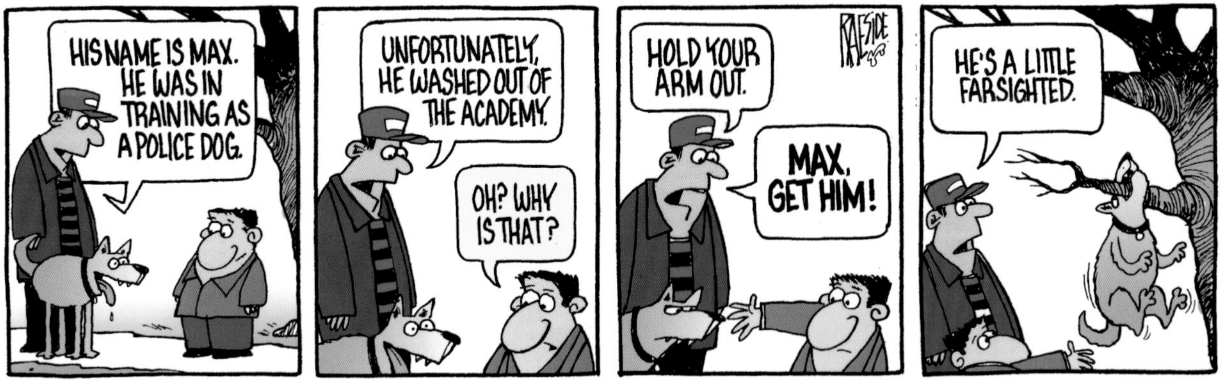
HIS NAME IS MAX. HE WAS IN TRAINING AS A POLICE DOG.
UNFORTUNATELY, HE WASHED OUT OF THE ACADEMY.
OH? WHY IS THAT?
HOLD YOUR ARM OUT.
MAX, GET HIM!
HE'S A LITTLE FARSIGHTED.

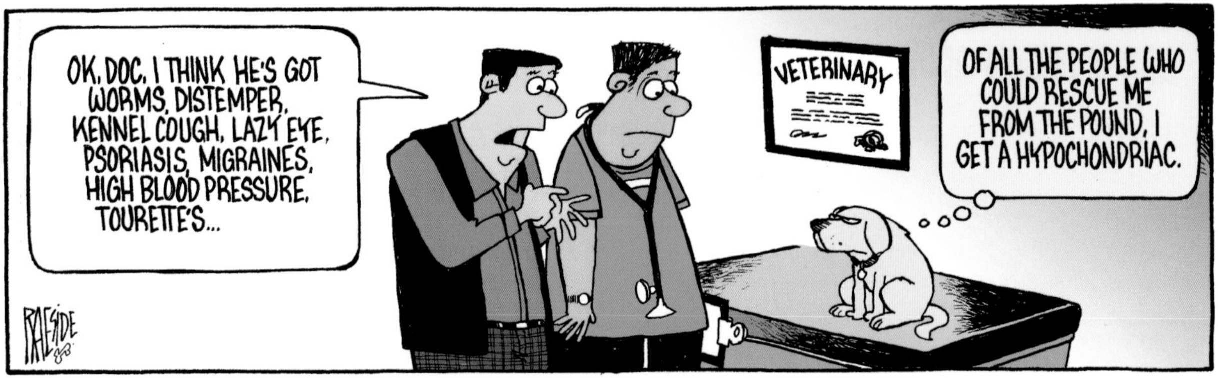
OK, DOC, I THINK HE'S GOT WORMS, DISTEMPER, KENNEL COUGH, LAZY EYE, PSORIASIS, MIGRAINES, HIGH BLOOD PRESSURE, TOURETTE'S...
VETERINARY
OF ALL THE PEOPLE WHO COULD RESCUE ME FROM THE POUND, I GET A HYPOCHONDRIAC.

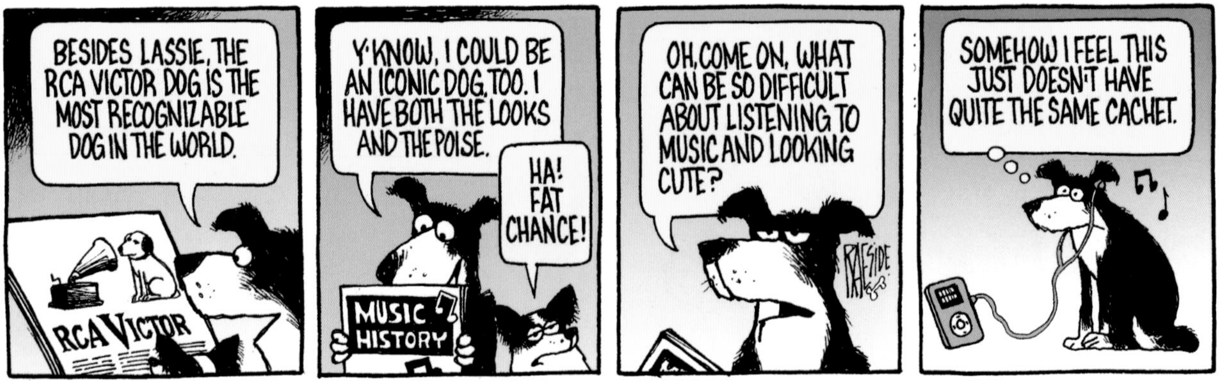
BESIDES LASSIE, THE RCA VICTOR DOG IS THE MOST RECOGNIZABLE DOG IN THE WORLD.
RCA VICTOR
Y'KNOW, I COULD BE AN ICONIC DOG, TOO. I HAVE BOTH THE LOOKS AND THE POISE.
HA! FAT CHANCE!
MUSIC HISTORY
OH, COME ON, WHAT CAN BE SO DIFFICULT ABOUT LISTENING TO MUSIC AND LOOKING CUTE?
SOMEHOW I FEEL THIS JUST DOESN'T HAVE QUITE THE SAME CACHET.

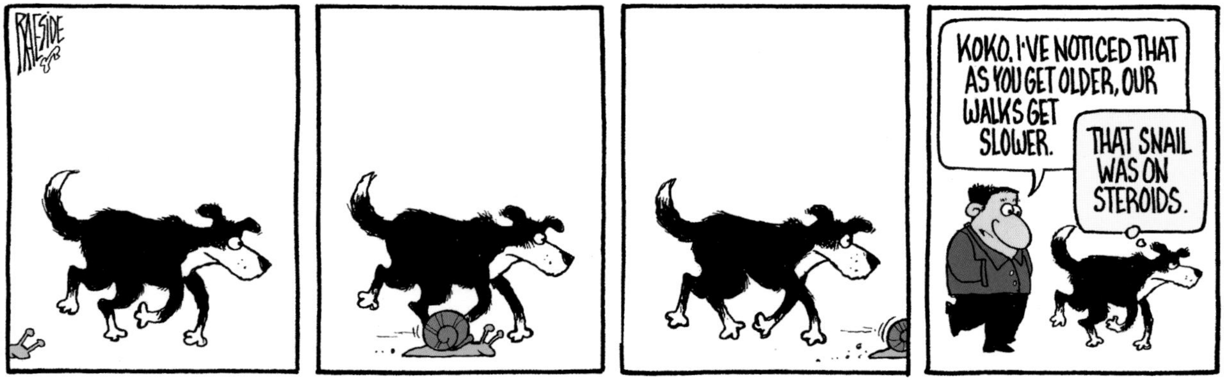
RAESIDE
KOKO, I'VE NOTICED THAT AS YOU GET OLDER, OUR WALKS GET SLOWER.
THAT SNAIL WAS ON STEROIDS.

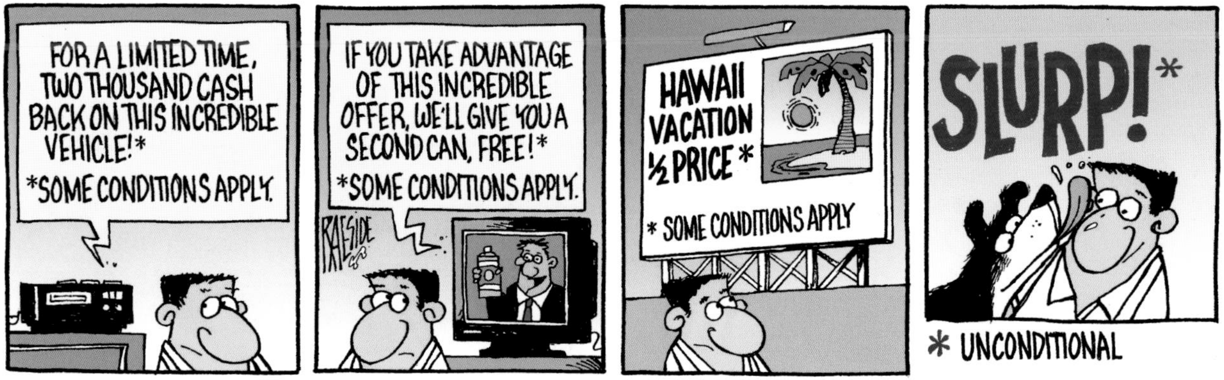
FOR A LIMITED TIME, TWO THOUSAND CASH BACK ON THIS INCREDIBLE VEHICLE!*
*SOME CONDITIONS APPLY.
IF YOU TAKE ADVANTAGE OF THIS INCREDIBLE OFFER, WE'LL GIVE YOU A SECOND CAN, FREE!*
*SOME CONDITIONS APPLY.
RAESIDE
HAWAII VACATION ½ PRICE *
* SOME CONDITIONS APPLY
SLURP!*
* UNCONDITIONAL

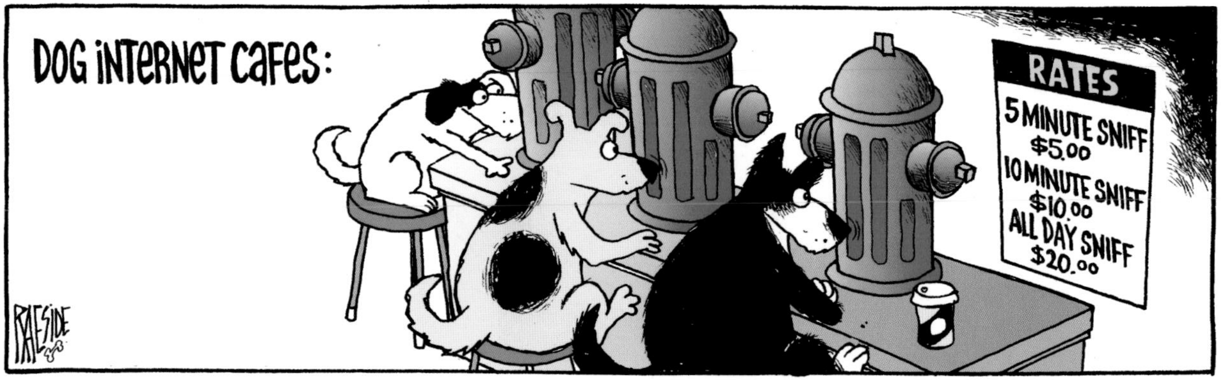
DOG INTERNET CAFES:
RATES
5 MINUTE SNIFF $5.00
10 MINUTE SNIFF $10.00
ALL DAY SNIFF $20.00
RAESIDE

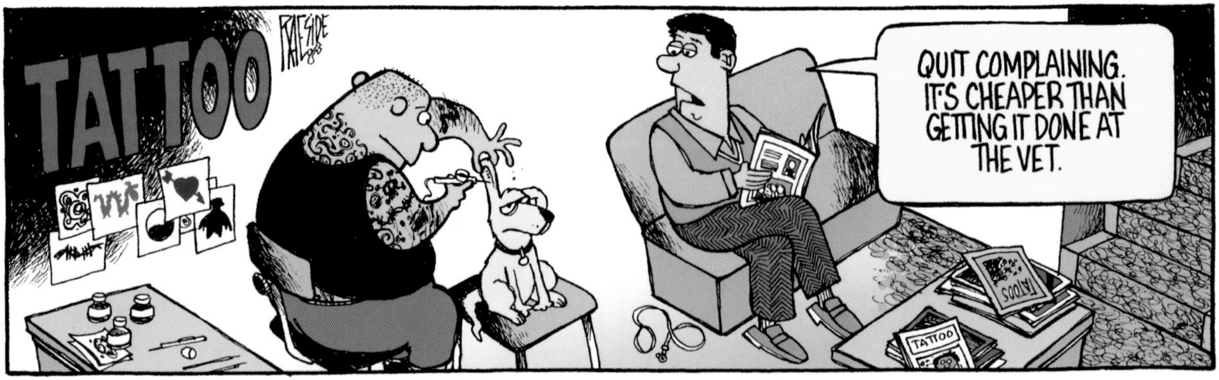
TATTOO
QUIT COMPLAINING. IT'S CHEAPER THAN GETTING IT DONE AT THE VET.
TATTOO

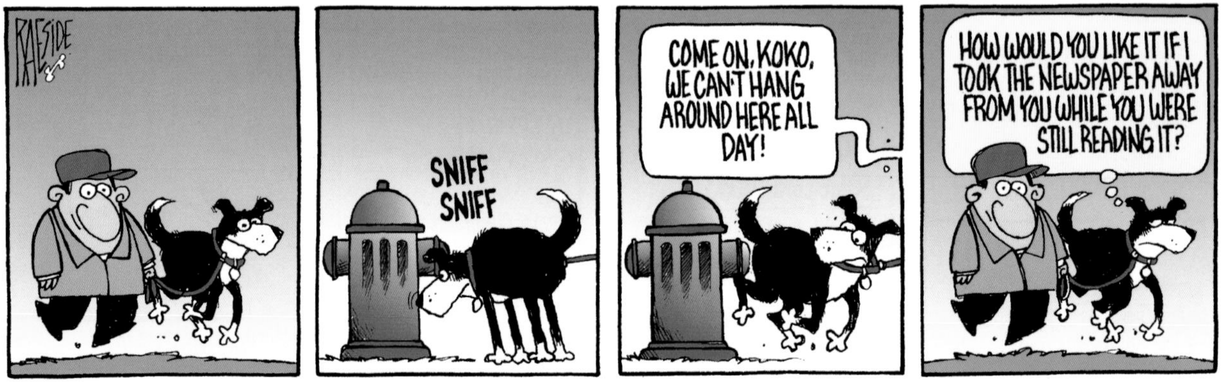
SNIFF SNIFF
COME ON, KOKO, WE CAN'T HANG AROUND HERE ALL DAY!
HOW WOULD YOU LIKE IT IF I TOOK THE NEWSPAPER AWAY FROM YOU WHILE YOU WERE STILL READING IT?

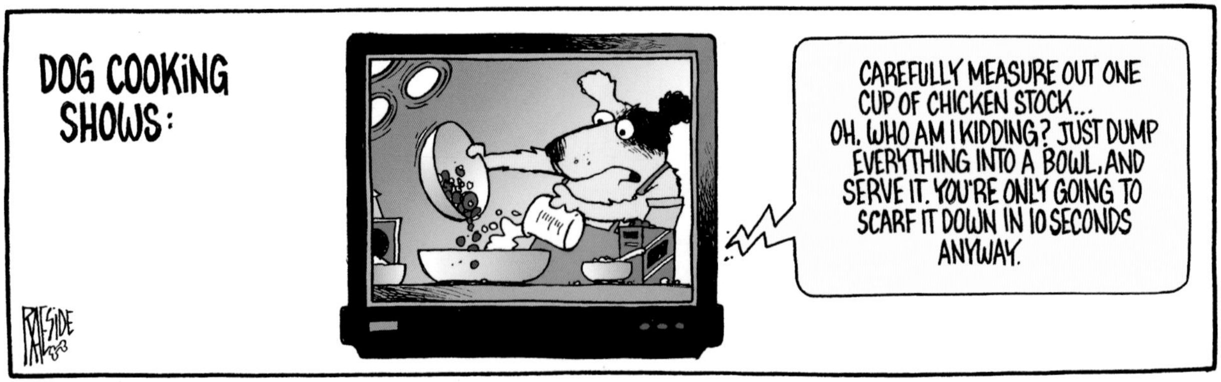
DOG COOKING SHOWS:
CAREFULLY MEASURE OUT ONE CUP OF CHICKEN STOCK... OH, WHO AM I KIDDING? JUST DUMP EVERYTHING INTO A BOWL, AND SERVE IT. YOU'RE ONLY GOING TO SCARF IT DOWN IN 10 SECONDS ANYWAY.

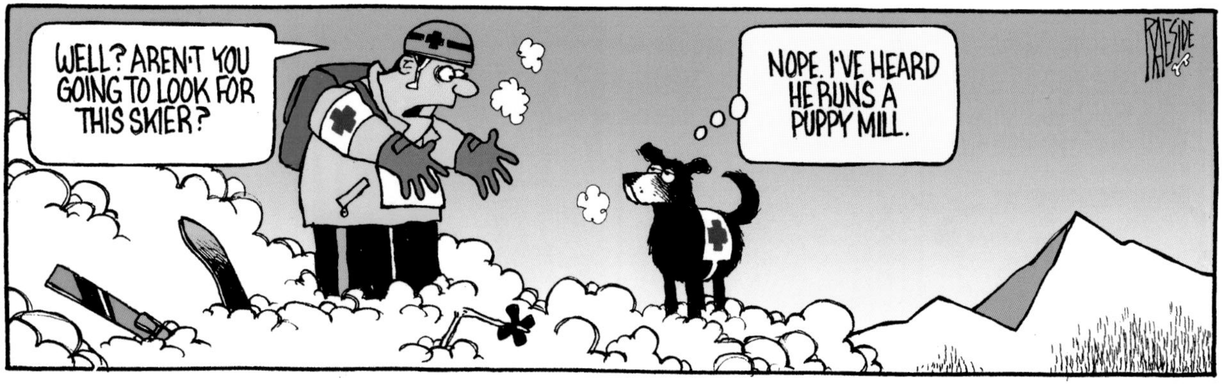
WELL? AREN'T YOU GOING TO LOOK FOR THIS SKIER?
NOPE. I'VE HEARD HE RUNS A PUPPY MILL.
RAESIDE

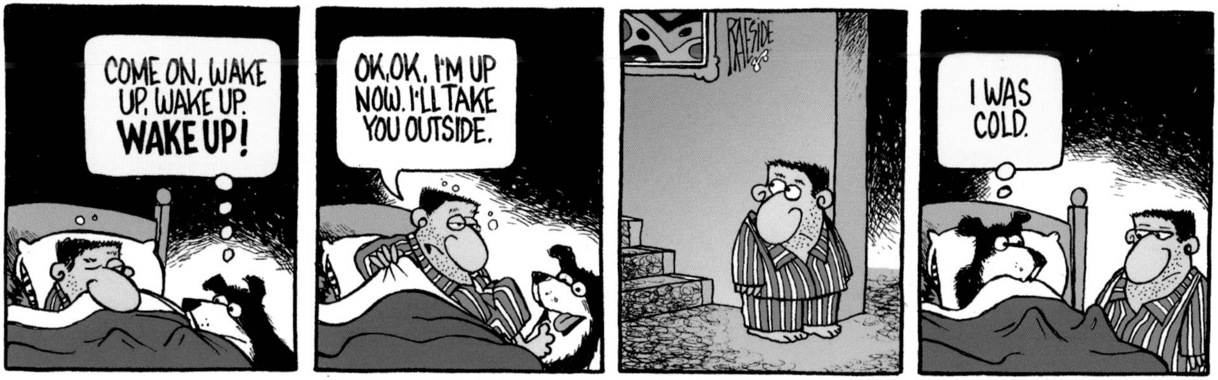
COME ON, WAKE UP, WAKE UP. WAKE UP!
OK, OK, I'M UP NOW. I'LL TAKE YOU OUTSIDE.
RAESIDE
I WAS COLD.

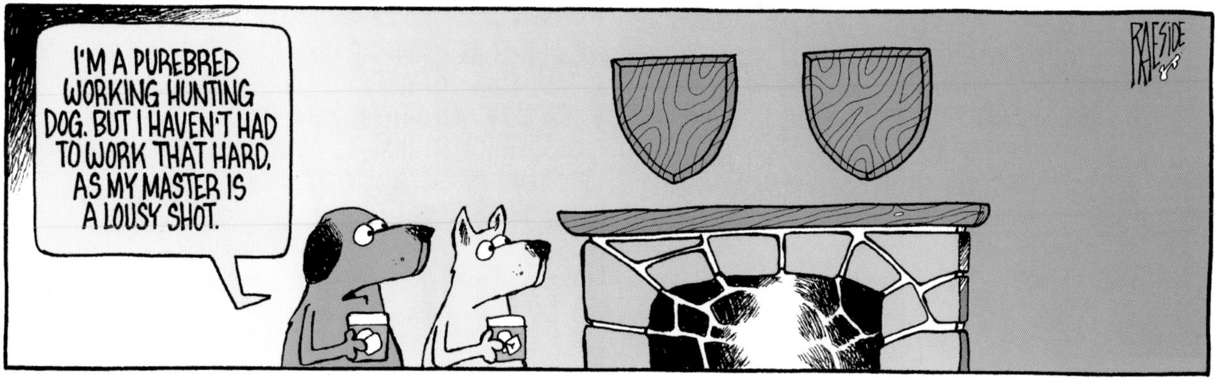
I'M A PUREBRED WORKING HUNTING DOG. BUT I HAVEN'T HAD TO WORK THAT HARD, AS MY MASTER IS A LOUSY SHOT.
RAESIDE

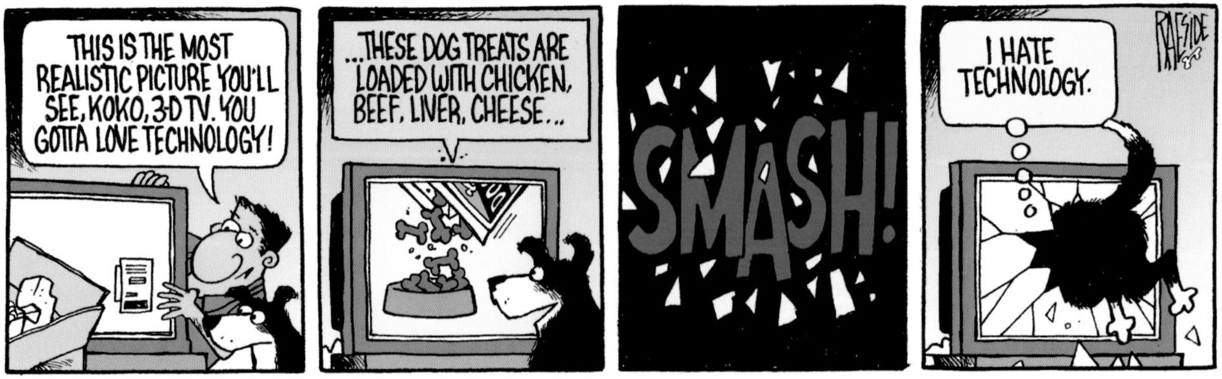
THIS IS THE MOST REALISTIC PICTURE YOU'LL SEE, KOKO, 3-D TV. YOU GOTTA LOVE TECHNOLOGY!
...THESE DOG TREATS ARE LOADED WITH CHICKEN, BEEF, LIVER, CHEESE...
SMASH!
I HATE TECHNOLOGY.
RAESIDE

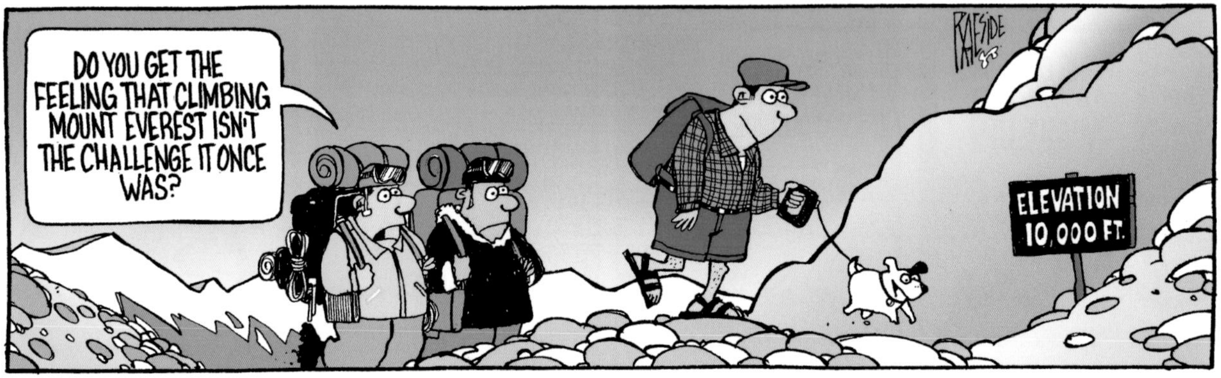
DO YOU GET THE FEELING THAT CLIMBING MOUNT EVEREST ISN'T THE CHALLENGE IT ONCE WAS?
ELEVATION 10,000 FT.
RAESIDE

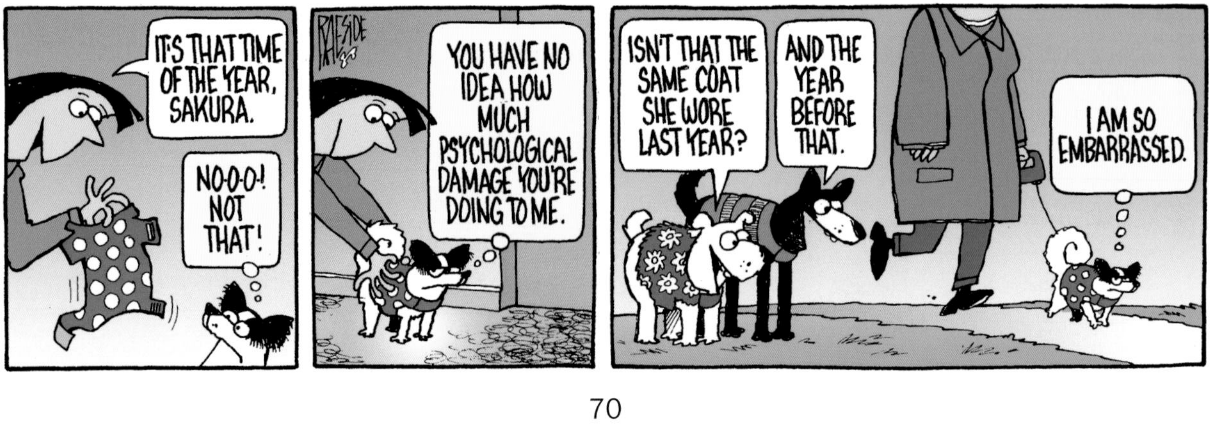
IT'S THAT TIME OF THE YEAR, SAKURA.
NO-O-O! NOT THAT!
RAESIDE
YOU HAVE NO IDEA HOW MUCH PSYCHOLOGICAL DAMAGE YOU'RE DOING TO ME.
ISN'T THAT THE SAME COAT SHE WORE LAST YEAR?
AND THE YEAR BEFORE THAT.
I AM SO EMBARRASSED.

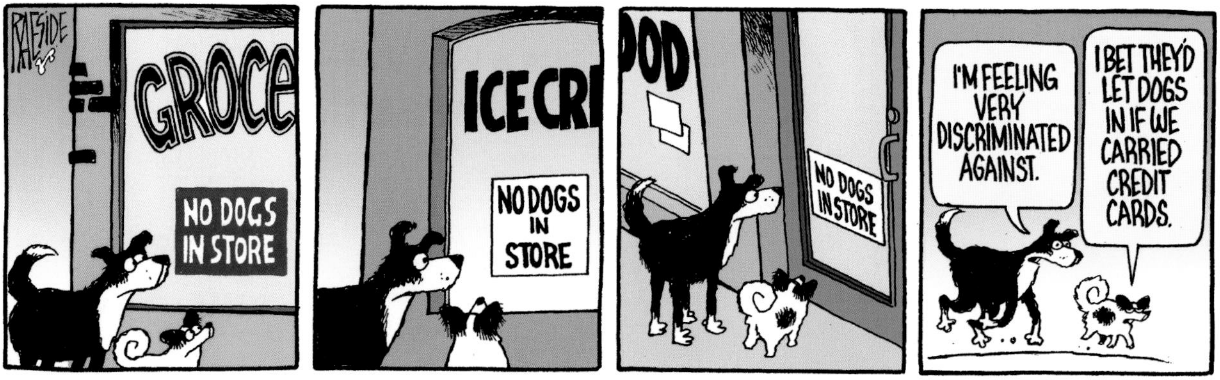
RAESIDE
GROCE
NO DOGS IN STORE
ICE CR
NO DOGS IN STORE
OOD
NO DOGS IN STORE
I'M FEELING VERY DISCRIMINATED AGAINST.
I BET THEY'D LET DOGS IN IF WE CARRIED CREDIT CARDS.

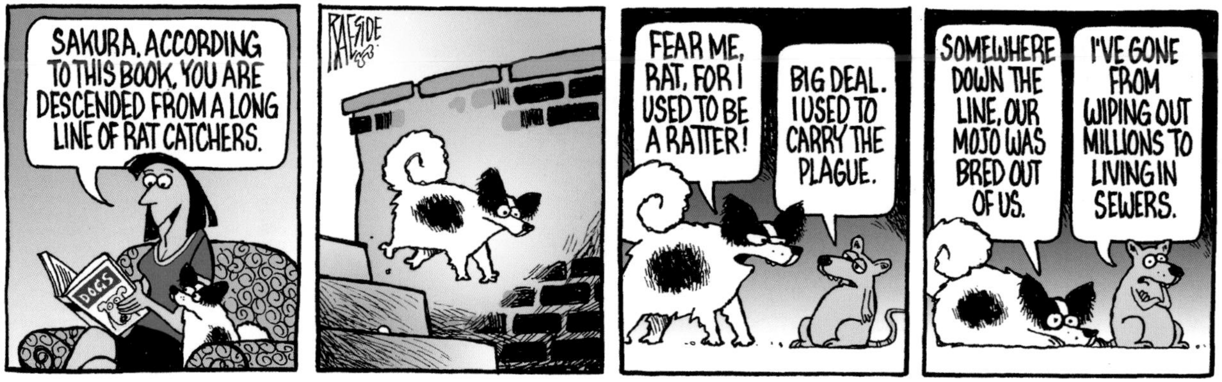
SAKURA, ACCORDING TO THIS BOOK, YOU ARE DESCENDED FROM A LONG LINE OF RAT CATCHERS.
DOGS
RAESIDE
FEAR ME, RAT, FOR I USED TO BE A RATTER!
BIG DEAL. I USED TO CARRY THE PLAGUE.
SOMEWHERE DOWN THE LINE, OUR MOJO WAS BRED OUT OF US.
I'VE GONE FROM WIPING OUT MILLIONS TO LIVING IN SEWERS.

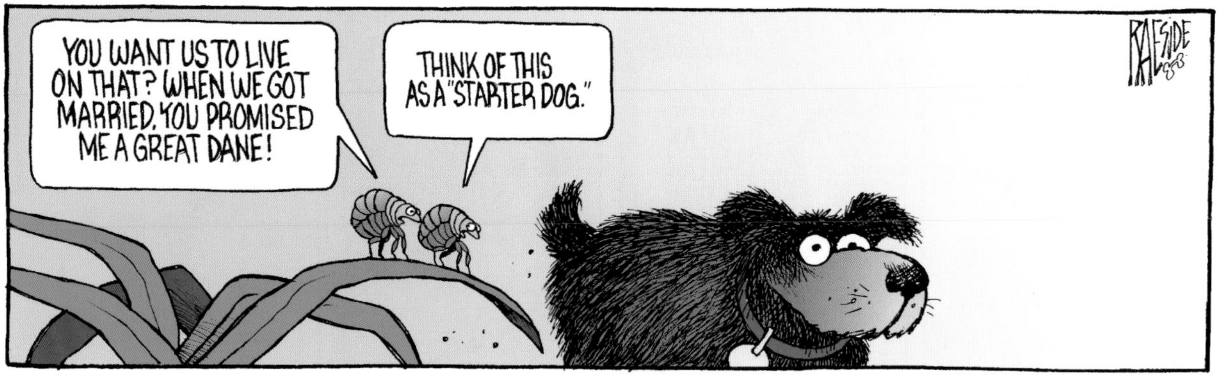
YOU WANT US TO LIVE ON THAT? WHEN WE GOT MARRIED, YOU PROMISED ME A GREAT DANE!
THINK OF THIS AS A "STARTER DOG."
RAESIDE

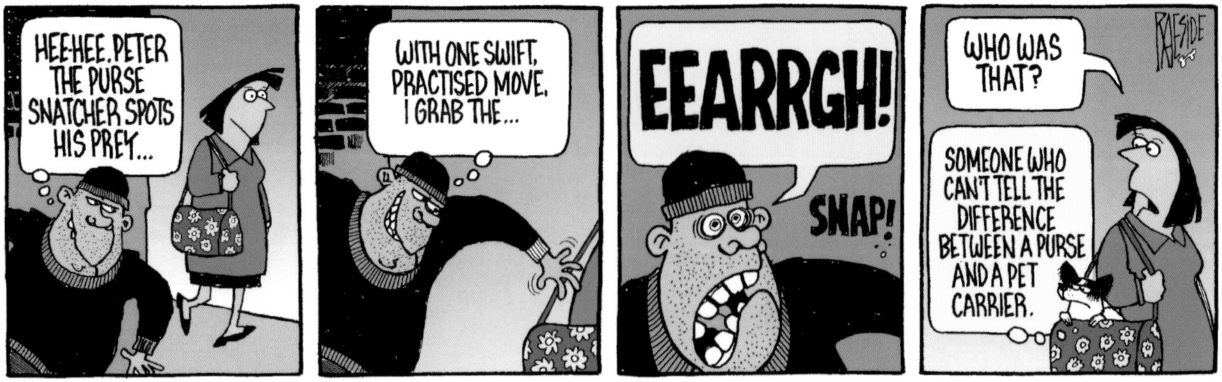
HEE-HEE. PETER THE PURSE SNATCHER SPOTS HIS PREY...
WITH ONE SWIFT, PRACTISED MOVE, I GRAB THE...
EEARRGH!
SNAP!
RAESIDE
WHO WAS THAT?
SOMEONE WHO CAN'T TELL THE DIFFERENCE BETWEEN A PURSE AND A PET CARRIER.

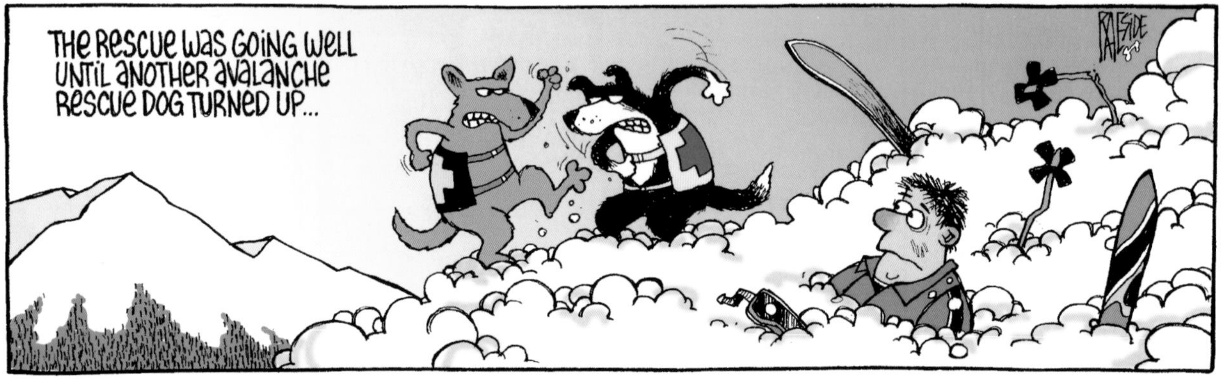
THE RESCUE WAS GOING WELL UNTIL ANOTHER AVALANCHE RESCUE DOG TURNED UP...
RAESIDE

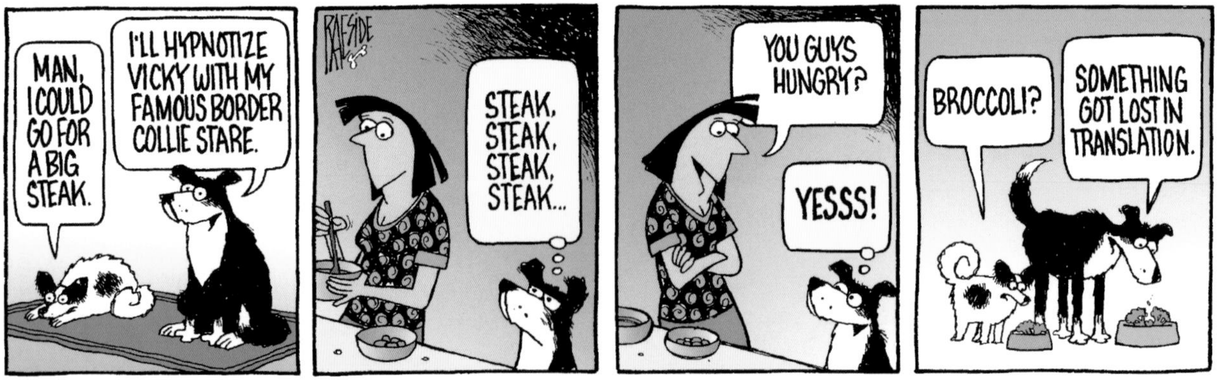
MAN, I COULD GO FOR A BIG STEAK.
I'LL HYPNOTIZE VICKY WITH MY FAMOUS BORDER COLLIE STARE.
RAESIDE
STEAK, STEAK, STEAK, STEAK...
YOU GUYS HUNGRY?
YESSS!
BROCCOLI?
SOMETHING GOT LOST IN TRANSLATION.

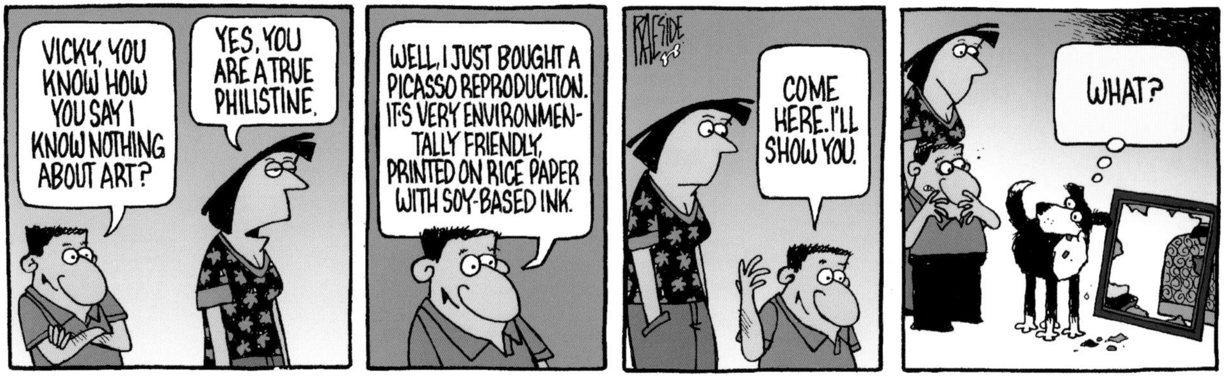
VICKY, YOU KNOW HOW YOU SAY I KNOW NOTHING ABOUT ART?
YES, YOU ARE A TRUE PHILISTINE.
WELL, I JUST BOUGHT A PICASSO REPRODUCTION. IT'S VERY ENVIRONMENTALLY FRIENDLY, PRINTED ON RICE PAPER WITH SOY-BASED INK.
COME HERE. I'LL SHOW YOU.
WHAT?

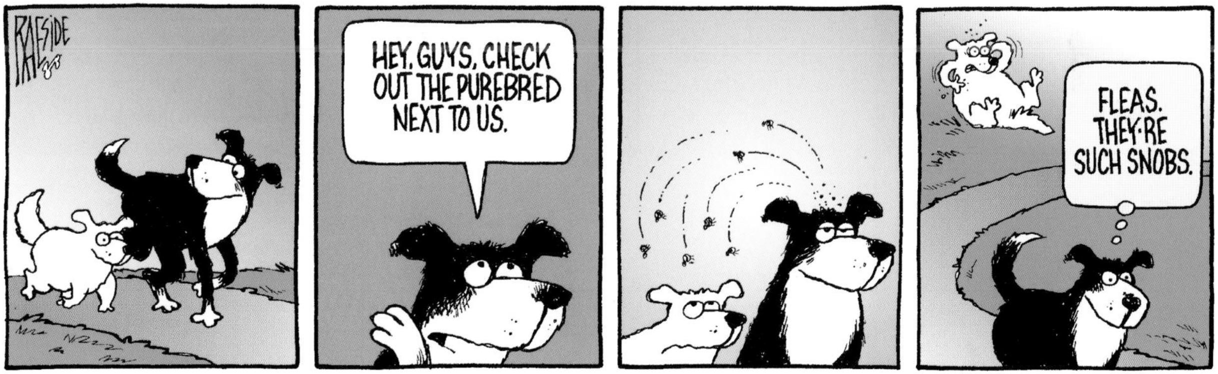
HEY, GUYS, CHECK OUT THE PUREBRED NEXT TO US.
FLEAS. THEY'RE SUCH SNOBS.

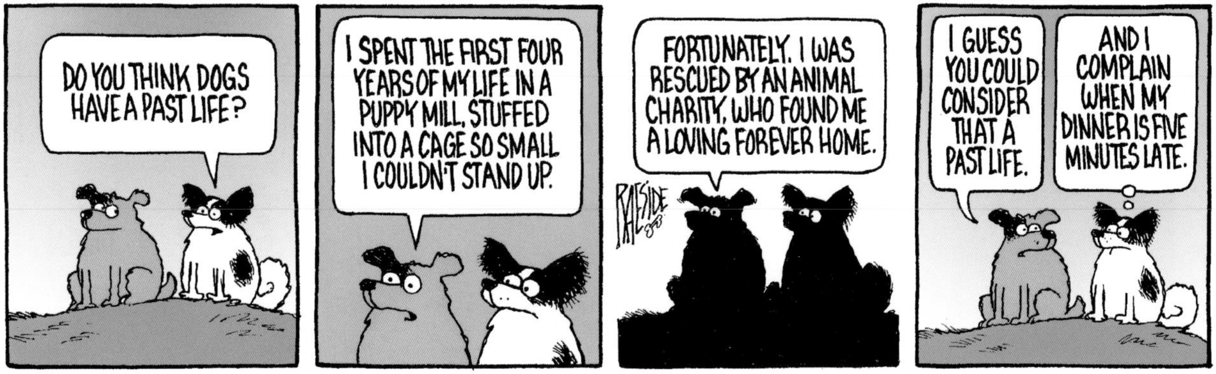
DO YOU THINK DOGS HAVE A PAST LIFE?
I SPENT THE FIRST FOUR YEARS OF MY LIFE IN A PUPPY MILL, STUFFED INTO A CAGE SO SMALL I COULDN'T STAND UP.
FORTUNATELY, I WAS RESCUED BY AN ANIMAL CHARITY, WHO FOUND ME A LOVING FOREVER HOME.
I GUESS YOU COULD CONSIDER THAT A PAST LIFE.
AND I COMPLAIN WHEN MY DINNER IS FIVE MINUTES LATE.

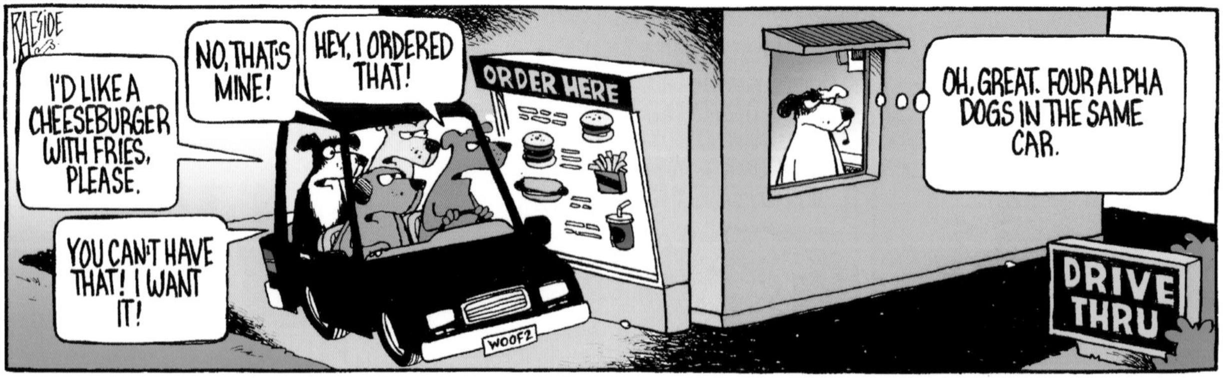
I'D LIKE A CHEESEBURGER WITH FRIES, PLEASE.
YOU CAN'T HAVE THAT! I WANT IT!
NO, THAT'S MINE!
HEY, I ORDERED THAT!
ORDER HERE
WOOF2
OH, GREAT. FOUR ALPHA DOGS IN THE SAME CAR.
DRIVE THRU

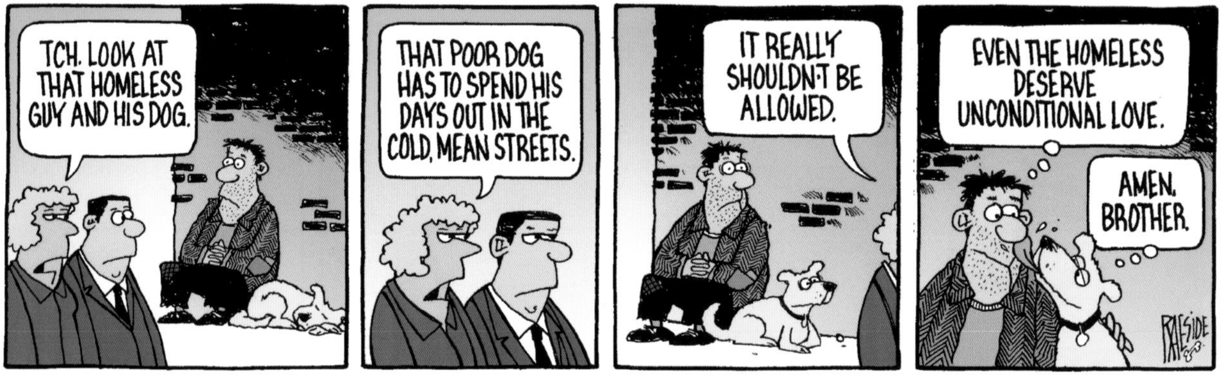
TCH. LOOK AT THAT HOMELESS GUY AND HIS DOG.
THAT POOR DOG HAS TO SPEND HIS DAYS OUT IN THE COLD, MEAN STREETS.
IT REALLY SHOULDN'T BE ALLOWED.
EVEN THE HOMELESS DESERVE UNCONDITIONAL LOVE.
AMEN, BROTHER.

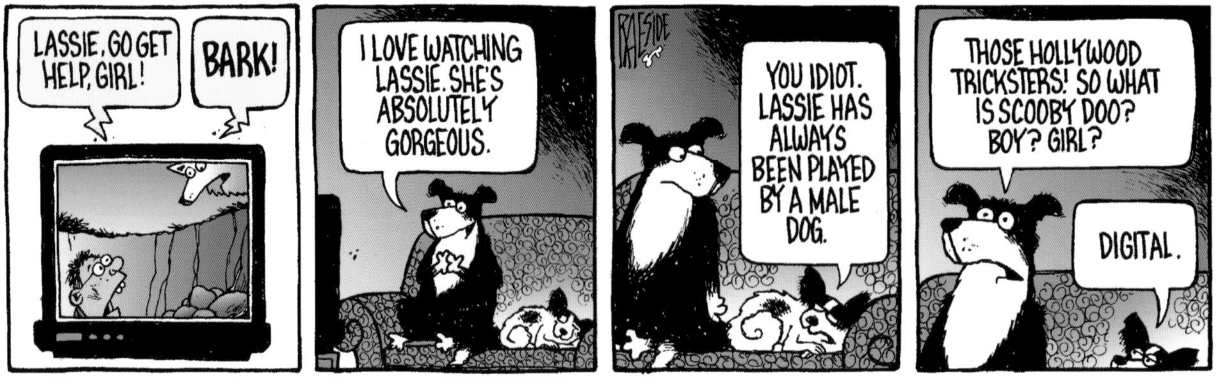
LASSIE, GO GET HELP, GIRL!
BARK!
I LOVE WATCHING LASSIE. SHE'S ABSOLUTELY GORGEOUS.
YOU IDIOT. LASSIE HAS ALWAYS BEEN PLAYED BY A MALE DOG.
THOSE HOLLYWOOD TRICKSTERS! SO WHAT IS SCOOBY DOO? BOY? GIRL?
DIGITAL.

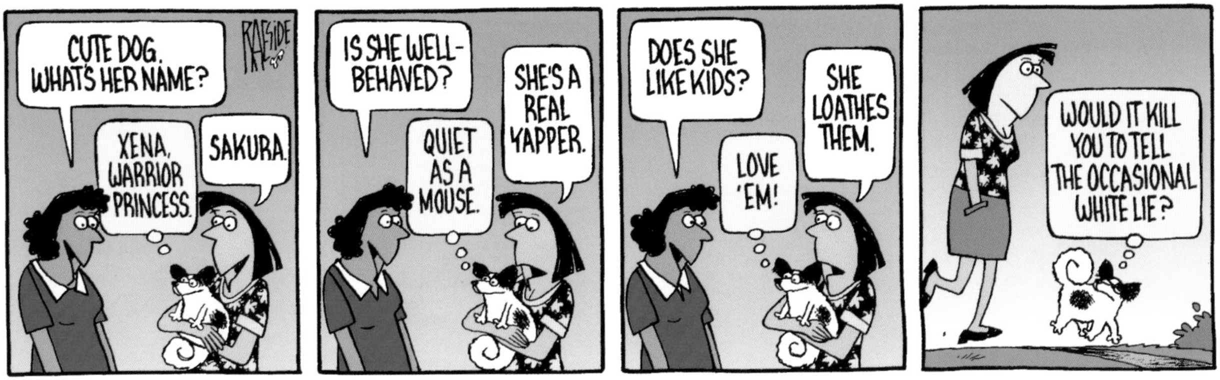
RAESIDE
CUTE DOG. WHAT'S HER NAME?
XENA, WARRIOR PRINCESS.
SAKURA.
IS SHE WELL-BEHAVED?
QUIET AS A MOUSE.
SHE'S A REAL YAPPER.
DOES SHE LIKE KIDS?
LOVE 'EM!
SHE LOATHES THEM.
WOULD IT KILL YOU TO TELL THE OCCASIONAL WHITE LIE?

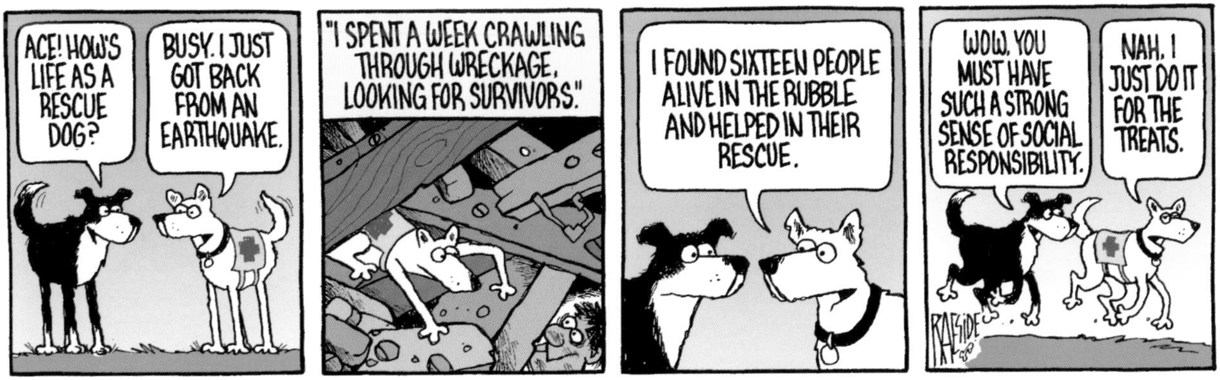
ACE! HOW'S LIFE AS A RESCUE DOG?
BUSY. I JUST GOT BACK FROM AN EARTHQUAKE.
"I SPENT A WEEK CRAWLING THROUGH WRECKAGE, LOOKING FOR SURVIVORS."
I FOUND SIXTEEN PEOPLE ALIVE IN THE RUBBLE AND HELPED IN THEIR RESCUE.
WOW, YOU MUST HAVE SUCH A STRONG SENSE OF SOCIAL RESPONSIBILITY.
NAH, I JUST DO IT FOR THE TREATS.
RAESIDE

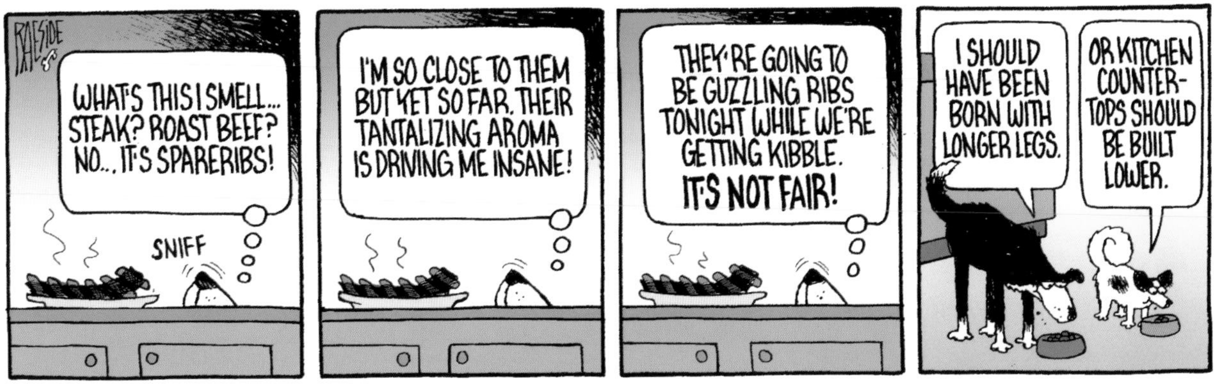
RAESIDE
WHAT'S THIS I SMELL... STEAK? ROAST BEEF? NO... IT'S SPARERIBS!
SNIFF
I'M SO CLOSE TO THEM BUT YET SO FAR. THEIR TANTALIZING AROMA IS DRIVING ME INSANE!
THEY'RE GOING TO BE GUZZLING RIBS TONIGHT WHILE WE'RE GETTING KIBBLE.
IT'S NOT FAIR!
I SHOULD HAVE BEEN BORN WITH LONGER LEGS.
OR KITCHEN COUNTER-TOPS SHOULD BE BUILT LOWER.

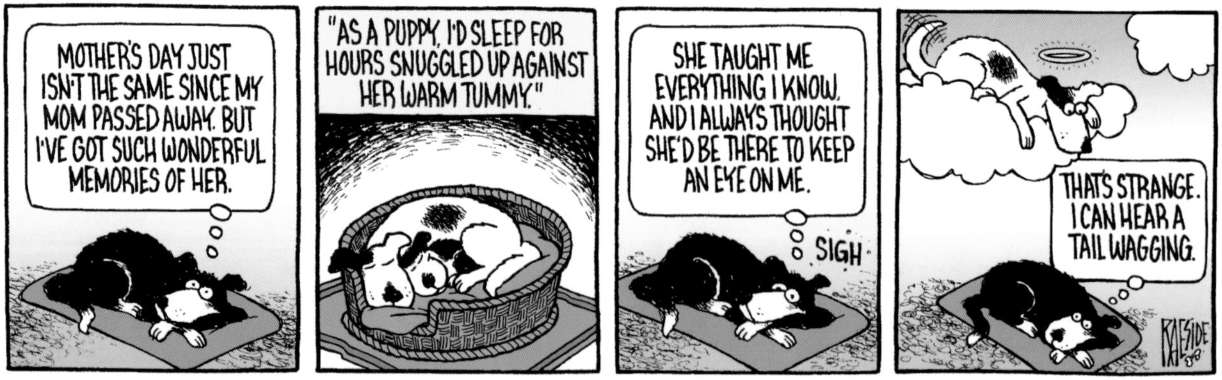
MOTHER'S DAY JUST ISN'T THE SAME SINCE MY MOM PASSED AWAY. BUT I'VE GOT SUCH WONDERFUL MEMORIES OF HER.
"AS A PUPPY, I'D SLEEP FOR HOURS SNUGGLED UP AGAINST HER WARM TUMMY."
SHE TAUGHT ME EVERYTHING I KNOW, AND I ALWAYS THOUGHT SHE'D BE THERE TO KEEP AN EYE ON ME.
SIGH
THAT'S STRANGE. I CAN HEAR A TAIL WAGGING.

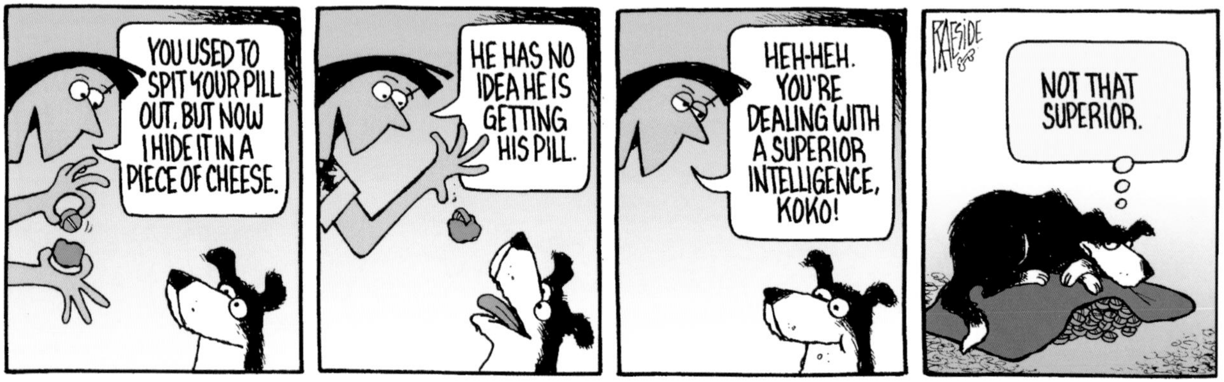
YOU USED TO SPIT YOUR PILL OUT, BUT NOW I HIDE IT IN A PIECE OF CHEESE.
HE HAS NO IDEA HE IS GETTING HIS PILL.
HEH-HEH. YOU'RE DEALING WITH A SUPERIOR INTELLIGENCE, KOKO!
NOT THAT SUPERIOR.

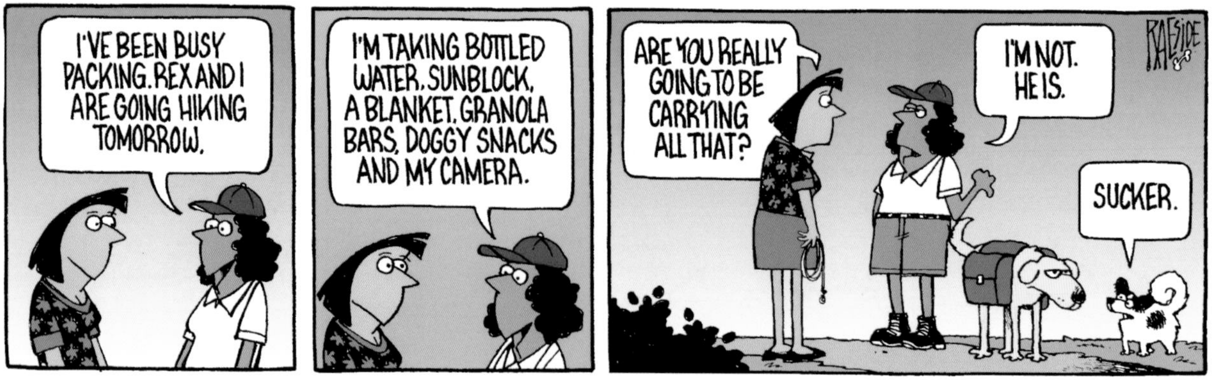
I'VE BEEN BUSY PACKING. REX AND I ARE GOING HIKING TOMORROW.
I'M TAKING BOTTLED WATER, SUNBLOCK, A BLANKET, GRANOLA BARS, DOGGY SNACKS AND MY CAMERA.
ARE YOU REALLY GOING TO BE CARRYING ALL THAT?
I'M NOT. HE IS.
SUCKER.

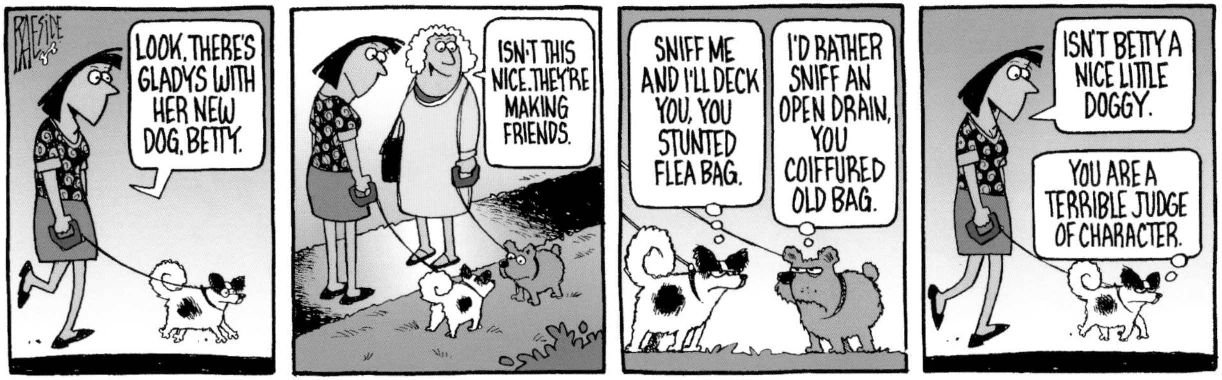
LOOK, THERE'S GLADYS WITH HER NEW DOG, BETTY.
ISN'T THIS NICE. THEY'RE MAKING FRIENDS.
SNIFF ME AND I'LL DECK YOU, YOU STUNTED FLEA BAG.
I'D RATHER SNIFF AN OPEN DRAIN, YOU COIFFURED OLD BAG.
ISN'T BETTY A NICE LITTLE DOGGY.
YOU ARE A TERRIBLE JUDGE OF CHARACTER.

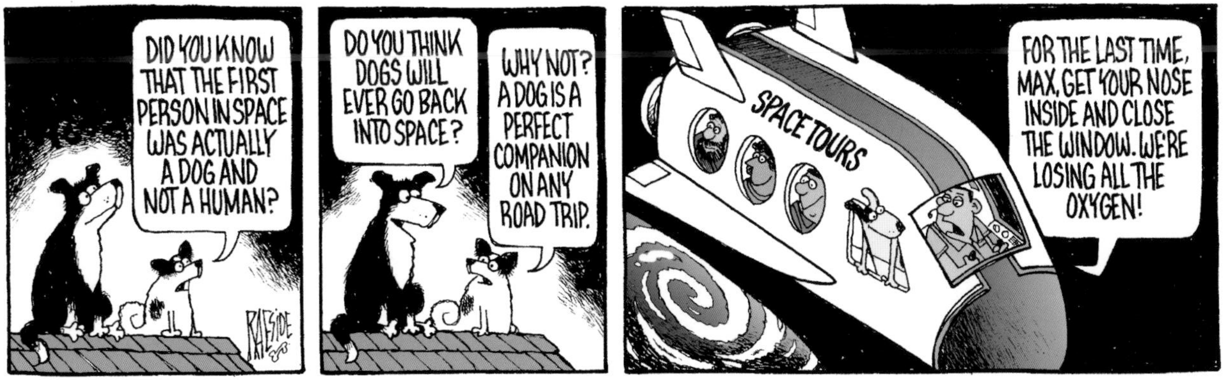
DID YOU KNOW THAT THE FIRST PERSON IN SPACE WAS ACTUALLY A DOG AND NOT A HUMAN?
DO YOU THINK DOGS WILL EVER GO BACK INTO SPACE?
WHY NOT? A DOG IS A PERFECT COMPANION ON ANY ROAD TRIP.
SPACE TOURS
FOR THE LAST TIME, MAX, GET YOUR NOSE INSIDE AND CLOSE THE WINDOW. WE'RE LOSING ALL THE OXYGEN!

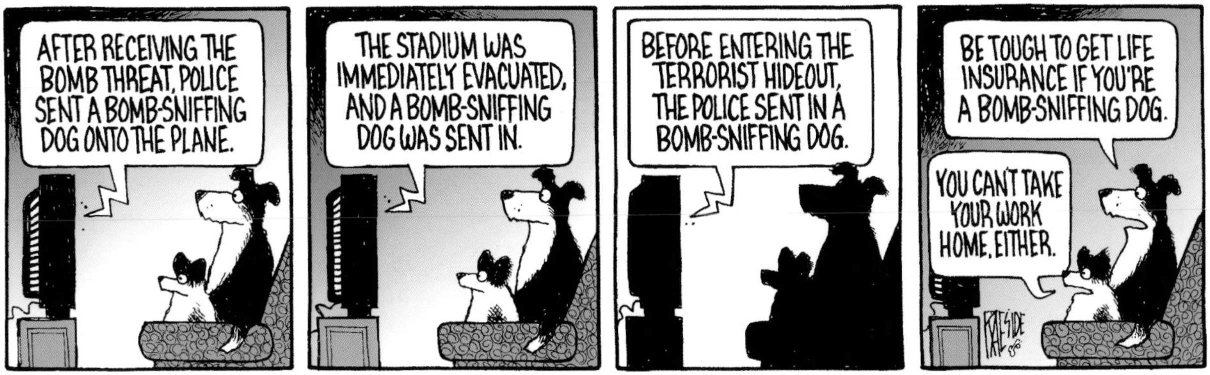
AFTER RECEIVING THE BOMB THREAT, POLICE SENT A BOMB-SNIFFING DOG ONTO THE PLANE.
THE STADIUM WAS IMMEDIATELY EVACUATED, AND A BOMB-SNIFFING DOG WAS SENT IN.
BEFORE ENTERING THE TERRORIST HIDEOUT, THE POLICE SENT IN A BOMB-SNIFFING DOG.
BE TOUGH TO GET LIFE INSURANCE IF YOU'RE A BOMB-SNIFFING DOG.
YOU CAN'T TAKE YOUR WORK HOME, EITHER.

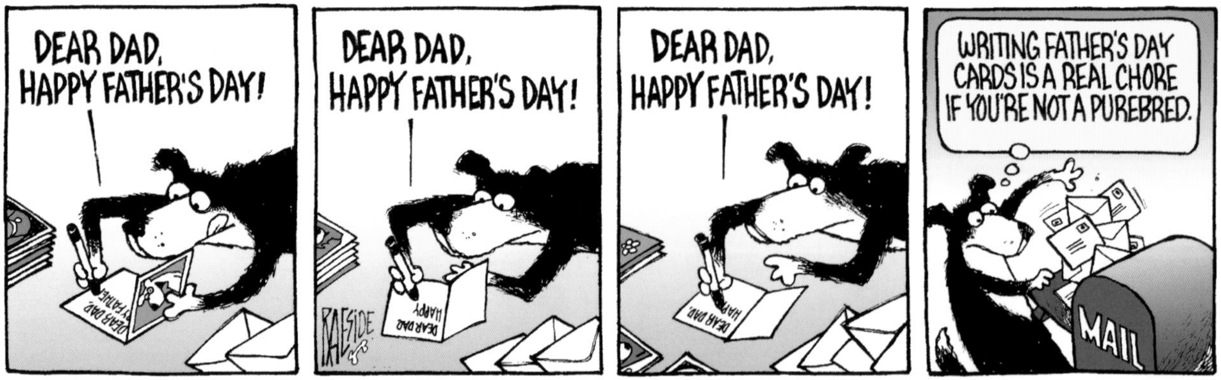
DEAR DAD,
HAPPY FATHER'S DAY!
DEAR DAD,
HAPPY FATHER'S DAY!
DEAR DAD,
HAPPY FATHER'S DAY!
WRITING FATHER'S DAY CARDS IS A REAL CHORE IF YOU'RE NOT A PUREBRED.
MAIL

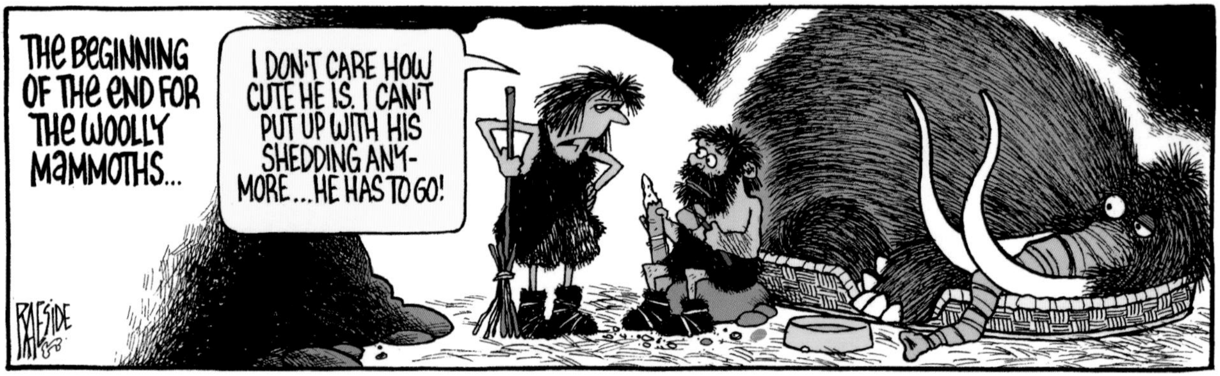
THE BEGINNING OF THE END FOR THE WOOLLY MAMMOTHS...
I DON'T CARE HOW CUTE HE IS. I CAN'T PUT UP WITH HIS SHEDDING ANY-MORE... HE HAS TO GO!

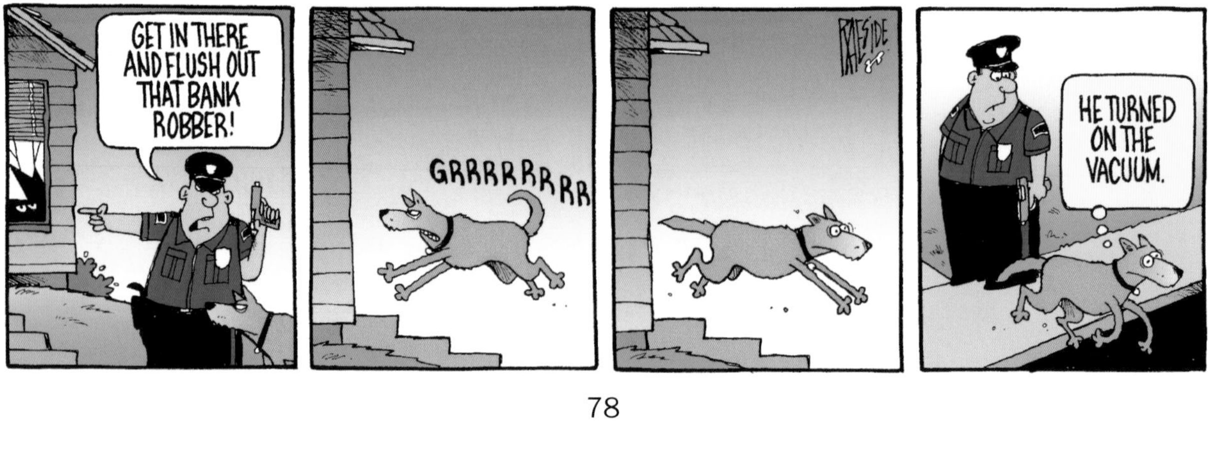
GET IN THERE AND FLUSH OUT THAT BANK ROBBER!
GRRRRRRRRR
HE TURNED ON THE VACUUM.

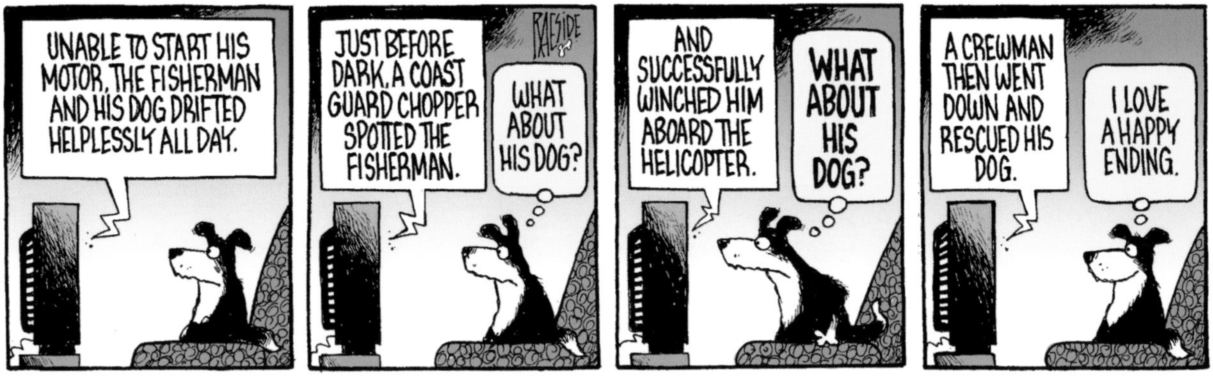

UNABLE TO START HIS MOTOR, THE FISHERMAN AND HIS DOG DRIFTED HELPLESSLY ALL DAY.
JUST BEFORE DARK, A COAST GUARD CHOPPER SPOTTED THE FISHERMAN.
WHAT ABOUT HIS DOG?
AND SUCCESSFULLY WINCHED HIM ABOARD THE HELICOPTER.
WHAT ABOUT HIS DOG?
A CREWMAN THEN WENT DOWN AND RESCUED HIS DOG.
I LOVE A HAPPY ENDING.

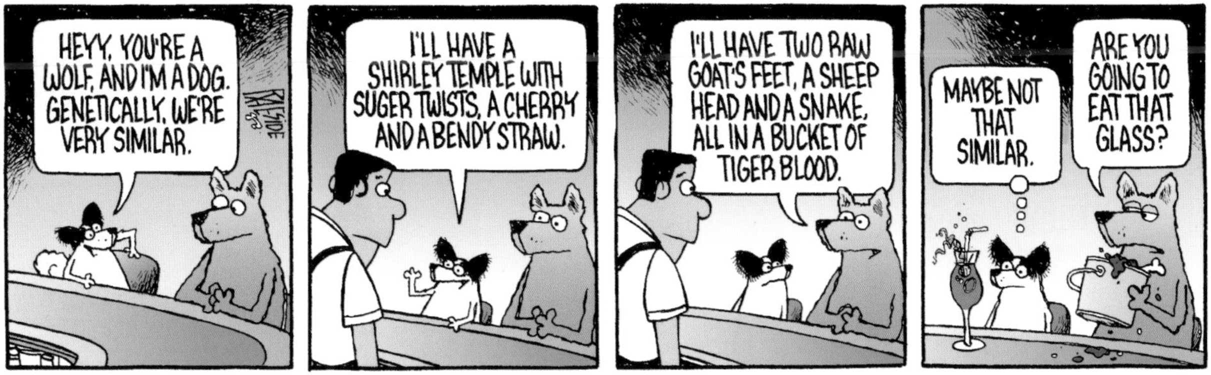

HEYY, YOU'RE A WOLF, AND I'M A DOG. GENETICALLY, WE'RE VERY SIMILAR.
I'LL HAVE A SHIRLEY TEMPLE WITH SUGER TWISTS, A CHERRY AND A BENDY STRAW.
I'LL HAVE TWO RAW GOAT'S FEET, A SHEEP HEAD AND A SNAKE, ALL IN A BUCKET OF TIGER BLOOD.
MAYBE NOT THAT SIMILAR.
ARE YOU GOING TO EAT THAT GLASS?

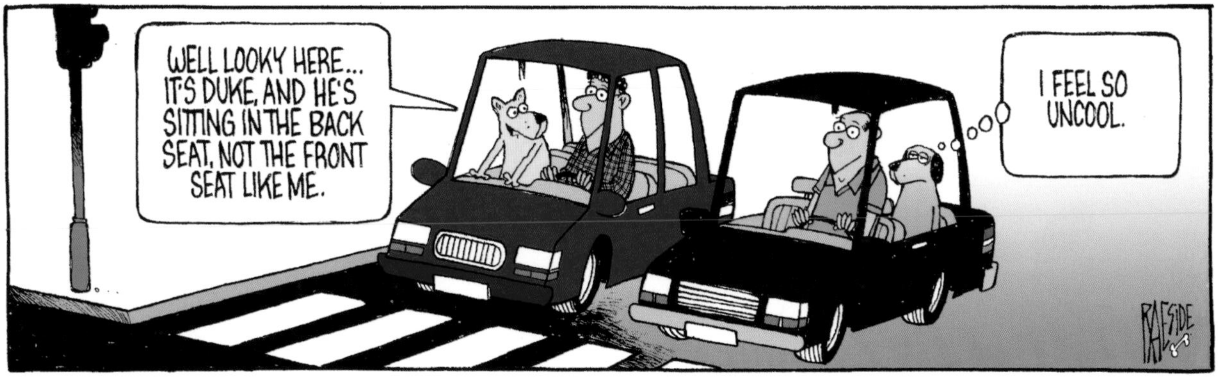

WELL LOOKY HERE... IT'S DUKE, AND HE'S SITTING IN THE BACK SEAT, NOT THE FRONT SEAT LIKE ME.
I FEEL SO UNCOOL.

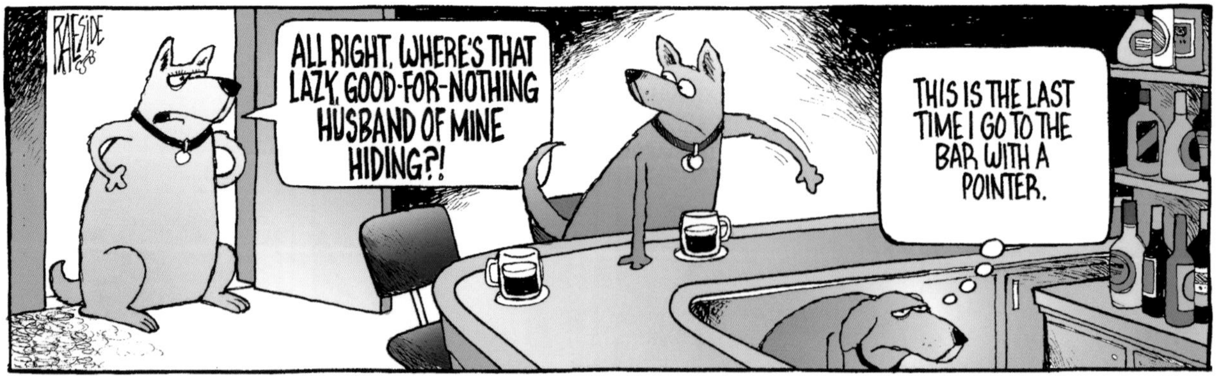
RAESIDE
ALL RIGHT, WHERE'S THAT LAZY, GOOD-FOR-NOTHING HUSBAND OF MINE HIDING?!
THIS IS THE LAST TIME I GO TO THE BAR WITH A POINTER.

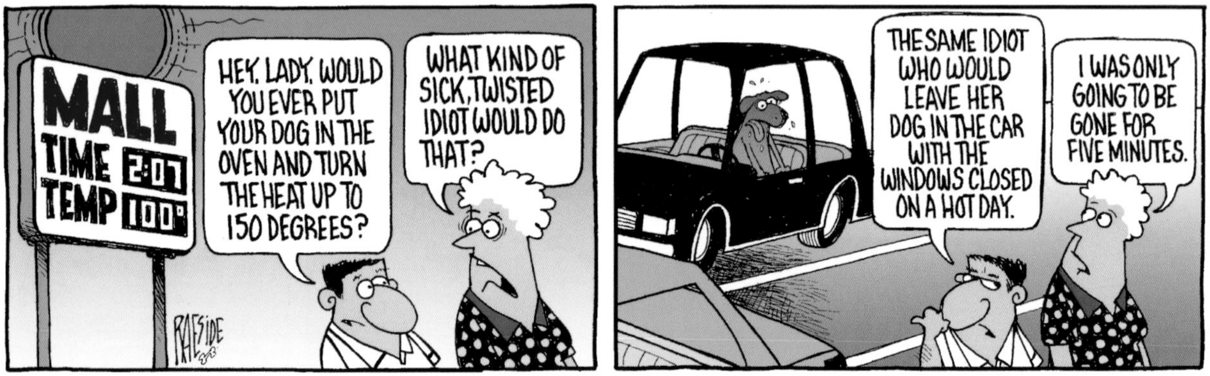
MALL
TIME 2:07
TEMP 100°
HEY, LADY, WOULD YOU EVER PUT YOUR DOG IN THE OVEN AND TURN THE HEAT UP TO 150 DEGREES?
WHAT KIND OF SICK, TWISTED IDIOT WOULD DO THAT?
RAESIDE
THE SAME IDIOT WHO WOULD LEAVE HER DOG IN THE CAR WITH THE WINDOWS CLOSED ON A HOT DAY.
I WAS ONLY GOING TO BE GONE FOR FIVE MINUTES.

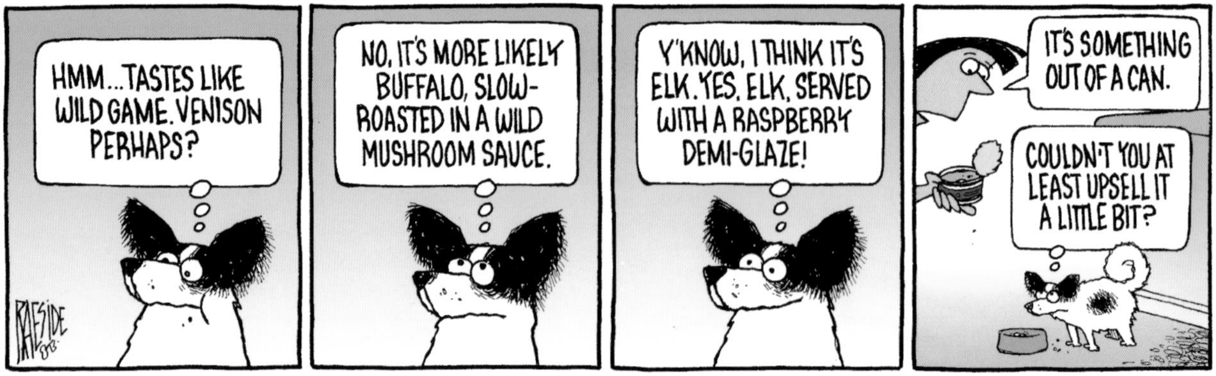
HMM...TASTES LIKE WILD GAME. VENISON PERHAPS?
RAESIDE
NO, IT'S MORE LIKELY BUFFALO, SLOW-ROASTED IN A WILD MUSHROOM SAUCE.
Y'KNOW, I THINK IT'S ELK. YES, ELK, SERVED WITH A RASPBERRY DEMI-GLAZE!
IT'S SOMETHING OUT OF A CAN.
COULDN'T YOU AT LEAST UPSELL IT A LITTLE BIT?

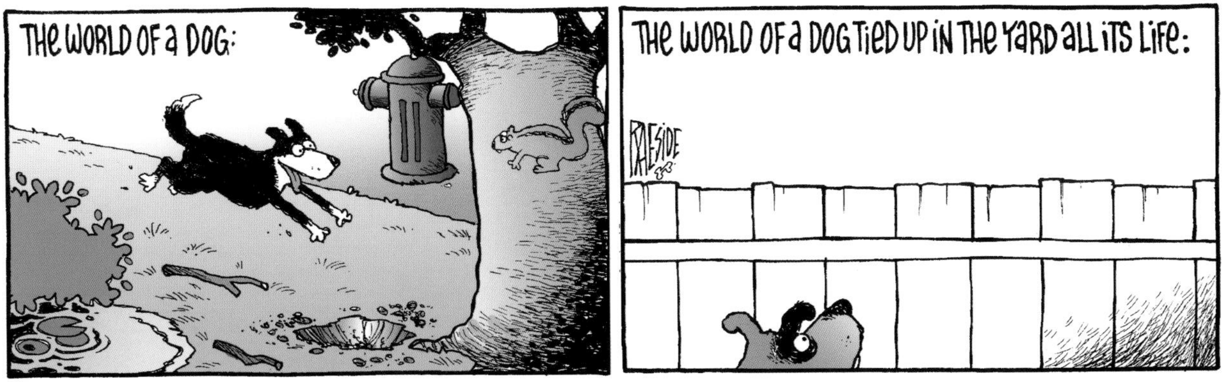
THE WORLD OF A DOG:
THE WORLD OF A DOG TIED UP IN THE YARD ALL ITS LIFE:

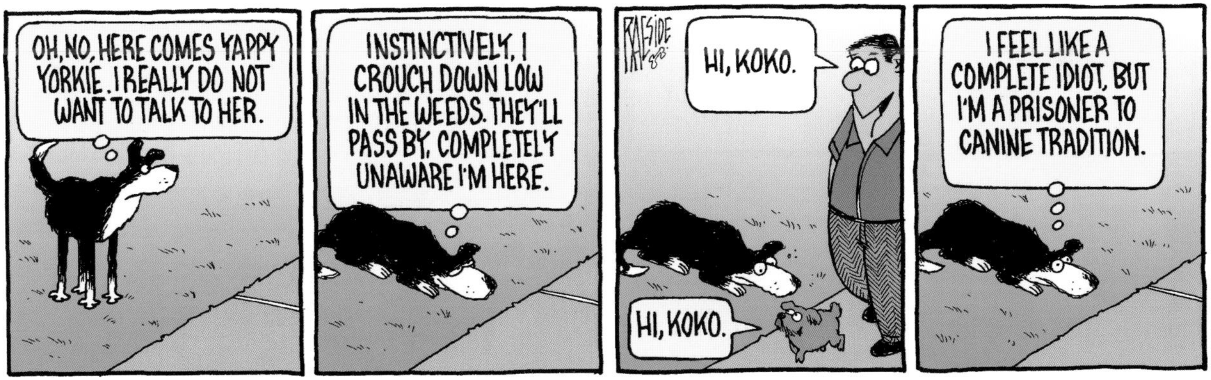
OH, NO, HERE COMES YAPPY YORKIE. I REALLY DO NOT WANT TO TALK TO HER.
INSTINCTIVELY, I CROUCH DOWN LOW IN THE WEEDS. THEY'LL PASS BY, COMPLETELY UNAWARE I'M HERE.
HI, KOKO.
HI, KOKO.
I FEEL LIKE A COMPLETE IDIOT, BUT I'M A PRISONER TO CANINE TRADITION.

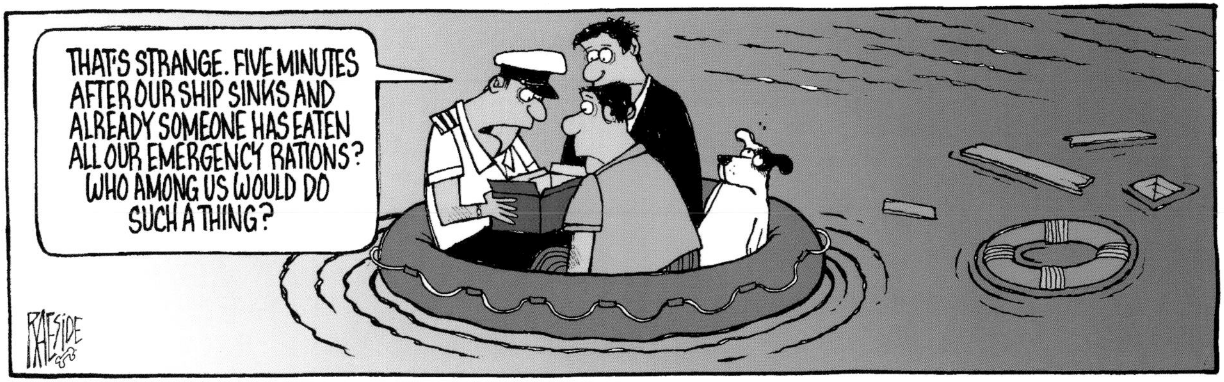
THAT'S STRANGE. FIVE MINUTES AFTER OUR SHIP SINKS AND ALREADY SOMEONE HAS EATEN ALL OUR EMERGENCY RATIONS? WHO AMONG US WOULD DO SUCH A THING?

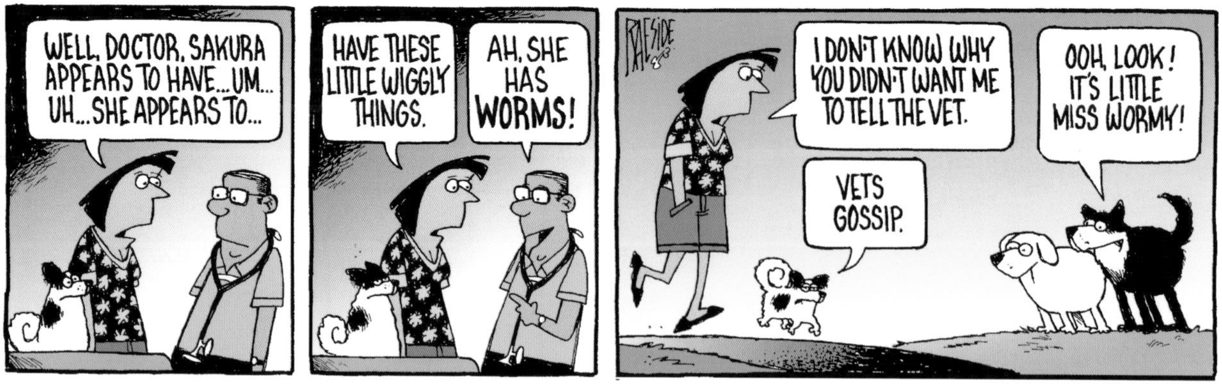
WELL, DOCTOR, SAKURA APPEARS TO HAVE...UM... UH...SHE APPEARS TO...
HAVE THESE LITTLE WIGGLY THINGS.
AH, SHE HAS WORMS!
I DON'T KNOW WHY YOU DIDN'T WANT ME TO TELL THE VET.
VETS GOSSIP.
OOH, LOOK! IT'S LITTLE MISS WORMY!

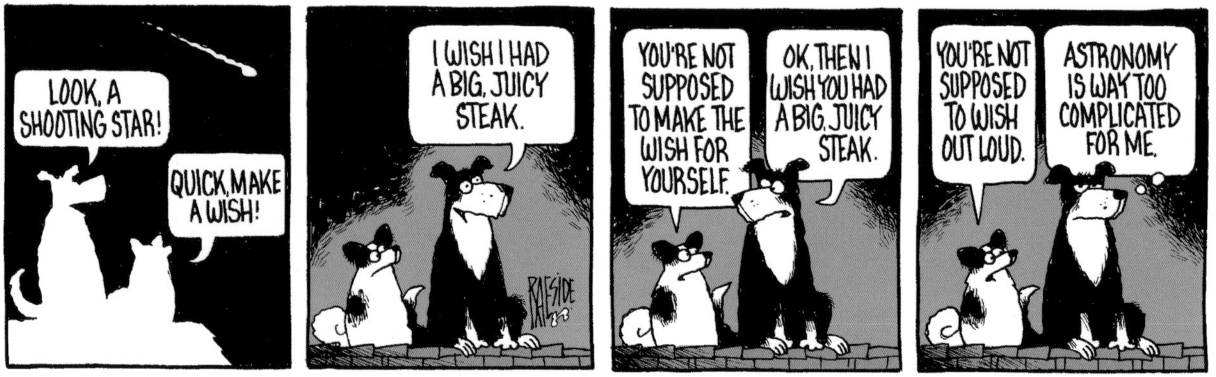
LOOK, A SHOOTING STAR!
QUICK, MAKE A WISH!
I WISH I HAD A BIG, JUICY STEAK.
YOU'RE NOT SUPPOSED TO MAKE THE WISH FOR YOURSELF.
OK, THEN I WISH YOU HAD A BIG, JUICY STEAK.
YOU'RE NOT SUPPOSED TO WISH OUT LOUD.
ASTRONOMY IS WAY TOO COMPLICATED FOR ME.

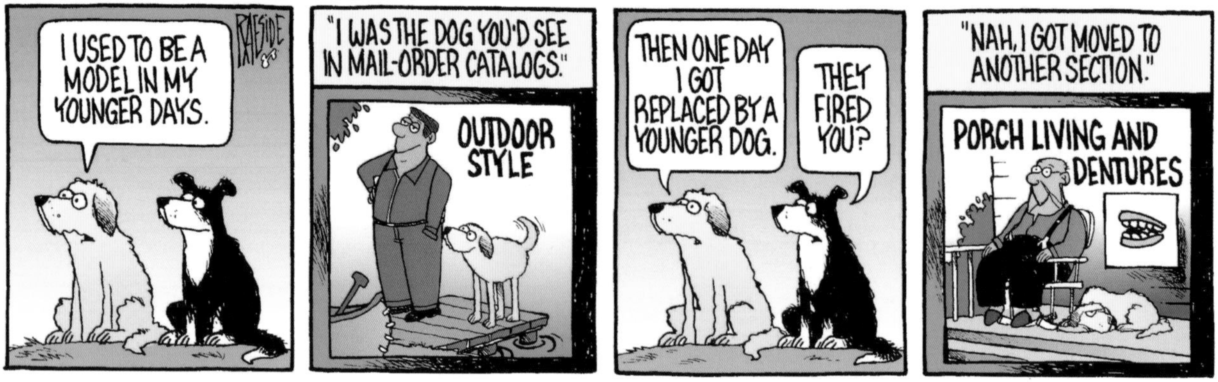
I USED TO BE A MODEL IN MY YOUNGER DAYS.
"I WAS THE DOG YOU'D SEE IN MAIL-ORDER CATALOGS."
OUTDOOR STYLE
THEN ONE DAY I GOT REPLACED BY A YOUNGER DOG.
THEY FIRED YOU?
"NAH, I GOT MOVED TO ANOTHER SECTION."
PORCH LIVING AND DENTURES

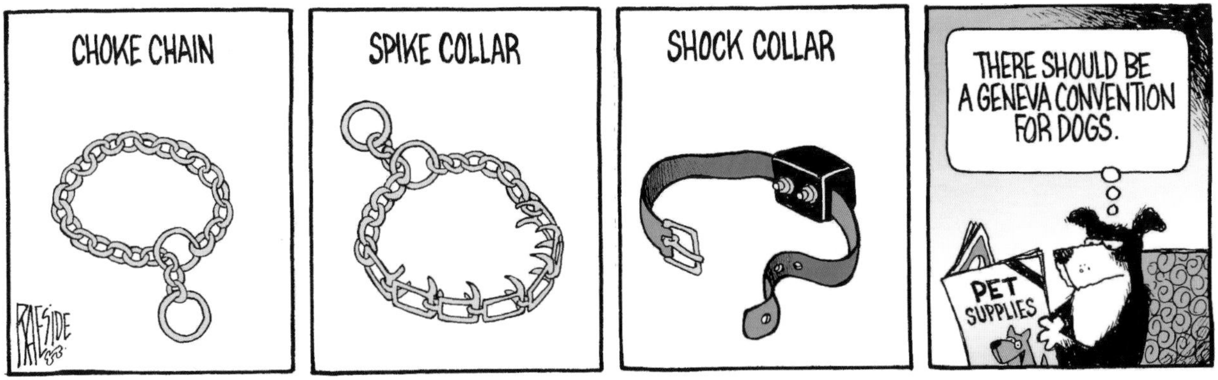
CHOKE CHAIN
SPIKE COLLAR
SHOCK COLLAR
THERE SHOULD BE A GENEVA CONVENTION FOR DOGS.
PET SUPPLIES

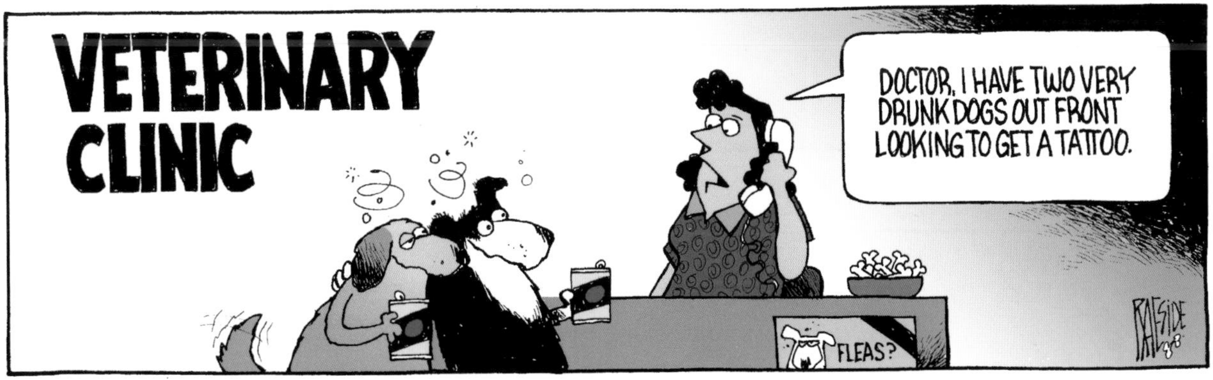
VETERINARY CLINIC
DOCTOR, I HAVE TWO VERY DRUNK DOGS OUT FRONT LOOKING TO GET A TATTOO.
FLEAS?

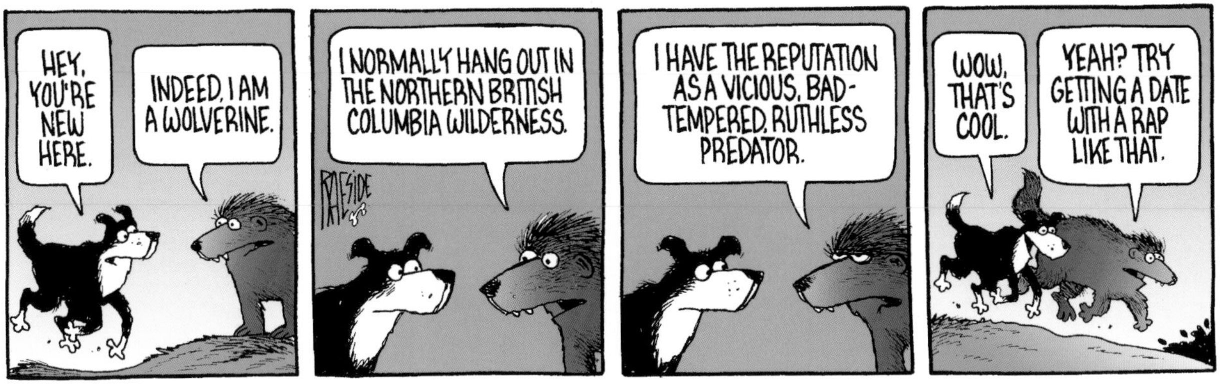
HEY, YOU'RE NEW HERE.
INDEED, I AM A WOLVERINE.
I NORMALLY HANG OUT IN THE NORTHERN BRITISH COLUMBIA WILDERNESS.
I HAVE THE REPUTATION AS A VICIOUS, BAD-TEMPERED, RUTHLESS PREDATOR.
WOW, THAT'S COOL.
YEAH? TRY GETTING A DATE WITH A RAP LIKE THAT.

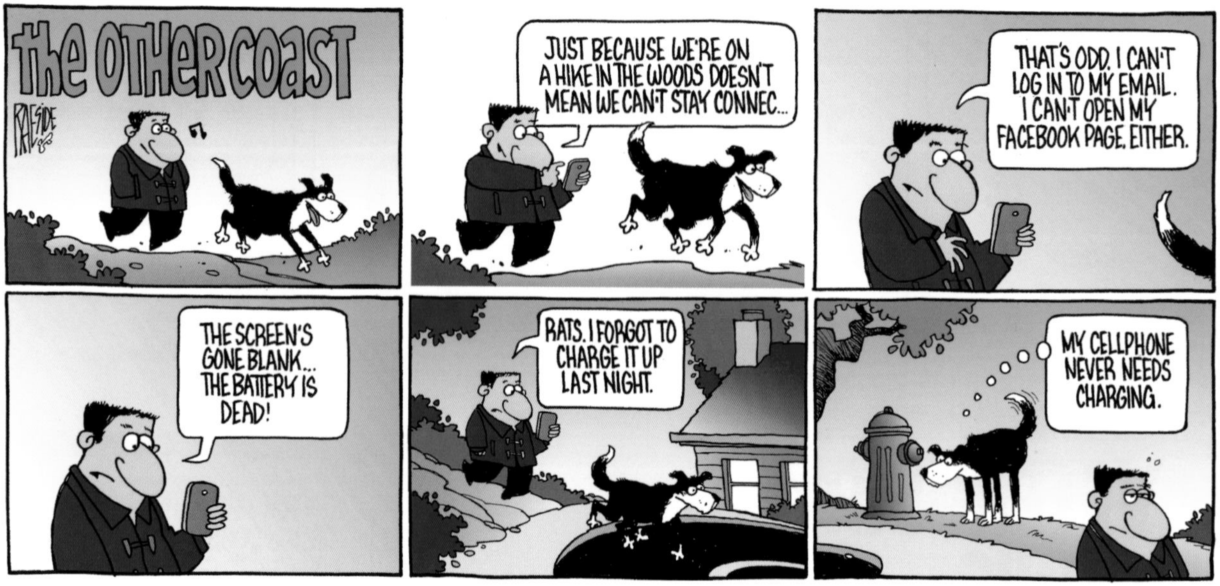
the OTHER COAST
RAESIDE
JUST BECAUSE WE'RE ON A HIKE IN THE WOODS DOESN'T MEAN WE CAN'T STAY CONNEC...
THAT'S ODD. I CAN'T LOG IN TO MY EMAIL. I CAN'T OPEN MY FACEBOOK PAGE, EITHER.
THE SCREEN'S GONE BLANK... THE BATTERY IS DEAD!
RATS. I FORGOT TO CHARGE IT UP LAST NIGHT.
MY CELLPHONE NEVER NEEDS CHARGING.

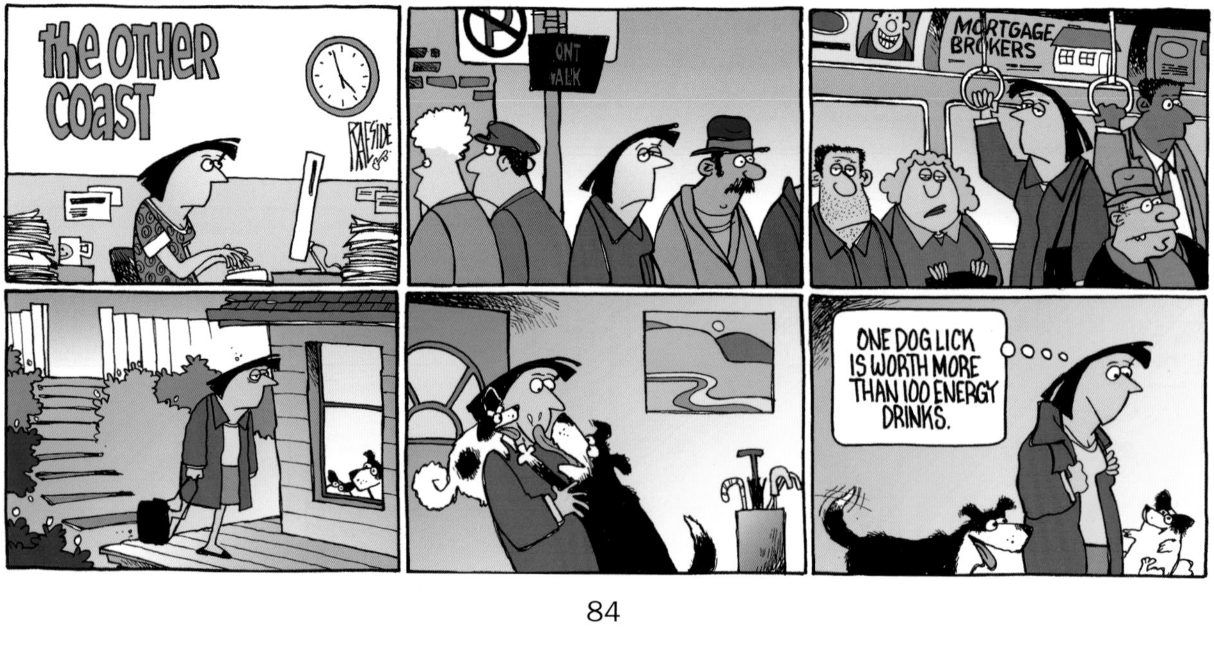
the OTHER COAST
RAESIDE
MORTGAGE BROKERS
ONE DOG LICK IS WORTH MORE THAN 100 ENERGY DRINKS.

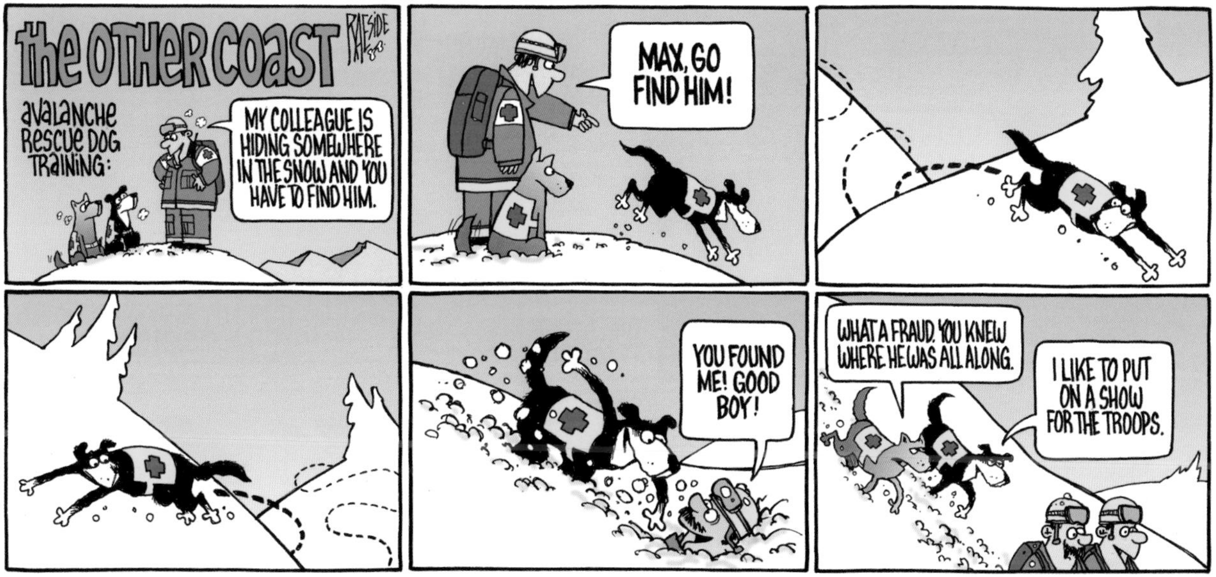
the OTHER COAST
RAESIDE
avalanche Rescue Dog Training:
MY COLLEAGUE IS HIDING SOMEWHERE IN THE SNOW AND YOU HAVE TO FIND HIM.
MAX, GO FIND HIM!
YOU FOUND ME! GOOD BOY!
WHAT A FRAUD. YOU KNEW WHERE HE WAS ALL ALONG.
I LIKE TO PUT ON A SHOW FOR THE TROOPS.

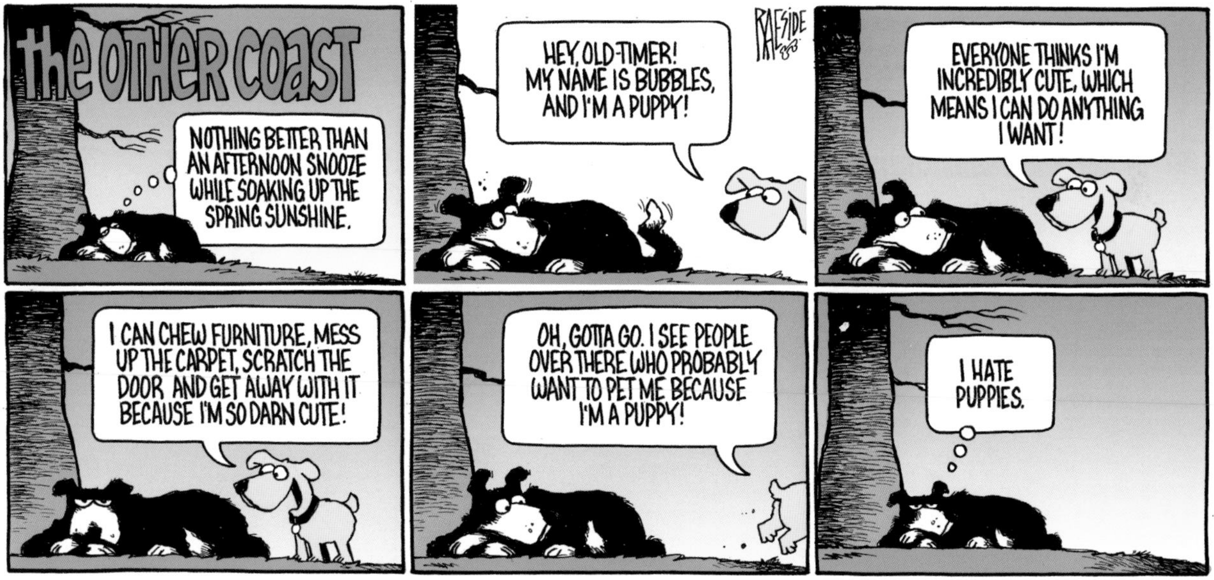
the OTHER COAST
NOTHING BETTER THAN AN AFTERNOON SNOOZE WHILE SOAKING UP THE SPRING SUNSHINE.
RAESIDE
HEY, OLD-TIMER! MY NAME IS BUBBLES, AND I'M A PUPPY!
EVERYONE THINKS I'M INCREDIBLY CUTE, WHICH MEANS I CAN DO ANYTHING I WANT!
I CAN CHEW FURNITURE, MESS UP THE CARPET, SCRATCH THE DOOR AND GET AWAY WITH IT BECAUSE I'M SO DARN CUTE!
OH, GOTTA GO. I SEE PEOPLE OVER THERE WHO PROBABLY WANT TO PET ME BECAUSE I'M A PUPPY!
I HATE PUPPIES.

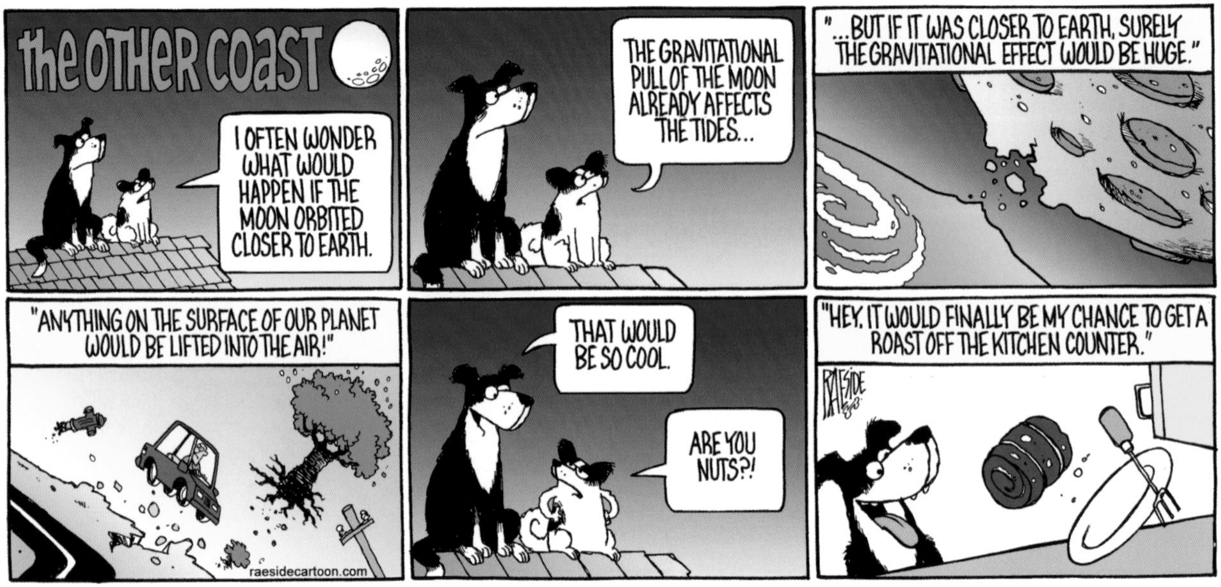
the OTHER COAST
I OFTEN WONDER WHAT WOULD HAPPEN IF THE MOON ORBITED CLOSER TO EARTH.
THE GRAVITATIONAL PULL OF THE MOON ALREADY AFFECTS THE TIDES...
"...BUT IF IT WAS CLOSER TO EARTH, SURELY THE GRAVITATIONAL EFFECT WOULD BE HUGE."
"ANYTHING ON THE SURFACE OF OUR PLANET WOULD BE LIFTED INTO THE AIR!"
raesidecartoon.com
THAT WOULD BE SO COOL.
ARE YOU NUTS?!
"HEY, IT WOULD FINALLY BE MY CHANCE TO GET A ROAST OFF THE KITCHEN COUNTER."
RAESIDE

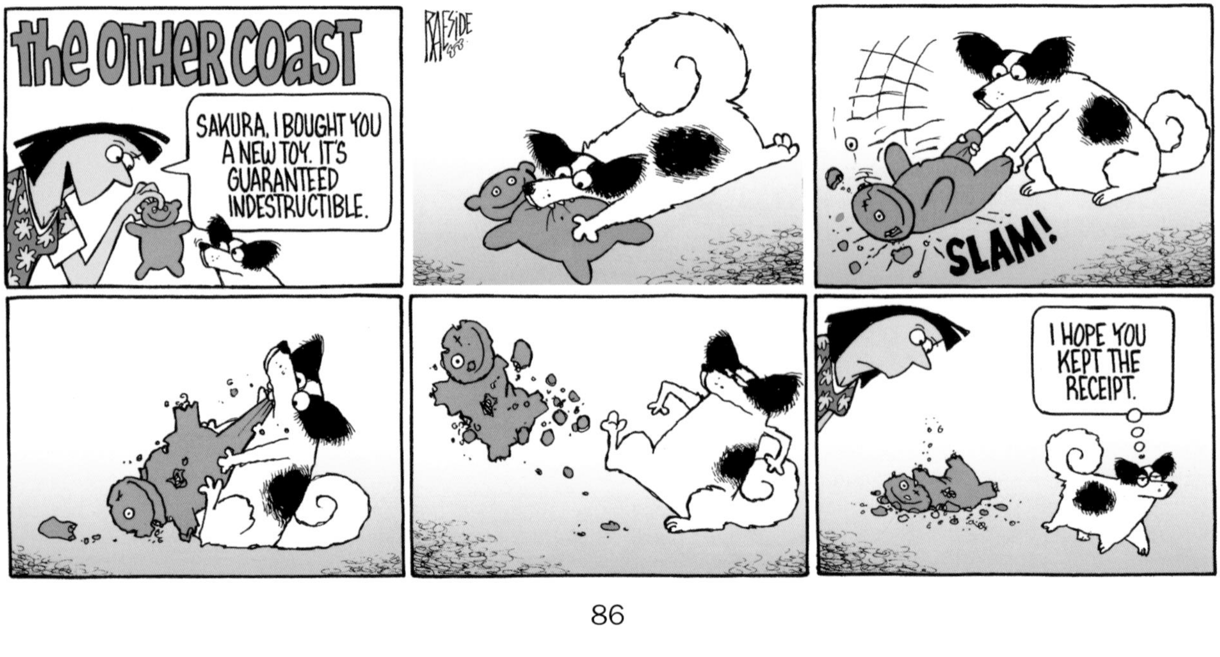
the OTHER COAST
SAKURA, I BOUGHT YOU A NEW TOY. IT'S GUARANTEED INDESTRUCTIBLE.
RAESIDE
SLAM!
I HOPE YOU KEPT THE RECEIPT.

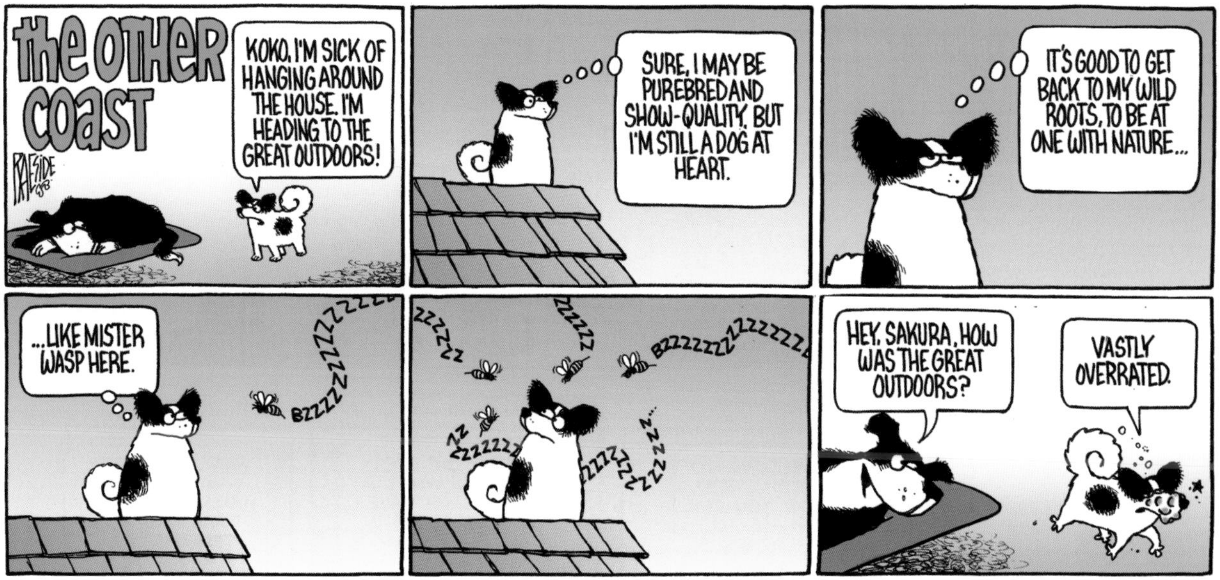
the OTHER COAST
RAESIDE
KOKO, I'M SICK OF HANGING AROUND THE HOUSE. I'M HEADING TO THE GREAT OUTDOORS!
SURE, I MAY BE PUREBRED AND SHOW-QUALITY, BUT I'M STILL A DOG AT HEART.
IT'S GOOD TO GET BACK TO MY WILD ROOTS, TO BE AT ONE WITH NATURE...
...LIKE MISTER WASP HERE.
BZZZZZZZZZZZZZZZ
HEY, SAKURA, HOW WAS THE GREAT OUTDOORS?
VASTLY OVERRATED.

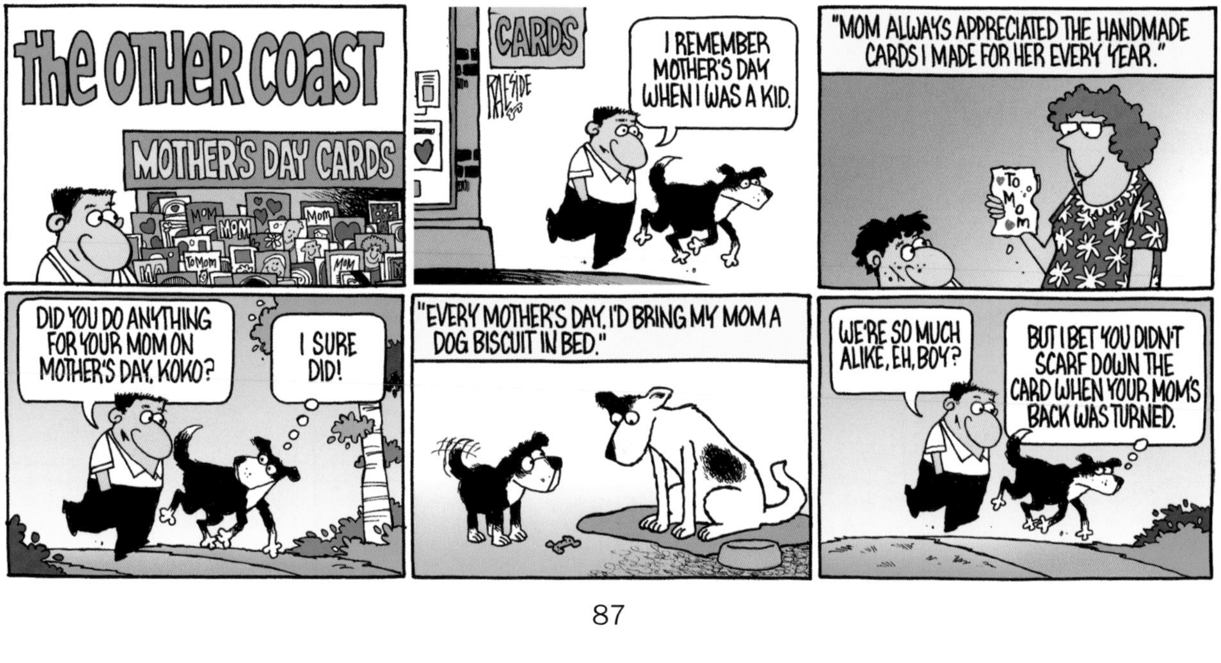
the OTHER COAST
MOTHER'S DAY CARDS
CARDS
RAESIDE
I REMEMBER MOTHER'S DAY WHEN I WAS A KID.
"MOM ALWAYS APPRECIATED THE HANDMADE CARDS I MADE FOR HER EVERY YEAR."
To MoM
DID YOU DO ANYTHING FOR YOUR MOM ON MOTHER'S DAY, KOKO?
I SURE DID!
"EVERY MOTHER'S DAY, I'D BRING MY MOM A DOG BISCUIT IN BED."
WE'RE SO MUCH ALIKE, EH, BOY?
BUT I BET YOU DIDN'T SCARF DOWN THE CARD WHEN YOUR MOM'S BACK WAS TURNED.

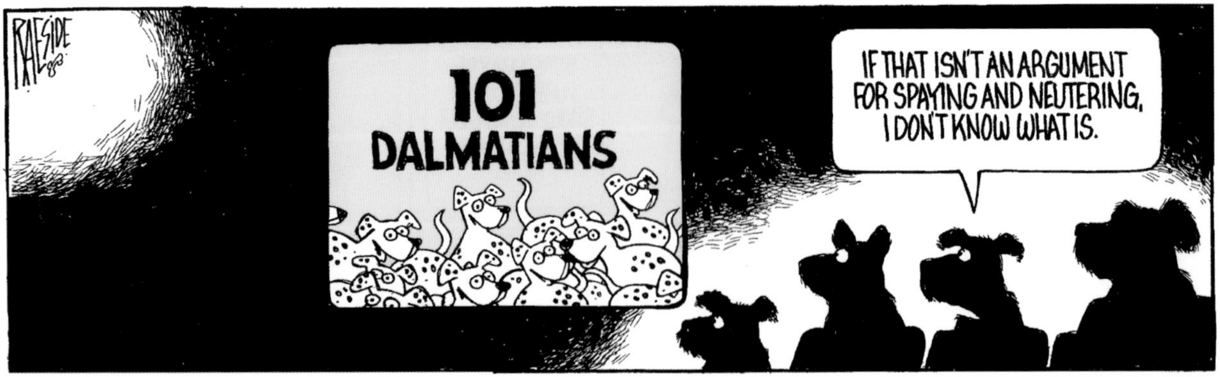
RAESIDE
101 DALMATIANS
IF THAT ISN'T AN ARGUMENT FOR SPAYING AND NEUTERING, I DON'T KNOW WHAT IS.

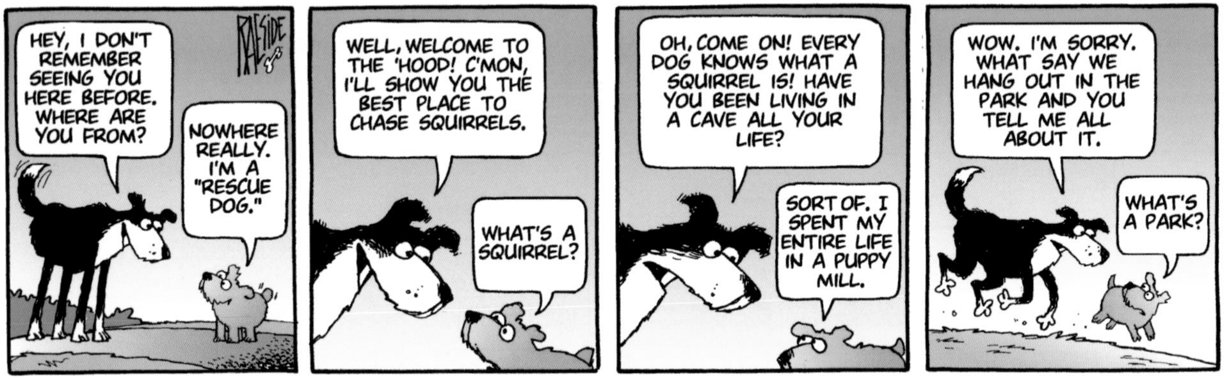
HEY, I DON'T REMEMBER SEEING YOU HERE BEFORE. WHERE ARE YOU FROM?
NOWHERE REALLY. I'M A "RESCUE DOG."
RAESIDE
WELL, WELCOME TO THE 'HOOD! C'MON, I'LL SHOW YOU THE BEST PLACE TO CHASE SQUIRRELS.
WHAT'S A SQUIRREL?
OH, COME ON! EVERY DOG KNOWS WHAT A SQUIRREL IS! HAVE YOU BEEN LIVING IN A CAVE ALL YOUR LIFE?
SORT OF. I SPENT MY ENTIRE LIFE IN A PUPPY MILL.
WOW. I'M SORRY. WHAT SAY WE HANG OUT IN THE PARK AND YOU TELL ME ALL ABOUT IT.
WHAT'S A PARK?

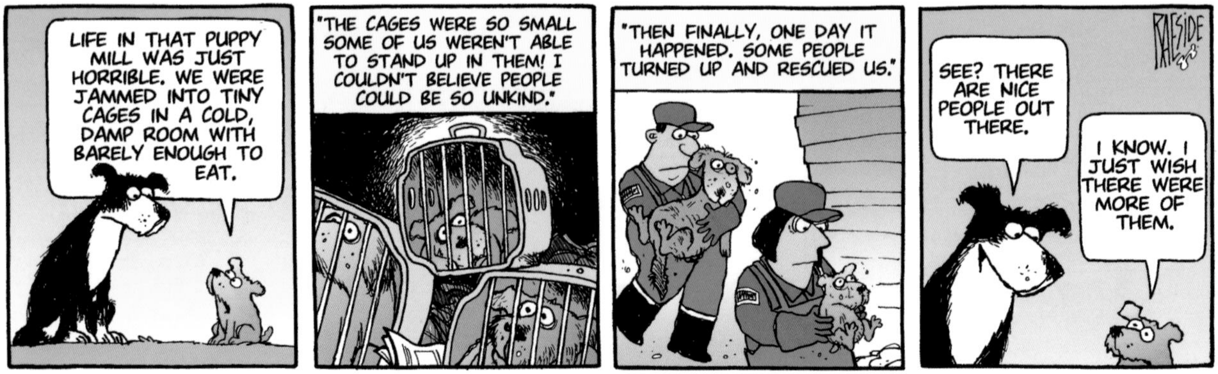
LIFE IN THAT PUPPY MILL WAS JUST HORRIBLE. WE WERE JAMMED INTO TINY CAGES IN A COLD, DAMP ROOM WITH BARELY ENOUGH TO EAT.
"THE CAGES WERE SO SMALL SOME OF US WEREN'T ABLE TO STAND UP IN THEM! I COULDN'T BELIEVE PEOPLE COULD BE SO UNKIND."
"THEN FINALLY, ONE DAY IT HAPPENED. SOME PEOPLE TURNED UP AND RESCUED US."
RAESIDE
SEE? THERE ARE NICE PEOPLE OUT THERE.
I KNOW. I JUST WISH THERE WERE MORE OF THEM.

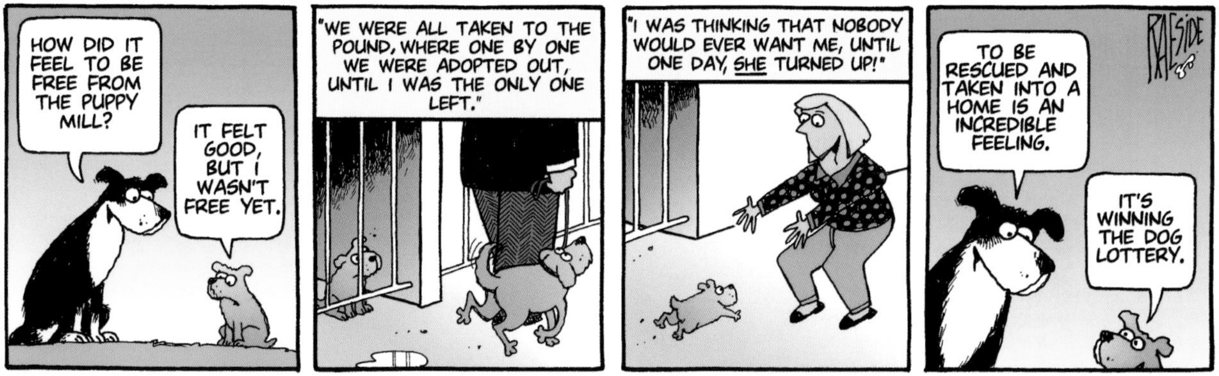
HOW DID IT FEEL TO BE FREE FROM THE PUPPY MILL?
IT FELT GOOD, BUT I WASN'T FREE YET.
"WE WERE ALL TAKEN TO THE POUND, WHERE ONE BY ONE WE WERE ADOPTED OUT, UNTIL I WAS THE ONLY ONE LEFT."
"I WAS THINKING THAT NOBODY WOULD EVER WANT ME, UNTIL ONE DAY, SHE TURNED UP!"
TO BE RESCUED AND TAKEN INTO A HOME IS AN INCREDIBLE FEELING.
IT'S WINNING THE DOG LOTTERY.

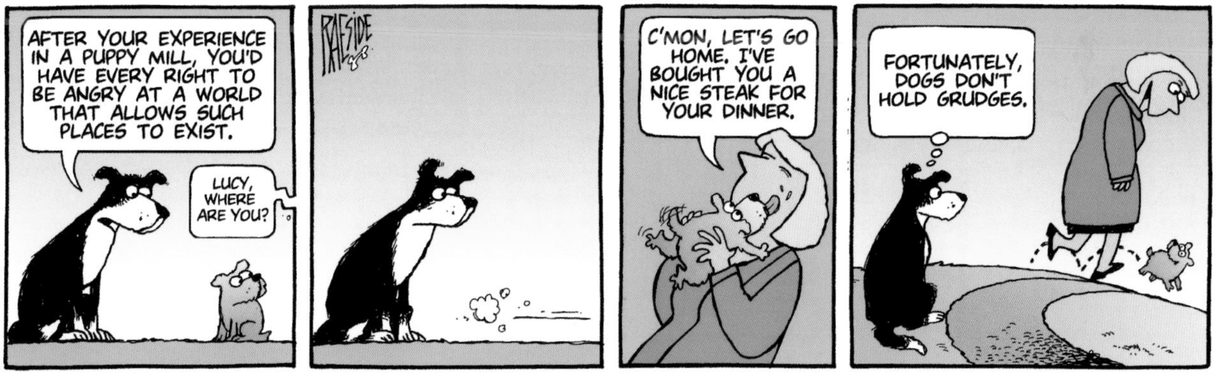
AFTER YOUR EXPERIENCE IN A PUPPY MILL, YOU'D HAVE EVERY RIGHT TO BE ANGRY AT A WORLD THAT ALLOWS SUCH PLACES TO EXIST.
LUCY, WHERE ARE YOU?
C'MON, LET'S GO HOME. I'VE BOUGHT YOU A NICE STEAK FOR YOUR DINNER.
FORTUNATELY, DOGS DON'T HOLD GRUDGES.

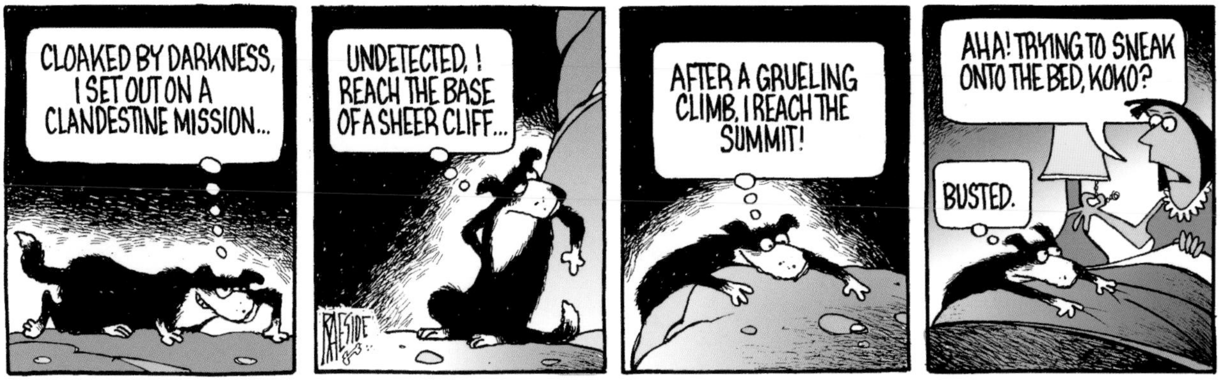
CLOAKED BY DARKNESS, I SET OUT ON A CLANDESTINE MISSION...
UNDETECTED, I REACH THE BASE OF A SHEER CLIFF...
AFTER A GRUELING CLIMB, I REACH THE SUMMIT!
AHA! TRYING TO SNEAK ONTO THE BED, KOKO?
BUSTED.

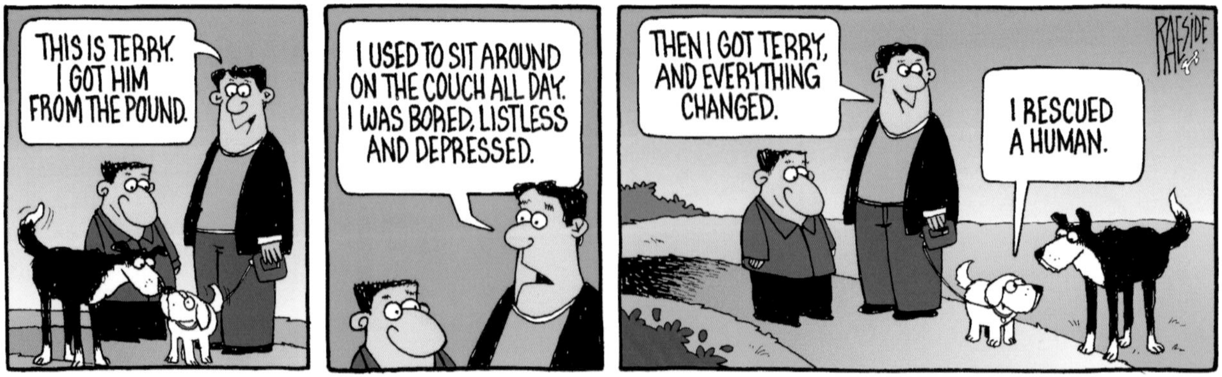
THIS IS TERRY. I GOT HIM FROM THE POUND.
I USED TO SIT AROUND ON THE COUCH ALL DAY. I WAS BORED, LISTLESS AND DEPRESSED.
THEN I GOT TERRY, AND EVERYTHING CHANGED.
I RESCUED A HUMAN.

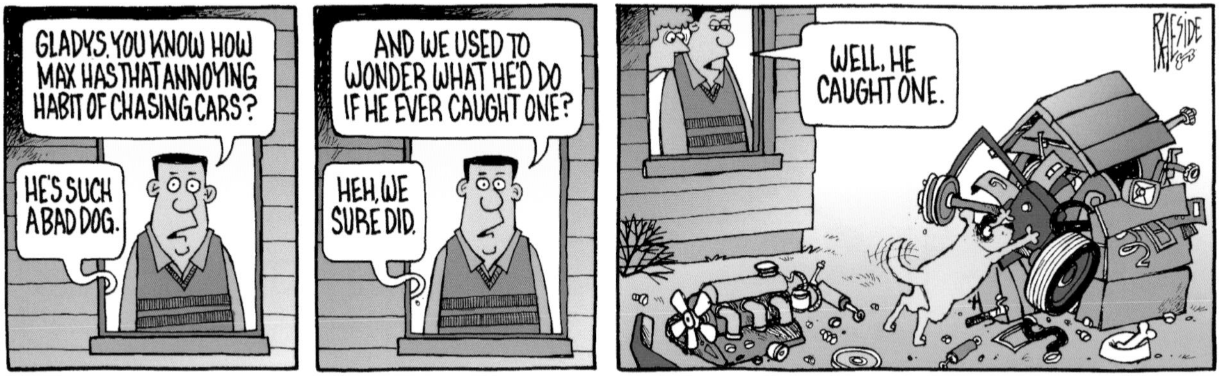
GLADYS, YOU KNOW HOW MAX HAS THAT ANNOYING HABIT OF CHASING CARS?
HE'S SUCH A BAD DOG.
AND WE USED TO WONDER WHAT HE'D DO IF HE EVER CAUGHT ONE?
HEH, WE SURE DID.
WELL, HE CAUGHT ONE.

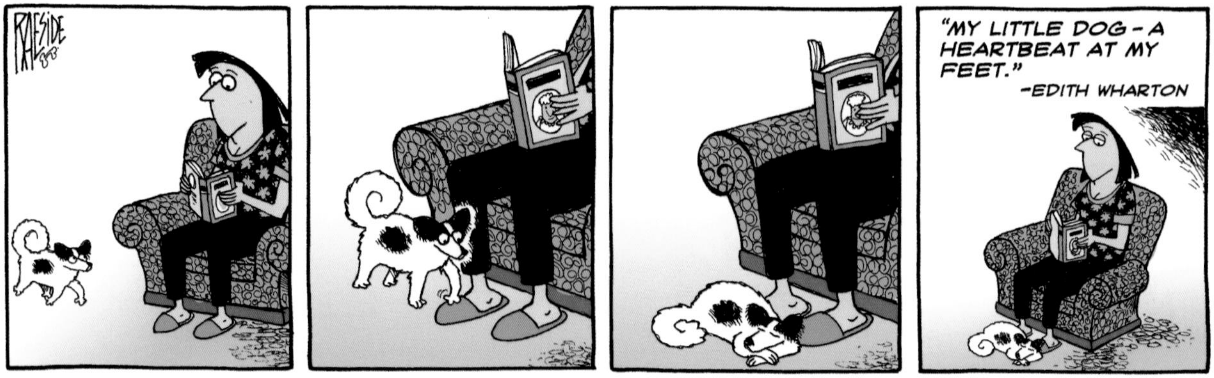
"MY LITTLE DOG – A HEARTBEAT AT MY FEET."
–EDITH WHARTON

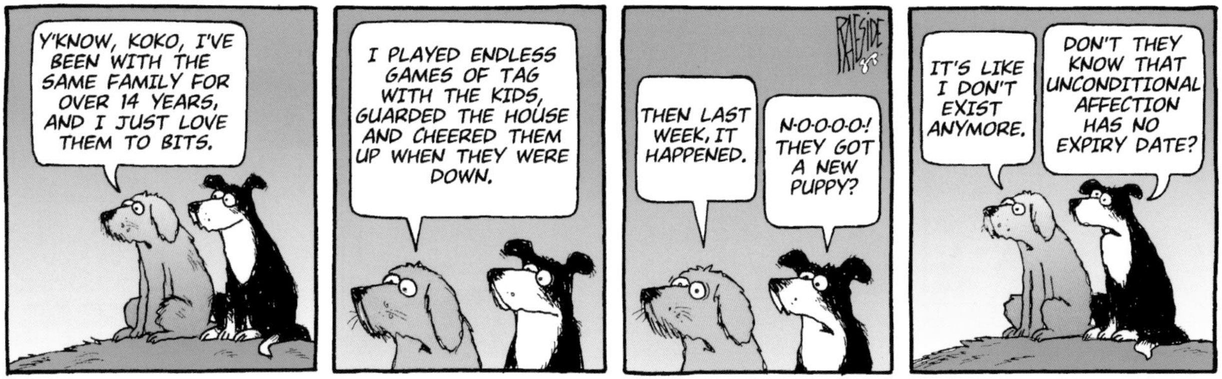
Y'KNOW, KOKO, I'VE BEEN WITH THE SAME FAMILY FOR OVER 14 YEARS, AND I JUST LOVE THEM TO BITS.
I PLAYED ENDLESS GAMES OF TAG WITH THE KIDS, GUARDED THE HOUSE AND CHEERED THEM UP WHEN THEY WERE DOWN.
THEN LAST WEEK, IT HAPPENED.
N-O-O-O-O-! THEY GOT A NEW PUPPY?
IT'S LIKE I DON'T EXIST ANYMORE.
DON'T THEY KNOW THAT UNCONDITIONAL AFFECTION HAS NO EXPIRY DATE?

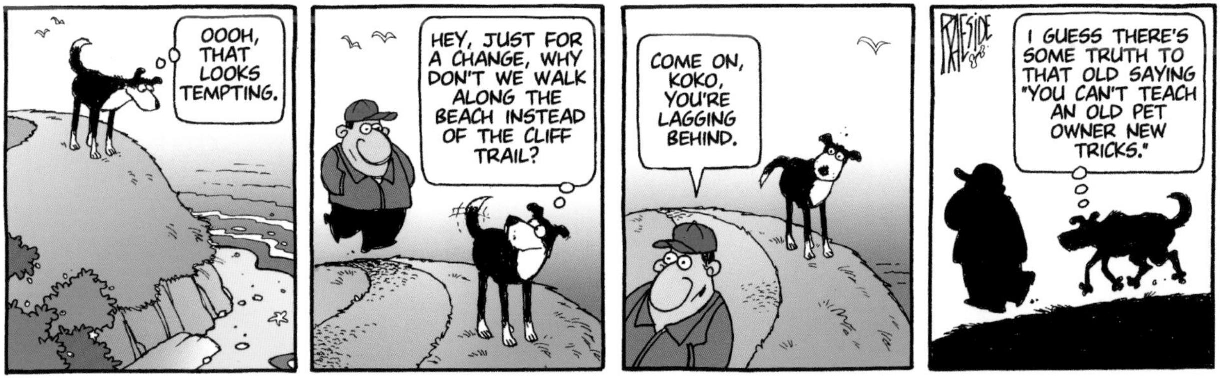
OOOH, THAT LOOKS TEMPTING.
HEY, JUST FOR A CHANGE, WHY DON'T WE WALK ALONG THE BEACH INSTEAD OF THE CLIFF TRAIL?
COME ON, KOKO, YOU'RE LAGGING BEHIND.
I GUESS THERE'S SOME TRUTH TO THAT OLD SAYING "YOU CAN'T TEACH AN OLD PET OWNER NEW TRICKS."

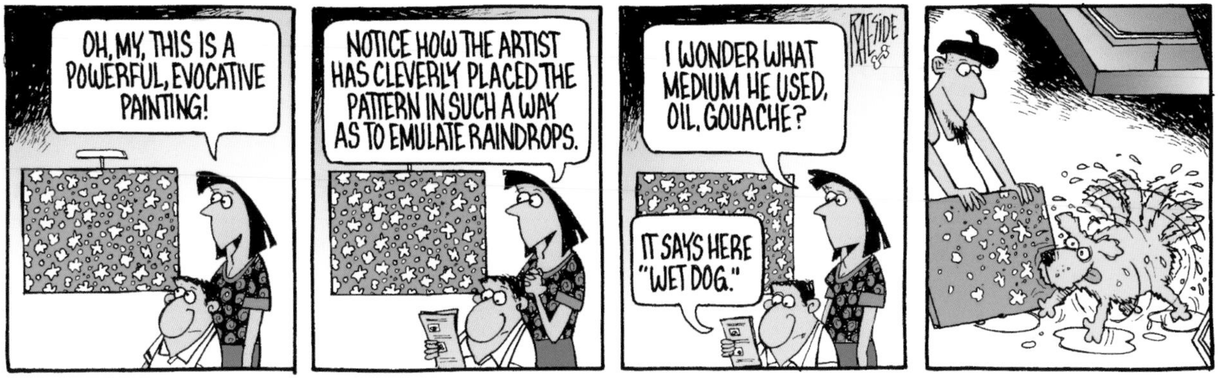
OH, MY, THIS IS A POWERFUL, EVOCATIVE PAINTING!
NOTICE HOW THE ARTIST HAS CLEVERLY PLACED THE PATTERN IN SUCH A WAY AS TO EMULATE RAINDROPS.
I WONDER WHAT MEDIUM HE USED. OIL, GOUACHE?
IT SAYS HERE "WET DOG."

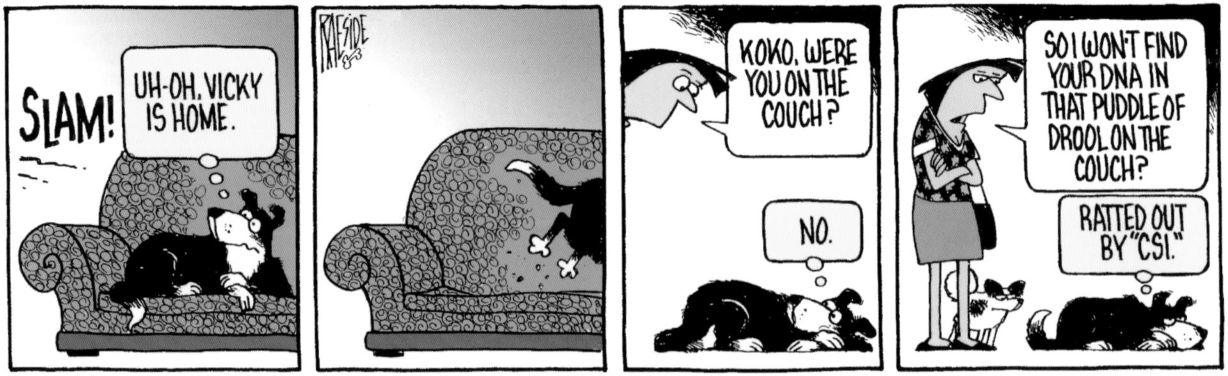
SLAM!
UH-OH, VICKY IS HOME.
KOKO, WERE YOU ON THE COUCH?
NO.
SO I WON'T FIND YOUR DNA IN THAT PUDDLE OF DROOL ON THE COUCH?
RATTED OUT BY "CSI."

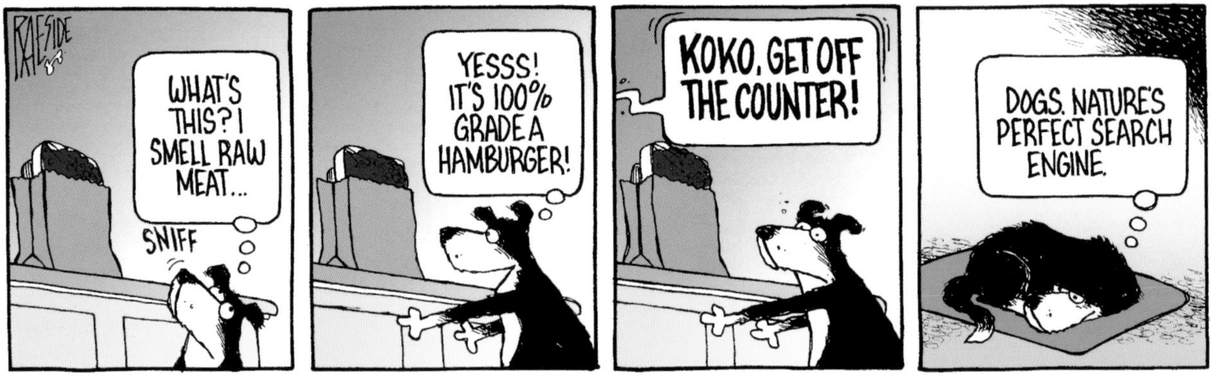
WHAT'S THIS? I SMELL RAW MEAT...
SNIFF
YESSS! IT'S 100% GRADE A HAMBURGER!
KOKO, GET OFF THE COUNTER!
DOGS. NATURE'S PERFECT SEARCH ENGINE.

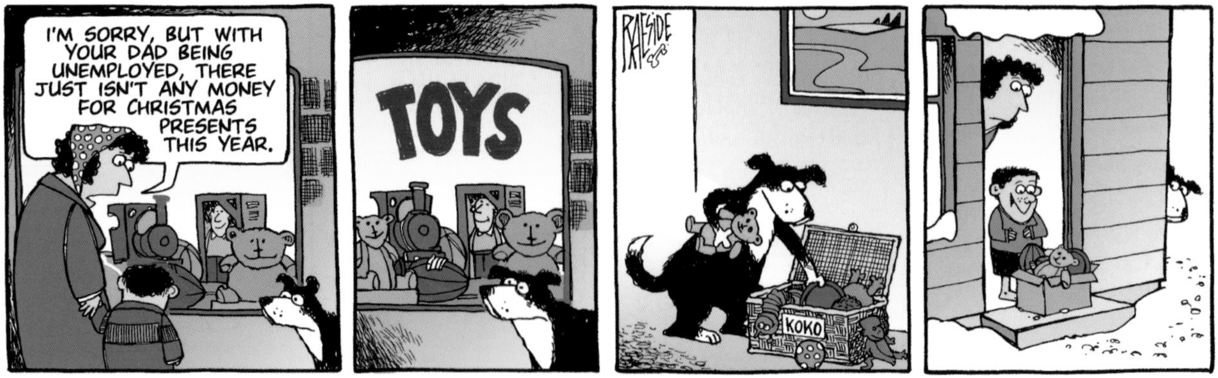
I'M SORRY, BUT WITH YOUR DAD BEING UNEMPLOYED, THERE JUST ISN'T ANY MONEY FOR CHRISTMAS PRESENTS THIS YEAR.
TOYS
KOKO

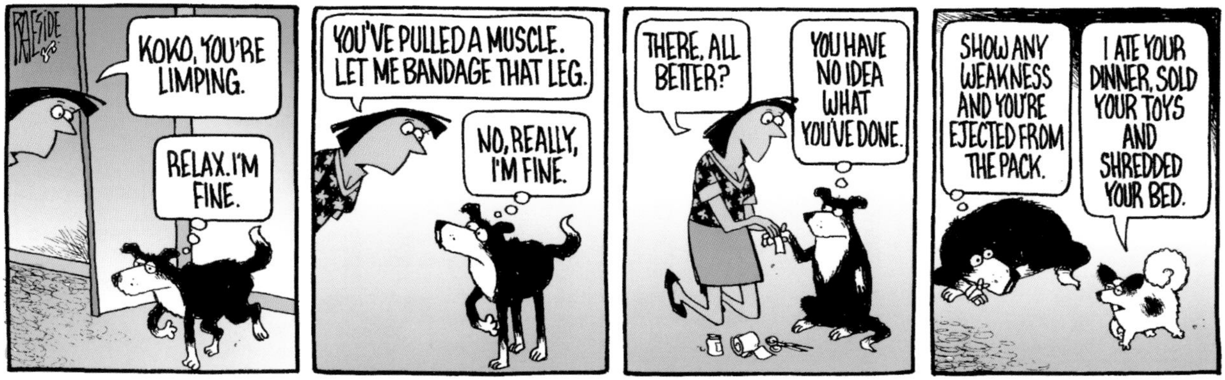
RAESIDE
KOKO, YOU'RE LIMPING.
RELAX. I'M FINE.
YOU'VE PULLED A MUSCLE. LET ME BANDAGE THAT LEG.
NO, REALLY, I'M FINE.
THERE, ALL BETTER?
YOU HAVE NO IDEA WHAT YOU'VE DONE.
SHOW ANY WEAKNESS AND YOU'RE EJECTED FROM THE PACK.
I ATE YOUR DINNER, SOLD YOUR TOYS AND SHREDDED YOUR BED.

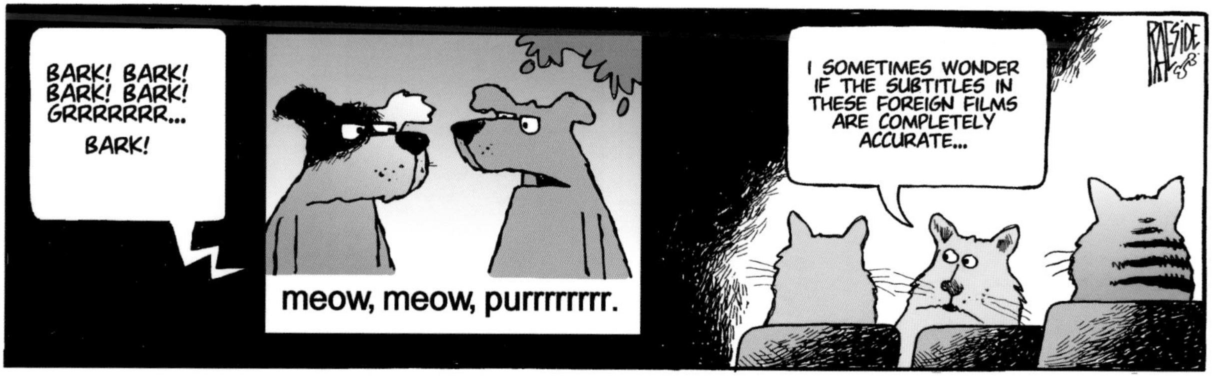
BARK! BARK! BARK! BARK! GRRRRRRR... BARK!
meow, meow, purrrrrrrr.
RAESIDE
I SOMETIMES WONDER IF THE SUBTITLES IN THESE FOREIGN FILMS ARE COMPLETELY ACCURATE...

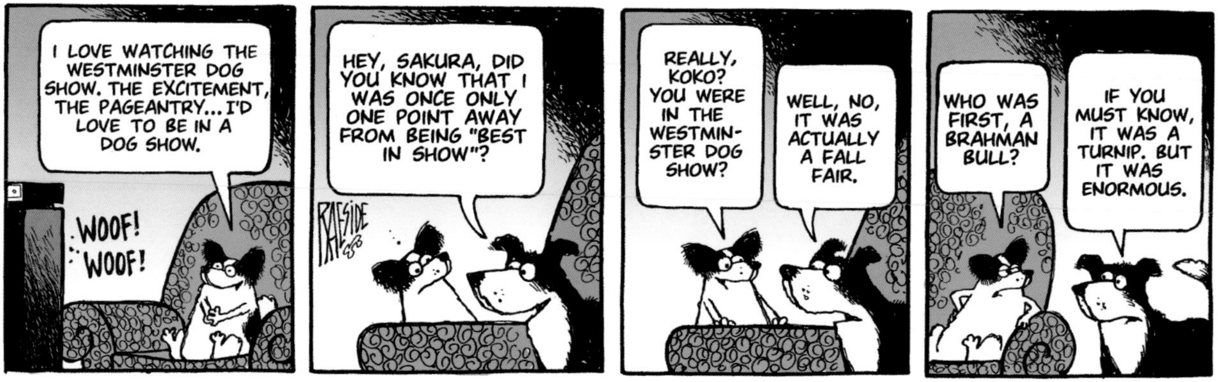
I LOVE WATCHING THE WESTMINSTER DOG SHOW. THE EXCITEMENT, THE PAGEANTRY... I'D LOVE TO BE IN A DOG SHOW.
WOOF! WOOF!
RAESIDE
HEY, SAKURA, DID YOU KNOW THAT I WAS ONCE ONLY ONE POINT AWAY FROM BEING "BEST IN SHOW"?
REALLY, KOKO? YOU WERE IN THE WESTMINSTER DOG SHOW?
WELL, NO, IT WAS ACTUALLY A FALL FAIR.
WHO WAS FIRST, A BRAHMAN BULL?
IF YOU MUST KNOW, IT WAS A TURNIP. BUT IT WAS ENORMOUS.

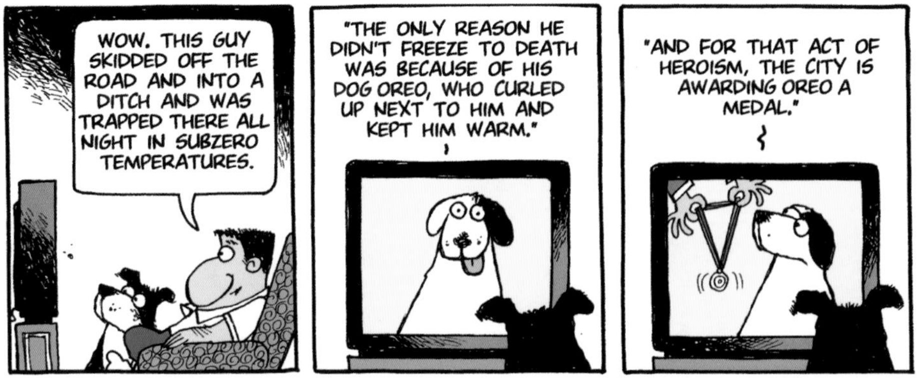
WOW. THIS GUY SKIDDED OFF THE ROAD AND INTO A DITCH AND WAS TRAPPED THERE ALL NIGHT IN SUBZERO TEMPERATURES.
"THE ONLY REASON HE DIDN'T FREEZE TO DEATH WAS BECAUSE OF HIS DOG OREO, WHO CURLED UP NEXT TO HIM AND KEPT HIM WARM."
"AND FOR THAT ACT OF HEROISM, THE CITY IS AWARDING OREO A MEDAL."
I'M SURE OREO IS REALLY HAPPY TO GET THAT MEDAL.
I'M SURE OREO WOULD HAVE PREFERRED A STEAK.

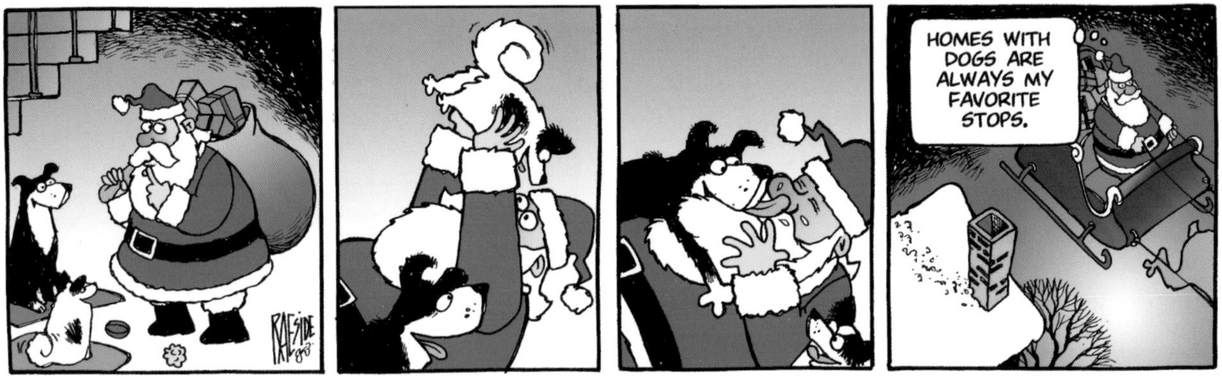
HOMES WITH DOGS ARE ALWAYS MY FAVORITE STOPS.

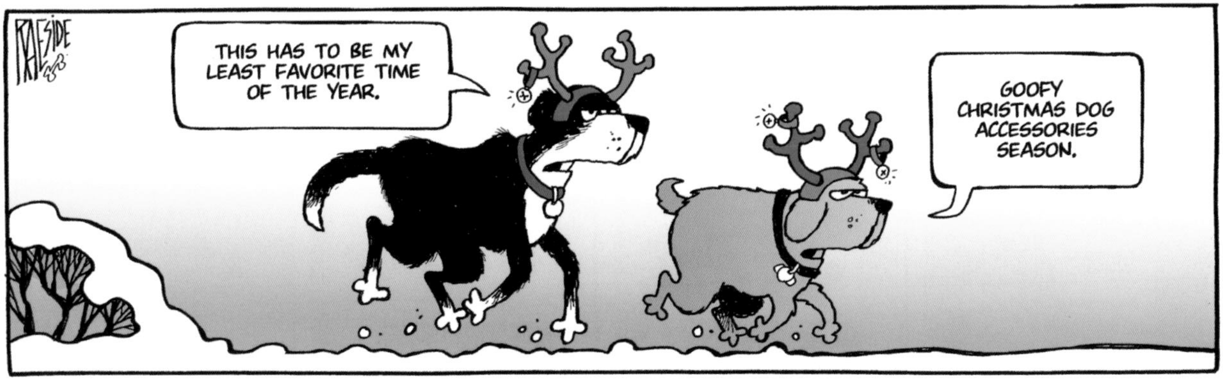
THIS HAS TO BE MY LEAST FAVORITE TIME OF THE YEAR.
GOOFY CHRISTMAS DOG ACCESSORIES SEASON.

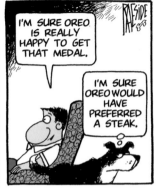

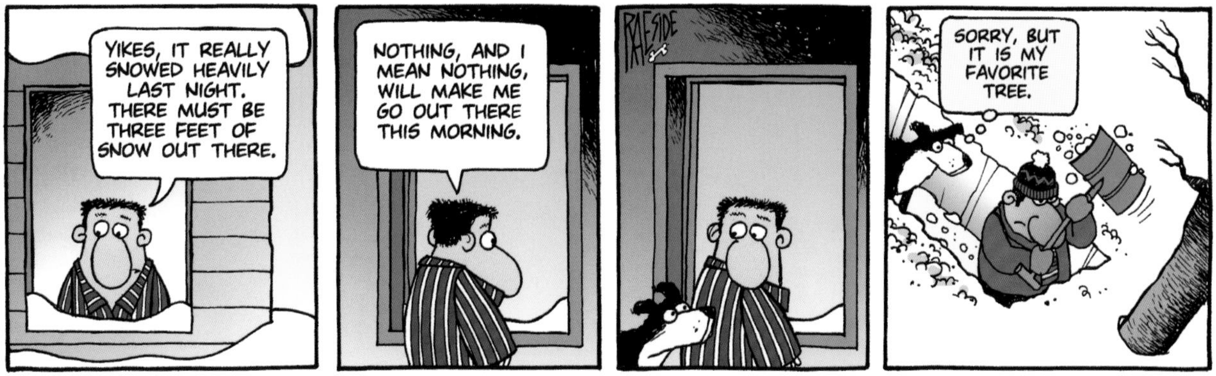
YIKES, IT REALLY SNOWED HEAVILY LAST NIGHT. THERE MUST BE THREE FEET OF SNOW OUT THERE.
NOTHING, AND I MEAN NOTHING, WILL MAKE ME GO OUT THERE THIS MORNING.
SORRY, BUT IT IS MY FAVORITE TREE.

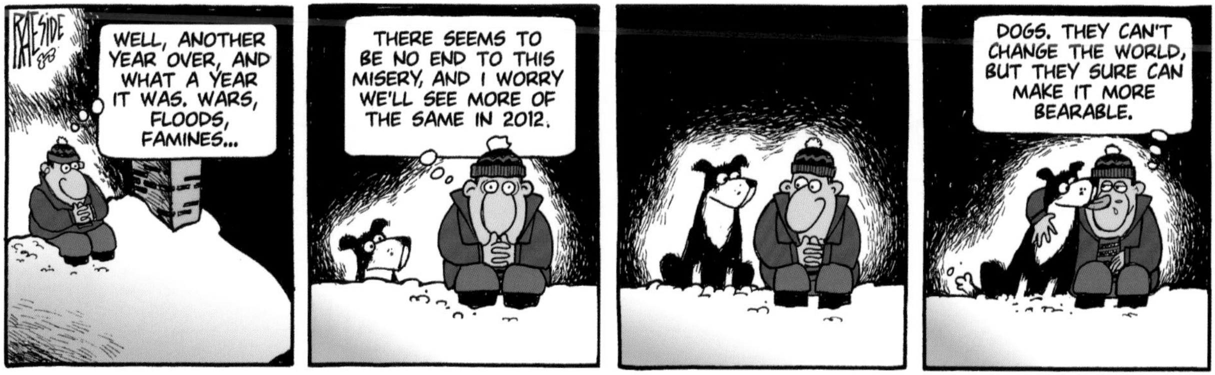
WELL, ANOTHER YEAR OVER, AND WHAT A YEAR IT WAS. WARS, FLOODS, FAMINES...
THERE SEEMS TO BE NO END TO THIS MISERY, AND I WORRY WE'LL SEE MORE OF THE SAME IN 2012.
DOGS. THEY CAN'T CHANGE THE WORLD, BUT THEY SURE CAN MAKE IT MORE BEARABLE.

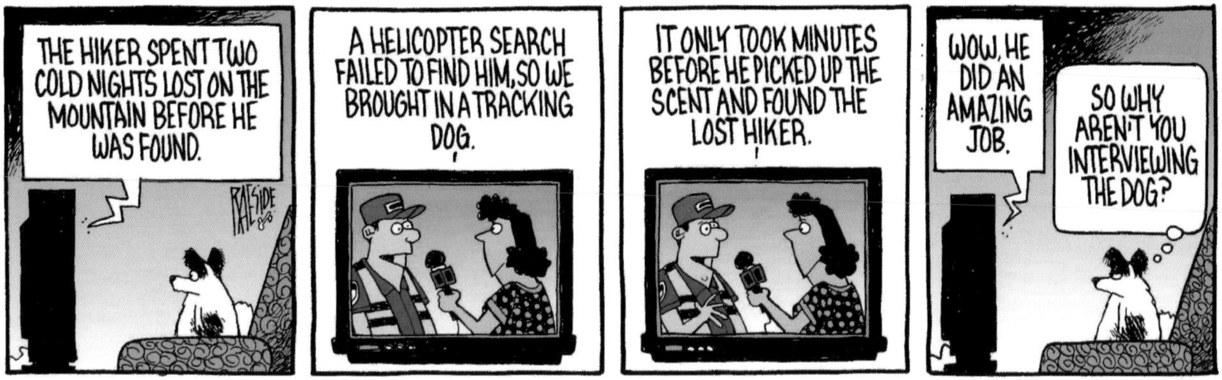
THE HIKER SPENT TWO COLD NIGHTS LOST ON THE MOUNTAIN BEFORE HE WAS FOUND.
A HELICOPTER SEARCH FAILED TO FIND HIM, SO WE BROUGHT IN A TRACKING DOG.
IT ONLY TOOK MINUTES BEFORE HE PICKED UP THE SCENT AND FOUND THE LOST HIKER.
WOW, HE DID AN AMAZING JOB.
SO WHY AREN'T YOU INTERVIEWING THE DOG?

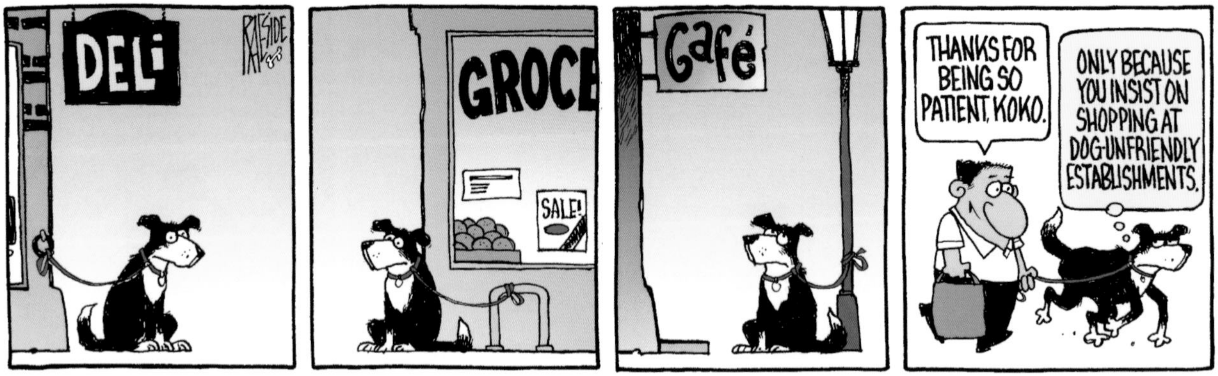
DELI
GROCE
SALE!
Café
THANKS FOR BEING SO PATIENT, KOKO.
ONLY BECAUSE YOU INSIST ON SHOPPING AT DOG-UNFRIENDLY ESTABLISHMENTS.

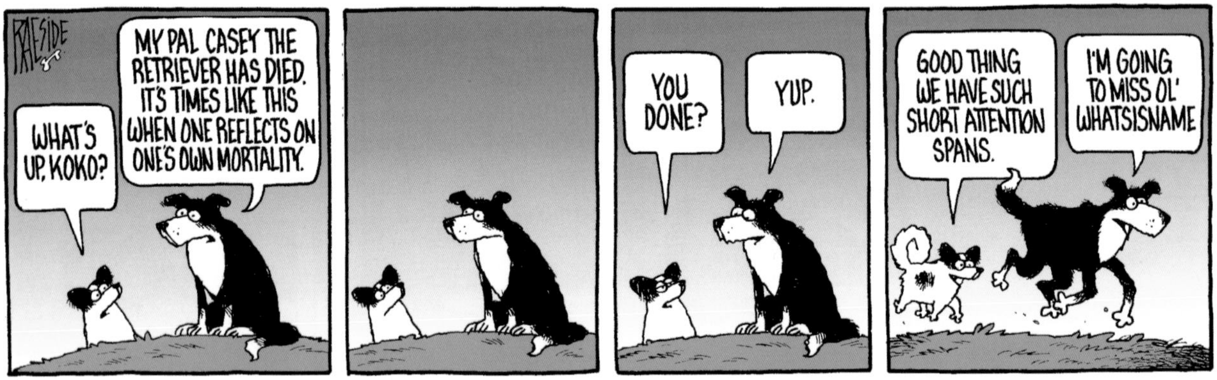
WHAT'S UP, KOKO?
MY PAL CASEY THE RETRIEVER HAS DIED. IT'S TIMES LIKE THIS WHEN ONE REFLECTS ON ONE'S OWN MORTALITY.
YOU DONE?
YUP.
GOOD THING WE HAVE SUCH SHORT ATTENTION SPANS.
I'M GOING TO MISS OL' WHATSISNAME

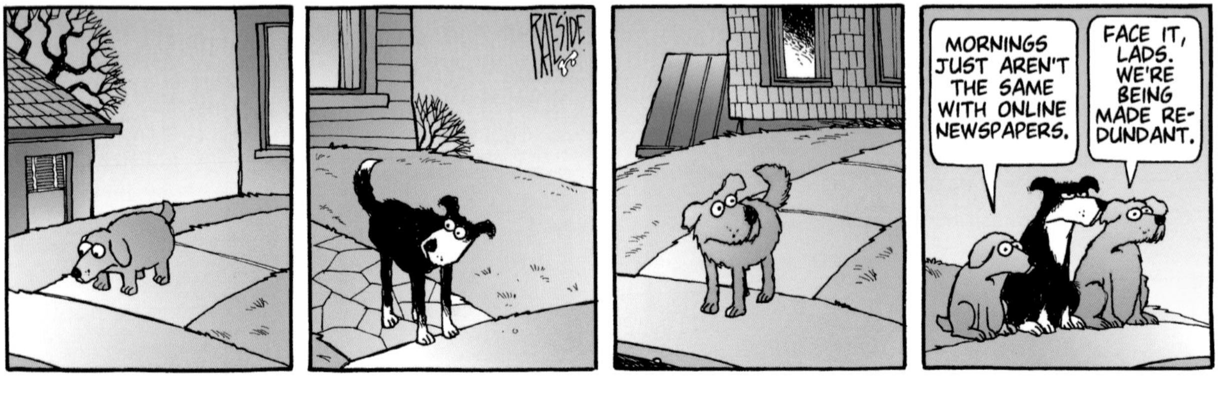
MORNINGS JUST AREN'T THE SAME WITH ONLINE NEWSPAPERS.
FACE IT, LADS. WE'RE BEING MADE RE-DUNDANT.

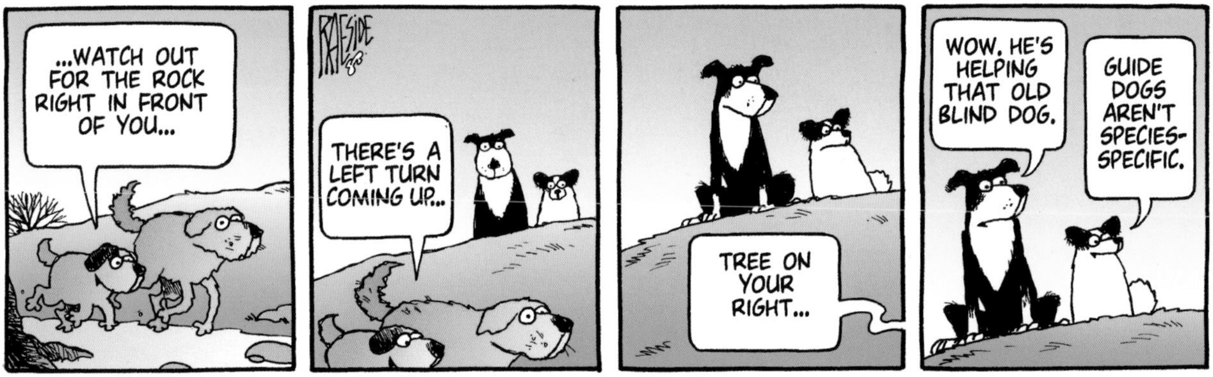
...WATCH OUT FOR THE ROCK RIGHT IN FRONT OF YOU...
THERE'S A LEFT TURN COMING UP...
TREE ON YOUR RIGHT...
WOW. HE'S HELPING THAT OLD BLIND DOG.
GUIDE DOGS AREN'T SPECIES-SPECIFIC.

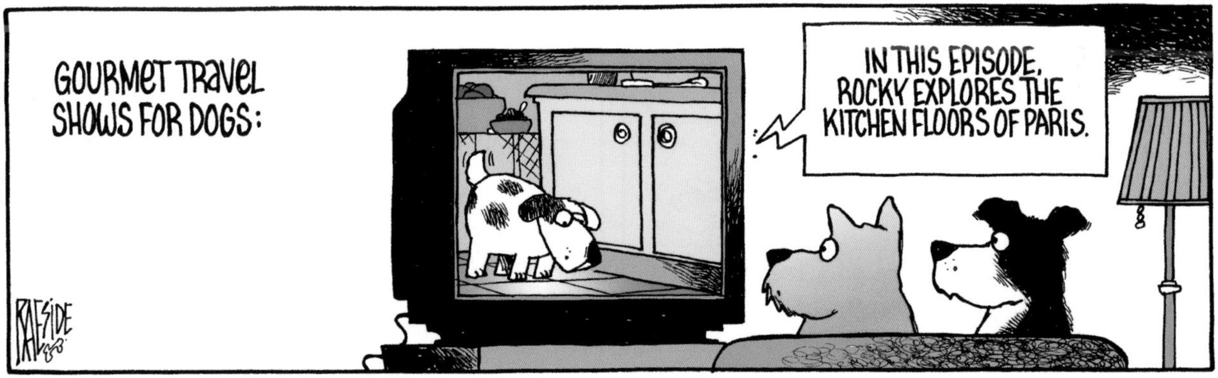
GOURMET TRAVEL SHOWS FOR DOGS:
IN THIS EPISODE, ROCKY EXPLORES THE KITCHEN FLOORS OF PARIS.

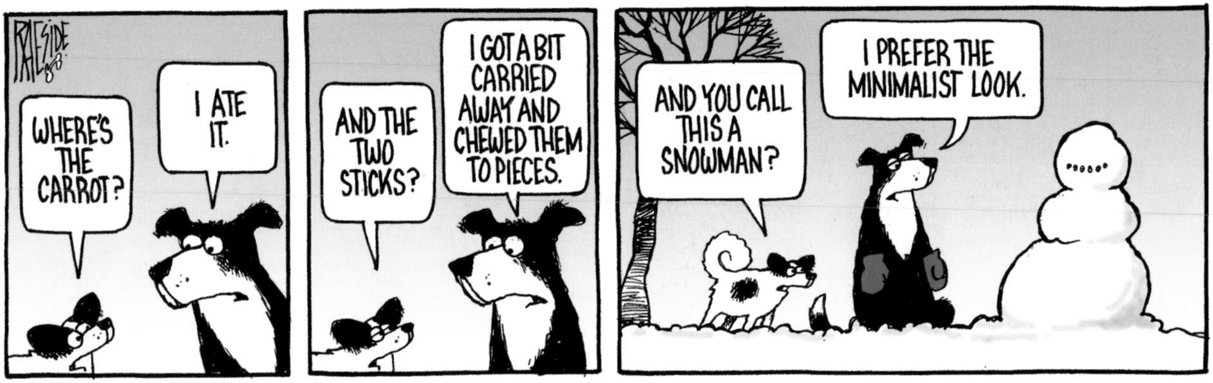
WHERE'S THE CARROT?
I ATE IT.
AND THE TWO STICKS?
I GOT A BIT CARRIED AWAY AND CHEWED THEM TO PIECES.
AND YOU CALL THIS A SNOWMAN?
I PREFER THE MINIMALIST LOOK.

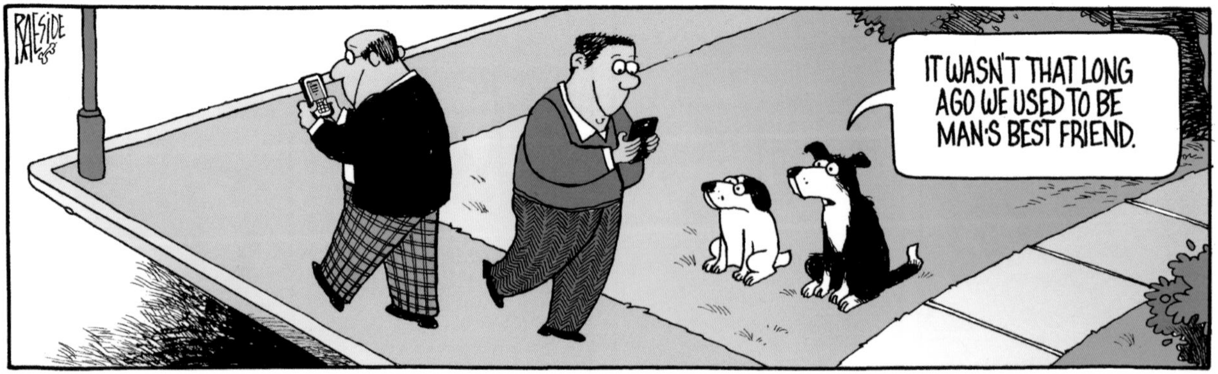
IT WASN'T THAT LONG AGO WE USED TO BE MAN'S BEST FRIEND.

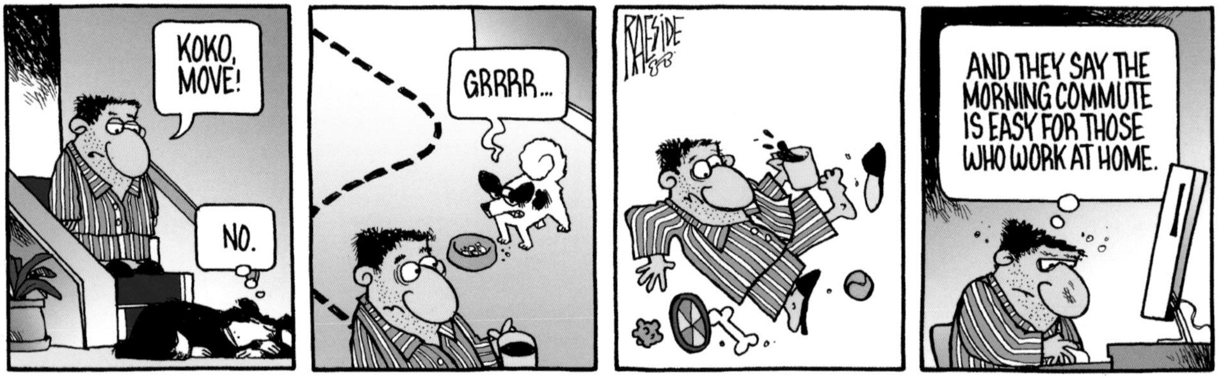
KOKO, MOVE!
NO.
GRRRR...
AND THEY SAY THE MORNING COMMUTE IS EASY FOR THOSE WHO WORK AT HOME.

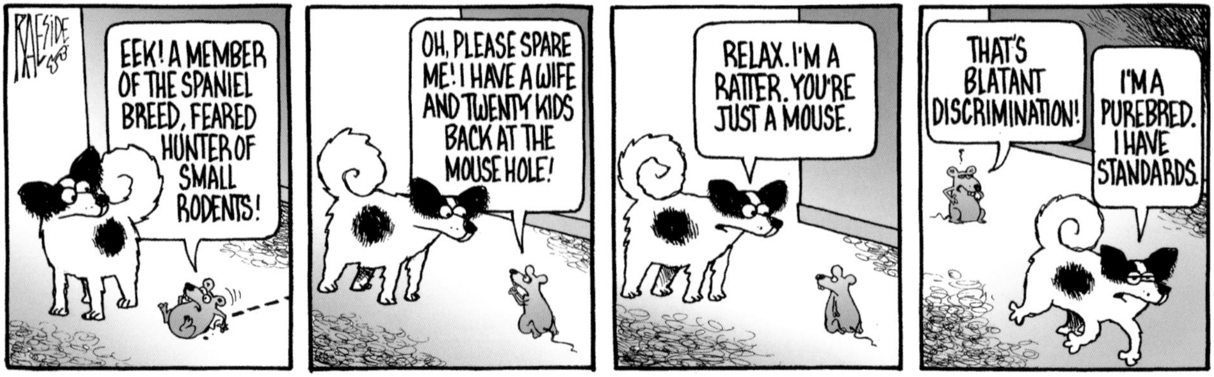
EEK! A MEMBER OF THE SPANIEL BREED, FEARED HUNTER OF SMALL RODENTS!
OH, PLEASE SPARE ME! I HAVE A WIFE AND TWENTY KIDS BACK AT THE MOUSE HOLE!
RELAX. I'M A RATTER. YOU'RE JUST A MOUSE.
THAT'S BLATANT DISCRIMINATION!
I'M A PUREBRED. I HAVE STANDARDS.

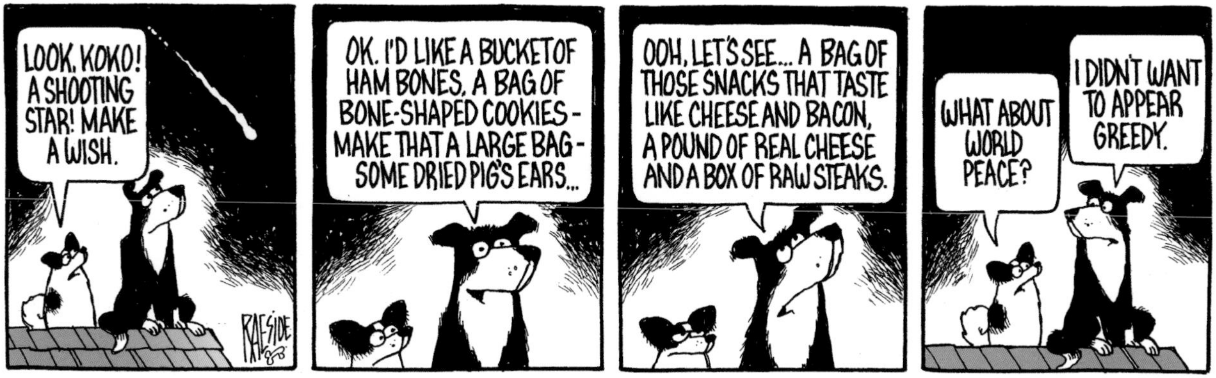
LOOK, KOKO! A SHOOTING STAR! MAKE A WISH.
OK. I'D LIKE A BUCKET OF HAM BONES, A BAG OF BONE-SHAPED COOKIES - MAKE THAT A LARGE BAG - SOME DRIED PIG'S EARS...
OOH, LET'S SEE... A BAG OF THOSE SNACKS THAT TASTE LIKE CHEESE AND BACON, A POUND OF REAL CHEESE AND A BOX OF RAW STEAKS.
WHAT ABOUT WORLD PEACE?
I DIDN'T WANT TO APPEAR GREEDY.

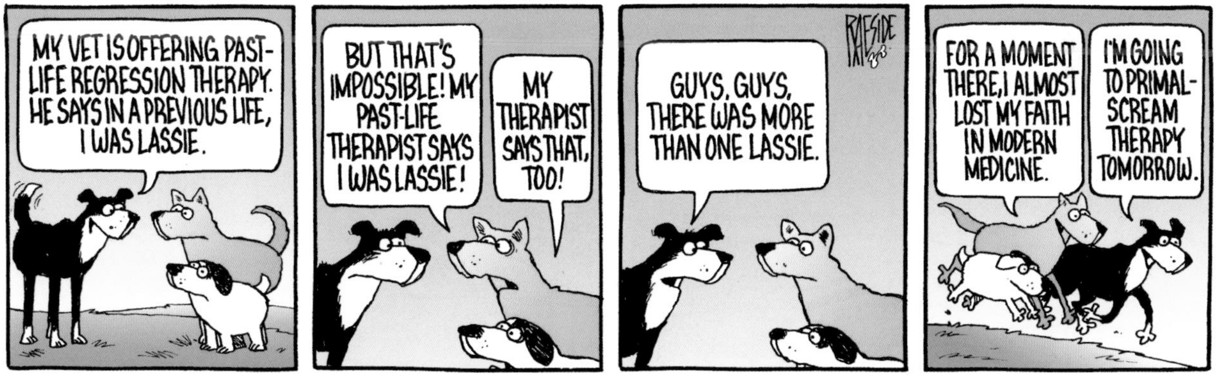
MY VET IS OFFERING PAST-LIFE REGRESSION THERAPY. HE SAYS IN A PREVIOUS LIFE, I WAS LASSIE.
BUT THAT'S IMPOSSIBLE! MY PAST-LIFE THERAPIST SAYS I WAS LASSIE!
MY THERAPIST SAYS THAT, TOO!
GUYS, GUYS, THERE WAS MORE THAN ONE LASSIE.
FOR A MOMENT THERE, I ALMOST LOST MY FAITH IN MODERN MEDICINE.
I'M GOING TO PRIMAL-SCREAM THERAPY TOMORROW.

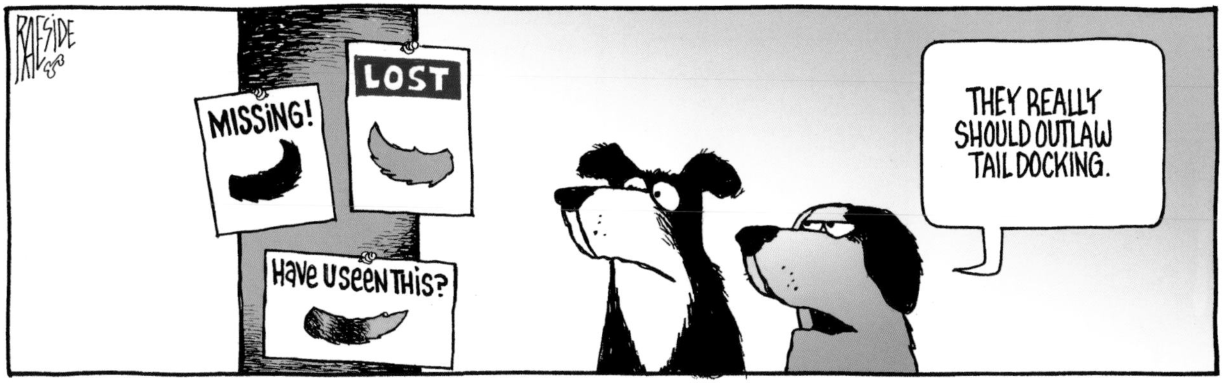
MISSING!
LOST
Have U seen THIS?
THEY REALLY SHOULD OUTLAW TAIL DOCKING.

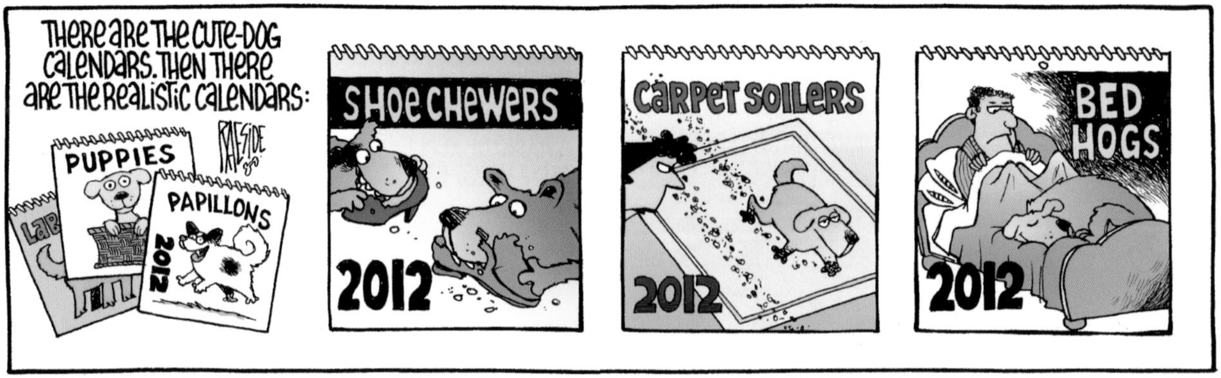
There are the cute-dog calendars. Then there are the realistic calendars:
PUPPIES
LAB
PAPILLONS
2012
SHOE CHEWERS
2012
CARPET SOILERS
2012
BED HOGS
2012

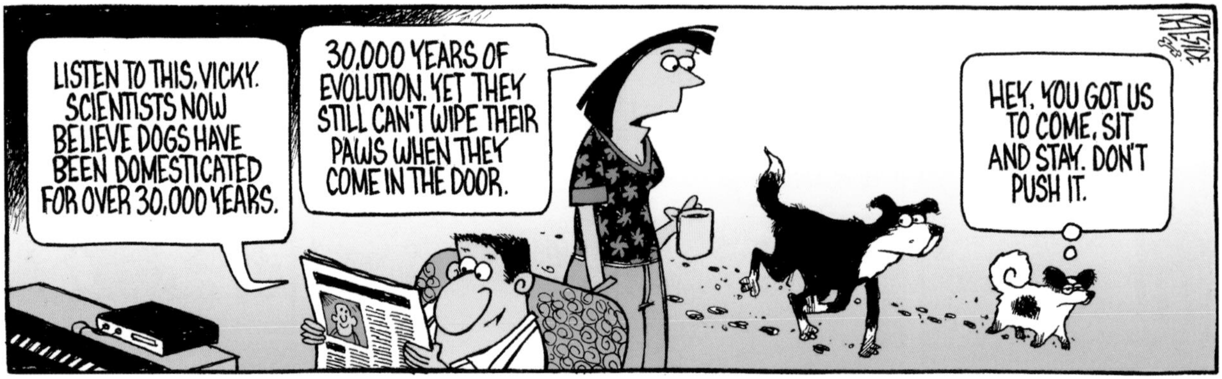
LISTEN TO THIS, VICKY. SCIENTISTS NOW BELIEVE DOGS HAVE BEEN DOMESTICATED FOR OVER 30,000 YEARS.
30,000 YEARS OF EVOLUTION. YET THEY STILL CAN'T WIPE THEIR PAWS WHEN THEY COME IN THE DOOR.
HEY, YOU GOT US TO COME, SIT AND STAY. DON'T PUSH IT.

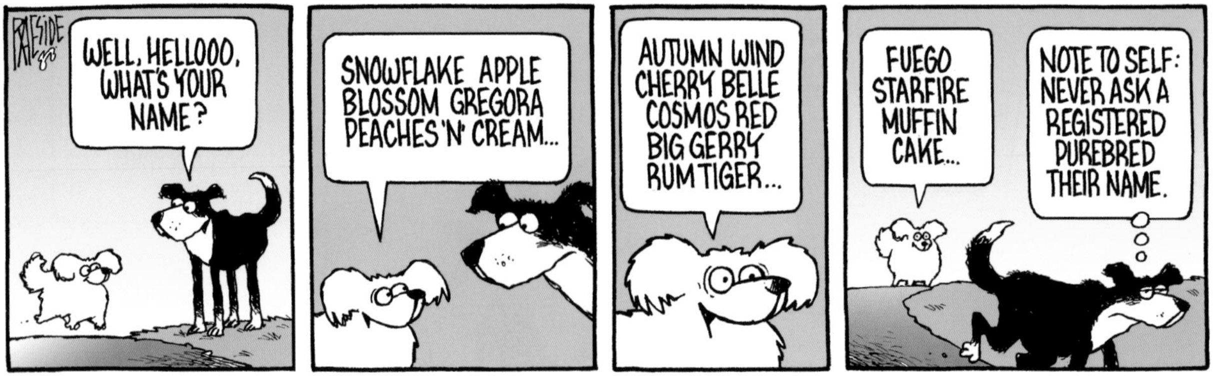
WELL, HELLOOO, WHAT'S YOUR NAME?
SNOWFLAKE APPLE BLOSSOM GREGORA PEACHES 'N' CREAM...
AUTUMN WIND CHERRY BELLE COSMOS RED BIG GERRY RUM TIGER...
FUEGO STARFIRE MUFFIN CAKE...
NOTE TO SELF: NEVER ASK A REGISTERED PUREBRED THEIR NAME.

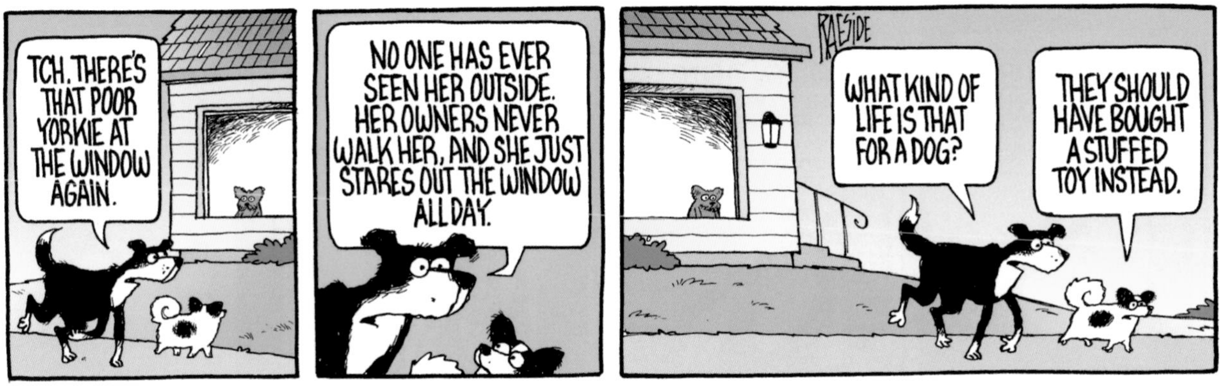
TCH. THERE'S THAT POOR YORKIE AT THE WINDOW AGAIN.
NO ONE HAS EVER SEEN HER OUTSIDE. HER OWNERS NEVER WALK HER, AND SHE JUST STARES OUT THE WINDOW ALL DAY.
RAESIDE
WHAT KIND OF LIFE IS THAT FOR A DOG?
THEY SHOULD HAVE BOUGHT A STUFFED TOY INSTEAD.

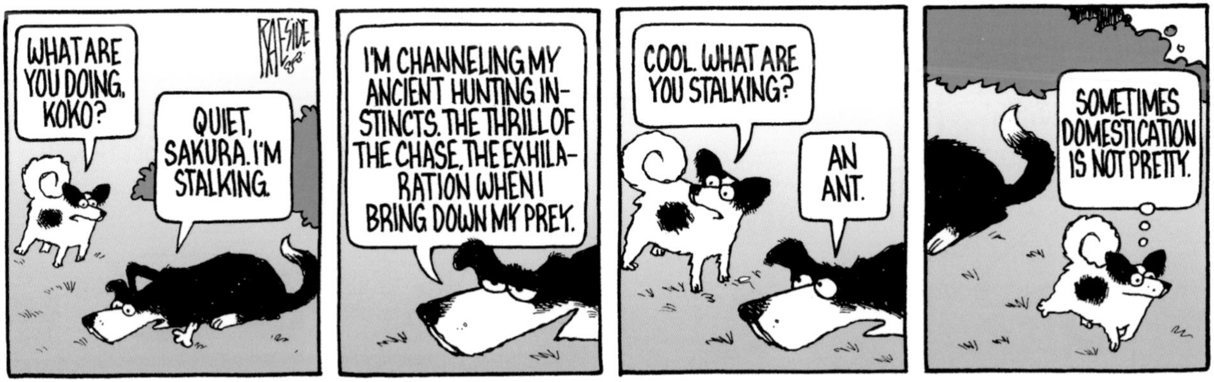
WHAT ARE YOU DOING, KOKO?
RAESIDE
QUIET, SAKURA. I'M STALKING.
I'M CHANNELING MY ANCIENT HUNTING IN-STINCTS. THE THRILL OF THE CHASE, THE EXHILA-RATION WHEN I BRING DOWN MY PREY.
COOL. WHAT ARE YOU STALKING?
AN ANT.
SOMETIMES DOMESTICATION IS NOT PRETTY.

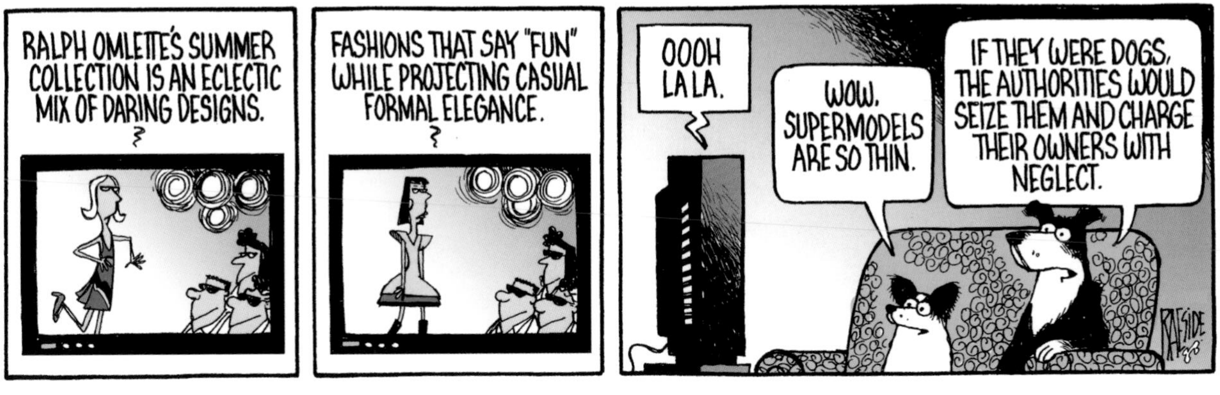
RALPH OMLETTE'S SUMMER COLLECTION IS AN ECLECTIC MIX OF DARING DESIGNS.
FASHIONS THAT SAY "FUN" WHILE PROJECTING CASUAL FORMAL ELEGANCE.
OOOH LA LA.
WOW, SUPERMODELS ARE SO THIN.
IF THEY WERE DOGS, THE AUTHORITIES WOULD SEIZE THEM AND CHARGE THEIR OWNERS WITH NEGLECT.
RAESIDE

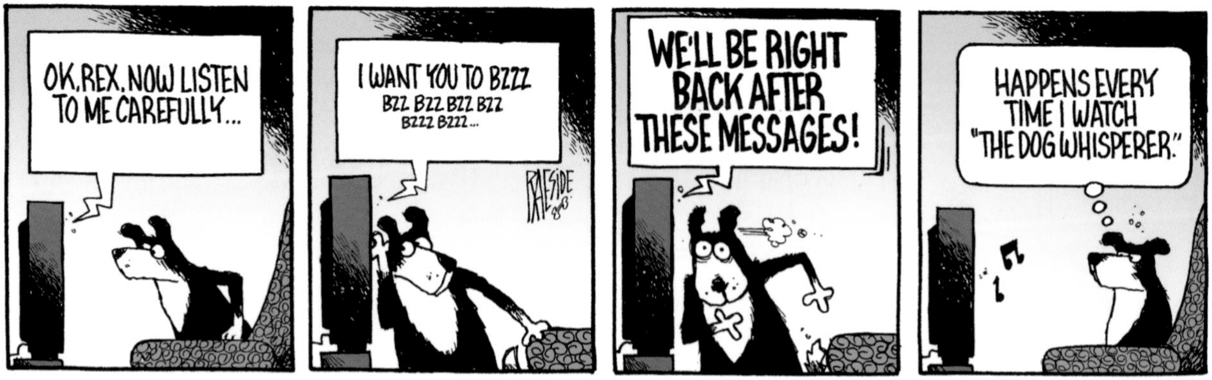
OK, REX, NOW LISTEN TO ME CAREFULLY...
I WANT YOU TO BZZZ BZZ BZZ BZZ BZZ BZZZ BZZZ...
WE'LL BE RIGHT BACK AFTER THESE MESSAGES!
HAPPENS EVERY TIME I WATCH "THE DOG WHISPERER."

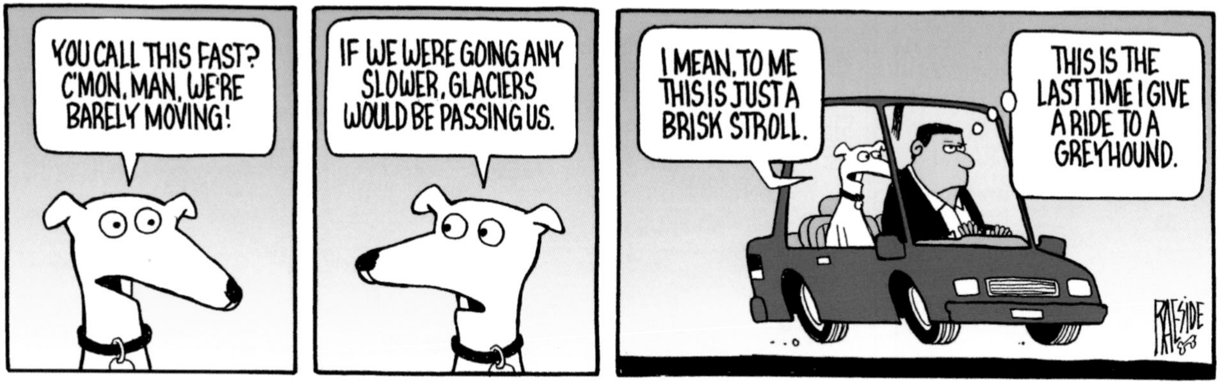
YOU CALL THIS FAST? C'MON, MAN, WE'RE BARELY MOVING!
IF WE WERE GOING ANY SLOWER, GLACIERS WOULD BE PASSING US.
I MEAN, TO ME THIS IS JUST A BRISK STROLL.
THIS IS THE LAST TIME I GIVE A RIDE TO A GREYHOUND.

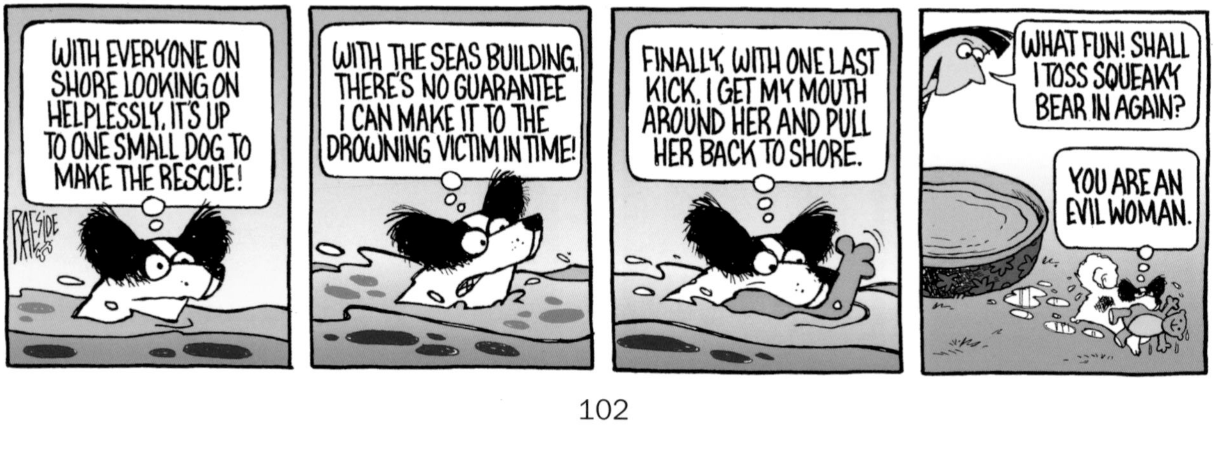
WITH EVERYONE ON SHORE LOOKING ON HELPLESSLY, IT'S UP TO ONE SMALL DOG TO MAKE THE RESCUE!
WITH THE SEAS BUILDING, THERE'S NO GUARANTEE I CAN MAKE IT TO THE DROWNING VICTIM IN TIME!
FINALLY, WITH ONE LAST KICK, I GET MY MOUTH AROUND HER AND PULL HER BACK TO SHORE.
WHAT FUN! SHALL I TOSS SQUEAKY BEAR IN AGAIN?
YOU ARE AN EVIL WOMAN.

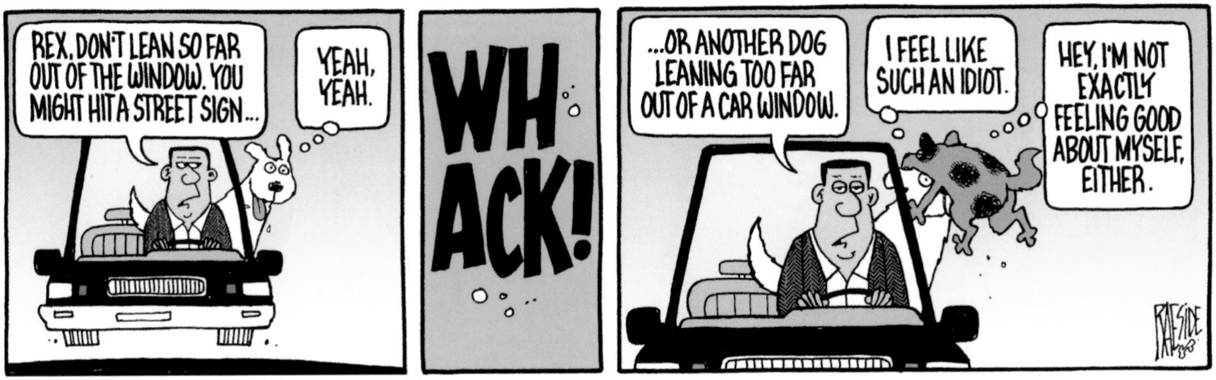
REX, DON'T LEAN SO FAR OUT OF THE WINDOW. YOU MIGHT HIT A STREET SIGN...
YEAH, YEAH.
WHACK!
...OR ANOTHER DOG LEANING TOO FAR OUT OF A CAR WINDOW.
I FEEL LIKE SUCH AN IDIOT.
HEY, I'M NOT EXACTLY FEELING GOOD ABOUT MYSELF, EITHER.
RAESIDE

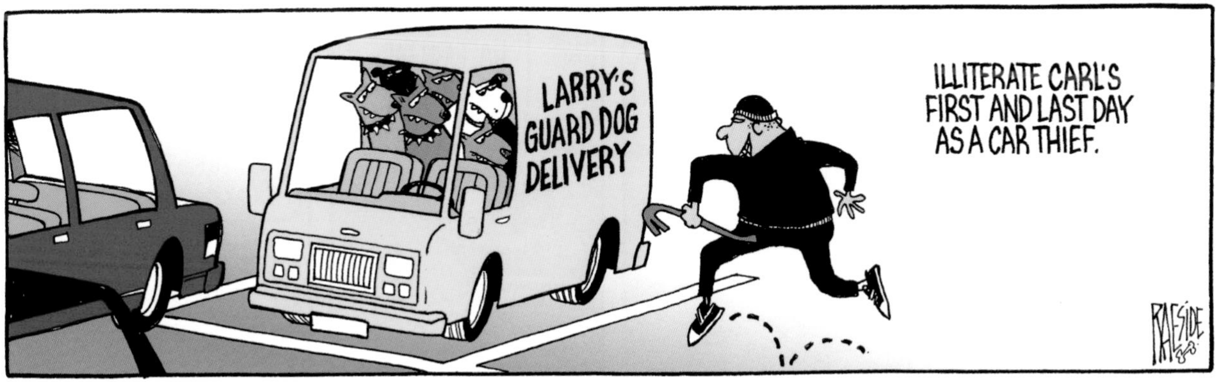
LARRY'S GUARD DOG DELIVERY
ILLITERATE CARL'S FIRST AND LAST DAY AS A CAR THIEF.
RAESIDE

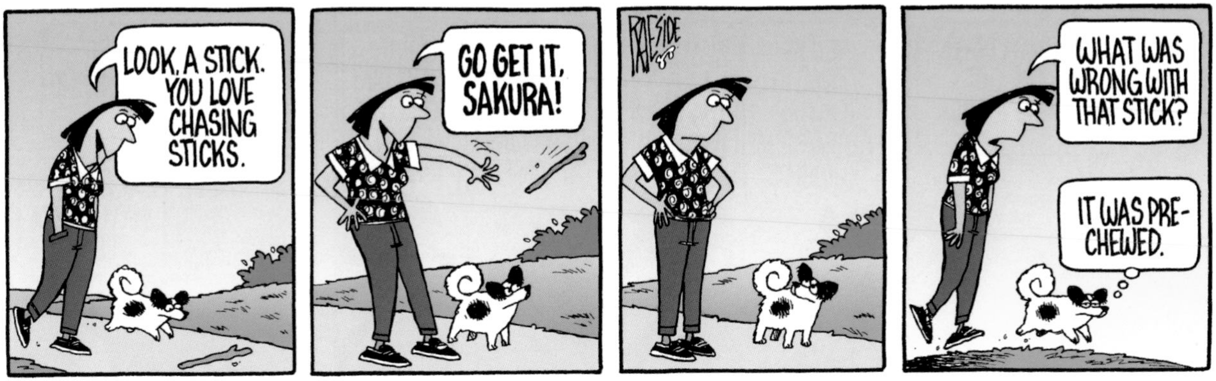
LOOK, A STICK. YOU LOVE CHASING STICKS.
GO GET IT, SAKURA!
RAESIDE
WHAT WAS WRONG WITH THAT STICK?
IT WAS PRE-CHEWED.

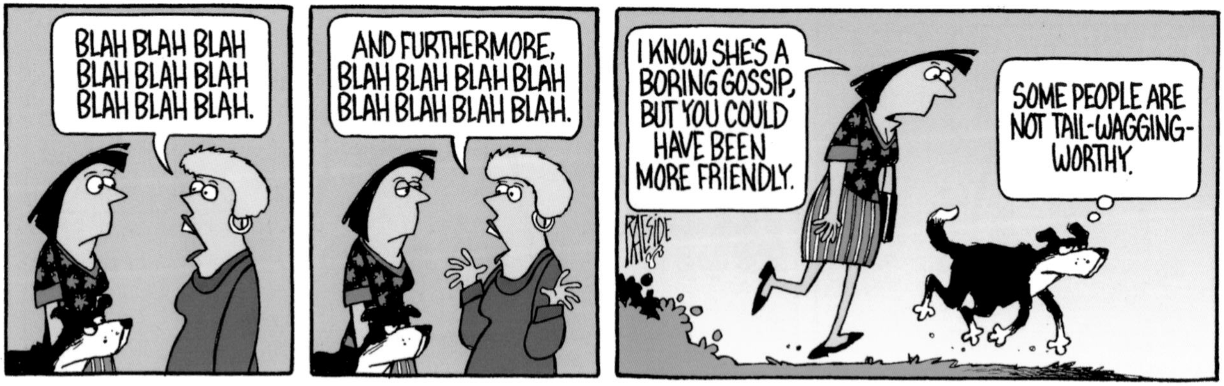
BLAH BLAH BLAH BLAH BLAH BLAH BLAH BLAH BLAH.
AND FURTHERMORE, BLAH BLAH BLAH BLAH BLAH BLAH BLAH BLAH.
I KNOW SHE'S A BORING GOSSIP, BUT YOU COULD HAVE BEEN MORE FRIENDLY.
SOME PEOPLE ARE NOT TAIL-WAGGING-WORTHY.

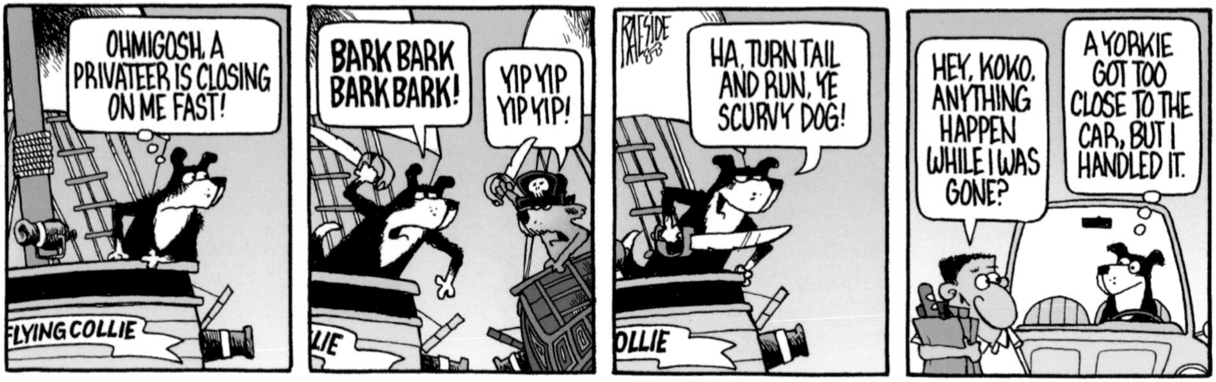
OHMIGOSH, A PRIVATEER IS CLOSING ON ME FAST!
FLYING COLLIE
BARK BARK BARK BARK!
YIP YIP YIP YIP!
HA, TURN TAIL AND RUN, YE SCURVY DOG!
HEY, KOKO, ANYTHING HAPPEN WHILE I WAS GONE?
A YORKIE GOT TOO CLOSE TO THE CAR, BUT I HANDLED IT.

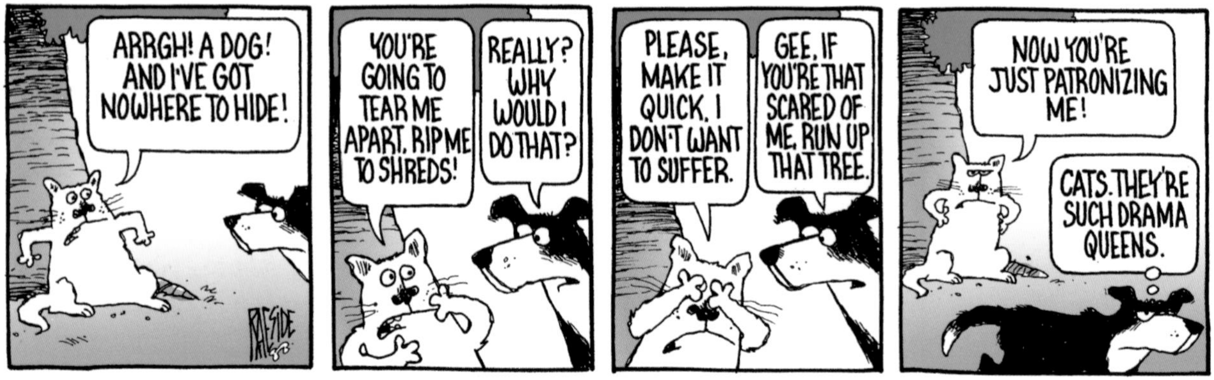
ARRGH! A DOG! AND I'VE GOT NOWHERE TO HIDE!
YOU'RE GOING TO TEAR ME APART, RIP ME TO SHREDS!
REALLY? WHY WOULD I DO THAT?
PLEASE, MAKE IT QUICK. I DON'T WANT TO SUFFER.
GEE, IF YOU'RE THAT SCARED OF ME, RUN UP THAT TREE.
NOW YOU'RE JUST PATRONIZING ME!
CATS. THEY'RE SUCH DRAMA QUEENS.

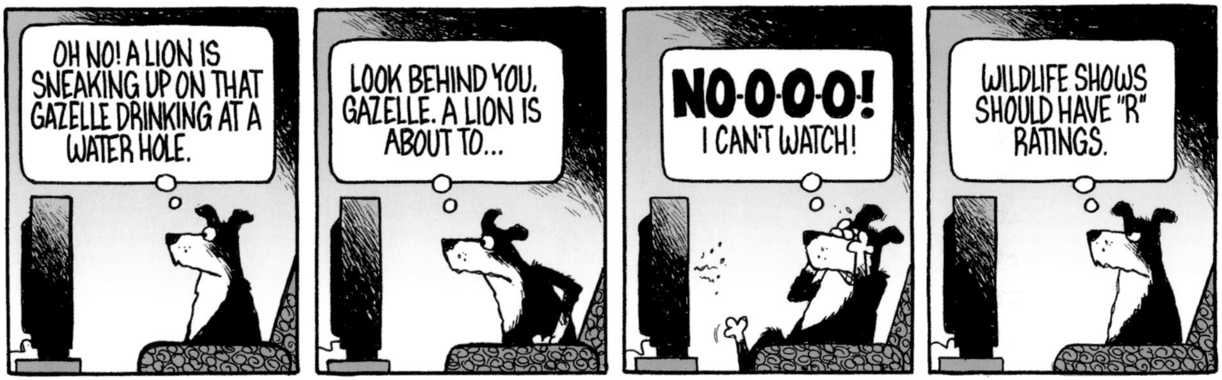
OH NO! A LION IS SNEAKING UP ON THAT GAZELLE DRINKING AT A WATER HOLE.
LOOK BEHIND YOU, GAZELLE. A LION IS ABOUT TO...
NO-O-O-O! I CAN'T WATCH!
WILDLIFE SHOWS SHOULD HAVE "R" RATINGS.

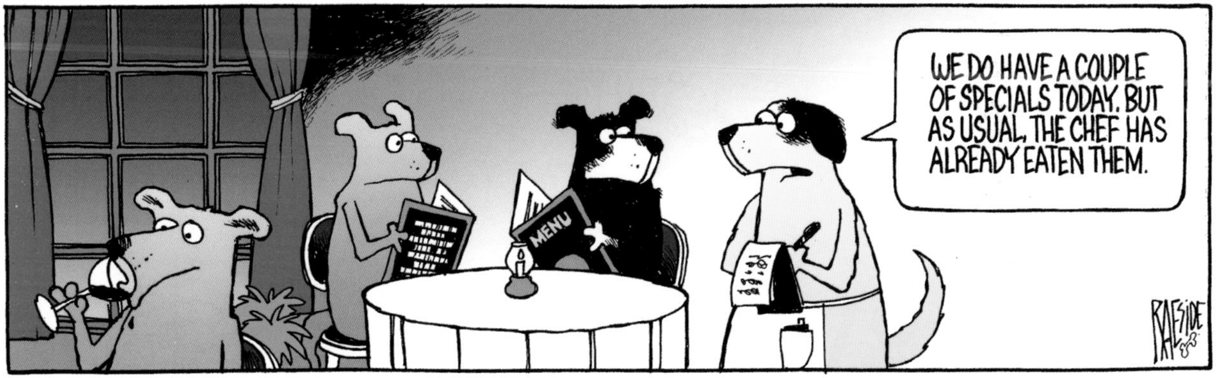
MENU
WE DO HAVE A COUPLE OF SPECIALS TODAY, BUT AS USUAL, THE CHEF HAS ALREADY EATEN THEM.
RAESIDE

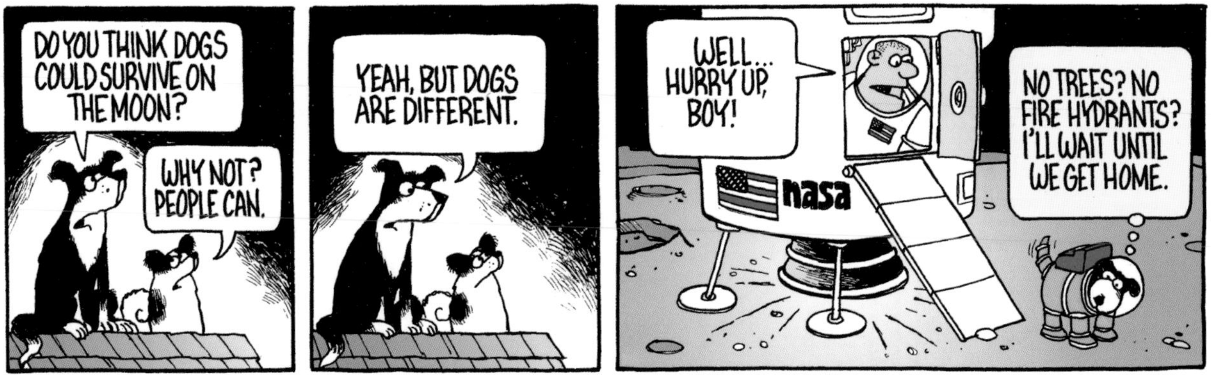
DO YOU THINK DOGS COULD SURVIVE ON THE MOON?
WHY NOT? PEOPLE CAN.
YEAH, BUT DOGS ARE DIFFERENT.
WELL... HURRY UP, BOY!
nasa
NO TREES? NO FIRE HYDRANTS? I'LL WAIT UNTIL WE GET HOME.

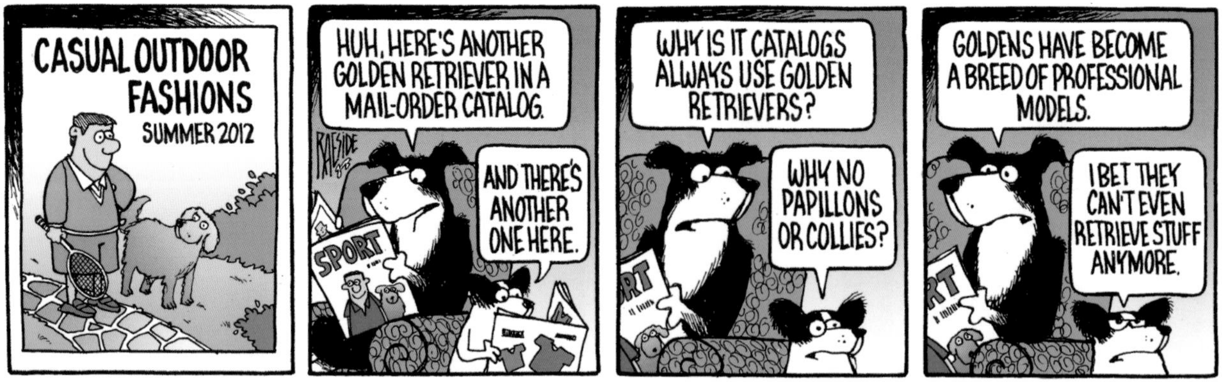
CASUAL OUTDOOR FASHIONS
SUMMER 2012
HUH, HERE'S ANOTHER GOLDEN RETRIEVER IN A MAIL-ORDER CATALOG.
AND THERE'S ANOTHER ONE HERE.
SPORT
RAESIDE
WHY IS IT CATALOGS ALWAYS USE GOLDEN RETRIEVERS?
WHY NO PAPILLONS OR COLLIES?
GOLDENS HAVE BECOME A BREED OF PROFESSIONAL MODELS.
I BET THEY CAN'T EVEN RETRIEVE STUFF ANYMORE.

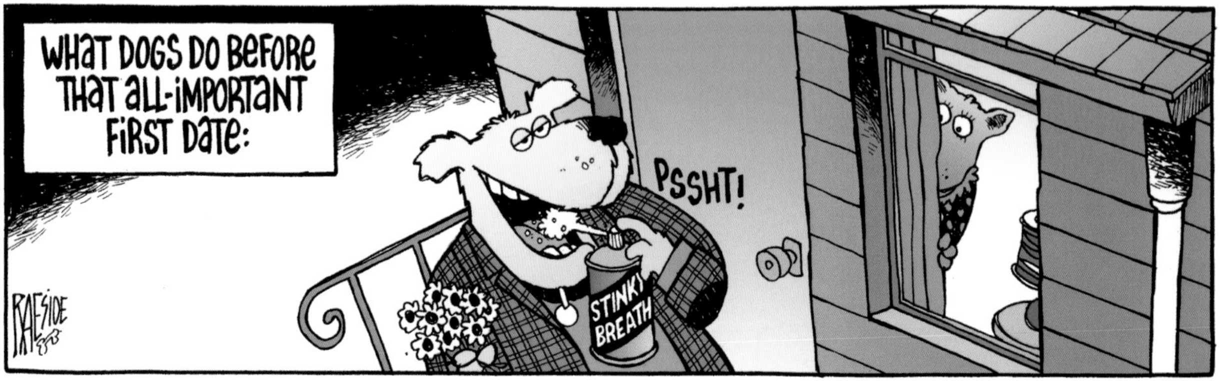
WHAT DOGS DO BEFORE THAT ALL-IMPORTANT FIRST DATE:
PSSHT!
STINKY BREATH
RAESIDE

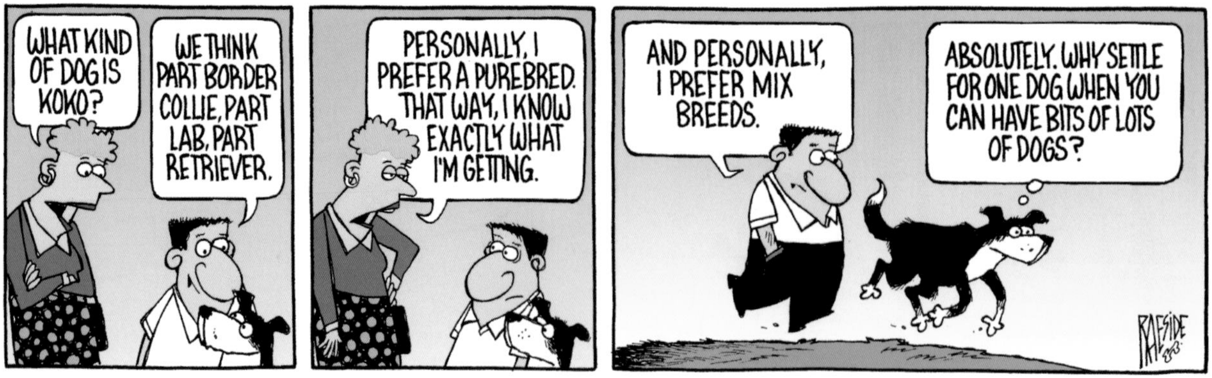
WHAT KIND OF DOG IS KOKO?
WE THINK PART BORDER COLLIE, PART LAB, PART RETRIEVER.
PERSONALLY, I PREFER A PUREBRED. THAT WAY, I KNOW EXACTLY WHAT I'M GETTING.
AND PERSONALLY, I PREFER MIX BREEDS.
ABSOLUTELY. WHY SETTLE FOR ONE DOG WHEN YOU CAN HAVE BITS OF LOTS OF DOGS?
RAESIDE

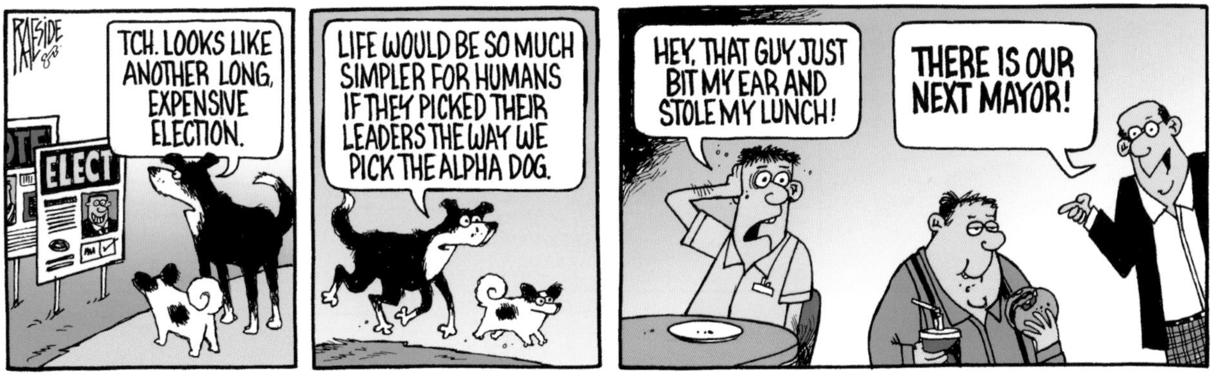

TCH. LOOKS LIKE ANOTHER LONG, EXPENSIVE ELECTION.
ELECT
LIFE WOULD BE SO MUCH SIMPLER FOR HUMANS IF THEY PICKED THEIR LEADERS THE WAY WE PICK THE ALPHA DOG.
HEY, THAT GUY JUST BIT MY EAR AND STOLE MY LUNCH!
THERE IS OUR NEXT MAYOR!

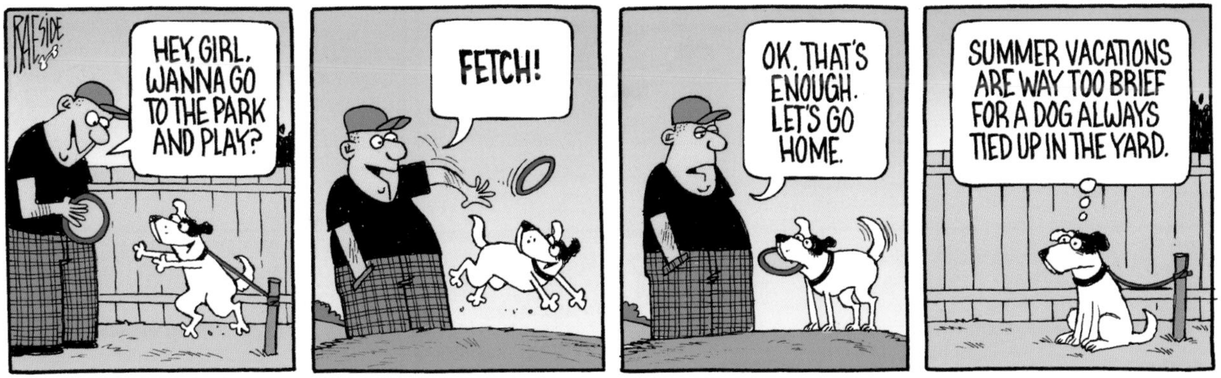

HEY, GIRL, WANNA GO TO THE PARK AND PLAY?
FETCH!
OK, THAT'S ENOUGH. LET'S GO HOME.
SUMMER VACATIONS ARE WAY TOO BRIEF FOR A DOG ALWAYS TIED UP IN THE YARD.

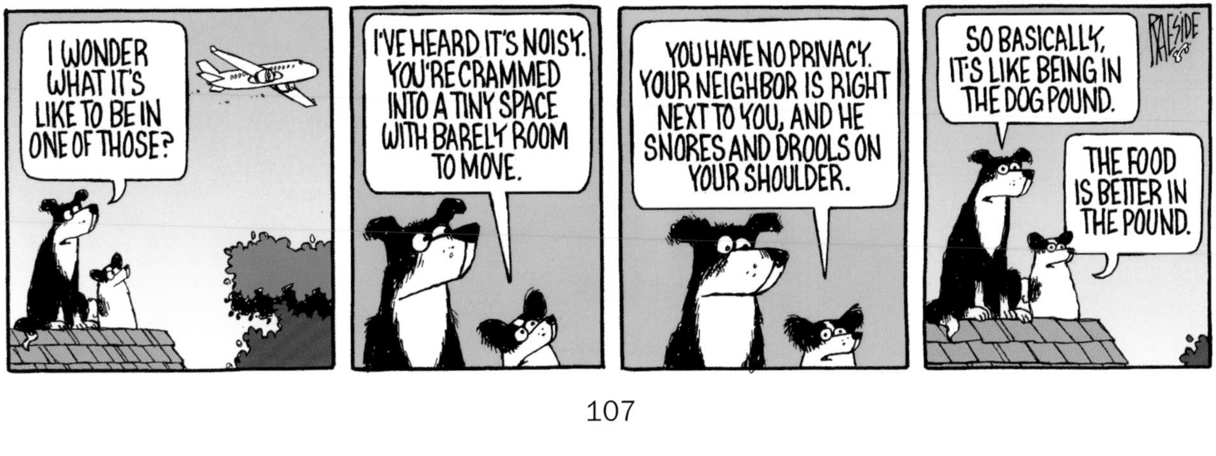

I WONDER WHAT IT'S LIKE TO BE IN ONE OF THOSE?
I'VE HEARD IT'S NOISY. YOU'RE CRAMMED INTO A TINY SPACE WITH BARELY ROOM TO MOVE.
YOU HAVE NO PRIVACY. YOUR NEIGHBOR IS RIGHT NEXT TO YOU, AND HE SNORES AND DROOLS ON YOUR SHOULDER.
SO BASICALLY, IT'S LIKE BEING IN THE DOG POUND.
THE FOOD IS BETTER IN THE POUND.

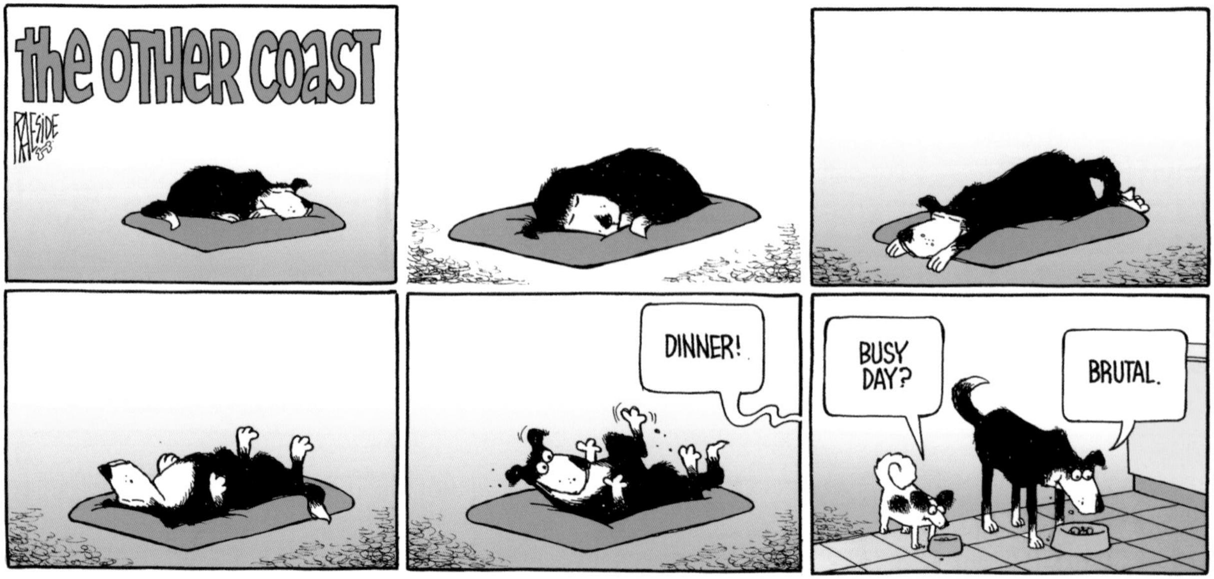
the OTHER COAST
DINNER!
BUSY DAY?
BRUTAL.

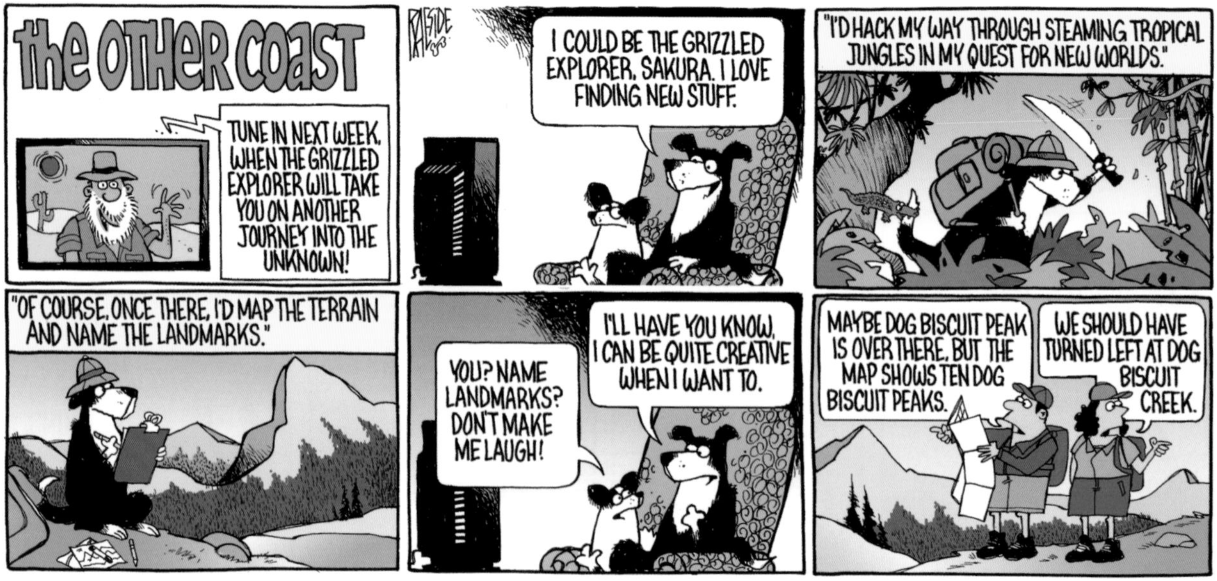
the OTHER COAST
TUNE IN NEXT WEEK, WHEN THE GRIZZLED EXPLORER WILL TAKE YOU ON ANOTHER JOURNEY INTO THE UNKNOWN!
I COULD BE THE GRIZZLED EXPLORER, SAKURA. I LOVE FINDING NEW STUFF.
"I'D HACK MY WAY THROUGH STEAMING TROPICAL JUNGLES IN MY QUEST FOR NEW WORLDS."
"OF COURSE, ONCE THERE, I'D MAP THE TERRAIN AND NAME THE LANDMARKS."
YOU? NAME LANDMARKS? DON'T MAKE ME LAUGH!
I'LL HAVE YOU KNOW, I CAN BE QUITE CREATIVE WHEN I WANT TO.
MAYBE DOG BISCUIT PEAK IS OVER THERE, BUT THE MAP SHOWS TEN DOG BISCUIT PEAKS.
WE SHOULD HAVE TURNED LEFT AT DOG BISCUIT CREEK.

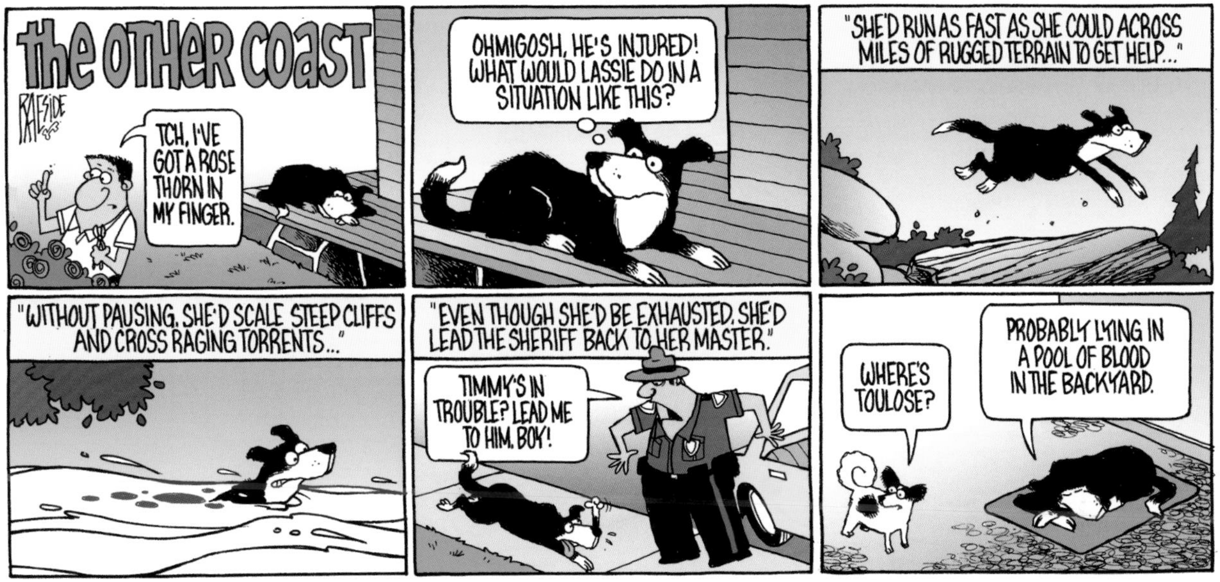
the OTHER COAST
RAESIDE
TCH, I'VE GOT A ROSE THORN IN MY FINGER.
OHMIGOSH, HE'S INJURED! WHAT WOULD LASSIE DO IN A SITUATION LIKE THIS?
"SHE'D RUN AS FAST AS SHE COULD ACROSS MILES OF RUGGED TERRAIN TO GET HELP..."
"WITHOUT PAUSING, SHE'D SCALE STEEP CLIFFS AND CROSS RAGING TORRENTS..."
"EVEN THOUGH SHE'D BE EXHAUSTED, SHE'D LEAD THE SHERIFF BACK TO HER MASTER."
TIMMY'S IN TROUBLE? LEAD ME TO HIM, BOY!
WHERE'S TOULOSE?
PROBABLY LYING IN A POOL OF BLOOD IN THE BACKYARD.

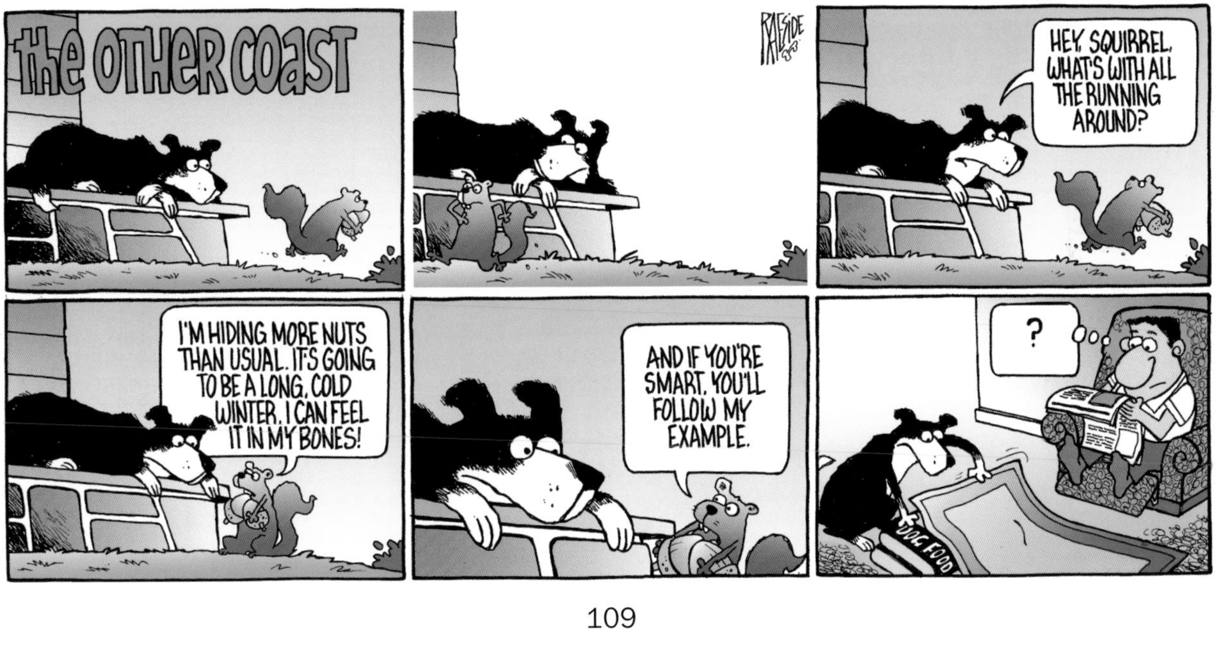
the OTHER COAST
RAESIDE
HEY, SQUIRREL, WHAT'S WITH ALL THE RUNNING AROUND?
I'M HIDING MORE NUTS THAN USUAL. IT'S GOING TO BE A LONG, COLD WINTER. I CAN FEEL IT IN MY BONES!
AND IF YOU'RE SMART, YOU'LL FOLLOW MY EXAMPLE.
?
DOG FOOD

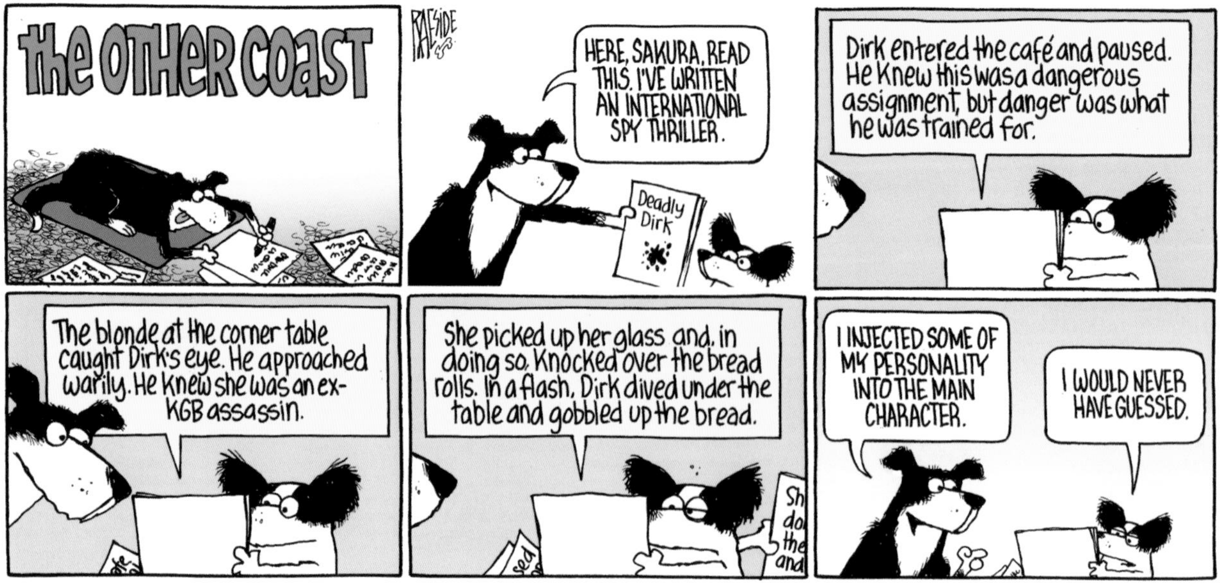
the OTHER COAST
RAESIDE
HERE, SAKURA, READ THIS. I'VE WRITTEN AN INTERNATIONAL SPY THRILLER.
Deadly Dirk
Dirk entered the café and paused. He knew this was a dangerous assignment, but danger was what he was trained for.
The blonde at the corner table caught Dirk's eye. He approached warily. He knew she was an ex-KGB assassin.
She picked up her glass and, in doing so, knocked over the bread rolls. In a flash, Dirk dived under the table and gobbled up the bread.
I INJECTED SOME OF MY PERSONALITY INTO THE MAIN CHARACTER.
I WOULD NEVER HAVE GUESSED.

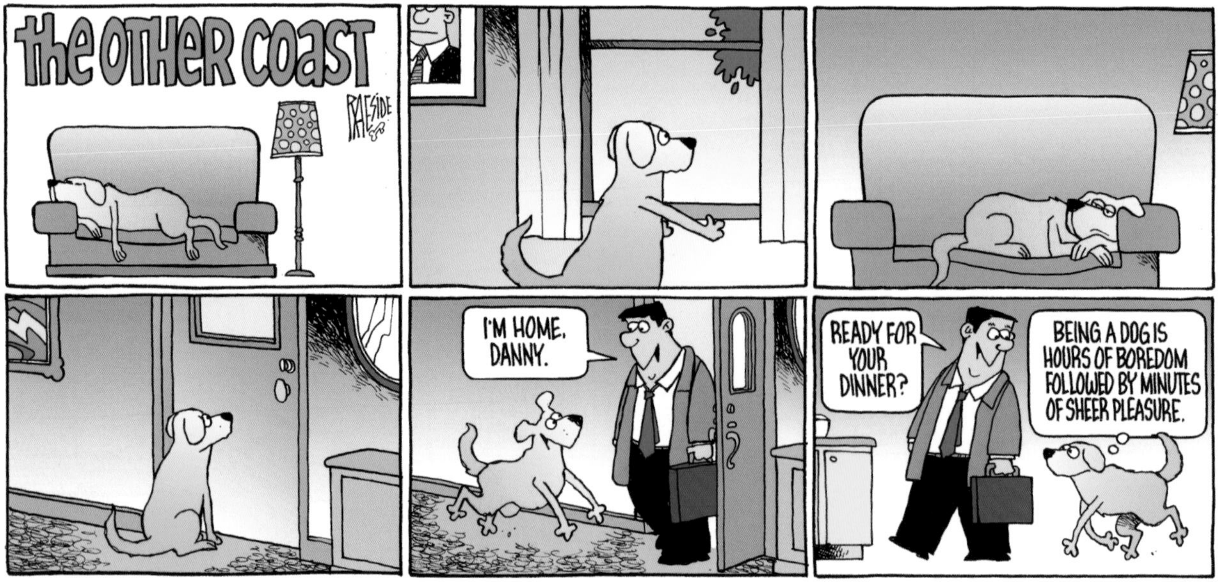
the OTHER COAST
RAESIDE
I'M HOME, DANNY.
READY FOR YOUR DINNER?
BEING A DOG IS HOURS OF BOREDOM FOLLOWED BY MINUTES OF SHEER PLEASURE.

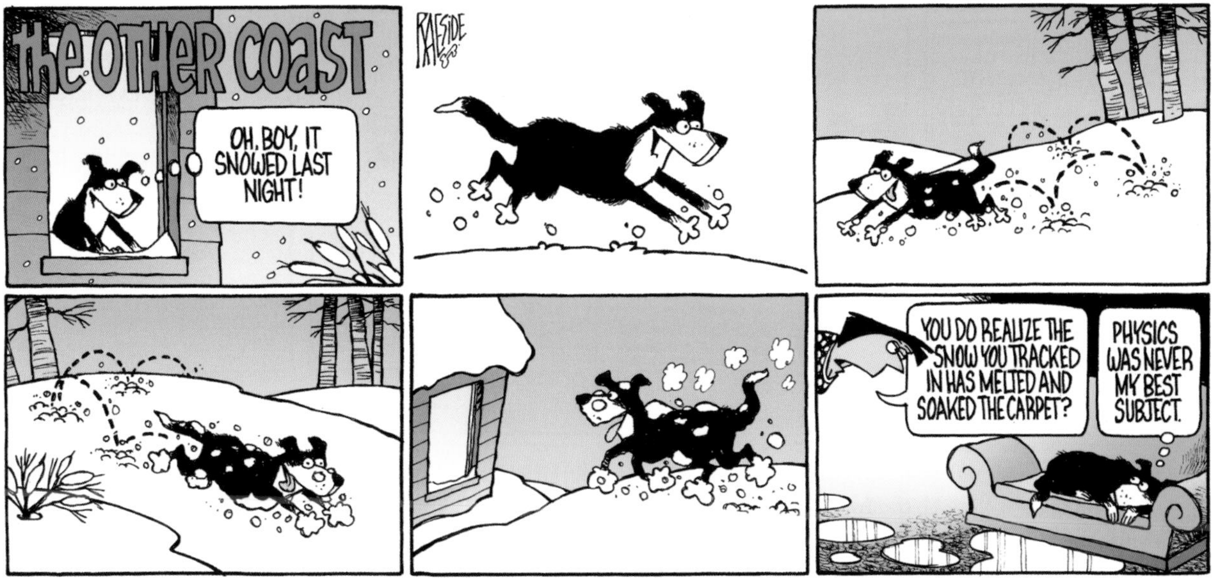
the OTHER COAST
RAESIDE
OH, BOY, IT SNOWED LAST NIGHT!
YOU DO REALIZE THE SNOW YOU TRACKED IN HAS MELTED AND SOAKED THE CARPET?
PHYSICS WAS NEVER MY BEST SUBJECT.

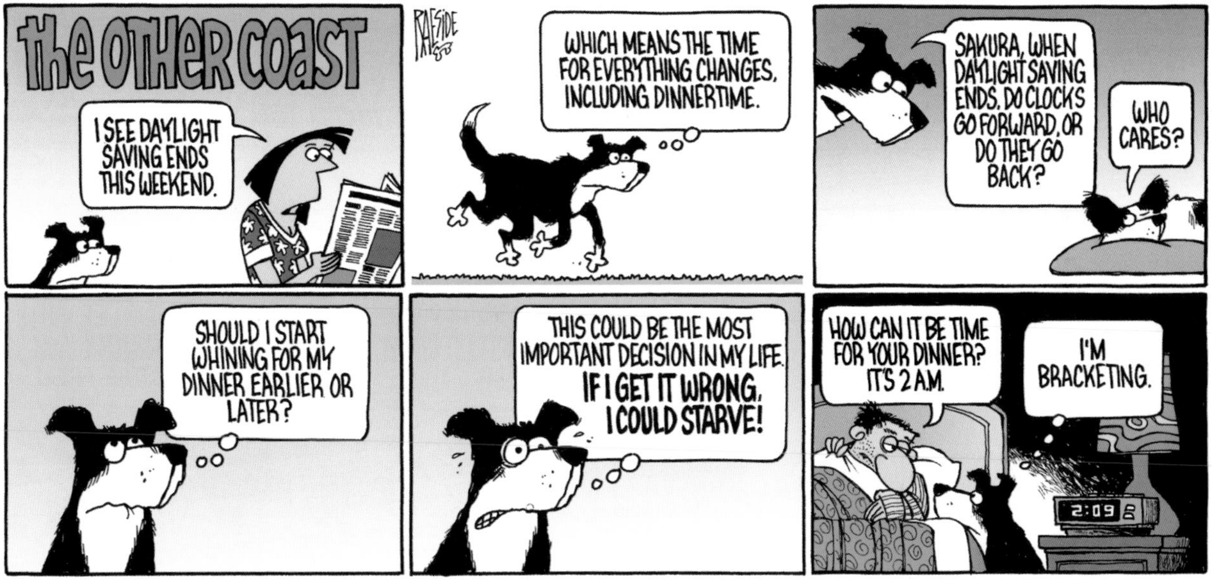
the OTHER COAST
RAESIDE
I SEE DAYLIGHT SAVING ENDS THIS WEEKEND.
WHICH MEANS THE TIME FOR EVERYTHING CHANGES, INCLUDING DINNERTIME.
SAKURA, WHEN DAYLIGHT SAVING ENDS, DO CLOCKS GO FORWARD, OR DO THEY GO BACK?
WHO CARES?
SHOULD I START WHINING FOR MY DINNER EARLIER OR LATER?
THIS COULD BE THE MOST IMPORTANT DECISION IN MY LIFE.
IF I GET IT WRONG, I COULD STARVE!
HOW CAN IT BE TIME FOR YOUR DINNER? IT'S 2 A.M.
I'M BRACKETING.
2:09

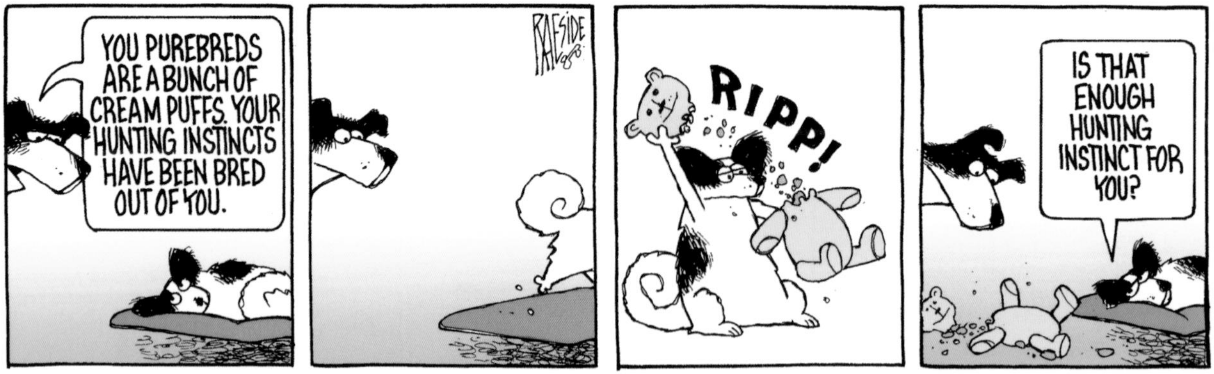
YOU PUREBREDS ARE A BUNCH OF CREAM PUFFS. YOUR HUNTING INSTINCTS HAVE BEEN BRED OUT OF YOU.
RIPP!
IS THAT ENOUGH HUNTING INSTINCT FOR YOU?

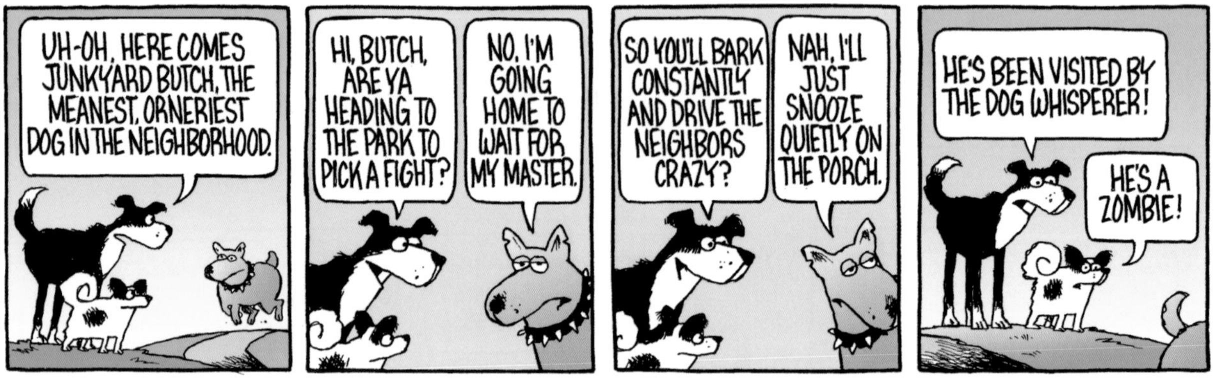
UH-OH, HERE COMES JUNKYARD BUTCH, THE MEANEST, ORNERIEST DOG IN THE NEIGHBORHOOD.
HI, BUTCH, ARE YA HEADING TO THE PARK TO PICK A FIGHT?
NO. I'M GOING HOME TO WAIT FOR MY MASTER.
SO YOU'LL BARK CONSTANTLY AND DRIVE THE NEIGHBORS CRAZY?
NAH, I'LL JUST SNOOZE QUIETLY ON THE PORCH.
HE'S BEEN VISITED BY THE DOG WHISPERER!
HE'S A ZOMBIE!

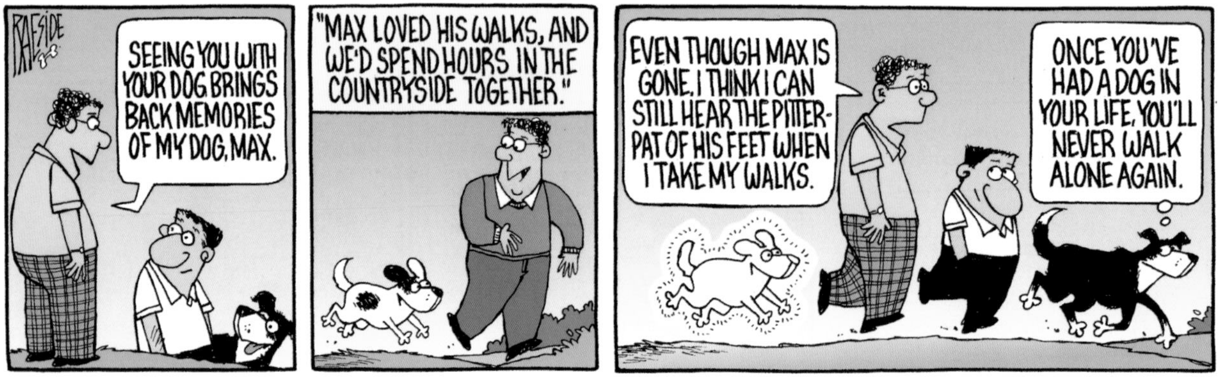
SEEING YOU WITH YOUR DOG BRINGS BACK MEMORIES OF MY DOG, MAX.
"MAX LOVED HIS WALKS, AND WE'D SPEND HOURS IN THE COUNTRYSIDE TOGETHER."
EVEN THOUGH MAX IS GONE, I THINK I CAN STILL HEAR THE PITTER-PAT OF HIS FEET WHEN I TAKE MY WALKS.
ONCE YOU'VE HAD A DOG IN YOUR LIFE, YOU'LL NEVER WALK ALONE AGAIN.

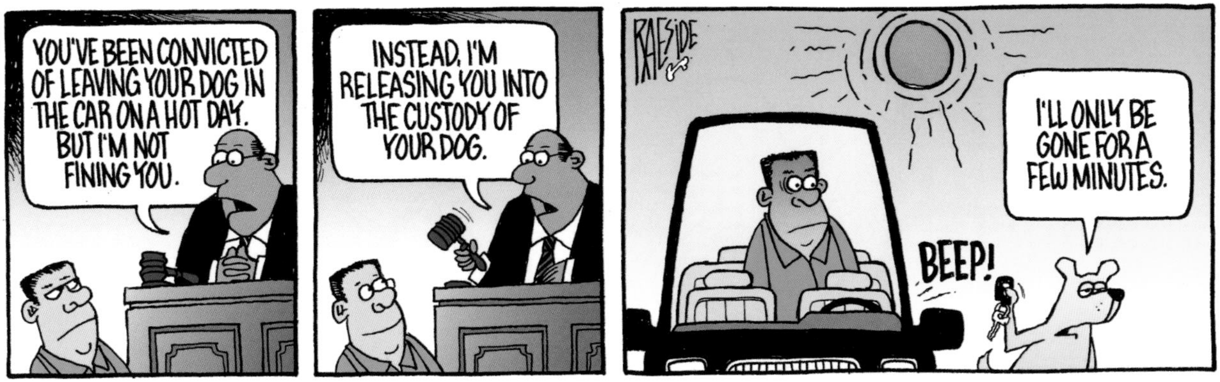
YOU'VE BEEN CONVICTED OF LEAVING YOUR DOG IN THE CAR ON A HOT DAY. BUT I'M NOT FINING YOU.
INSTEAD, I'M RELEASING YOU INTO THE CUSTODY OF YOUR DOG.
RAESIDE
I'LL ONLY BE GONE FOR A FEW MINUTES.
BEEP!

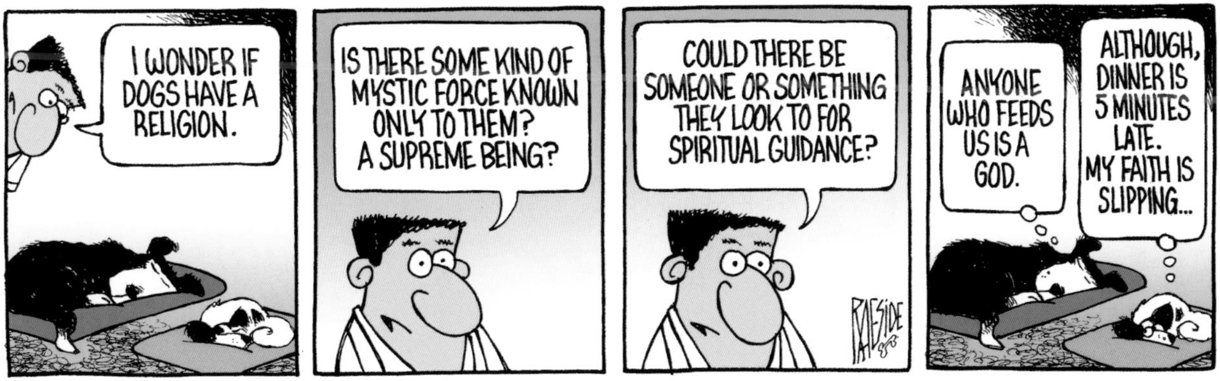
I WONDER IF DOGS HAVE A RELIGION.
IS THERE SOME KIND OF MYSTIC FORCE KNOWN ONLY TO THEM? A SUPREME BEING?
COULD THERE BE SOMEONE OR SOMETHING THEY LOOK TO FOR SPIRITUAL GUIDANCE?
RAESIDE
ANYONE WHO FEEDS US IS A GOD.
ALTHOUGH, DINNER IS 5 MINUTES LATE. MY FAITH IS SLIPPING...

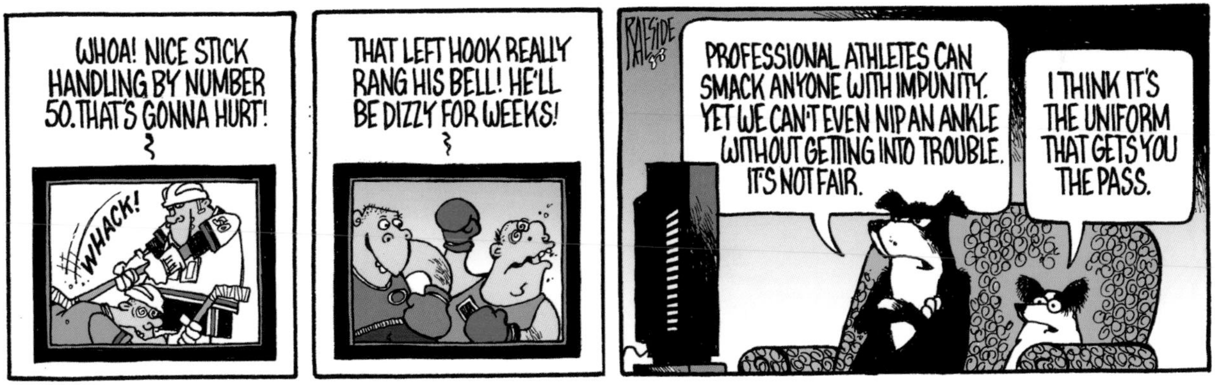
WHOA! NICE STICK HANDLING BY NUMBER 50. THAT'S GONNA HURT!
WHACK!
THAT LEFT HOOK REALLY RANG HIS BELL! HE'LL BE DIZZY FOR WEEKS!
RAESIDE
PROFESSIONAL ATHLETES CAN SMACK ANYONE WITH IMPUNITY. YET WE CAN'T EVEN NIP AN ANKLE WITHOUT GETTING INTO TROUBLE. IT'S NOT FAIR.
I THINK IT'S THE UNIFORM THAT GETS YOU THE PASS.

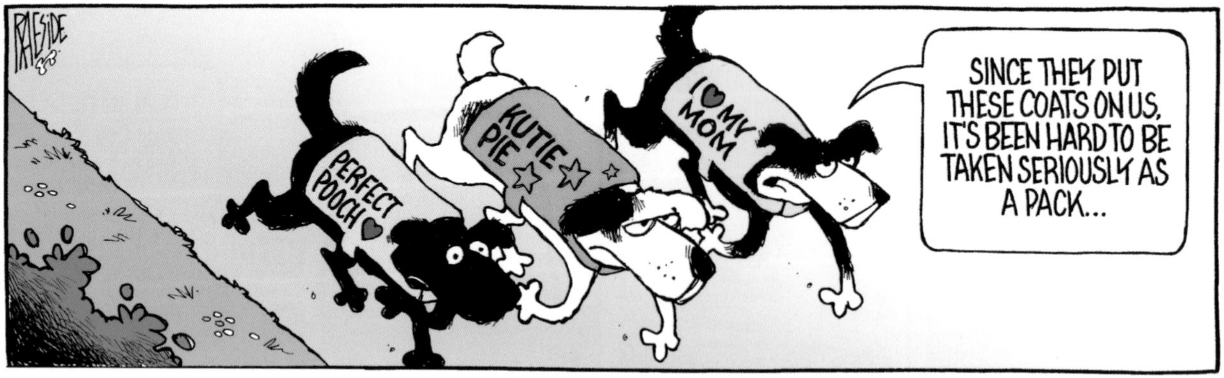
RAESIDE
PERFECT POOCH
KUTIE PIE
I ♥ MY MOM
SINCE THEY PUT THESE COATS ON US, IT'S BEEN HARD TO BE TAKEN SERIOUSLY AS A PACK...

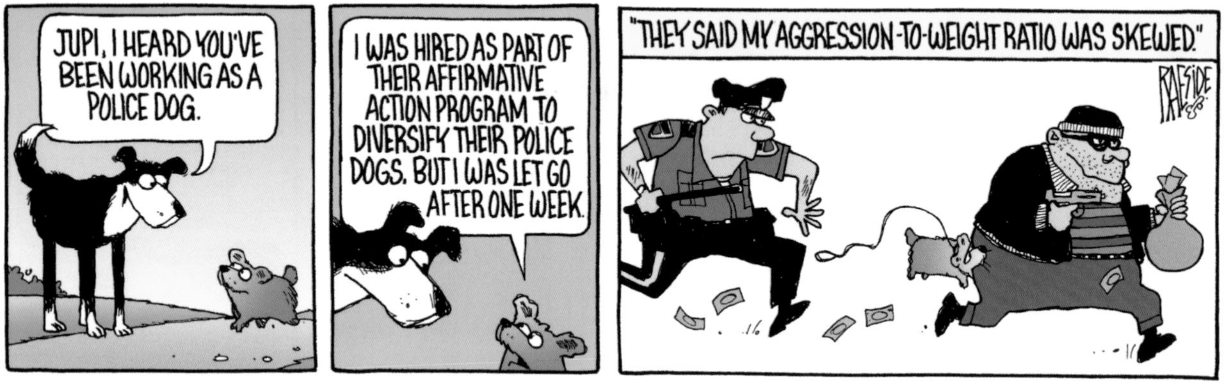
JUPI, I HEARD YOU'VE BEEN WORKING AS A POLICE DOG.
I WAS HIRED AS PART OF THEIR AFFIRMATIVE ACTION PROGRAM TO DIVERSIFY THEIR POLICE DOGS. BUT I WAS LET GO AFTER ONE WEEK.
"THEY SAID MY AGGRESSION-TO-WEIGHT RATIO WAS SKEWED."
RAESIDE

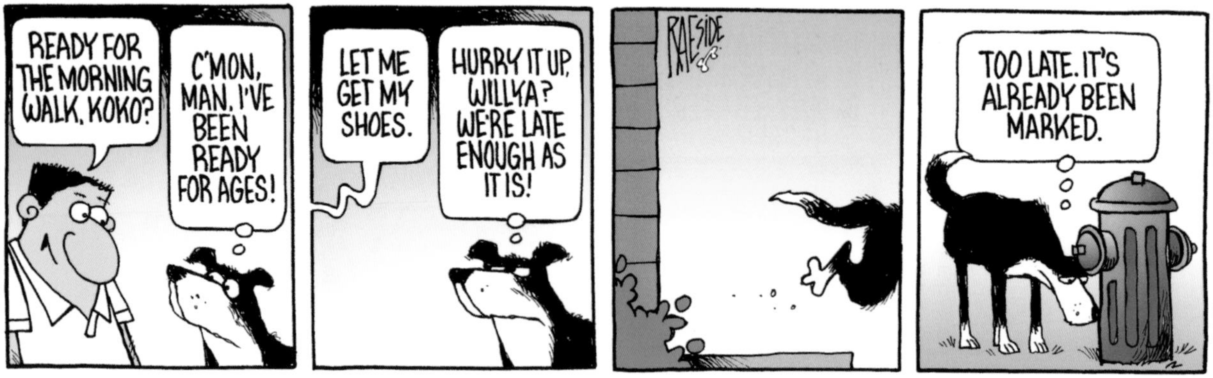
READY FOR THE MORNING WALK, KOKO?
C'MON, MAN, I'VE BEEN READY FOR AGES!
LET ME GET MY SHOES.
HURRY IT UP, WILLYA? WE'RE LATE ENOUGH AS IT IS!
RAESIDE
TOO LATE. IT'S ALREADY BEEN MARKED.

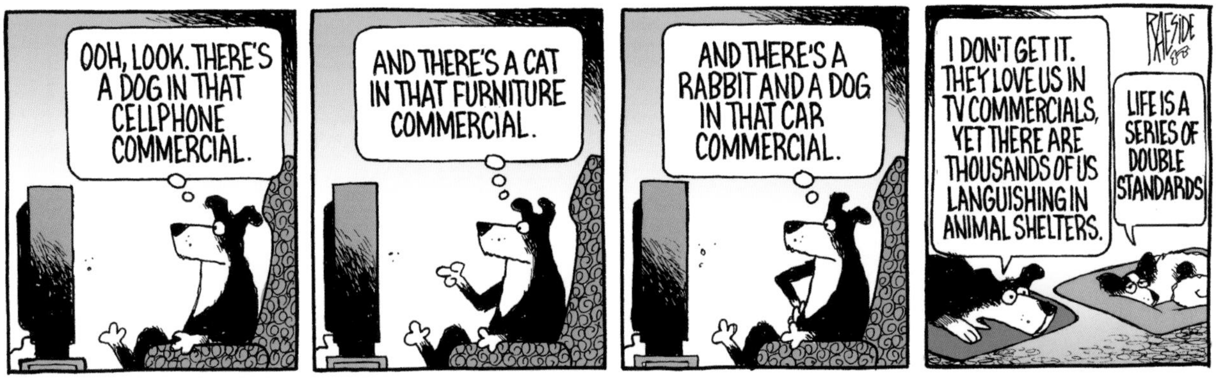
OOH, LOOK. THERE'S A DOG IN THAT CELLPHONE COMMERCIAL.
AND THERE'S A CAT IN THAT FURNITURE COMMERCIAL.
AND THERE'S A RABBIT AND A DOG IN THAT CAR COMMERCIAL.
I DON'T GET IT. THEY LOVE US IN TV COMMERCIALS, YET THERE ARE THOUSANDS OF US LANGUISHING IN ANIMAL SHELTERS.
LIFE IS A SERIES OF DOUBLE STANDARDS

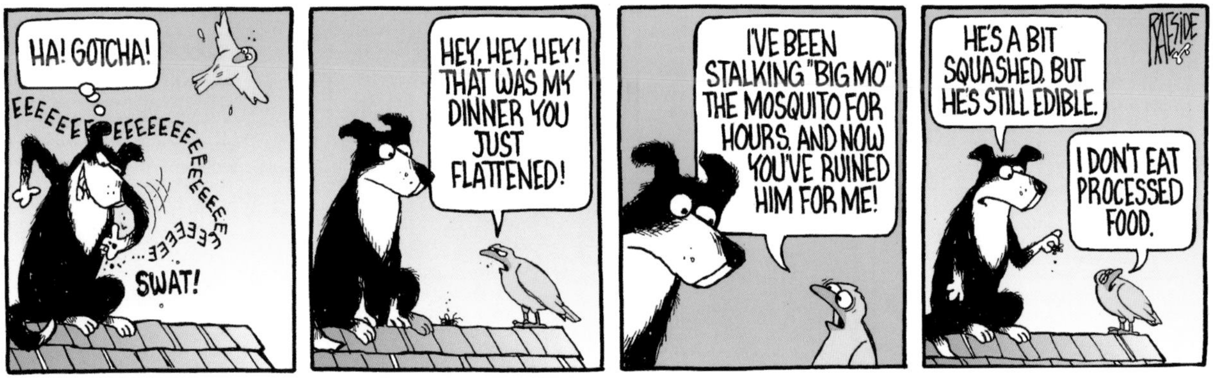
HA! GOTCHA!
EEEEEEEEEEEEEEEEEEEEEEEEEEEEEEE
SWAT!
HEY, HEY, HEY! THAT WAS MY DINNER YOU JUST FLATTENED!
I'VE BEEN STALKING "BIG MO" THE MOSQUITO FOR HOURS, AND NOW YOU'VE RUINED HIM FOR ME!
HE'S A BIT SQUASHED, BUT HE'S STILL EDIBLE.
I DON'T EAT PROCESSED FOOD.

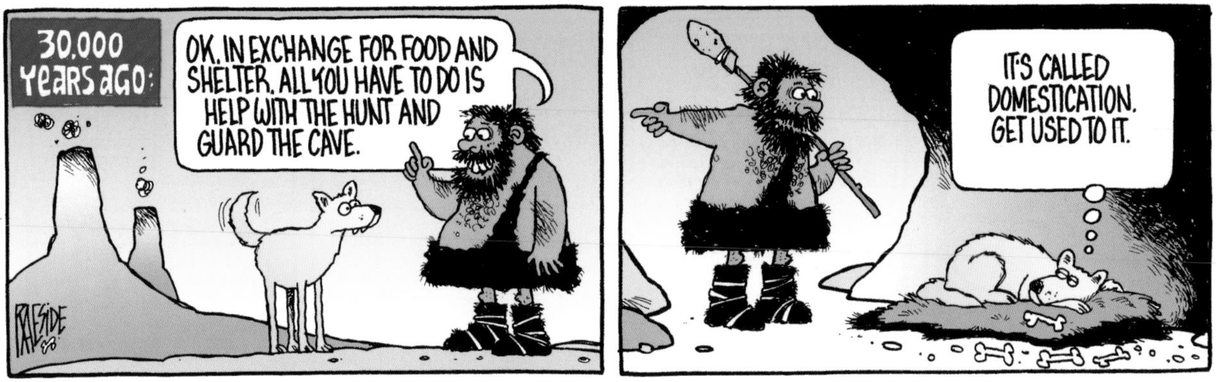
30,000 YEARS AGO:
OK, IN EXCHANGE FOR FOOD AND SHELTER, ALL YOU HAVE TO DO IS HELP WITH THE HUNT AND GUARD THE CAVE.
IT'S CALLED DOMESTICATION. GET USED TO IT.

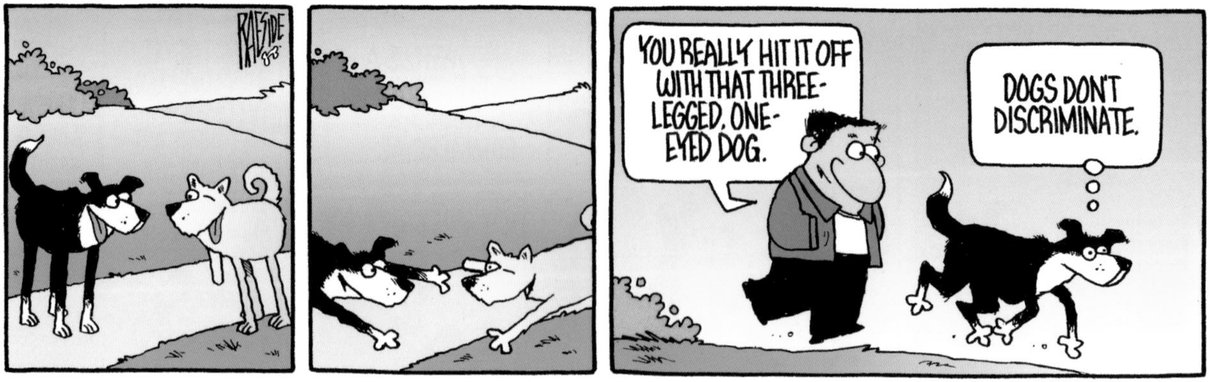
YOU REALLY HIT IT OFF WITH THAT THREE-LEGGED, ONE-EYED DOG.
DOGS DON'T DISCRIMINATE.

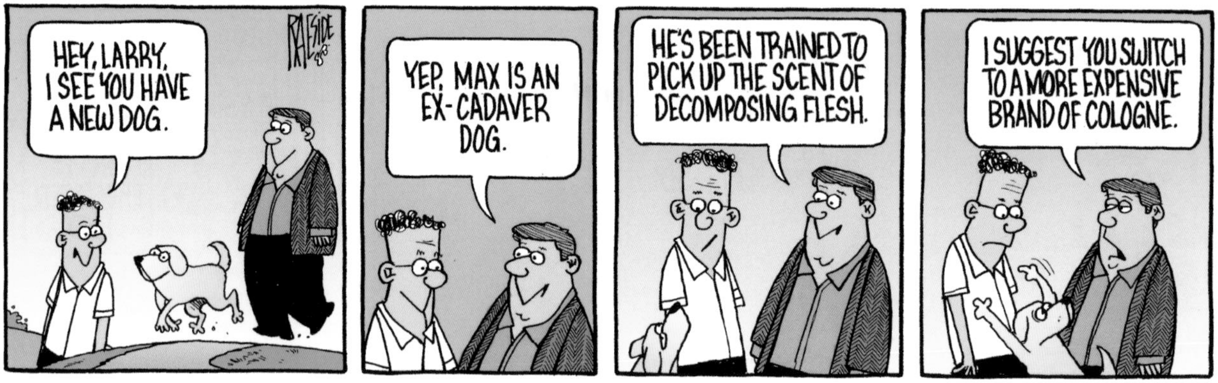
HEY, LARRY, I SEE YOU HAVE A NEW DOG.
YEP, MAX IS AN EX-CADAVER DOG.
HE'S BEEN TRAINED TO PICK UP THE SCENT OF DECOMPOSING FLESH.
I SUGGEST YOU SWITCH TO A MORE EXPENSIVE BRAND OF COLOGNE.

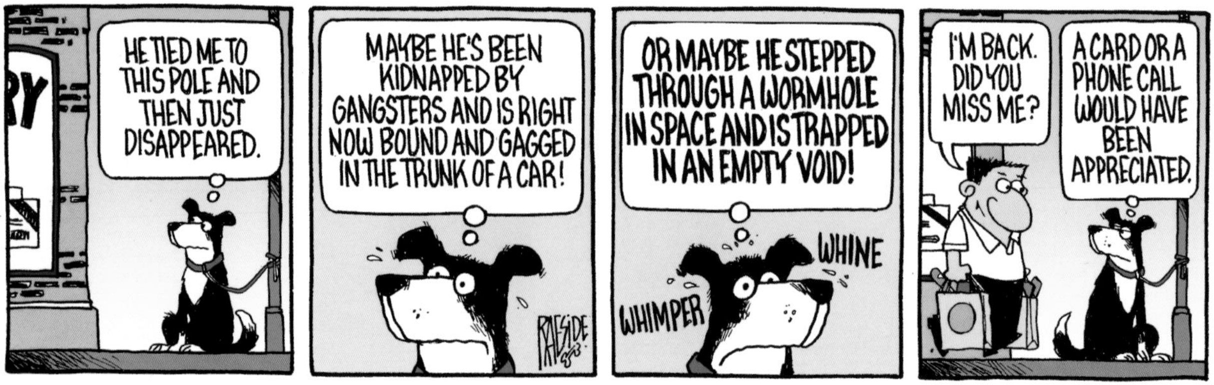
HE TIED ME TO THIS POLE AND THEN JUST DISAPPEARED.
MAYBE HE'S BEEN KIDNAPPED BY GANGSTERS AND IS RIGHT NOW BOUND AND GAGGED IN THE TRUNK OF A CAR!
OR MAYBE HE STEPPED THROUGH A WORMHOLE IN SPACE AND IS TRAPPED IN AN EMPTY VOID!
WHINE
WHIMPER
I'M BACK. DID YOU MISS ME?
A CARD OR A PHONE CALL WOULD HAVE BEEN APPRECIATED.

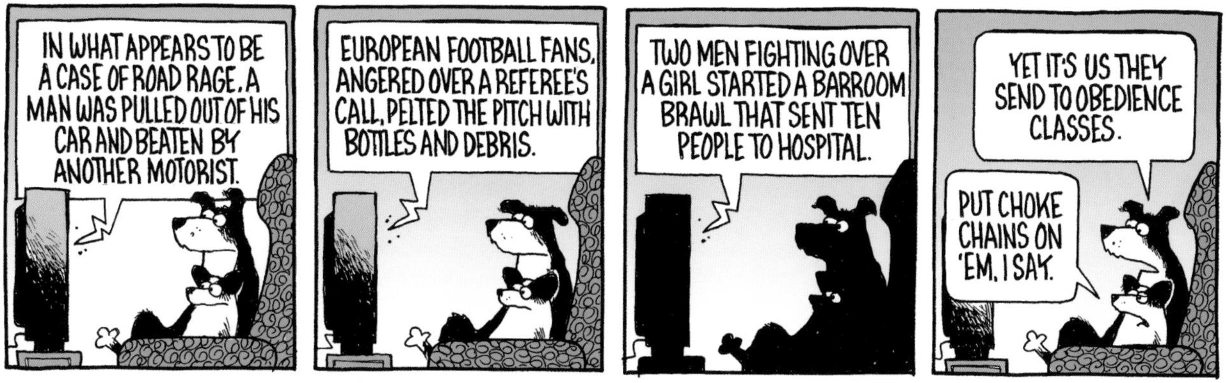
IN WHAT APPEARS TO BE A CASE OF ROAD RAGE, A MAN WAS PULLED OUT OF HIS CAR AND BEATEN BY ANOTHER MOTORIST.
EUROPEAN FOOTBALL FANS, ANGERED OVER A REFEREE'S CALL, PELTED THE PITCH WITH BOTTLES AND DEBRIS.
TWO MEN FIGHTING OVER A GIRL STARTED A BARROOM BRAWL THAT SENT TEN PEOPLE TO HOSPITAL.
YET IT'S US THEY SEND TO OBEDIENCE CLASSES.
PUT CHOKE CHAINS ON 'EM, I SAY.

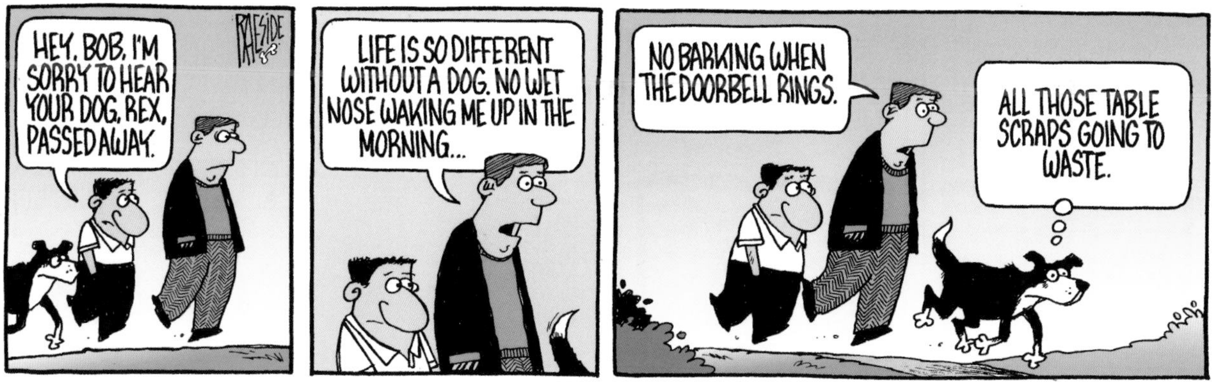
HEY, BOB, I'M SORRY TO HEAR YOUR DOG, REX, PASSED AWAY.
LIFE IS SO DIFFERENT WITHOUT A DOG. NO WET NOSE WAKING ME UP IN THE MORNING...
NO BARKING WHEN THE DOORBELL RINGS.
ALL THOSE TABLE SCRAPS GOING TO WASTE.

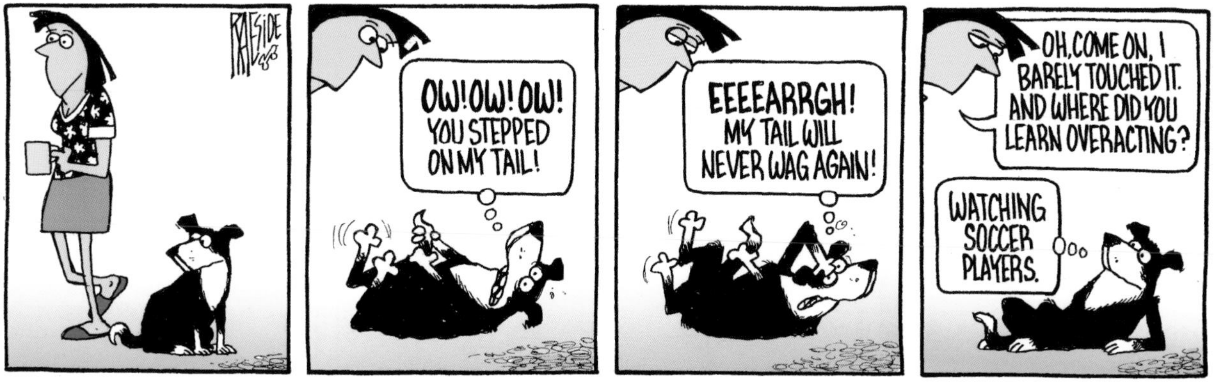
OW! OW! OW! YOU STEPPED ON MY TAIL!
EEEEARRGH! MY TAIL WILL NEVER WAG AGAIN!
OH, COME ON, I BARELY TOUCHED IT. AND WHERE DID YOU LEARN OVERACTING?
WATCHING SOCCER PLAYERS.

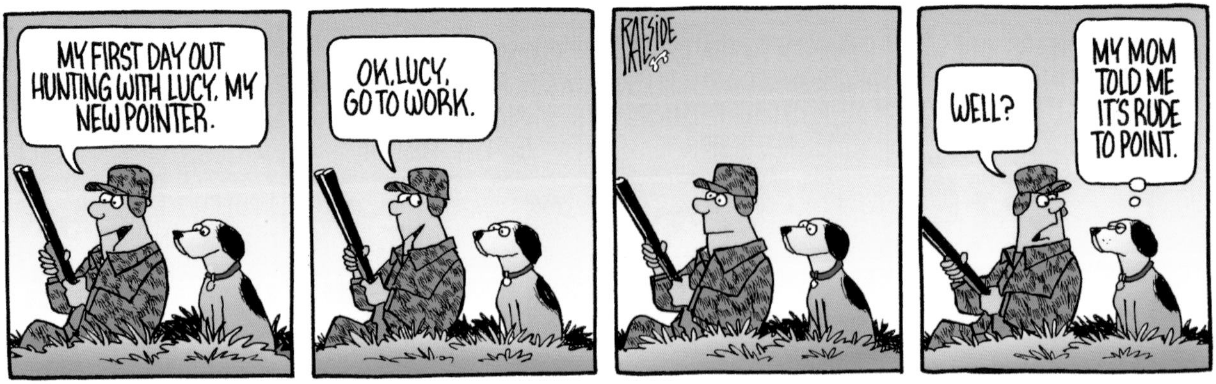
MY FIRST DAY OUT HUNTING WITH LUCY, MY NEW POINTER.
OK, LUCY, GO TO WORK.
WELL?
MY MOM TOLD ME IT'S RUDE TO POINT.

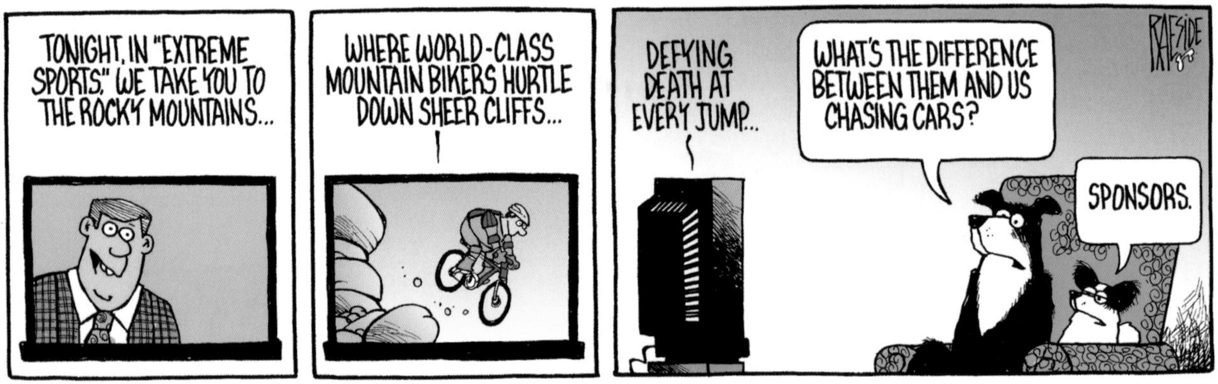
TONIGHT, IN "EXTREME SPORTS," WE TAKE YOU TO THE ROCKY MOUNTAINS...
WHERE WORLD-CLASS MOUNTAIN BIKERS HURTLE DOWN SHEER CLIFFS...
DEFYING DEATH AT EVERY JUMP...
WHAT'S THE DIFFERENCE BETWEEN THEM AND US CHASING CARS?
SPONSORS.

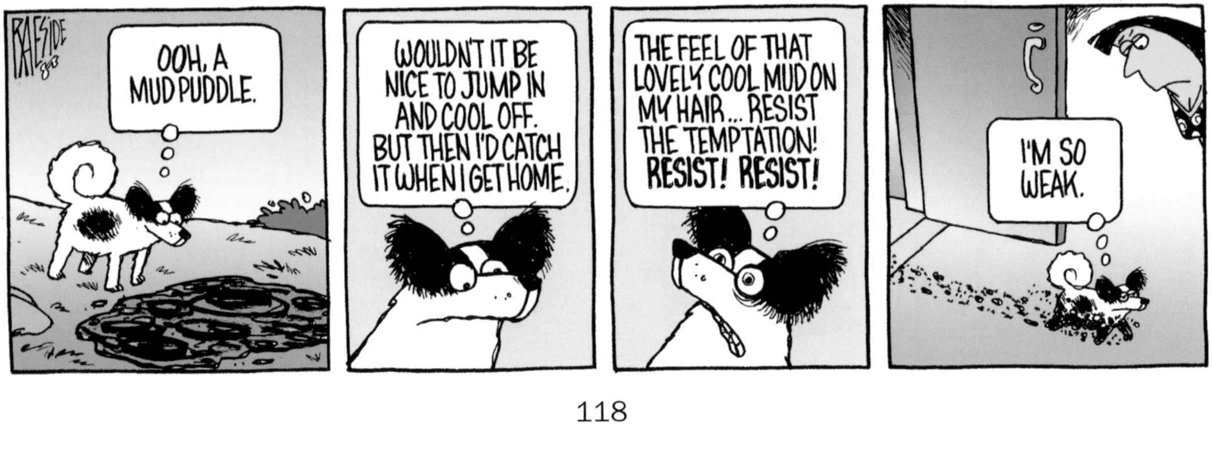
OOH, A MUD PUDDLE.
WOULDN'T IT BE NICE TO JUMP IN AND COOL OFF. BUT THEN I'D CATCH IT WHEN I GET HOME.
THE FEEL OF THAT LOVELY COOL MUD ON MY HAIR... RESIST THE TEMPTATION! RESIST! RESIST!
I'M SO WEAK.

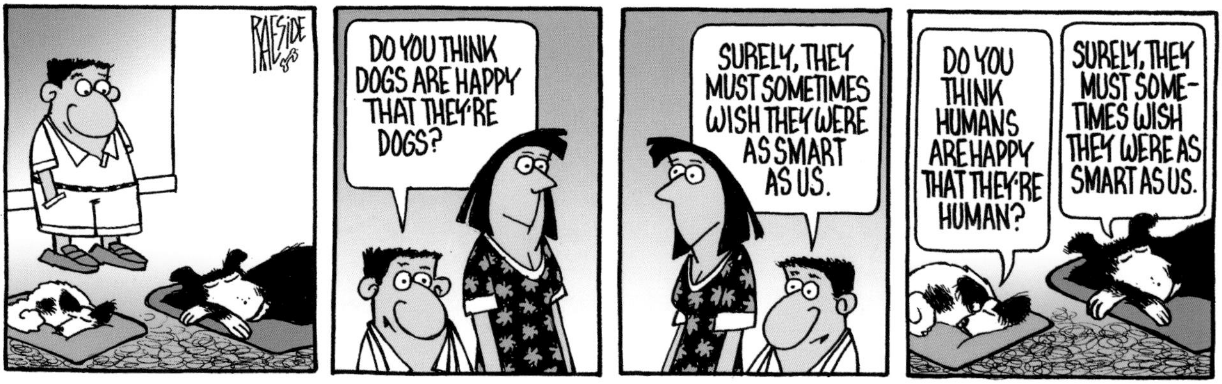
RAESIDE
DO YOU THINK DOGS ARE HAPPY THAT THEY'RE DOGS?
SURELY, THEY MUST SOMETIMES WISH THEY WERE AS SMART AS US.
DO YOU THINK HUMANS ARE HAPPY THAT THEY'RE HUMAN?
SURELY, THEY MUST SOME-TIMES WISH THEY WERE AS SMART AS US.

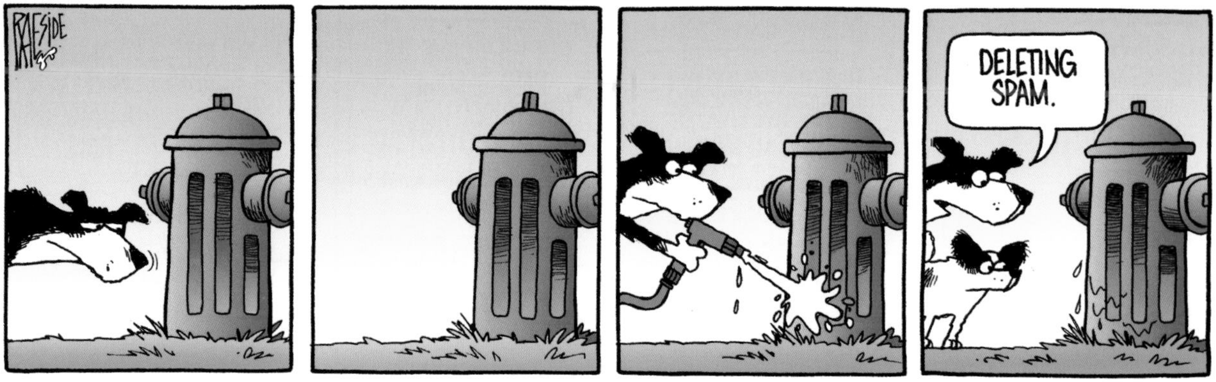
RAESIDE
DELETING SPAM.

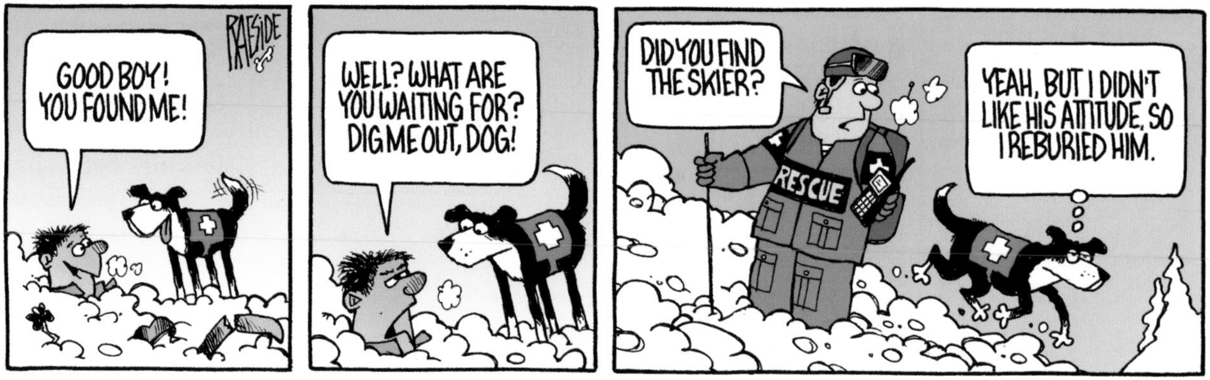
RAESIDE
GOOD BOY! YOU FOUND ME!
WELL? WHAT ARE YOU WAITING FOR? DIG ME OUT, DOG!
DID YOU FIND THE SKIER?
RESCUE
YEAH, BUT I DIDN'T LIKE HIS ATTITUDE, SO I REBURIED HIM.

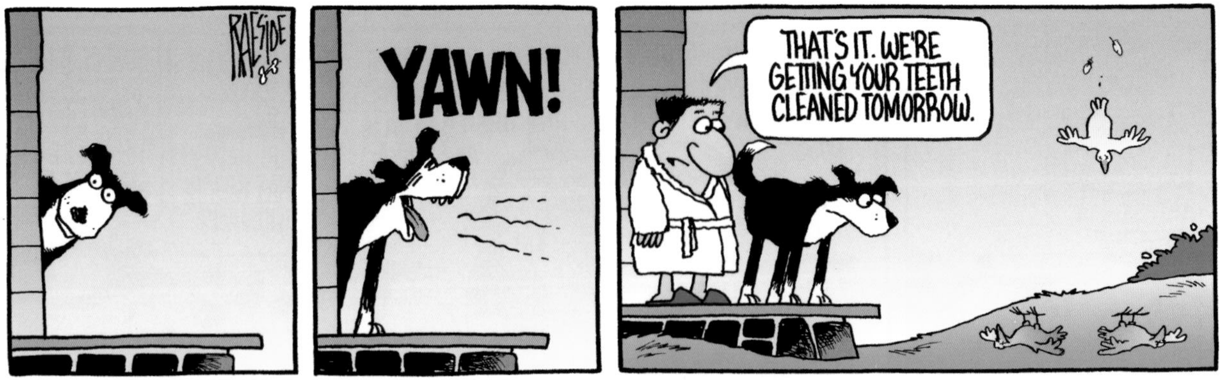
YAWN!
THAT'S IT. WE'RE GETTING YOUR TEETH CLEANED TOMORROW.

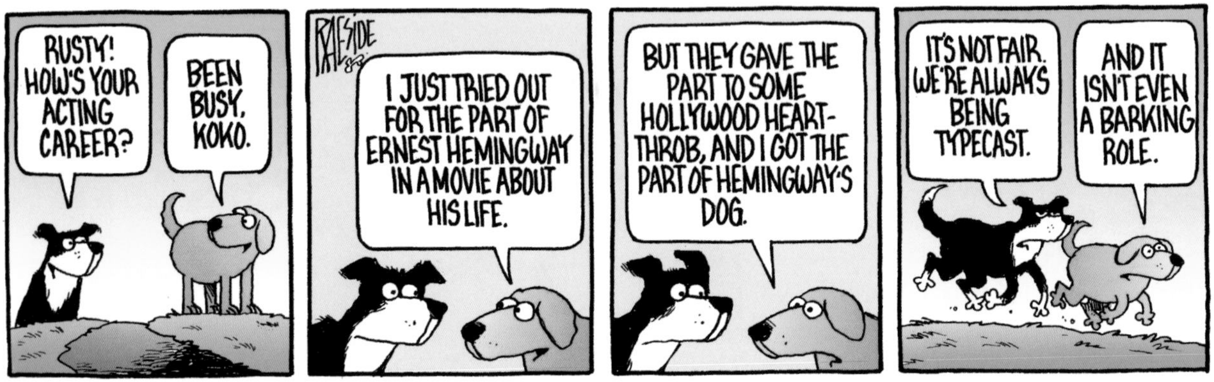
RUSTY! HOW'S YOUR ACTING CAREER?
BEEN BUSY, KOKO.
I JUST TRIED OUT FOR THE PART OF ERNEST HEMINGWAY IN A MOVIE ABOUT HIS LIFE.
BUT THEY GAVE THE PART TO SOME HOLLYWOOD HEART-THROB, AND I GOT THE PART OF HEMINGWAY'S DOG.
IT'S NOT FAIR. WE'RE ALWAYS BEING TYPECAST.
AND IT ISN'T EVEN A BARKING ROLE.

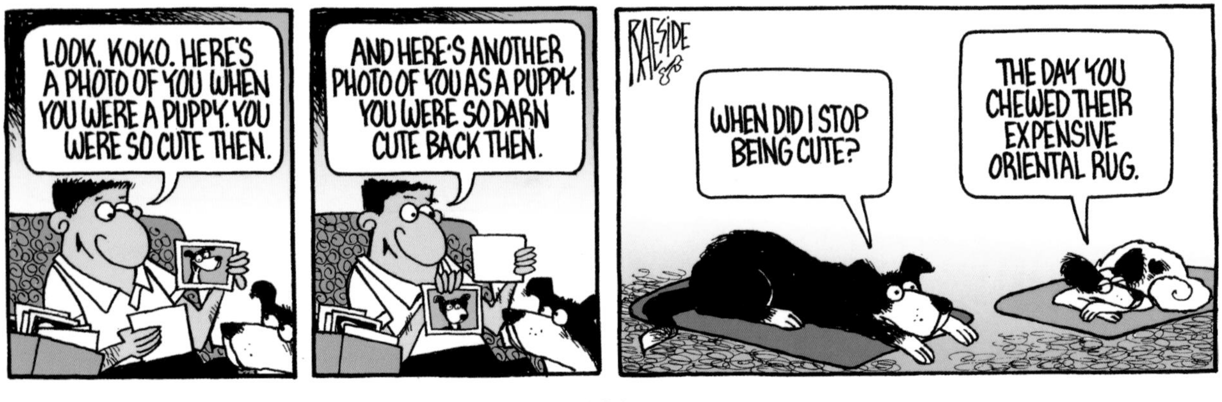
LOOK, KOKO. HERE'S A PHOTO OF YOU WHEN YOU WERE A PUPPY. YOU WERE SO CUTE THEN.
AND HERE'S ANOTHER PHOTO OF YOU AS A PUPPY. YOU WERE SO DARN CUTE BACK THEN.
WHEN DID I STOP BEING CUTE?
THE DAY YOU CHEWED THEIR EXPENSIVE ORIENTAL RUG.

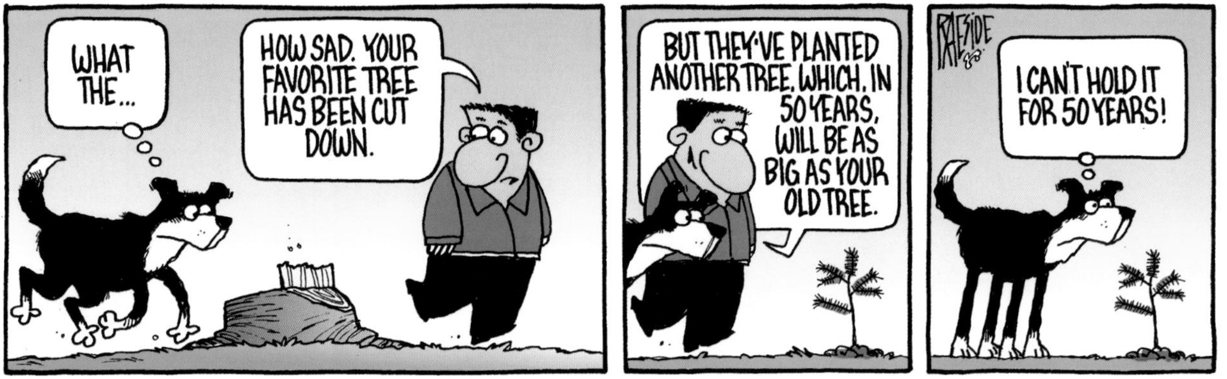
WHAT THE...
HOW SAD. YOUR FAVORITE TREE HAS BEEN CUT DOWN.
BUT THEY'VE PLANTED ANOTHER TREE, WHICH, IN 50 YEARS, WILL BE AS BIG AS YOUR OLD TREE.
RAESIDE
I CAN'T HOLD IT FOR 50 YEARS!

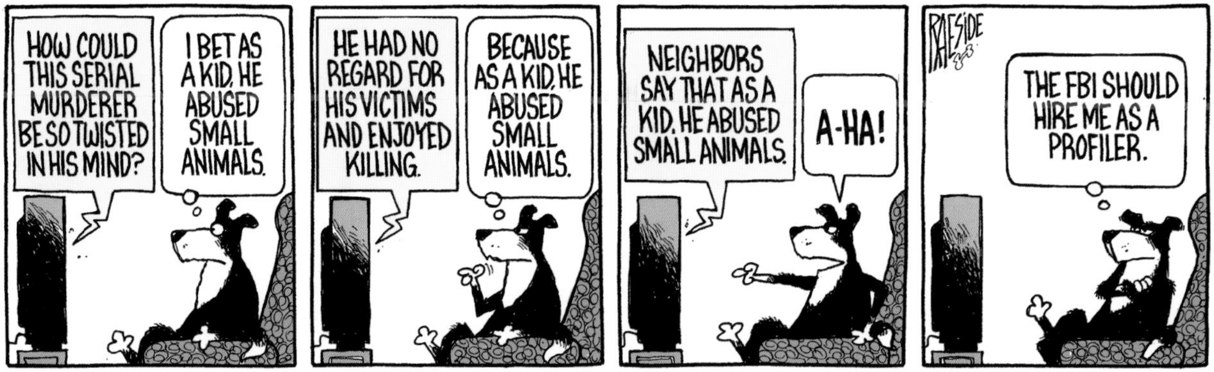
HOW COULD THIS SERIAL MURDERER BE SO TWISTED IN HIS MIND?
I BET AS A KID, HE ABUSED SMALL ANIMALS.
HE HAD NO REGARD FOR HIS VICTIMS AND ENJOYED KILLING.
BECAUSE AS A KID, HE ABUSED SMALL ANIMALS.
NEIGHBORS SAY THAT AS A KID, HE ABUSED SMALL ANIMALS.
A-HA!
RAESIDE
THE FBI SHOULD HIRE ME AS A PROFILER.

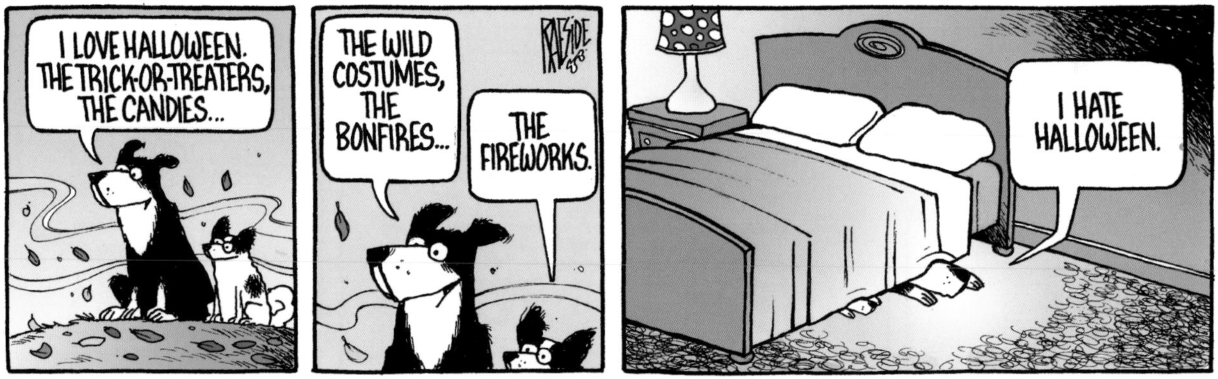
I LOVE HALLOWEEN. THE TRICK-OR-TREATERS, THE CANDIES...
THE WILD COSTUMES, THE BONFIRES...
RAESIDE
THE FIREWORKS.
I HATE HALLOWEEN.

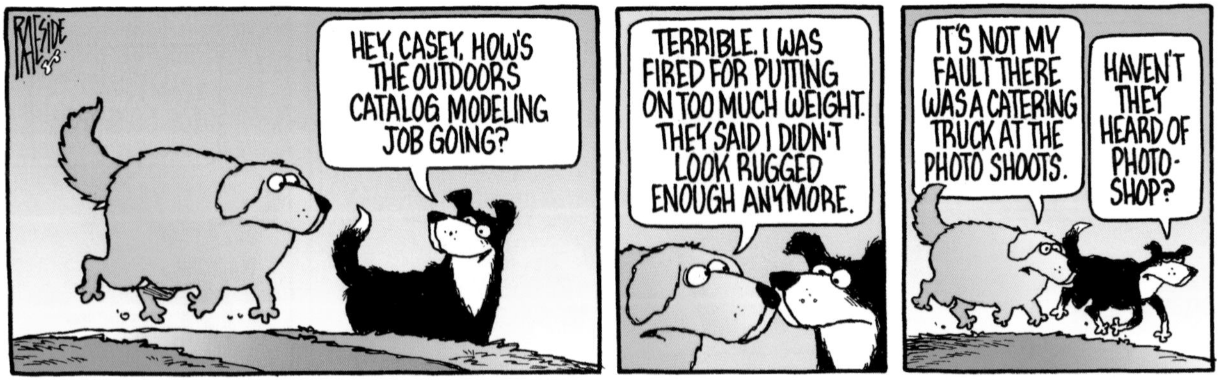
HEY, CASEY, HOW'S THE OUTDOORS CATALOG MODELING JOB GOING?
TERRIBLE. I WAS FIRED FOR PUTTING ON TOO MUCH WEIGHT. THEY SAID I DIDN'T LOOK RUGGED ENOUGH ANYMORE.
IT'S NOT MY FAULT THERE WAS A CATERING TRUCK AT THE PHOTO SHOOTS.
HAVEN'T THEY HEARD OF PHOTO-SHOP?

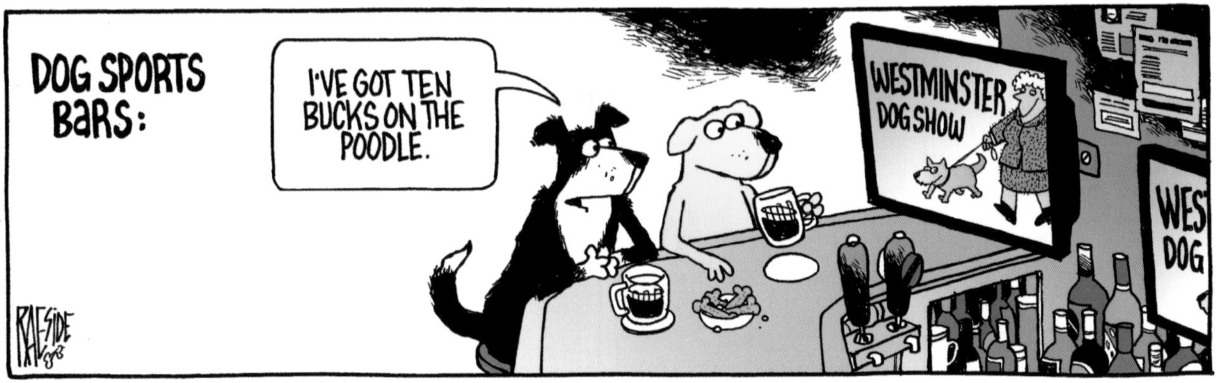
DOG SPORTS BARS:
I'VE GOT TEN BUCKS ON THE POODLE.
WESTMINSTER DOG SHOW

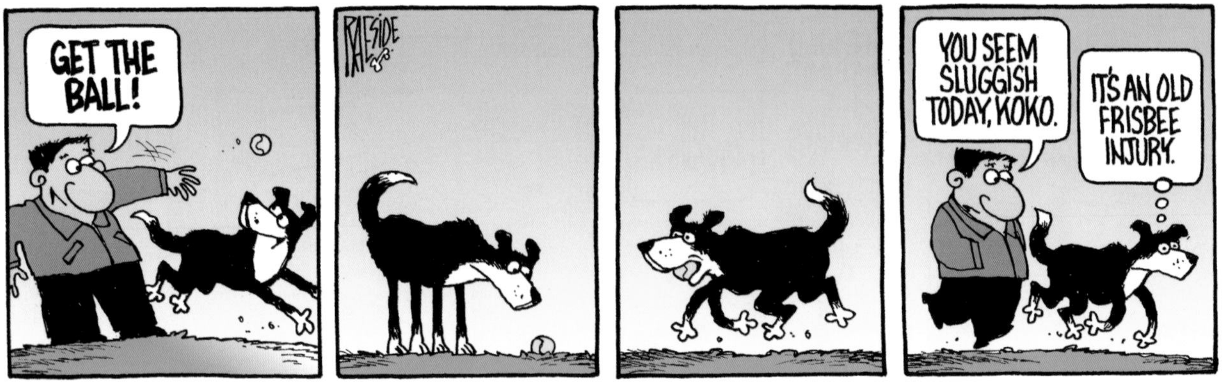
GET THE BALL!
YOU SEEM SLUGGISH TODAY, KOKO.
IT'S AN OLD FRISBEE INJURY.

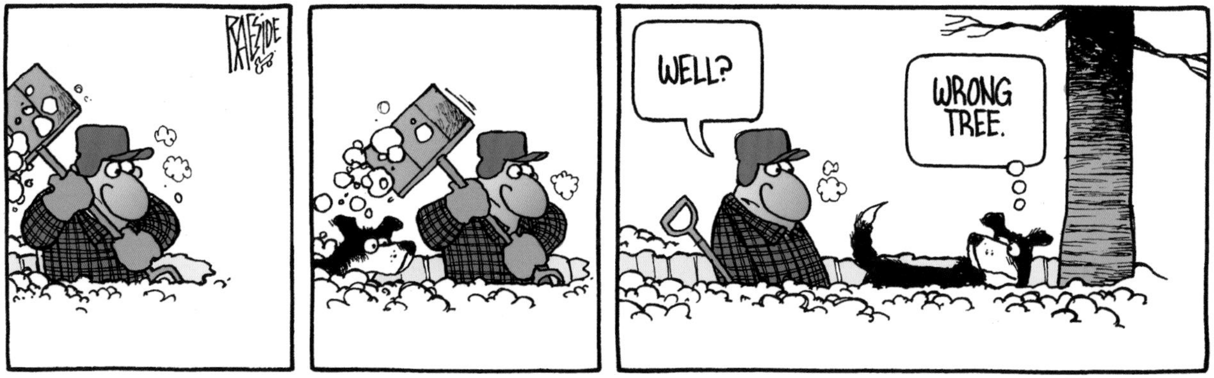
WELL?
WRONG TREE.

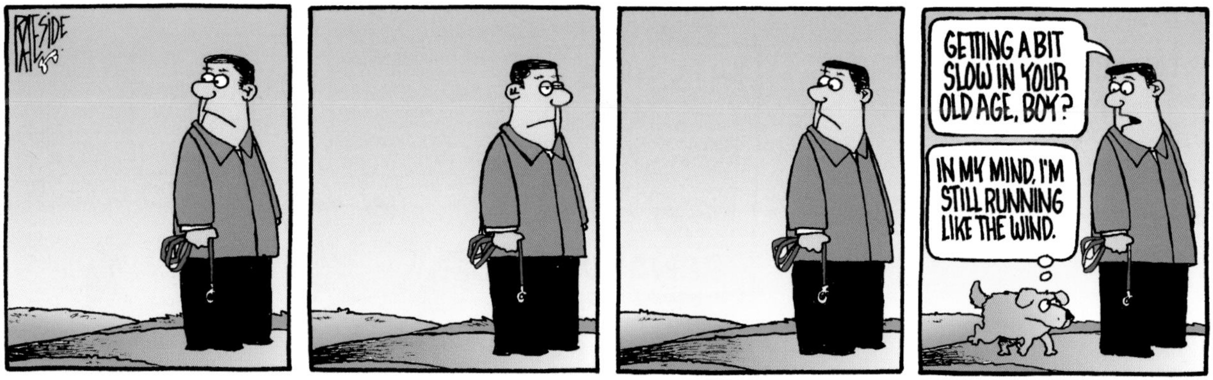
GETTING A BIT SLOW IN YOUR OLD AGE, BOY?
IN MY MIND, I'M STILL RUNNING LIKE THE WIND.

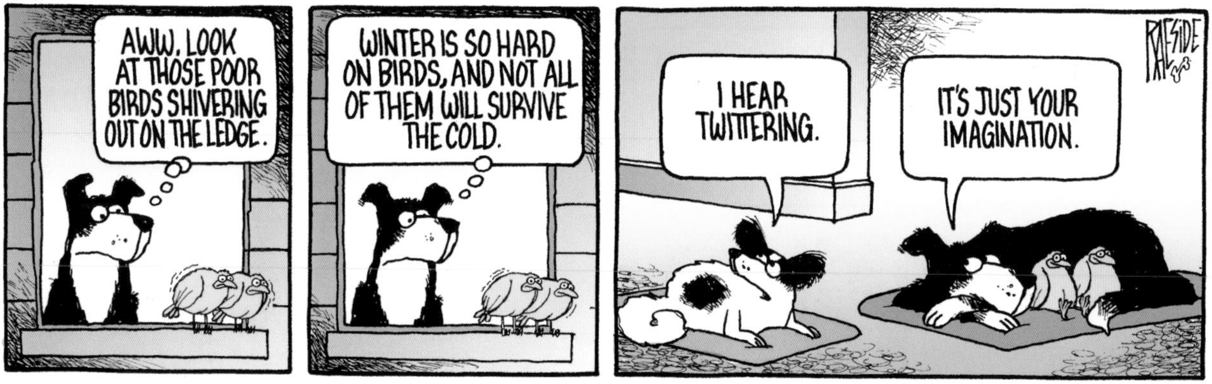
AWW, LOOK AT THOSE POOR BIRDS SHIVERING OUT ON THE LEDGE.
WINTER IS SO HARD ON BIRDS, AND NOT ALL OF THEM WILL SURVIVE THE COLD.
I HEAR TWITTERING.
IT'S JUST YOUR IMAGINATION.

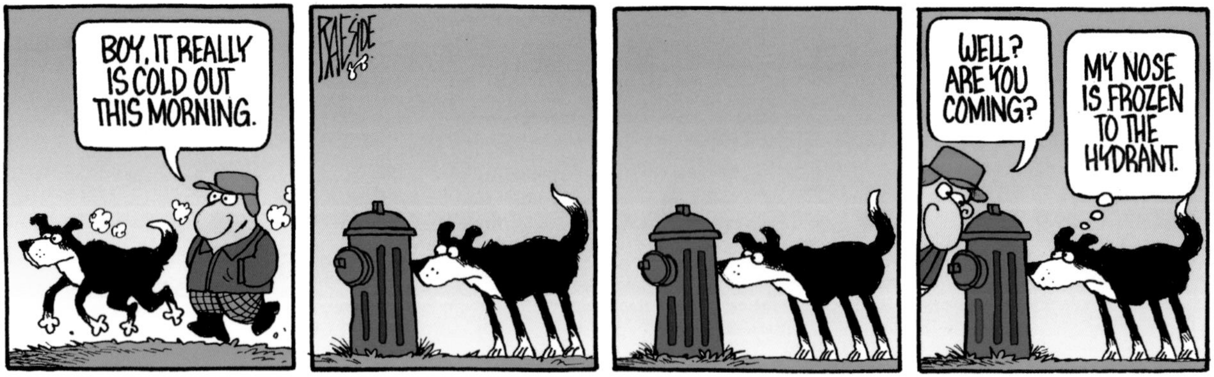
BOY, IT REALLY IS COLD OUT THIS MORNING.
WELL? ARE YOU COMING?
MY NOSE IS FROZEN TO THE HYDRANT.

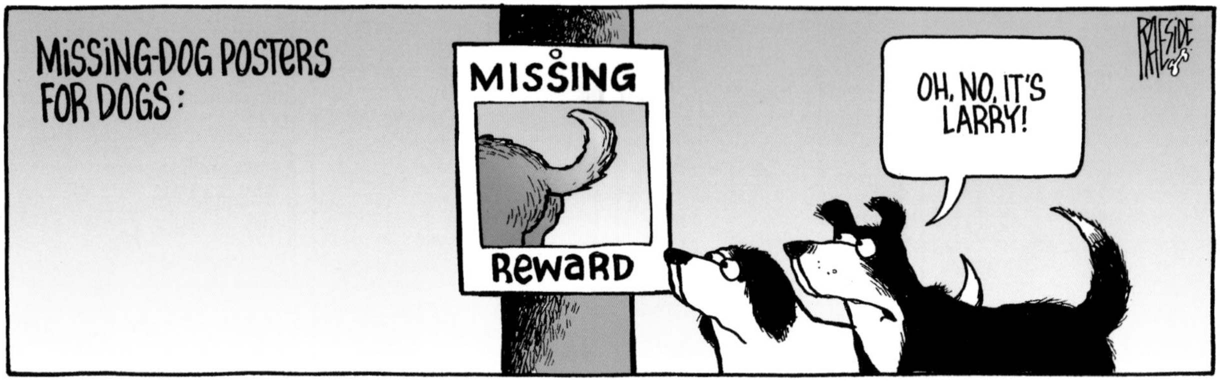
MISSING-DOG POSTERS FOR DOGS:
MISSING
REWARD
OH, NO, IT'S LARRY!

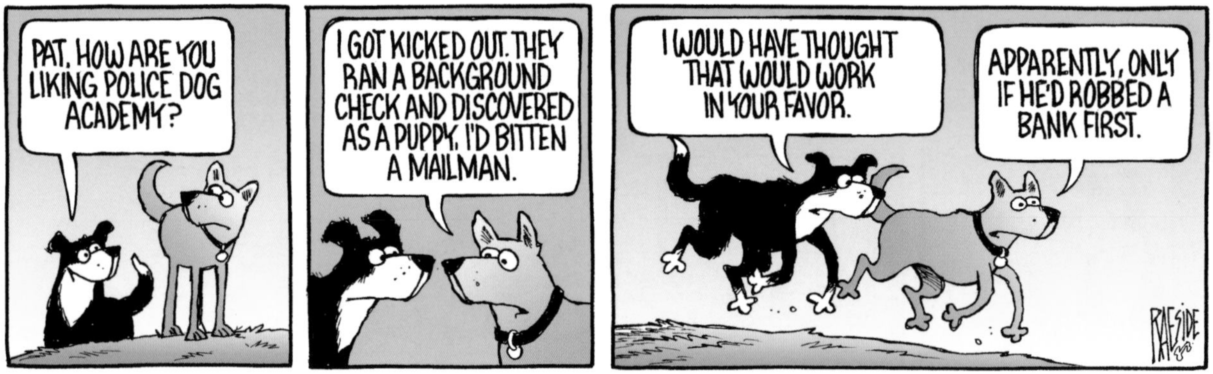
PAT, HOW ARE YOU LIKING POLICE DOG ACADEMY?
I GOT KICKED OUT. THEY RAN A BACKGROUND CHECK AND DISCOVERED AS A PUPPY, I'D BITTEN A MAILMAN.
I WOULD HAVE THOUGHT THAT WOULD WORK IN YOUR FAVOR.
APPARENTLY, ONLY IF HE'D ROBBED A BANK FIRST.

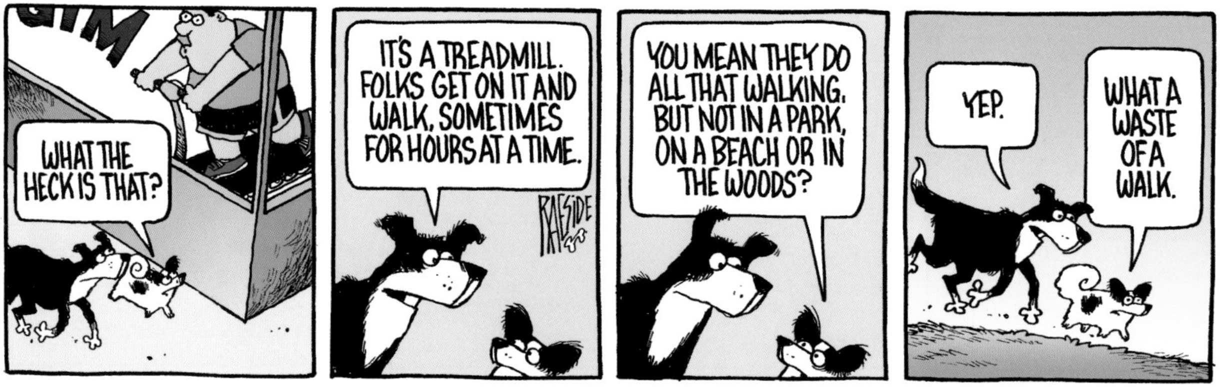
WHAT THE HECK IS THAT?
IT'S A TREADMILL. FOLKS GET ON IT AND WALK, SOMETIMES FOR HOURS AT A TIME.
RAESIDE
YOU MEAN THEY DO ALL THAT WALKING, BUT NOT IN A PARK, ON A BEACH OR IN THE WOODS?
YEP.
WHAT A WASTE OF A WALK.

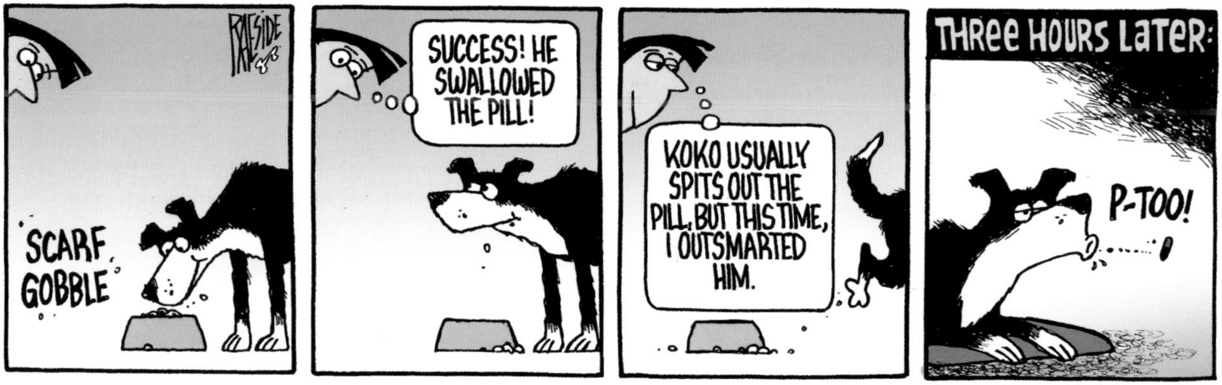
RAESIDE
SCARF GOBBLE
SUCCESS! HE SWALLOWED THE PILL!
KOKO USUALLY SPITS OUT THE PILL, BUT THIS TIME, I OUTSMARTED HIM.
THREE HOURS LATER:
P-TOO!

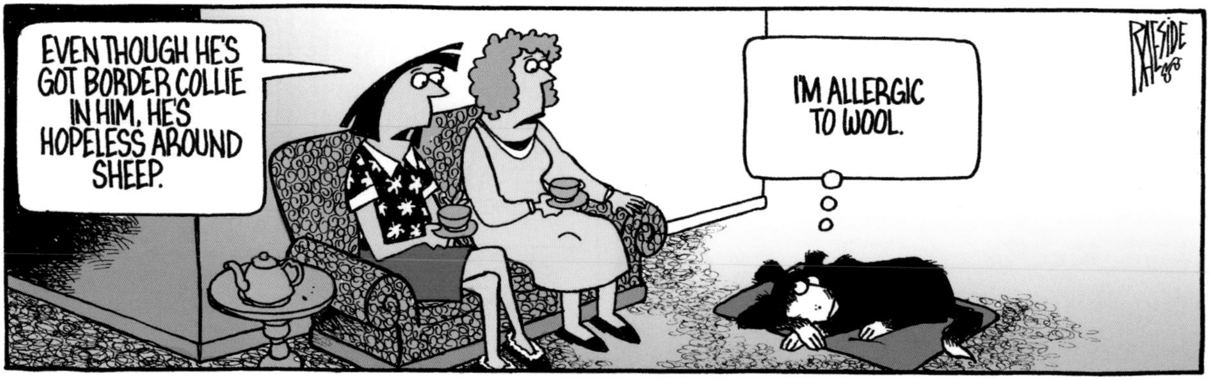
EVEN THOUGH HE'S GOT BORDER COLLIE IN HIM, HE'S HOPELESS AROUND SHEEP.
I'M ALLERGIC TO WOOL.
RAESIDE

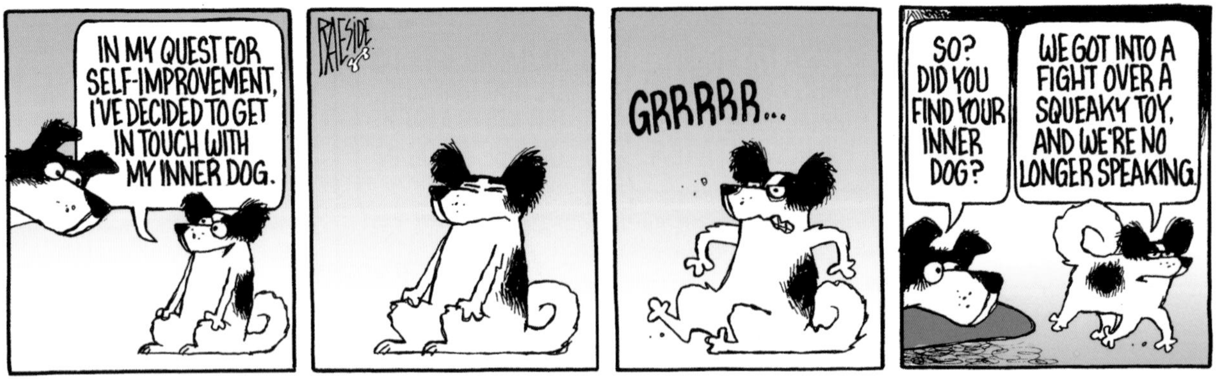
IN MY QUEST FOR SELF-IMPROVEMENT, I'VE DECIDED TO GET IN TOUCH WITH MY INNER DOG.
GRRRRR...
SO? DID YOU FIND YOUR INNER DOG?
WE GOT INTO A FIGHT OVER A SQUEAKY TOY, AND WE'RE NO LONGER SPEAKING.

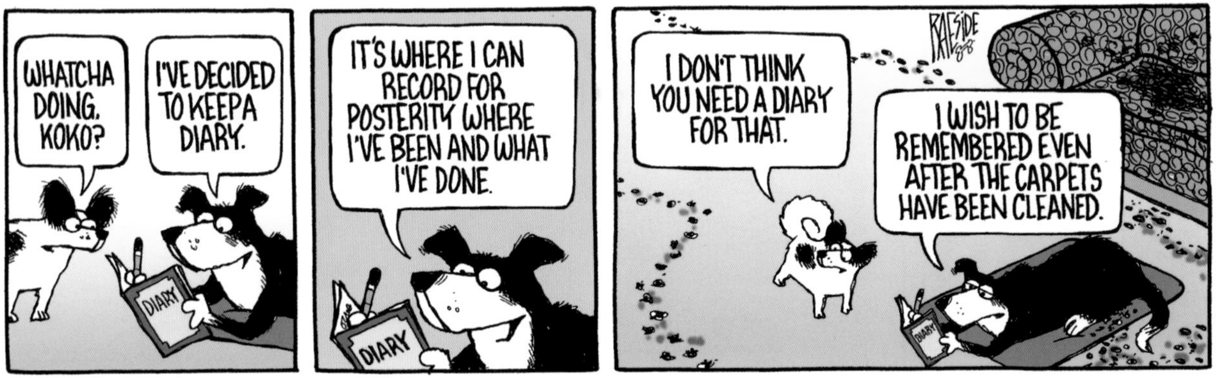
WHATCHA DOING, KOKO?
I'VE DECIDED TO KEEP A DIARY.
DIARY
IT'S WHERE I CAN RECORD FOR POSTERITY WHERE I'VE BEEN AND WHAT I'VE DONE.
DIARY
I DON'T THINK YOU NEED A DIARY FOR THAT.
I WISH TO BE REMEMBERED EVEN AFTER THE CARPETS HAVE BEEN CLEANED.

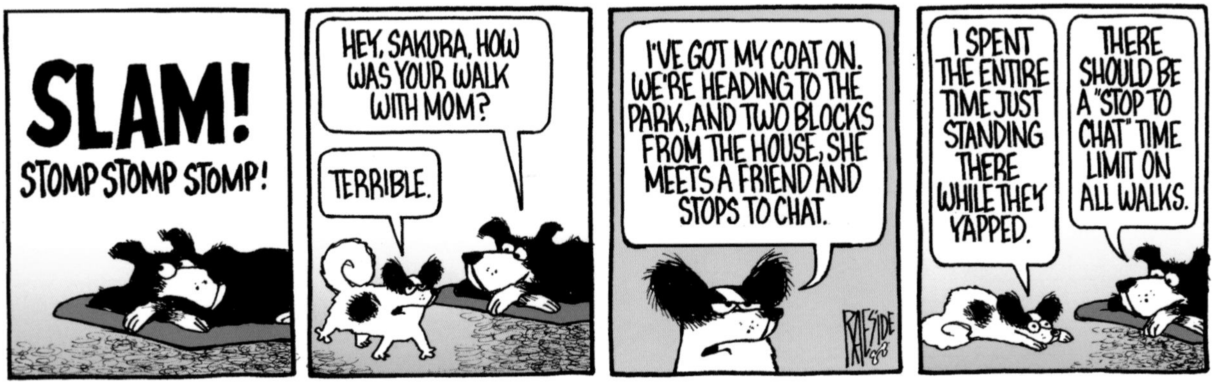
SLAM!
STOMP STOMP STOMP!
HEY, SAKURA, HOW WAS YOUR WALK WITH MOM?
TERRIBLE.
I'VE GOT MY COAT ON. WE'RE HEADING TO THE PARK, AND TWO BLOCKS FROM THE HOUSE, SHE MEETS A FRIEND AND STOPS TO CHAT.
I SPENT THE ENTIRE TIME JUST STANDING THERE WHILE THEY YAPPED.
THERE SHOULD BE A "STOP TO CHAT" TIME LIMIT ON ALL WALKS.

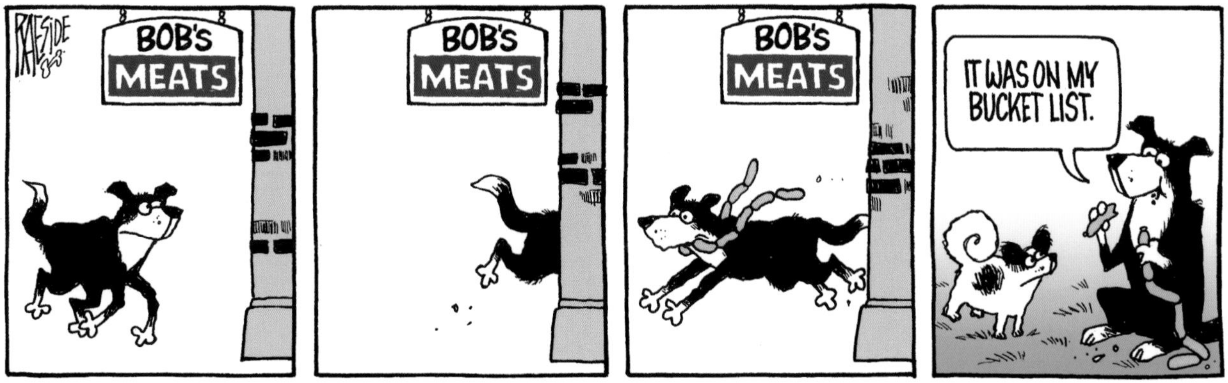
RAESIDE
BOB'S MEATS
BOB'S MEATS
BOB'S MEATS
IT WAS ON MY BUCKET LIST.

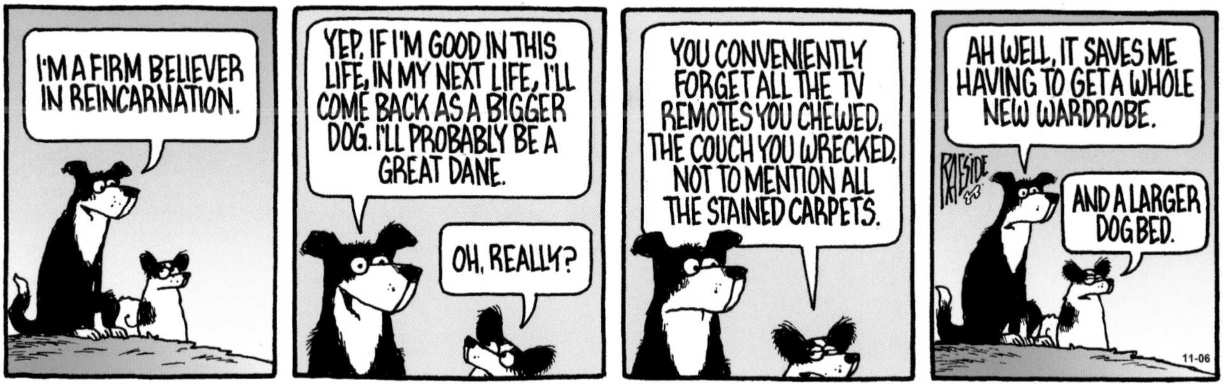
I'M A FIRM BELIEVER IN REINCARNATION.
YEP, IF I'M GOOD IN THIS LIFE, IN MY NEXT LIFE, I'LL COME BACK AS A BIGGER DOG. I'LL PROBABLY BE A GREAT DANE.
OH, REALLY?
YOU CONVENIENTLY FORGET ALL THE TV REMOTES YOU CHEWED, THE COUCH YOU WRECKED, NOT TO MENTION ALL THE STAINED CARPETS.
AH WELL, IT SAVES ME HAVING TO GET A WHOLE NEW WARDROBE.
RAESIDE
AND A LARGER DOG BED.
11-06

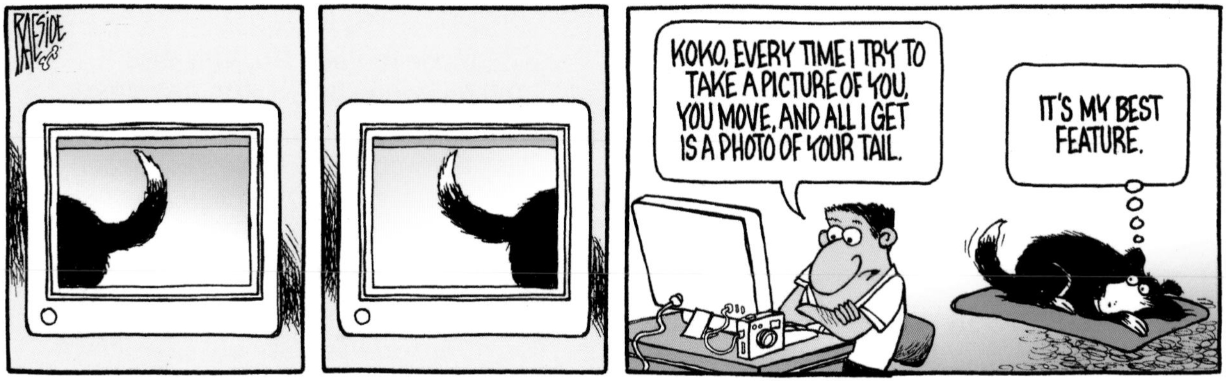
RAESIDE
KOKO, EVERY TIME I TRY TO TAKE A PICTURE OF YOU, YOU MOVE, AND ALL I GET IS A PHOTO OF YOUR TAIL.
IT'S MY BEST FEATURE.

ALSO BY ADRIAN RAESIDE...

THE RAINBOW BRIDGE: A Visit To Pet Paradise is a magical tale of adventure and a valuable fable for anyone who cherishes the companionship of a family pet.

Seven-year-old Rick and his beloved dog Koko are inseparable. They cavort in the swimming hole, chase each other through the fields, play fetch and wrestle. But their relationship changes as Koko grows old and his health declines.

With Koko's passing, Rick is devastated. But on Christmas Eve he is woken by Buster, a flatulent but well-intentioned messenger dog, who suddenly appears at the boy's bedside. Buster ferries Rick to a magical paradise for pets where Rick is reunited with Koko; it fills Rick's heart with joy. It's a place where cats burrow through fields of catnip, no couch is off-limits to dogs and frisbees are flung endlessly. This mysterious adventure is truly a holiday miracle!

Adrian Raeside captures the special bond between humans and their pets, and with marvellous illustrations, brings a gentle humour to a story that will resonate with children and pet lovers of all ages.

ISBN 978-1-55017-584-4
paperback / colour illustrations
8" x 8" / 32 pages

ADRIAN RAESIDE
THE RAINBOW BRIDGE
A Visit to Pet Paradise

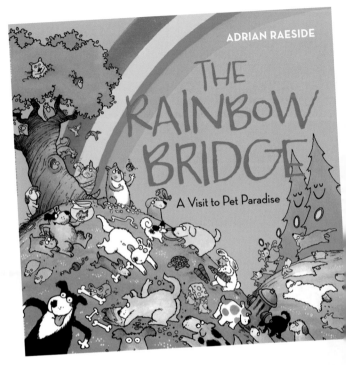

Available at your local bookstore or from

Harbour Publishing
P.O. Box 219
Madeira Park, BC, V0N 2H0
Toll-free order line: 1-800-667-2988

Visit our website for more information on all our titles and authors:

www.harbourpublishing.com

For more laughs visit Adrian Raeside's website:

www.raesidecartoon.com